British Military Spectacle

British Military Spectacle

From the Napoleonic Wars through the Crimea

SCOTT HUGHES MYERLY

HARVARD UNIVERSITY PRESS

Cambridge, Massachusetts / London, England / 1996

Copyright © 1996 by the President and Fellows of Harvard College
All rights reserved
Printed in the United States of America

Library of Congress Cataloging-in-Publication Data
Myerly, Scott Hughes.
British military spectacle : from the Napoleonic Wars through
the Crimea / Scott Hughes Myerly.
p. cm.
Includes bibliographical references (p.) and index.
ISBN 0-674-08249-4 (alk. paper)
1. Great Britain—History, Military—19th century. 2. Rites and ceremonies—Great
Britain—History—10th century. 3. Napoleonic Wars, 1800–1815. 4. Crimean War,
1853–1856. 5. Spectacular, The.
I. Title.
DA68.M94 1996
355.1′7′094109034—dc20   96-17260

For Tamara

CONTENTS

ILLUSTRATIONS

All references to the Brown Collection *Catalogue* are to Peter Harrington, *Catalogue to the Anne S. K. Brown Military Collection: The British Prints, Drawings and Watercolours*, vol. 1 (New York: Garland Publishing, 1987).

FOLLOWING PAGE 86

"Tenth Royal Regiment of Hussars." Lithograph by L. Mansion and S. Eschauzier, *Spooner's Upright Series*, no. 18 (London: W. Spooner, 1833–1836), Brown Collection, *Catalogue*, no. 2,209.

"The Great Army Tailoring Question," *Punch*, 16 (1849).

"The Eighteenth Regiment of Foot." Lithograph by J. Graf (London: William Spooner, *c.* 1844), Brown Collection, *Catalogue*, no. 2,150.

"The Black Choker," *Punch*, 26 (1854).

"Choking and Overloading Our Guards," *Punch*, 26 (1854).

"The Sixth Regiment of Foot, 1839." Lithograph by G. E. Madeley, *Cannon's Historical Records*, no. 32 (Longman, Orme & Co., 1839).

"Regiments of Light Infantry." By J. H. Lynch after M. A. Hayes, *Spooner's Oblong Series: "The British Army,"* no. 48, 1844.

"The Dandy Taylor [Planning] a New Hungry Dress." Huntington Library, print no. BM 13,237. Reproduced by permission of the Huntington Library, San Marino, California.

"Rifle Brigade, First Battalion." Lithograph plate by W. & J. O. Clerk after S. Eschauzier, *Spooner's Small Oblong Series*, no. 10 (London: Lefevre & Kohler, *c.* 1834–1835), Brown Collection, *Catalogue*, no. 2,224.

"Charge of the Third Dragoon Guards." Lithograph by L. Haghe after T. L. Rowbotham and W. Miller (Bristol: George Davey, 1831), Brown Collection, *Catalogue*, no. 1,038.

"A Scene in Downing Street." Hand-colored lithograph by W. I. M., 1830, Brown Collection, *Catalogue*, no. 549.

"Mars in Disguise." Library of Congress Collection.

"Maj. Everard William Bouverie." Lithograph after a painting by A. J. Dubois Drahonet.

"The King and the Duke." Superimposed lithograph (London: William Spooner, *c.* 1830), Brown Collection, *Catalogue*, no. 548.

"The Seventy-fourth Highlanders." Engraved by J. Harris after Henry Martins, *Ackermann's Costumes of the British Army*, no. 51 (London: R. Ackermann, 1853), Brown Collection, *Catalogue*, no. 2,203.

"A Charming Young Sentinel." Color lithograph by R. Evan Sly, no. 2 of R. Evan Sly's *New & Amusing Mechanical Prints* (London: Charles Edmonds, *c.* 1845), Brown Collection, *Catalogue*, no. 567.

FOLLOWING PAGE 150

"Sixth Dragoon Guards (Carabiniers), Officer." By J. Harris after H. de Daubrawa, *Ackermann's Costumes of the British Army*, I (London: R. Ackermann, 1844).

Frontispiece from Eric H. Underwood, ed., Andrei Nikolaievitch Alexandrov, trans., *The Battle of Waterloo, or the Countess Phedora's Curse: A True and Stirring Representation in Fourteen Scenes of the Duke of Wellington's Glorious Victory, and the Final Overthrow of the Corsican Tyrant!* (London: Pollock's Toy Theatres, Ltd., 1840; reprint ed., London: Eric Underwood, 1970). Pollock's Toy Museum is still in business at 1 Scala St., London.

"Up the Alma's Height." Illustrated music sheet cover by T. S. Seccombe (London: Cramer & Co., 1854), Brown Collection, GrBM 1,854.

"The Victory Polka." Illustrated music sheet cover by T. Packer (London: Stannard & Dixon, 1855), Brown Collection, GrBM 1,855.

"First Regiment, Grenadier Guards, Drummer." Lithograph by M. Gauci after

E. Hull, *Hull's Costume of the British Army in MDCCCXXVIII*, no. 38 (London: Engelmann, Graf, Coinet & Co., 1829), Brown Collection.

Militaria. Photograph by Sheperd Paine.

Appointments and Militaria. Photograph by Sheperd Paine.

"Making a Lancer." *William Heath's Cavalry Caricatures*, no. 3 (London: Thos. McLean, *c.* 1830–1834), Brown Collection, *Catalogue*, no. 608.

"Col. Sir Wm. Payne Bart." Hand-colored engraving by S. & J. Fuller after Henry Alken, *Alken Prints* (London: S. & J. Fuller, 1817), Brown Collection, *Catalogue*, no. 2,144.

"British Royal Horse Artillery." Lithograph by William Heath, *Heath's Royal Artillery Prints* (London: Colnaghi & Co., *c.* 1830), Brown Collection, *Catalogue*, no. 2,184.

"Pall Mall." Hand-colored steel engraving by Chavanne after Read (London, *c.* 1853), Brown Collection, *Catalogue*, no. 1,087.

Officer's shoulder belt plate. Photograph by Sheperd Paine.

"The Review in the Park at Windsor." Colored lithograph by L. Huard after G. H. Thomas, *Thomas Prints* (London: Paul & Dominic Colnaghi & Co., 1855), Brown Collection, *Catalogue*, no. 1,214.

"Officer, Royal Horse Artillery (Horse Brigade) Review Order." By L. Mansion and S. Eschauzier, *Spooner's Upright Series*, no. 56 (London: W. Spooner, 1833–1836).

"First Visit to Waterloo Bridge." Aquatint (London: R. Ackermann, 1817), Brown Collection, *Catalogue*, no. 1,014.

"Officer, Review Order." By L. Mansion and S. Eschauzier, *Spooner's Upright Series*, no. 18 (London: W. Spooner, 1833–1836).

Introduction:
Army Life

The author of a nineteenth-century memoir recalled that in 1871, as a new recruit in the British army, he had asked his mates: "'Is this a fightin' machine, or a blinking circus?' The self-appointed commission of recruits voted unanimously for the circus. [The army] was not trained solely, nor even principally for war."[1] This is an extraordinary statement about an army that in the nineteenth century fought an almost uninterrupted series of campaigns and conquered a quarter of the world. What makes it even more remarkable is that these lines were written, not by a would-be satirist, critic, or slacker, but by a veteran who was proud of his service; nor were such views by any means rare among soldiers.

The statement highlights the importance of fancy uniforms and display in the British army and indicates an apparent contradiction: that looks superseded the fundamental task of wielding armed force. This curious phenomenon is further highlighted by the sometimes severe inadequacies in training and equipment.

Rather than referring to "the army," in the first half of the nineteenth century it is more accurate to say that a collection of regiments was brought together temporarily to act in combination. The focus of life in the army for the vast majority of soldiers was the separate little world of the regiment. The character of the regimental colonel in command and his sense of duty to a great extent determined the conditions in each unit. Although some colonels were extremely competent, others were teenaged nobles who saw their responsibility as a way to escape boredom. Such a colonel was said to be "unmindful of the finances and comforts of those he commands."[2] The full-colonel usually lived permanently in Great Britain; he made decisions pertaining to the dress and display of the regiments, though he might ask the advice of others. Units were often run in the field by the lieutenant-colonels (also called colonels), who might decide on extra ornaments if the full-colonel so allowed or was too far away to exercise control.

The subordinate regimental officers also enjoyed great authority, yet the army was hardly an advantageous situation for them. Sometimes they were "abominably housed," and when on campaign abroad they might well live in "wretchedness."[3] With a few exceptions, all officers purchased both their commissions and their promotions. Their pay, which had been fixed in 1797, remained the same through the nineteenth century.[4] By 1811, many officers could not meet their expenses without outside incomes. The duke of Wellington told a Select Committee on Naval and Military Appointments that "three-fourths of the whole number (of officers) receive but little for their service besides the honour of serving the king."[5]

In addition to the cost of the uniform and kit, expenses included contributions for the regimental band (obligatory after 1823) and the officers' mess. Many officers were bitter about the high cost of the service, which resulted from "the richness of the appointments [equipment], the expense of the mess, and the frequency of quartering on inns instead of barracks."[6] The uniform and kit alone might well absorb the first year's pay, and if a full dress uniform was ruined, the officer would have to purchase another. Dr. Douglas Reid, a regimental surgeon in the Nine-tieth Foot, received 7s./6d. per day during the Crimean War and was in debt for more than a year to clear his outlay cost.[7]

Regimental officers were also important in determining the condition of their units; some were lazy, foolish, or worthless dandies, while others were both intelligent and competent. Some were sadistic monsters, but others were humane, generous, and even self-sacrificing in pursuit of their mens' welfare. There were many complaints about young fools who joined, not because of their love of the service and desire for glory, but because they wanted to indulge their vanity or advance their social status.[8] Wellington commented acidly in 1812 that "nobody . . . ever reads a regulation or an order as if it were to be a guide for his conduct, or in any other manner than as an amusing novel; and the consequence is, that when complicated arrangements are to be carried into execution . . . every gentleman proceeds according to his own fancy."[9] As a group, they frequently left management to the noncommissioned officers, and it was not unusual for the sergeant-major to actually run the unit. Indeed, the sergeants were the army's backbone, having risen from the most competent of the privates. Sergeants frequently took on the role of an old family servant, guiding young and inexperienced officers in the ways of the service.[10]

The privates were recruited from the lowest, most despised levels of society. Many joined in hopes of escaping extreme poverty, but it was difficult to attract decent men with families because the army made no provision for dependents, who were abandoned when the unit was shipped out. Wellington noted: "What is the consequence? That none but the worst description of men enter the regular service."[11] Consequently, the army was composed of an eclectic group of men often desperate from poverty or criminality, including outcasts, tramps, petty criminals, adventurers, bumpkins, fools, and idealists. "You can hardly conceive such a set brought together," as Wellington said of them.[12]

For the Other Ranks, the service was generally a bad bargain, and before the post-Crimean reforms conditions were frequently harsh. As one historian has noted, "Hard as an employer might be, he did not exercise a control over one's clothing, appointments and mode of walking. A merciless employer might be left; the penalty for desertion was death."[13] Most enlistments were for "life," which actually meant that a man was discharged after twenty-one years, or (in most cases) earlier if he was physically incapable of service. But very few survived their term of enlistment, for service in relatively healthy climates like Britain was usually short, whereas assignments in unhealthy ones—especially India—were frequently quite lengthy.[14] Thus poor families were usually devastated when their sons enlisted, and they did not expect to see them again.[15]

Living conditions did not alleviate these harsh circumstances. In 1813, common soldiers' food consisted of an unvaried daily diet of three-quarters of a pound of beef, usually of very poor quality with the fat, bone, and gristle left on, and one pound of bread, to which an additional one-half pound was added in 1833. Soldiers ran the risk of getting a piece of bone instead of meat in this already inadequate meal. Moreover, in many units the food was always prepared in the same monotonous way. On foreign service the meat ration might be altered to salt-pork instead of beef, but otherwise this unvaried fare was expected to sustain a soldier for a lifetime enlistment of twenty-one years. Until 1840, when a third meal was added,[16] the army provided only breakfast and dinner for its troops, which left many in a perpetual state of hunger, and even the additional food often proved to be inadequate.[17]

Yet circumstances varied from unit to unit. The traditional view of the army, expressed in Fortescue's *History*, has been that of an almost unmitigated misery for the Other Ranks, but though some conditions, such as the state of the barracks, were uniform throughout most of the army, many other factors could vary a good deal.[18]

Conditions were sometimes better on the march, where the men bought their own dinners,[19] though there was always the possibility that they would be quartered at inns of the worst description where food was "scantily prepared, and of the worst kind, and they [paid] dearly for it." The beds in such places were often "an antidote against rest . . . filthy and hard," and the rooms "seldom as good as where the hens roost."[20] Until 1827, soldiers in barracks slept four together in cribs, and though the minimum space was supposed to be 450 cubic feet per man, in some it was as few as 225 cubic feet. This was a smaller area than that provided by any workhouse, jail, or prison in the entire realm,[21] and barracks were compared to conditions on slave ships.[22] It was not uncommon for bedclothes to remain unwashed for years, and wooden urine tubs were the only receptacles provided at night for any sort of filth or refuse. These same tubs, after being emptied (but not always washed out), served as wash basins in the morning. No other furniture or amenities of any kind were provided in barracks.[23] Consequently, disease was an "extraordinary" problem, "hospitalizing 37% of the rank and file in 1860 alone," the cause of which was directly linked to the soldier's environment.[24]

The pay of a shilling per day, raised from eight pence in the 1790s, contrasts poorly with a bricklayer's pay of 3s./9d. per day in that same period, and the era of the French wars was one of rapid inflation.[25] Pay was further reduced by deductions for clothing, necessaries, and the mess bill (minus bread, which the public paid for after 1806). In some units what meager pay was left was withheld under some other pretext; not only did men of the Seventh Dragoon Guards sometimes have to go without rations during the Seventh "Kaffir" War of 1846–1847, but food deductions were still withheld from their pay and they were never compensated.[26] In 1853, a private of the Thirty-second Foot in India wrote that his unit had been served such bad food that a board of officers condemned it, and many soldiers ate nothing. The regimental quartermaster and commissary then robbed the men of their next meal, by which the quartermaster "greatly increased his income."[27]

Those in authority found many ways to victimize privates. A military satire, Francis Grose's *The Mirror's Image*, addresses the Other Ranks concerning officers who "are constantly endeavouring to withhold from you all your just dues."[28] Superiors might rob them with impunity, and brave indeed was the man who dared to complain; even if falsely accused of a crime, he had better remain silent: "If a man, when accused by superiors of something of which he was not guilty, ventured to speak in his own defence, he was called a lawyer, and desired to give no reply. If he said that he thought it was hard . . . the answer was, 'D——n you sir, you have no right to think . . . do what you are ordered, sir, right or wrong.'"[29] A guardsman who was ordered to buy new trousers even though his colonel was obligated by regulation to supply a free pair waited to complain until he was punished for not being presentable on parade. The complaint secured the trousers for him and the rest of his troop, but he was soon falsely charged with a crime and court-martialed. After two months of solitary confinement he was sentenced to seven years' transportation to Australia.[30]

Such fiscal abuses were easy to get away with. An investigation ordered by Secretary at War Hardinge in 1828 revealed that of forty-nine units stationed in Ireland, only four kept accurate books.[31] Fortescue states that even when the regulations were followed, "the life of a soldier, so far as the state was concerned with him sounds almost unendurable."[32]

Even the very small amount of pay left after deductions could be further reduced if the colonel ordered that extra ornaments be added to the uniform, and regimental commanders often evaded army dress regulations: "There are scarcely three regiments in the service, that do not deviate more or less from His Majesty's instructions."[33] Colonels still controlled the supply of clothing, and this was a major source of their expected profit from running a regiment. They purchased items in bulk and sold them to the men for a profit, but they had other sources of income too. For example, the average manpower deficiency for each battalion for the ten years preceding 1811 was 202 men, yet colonels still received and pocketed the clothing money earmarked for them. In 1811 this averaged £2 6s./9d. per man, or a total of £472 per battalion. This was the "casual" part, or the "off-reckonings," of the colonel's income.[34]

The army expected profit-making because the colonels' pay was so low, being the same in 1811 as it was in Marlborough's day. There was no guarantee that the colonels would make money, however, and they might even lose large sums on clothing. A unit might be stationed on the other side of the globe with clothing or equipment that was shoddy and would have to be replaced locally, with the cost being borne by the colonel or passed on to the men. Sometimes the delivery of official supplies was so irregular at foreign stations that colonels had to make up their troops' equipment in whatever way they could. The Dundas report of 1811 complained that "regiments are frequently so dispersed, particularly on foreign stations, as to make it difficult to ascertain within any reasonable space of time, the quantities of clothing actually delivered to their men."[35] A sudden change of station—which was not infrequent—might also render either full dress or tropical clothing unnecessary, and the colonel would have to take the loss on items he had already paid for. Colonels were required to pay out large sums and were subject to "ruinous delays" in settling their accounts, for they had to deal with the regimental agents, who in turn dealt with the paymaster-general and the clothiers. Even if the corps might be able to use this clothing later, there were problems with deterioration or damage while it was in store. These conditions made it easier for the colonels to alter their units' dress, and many thus tailored the styles according to their own preferences. "Regiments of the line serve . . . three-fourths of their time in our colonies . . . No reference can be made to higher authority, or any assistance sought after from without . . . But few who have ever been in the army can understand the almost unlimited power of the colonel of a regiment."[36]

The regiments were for the most part self-contained institutions, and the particular customs of each depended to a great extent upon the colonel.[37] Many tried to make a large profit (the "clothing colonels") by ordering their men to buy unauthorized items.[38] But if the colonel was wealthy and indifferent to expenses, he might pay out of his own pocket to create a more extravagant appearance, adding a more showy kit or additional items. Some lavished money on their units, including Lord Cardigan, who spent £10,000 per year on the Eleventh Hussars.[39] Others made a less showy appearance by using shoddy materials to increase profits.

The colonels thus varied a good deal in managing their units; some cheated their men or treated them with brutality, whereas others were decent, conscientious leaders. Some even used their own money to provide the soldiers with food and comforts in times of hardship and tried to be fathers to their men.[40] Private James Fitzgibbon "looked upon [his colonel] as the father of the regiment."[41] The authorities expected the colonel to animate the unit as a whole; as the Horse Guards informed them, "To him [the colonel] should each individual look up for example, instruction, and encouragement."[42] This emphasis on the colonel as a paternal figure is intrinsic to the regimental system, for enlistment meant that soldiers became virtually cut off from any other home and family life. This notion was officially encouraged: "It is wished that every non-commissioned officer and soldier should consider his regiment in a great degree as his home," and soldiers themselves frequently described the regiment as a family.[43]

The family setting was partly a result of the constant movement of units, which rarely stayed in any one post for very long. Consequently, soldiers could not hope to associate for any length of time with anyone outside the regiment, and those who married often paired up with other soldiers' daughters. Thus each regiment was a tight-knit, nomadic unit: "In civil life men have homes [and families, but in the army] they become dependent upon friends. Nowhere is friendship more true, more warm, more exalted, than in the army; absence from the mother-country, privation, peril, the pursuit and attainment of honor, are so many ties which bind soul to soul, in bonds bright and indestructible."[44]

For some the regiment was the best family they had ever known, and many officers firmly believed that no family could equal the precious rewards that were gained by the comradeship, solidarity, self-sacrifice, and honor of a first-rate regiment: "The hours of friendship and fellowship, the mutual support of hand and heart, of one purse and one mind . . . I ever found in military life, and there exclusively."[45] Unless a newly enlisted soldier was a complete loner—in which case his life would likely be made difficult—he was forced to participate in his unit's social life and to abide by whatever norms of behavior existed there.[46]

Yet even in the best of circumstances, army life was a bad bargain for almost everyone, involving as it did low pay, poor conditions, and isolation from the usual patterns of family life. But it was vital for the commanders that soldiers perform their duty exactly as ordered. Despite dreadful conditions endured by armed men whose work was to wield deadly force, maintaining the effectiveness and reliability of the regiments was absolutely essential for the state.

The manipulation of military spectacle was central to this process, and a major factor was the dress, which consisted of colorful, brilliant clothing, elaborate headgear, gaudy equipment, badges, and regimental distinctions. These elements, along with weapons, flags, music, and musical instruments, were displayed through the carefully regulated deployment and movements of men, animals, and their gear. Together they constituted the many ceremonies and rituals in military life, including parades and reviews, as well as the daily exercises, inspections, drills, guard mounting, and other duties.

The symbolic associations of these elements made them vital components in managing the deadly military machine. Here is the reason for the apparent contradiction that mere looks seemed to supersede the fundamental task of wielding armed force. This military show promoted goals of much greater importance than simply identifying the soldiers' occupation, preventing desertion, or gratifying a superficial whim for display. The martial spectacle could inspire powerful and sometimes conflicting emotions; the pristine image was upheld by endless drill and inspections that maintained a rigid discipline and order. Yet soldiers would literally die for what these military images symbolized, and even for the physical objects that conveyed the symbolism.[47] Maintaining and setting into motion this martial spectacle required a considerable amount of time, effort, and money, and the army was very much a theatrical institution.[48] Great emphasis was thus put upon the importance of fancy uniforms and display in the British army.

The uniform was the army's trademark and symbol—a distinctive dress that immediately set the soldier off from everyone else. Whereas civilians' dress is a personal proclamation of identity, the army's carefully constructed image was a matter of regulation and command, and dire punishments could result if common soldiers deviated in any way from the correct appearance. From the moment a potential recruit considered joining the service until the day he was either discharged or died, imagery constituted a vital dimension of every duty he carried out. Spectacle thus permeated military life and linked it from top to bottom.

Yet the visual and cultural dimension of military institutions has often been overlooked as a subject for critical analysis. Although there are many antiquarian and collector books about military dress, a number of which are supported by excellent research, only rarely has the subject been deemed worthy of scholarly analysis.[49] This is surprising, considering that warriors have always clothed themselves in striking costumes, and military uniforms, parades, and other displays have long been popular entertainments in Britain and other Western countries.

State-controlled military forces in the modern era have utilized uniforms whenever possible since the standing army in Europe reappeared in the mid-seventeenth century.[50] This emergence was a part of the growth of state power, as new, permanent armies gradually superseded the old, temporary mercenary regiments. States have always utilized visual images to enhance their prestige—and hence power—in many contexts, including court life and culture, art, and architecture, because visual images can exert a profound impact upon human emotion and thus significantly influence belief and action.[51] This ability to arouse people's emotions, and thus affect behavior, is a potent source of power. Because the most vital manifestation of state power is the army, the military's adoption of visual images is thus a phenomenon of considerable importance.

Martial images have always been a basic element of English state spectacle.[52] But from the mid-eighteenth century, European armies imitated the Prussian art of war, which was essentially the creation of King Frederick William I and a focal point for his martial obsessions, including a fixation on military uniforms.[53] The victories of his son Frederick II made the Prussian army the subsequent model for modern militarism and defined many features in the development of the military uniform.

This study focuses on the British army in the first half of the nineteenth century, examining the role and functions of its imagery and spectacle, especially the uniform. The influence of the military show became particularly strong in this era, probably stronger than at any time in British history.[54] The following chapters will show how martial spectacle functioned—what both soldiers and civilians felt as well as observed from the behavior of others. This concerns both the uses of the show and its perception, and perception is the key word, for the significance of images is primarily a matter of how people perceive them.

The era of 1800–1856 is particularly intriguing, for there were sharp contradictions in both civilians' and soldiers' perceptions of martial images. Many Britons clearly took pride in the army as a symbol of Britain's superiority, and many experienced vicarious feelings of honor, glory, valor, and national pride at the sight of gleaming steel and brilliant colors featured in the military show. Yet large numbers of Britons hated and feared the military as an engine of repression and believed that a peacetime army was an unconstitutional, un-English, and illegal institution. They complained about the army's cost and the violent and often morally reprehensible behavior of off-duty soldiers and officers. But the public still flocked by the tens of thousands and more to watch military reviews. And ironically, though military imagery was a fundamental part of state symbolism, organized groups who fought against the state often adopted it for their own use.

Although the army was a symbol for tyranny in this era, it still experienced significant reforms; but overall, there was a great degree of continuity both in its spectacle and in how it was managed. The show's significance does not end with the reforms subsequent to 1854 (although the more extreme aspects of both army management and spectacle started to diminish in the 1830s). Battlefield triumphs and the distinctive red coat contributed to the army's brilliant reputation through the nineteenth century and beyond, and one of its most noteworthy aspects is the continuity of its traditions and management methods, which have done much to maintain the British army's rich heritage.

The spectacle's trappings exerted a strong psychological and emotional influence on the soldiers, and thus were a vital tool in maintaining the dependability of the military instrument. For any state struggling to maintain control and authority in situations where its forces are insufficient for the task, as was the case in Great Britain, the manipulation of visual images is especially significant in the exercise of power. In addressing this management problem, the state had to mold and shape to the greatest possible extent the beliefs, opinions, and actions of its soldiers in order to make them into effective—and reliable—tools of war.

The primary goal of this book is to show how this imagery was an essential component of military management in the British army. Militaria and related features of the martial spectacle were essential in communicating to soldiers the fundamental values embedded in the military model: bravery and duty, discipline, self-control, conformity, order, and hierarchy; unity and solidarity of purpose; motivation, efficiency, and self-sacrifice for a higher goal; and, above all, loyalty to those in command. This system of values thus formed the "military virtues," and from the perspective of the commanders, these were the concepts and values they had to instill in their subordinates.

Soldiers had strong reasons to oppose the system, especially considering the larger conflicts between the rich and poor in British society. The management of these men was therefore a formidable task. In tackling this difficult problem, commanders had to manipulate the soldiers' emotions to invoke the desired response, and it was therefore essential that the spectacle be charismatic in nature.

But this show exerted a much wider appeal in British society, and broader, more fundamental questions are raised about the phenomenon. The values symbolized by the imagery exerted profound effects that reached well beyond the relatively circumscribed boundaries of the military subculture, and the basic meanings and principles of the earlier themes have continued beyond 1856, and remain strong to the present day.

This dovetails in part with the observation made at the turn of the century by Max Weber, who claimed that the discipline of armies has had lasting effects upon the political and social order, forming a model for the operation of the farm, factory, and office. But this thesis included only minimal evidence for its support, and it has not been explained how and why the martial model was adopted; nor have the reasons for this adoption been much explored.[55]

A secondary goal of this work is to show evidence supporting Weber's thesis, but within a somewhat modified context. This system of "military virtues" formed a complex of values, or a paradigm, which, being presented in the most positive light possible, constituted an ideal. This served as a managerial model outside of the military, and sometimes elements of the martial spectacle itself were adopted; an important example is civilian use of the military's inspirational and bureaucratic language.

This ideal thus manifested the notion of how any large-scale operation ought to function, especially from a management perspective; ideally, all subordinates would be totally dedicated to the goals set by those in authority. They would act as the passive cogs in a great machine, and do exactly what they were told, acting only as ordered. Such is the idealized vision for operations in any large-scale modern institution (however contrary its actual workings may be).

But the martial vision did not instruct how to produce goods or structure the finances of economic and governmental institutions; armies exist to threaten the state's enemies and to fight—not to produce commodities or cope with social problems. Rather, the martial paradigm displayed an idealized model of organization that was projected as a vision, and as a result it tended to aid in the imposition of social control on civilian society—whether enforced or voluntary—in a wide variety of contexts. It promoted what state leaders considered the proper spirit—and image— for soldiers. But in the civilian world, too, this ideal was adopted by some Britons as a guide for working and even living in the new and troubling world of urbanization, institutionalization, and industrialization. The relevance of this subject thus extends far beyond the boundaries of conventional military history.[56]

This process of change is also a cultural one, however, and the paradigm significantly influenced various genres of entertainment and pleasure. These cultural themes thus expand the scope of this study from the more circumscribed world of the military to that of civilians. I will argue that the appeal of the military model played a significant role in spreading the army's servile values throughout British society, promoting and advertising the adoption of the "military virtues" far beyond the military subculture.

This correlates with and is in part intended to complement the works of Lewis Mumford, who has written extensively on the influence of the concept of the machine, which he calls the "megamachine," in the development of civilization. Mumford argues that the ideas and values associated with the megamachine—regularity, order, and predictable, repeatable physical effects, as well as the manipulation of both the natural world and human beings—have all played important roles in the development of Western civilization. This includes political and economic activity, science, belief, leisure, and art. In short, he argues that all aspects of human thought and culture have been touched by this concept; it has both stimulated and enhanced the development of centralized political and economic power in the history of Western civilization, and thus is integral to the development of the state.

Military institutions are situated at the heart of state power, and the megamachine has greatly influenced the art of war throughout Western history. The values embedded in the nineteenth-century martial paradigm in particular have been deeply rooted in the idea of the machine. Mumford noted that "through the army . . . the standard model of the megamachine was transmitted from culture to culture." But he provided only a sketchy account of the army's actual role in this process and only briefly discussed the emergence of uniforms in the later Middle Ages. He pointed out that uniforms were "an outward token of inner unison" and that the "drill made [soldiers] act as one, discipline made them respond as one, and the uniform made them look as one."[57] But beyond these platitudes, Mumford did not analyze the significance of the role of spectacle in transmitting—and more important, in advertising—the concept of the megamachine.

Although this book expands on the ideas of Weber and Mumford, it is primarily a departure from them, and is a foray into territory that is familiar to everyone, yet largely passed over for serious inquiry. It focuses upon the theme of martial spectacle as an inspiring, charismatic model for military and other institutional management, elaborating on the martial values that were most useful—and essential—for those in authority.

CHAPTER ONE

The Spectacular Image

T he ideal of perfection was central to the art of nineteenth-century military management, especially in connection with martial display.[1] This emphasis on high standards frequently superseded all other priorities on home service (and often hampered foreign service), even to the direct detriment of the soldier's comfort and health. The concern accorded to appearances also rendered some weapons less effective, diminished the usefulness of certain aspects of training, and could be harmful to army horses.

Officers were sometimes obsessed with presenting a correct and pleasing appearance, which often resulted in the total neglect of other significant considerations, even if these were vital to the army's success. They were said to "attribute the glorious victories of the king of Prussia to these [appearances] and have therefore . . . introduced the Prussian exercise, [which reflected the] presumption that strength and beauty combine and move together by innate correspondence."[2] An eighteenth-century general complained that "those who embrace this profession take little or no pains to study it. They seem to think, that the knowledge of a few insignificant and useless trifles [constitutes] a great officer."

These "numberless and insignificant trifles" were the chief concern of officers whose "only science is reduced to adjust a hat, a button, etc., and such other important matters in which the merit of an officer entirely consists."[3] In 1831, one veteran colonel wrote of his disgust with "old musty general officers who had never seen service . . . All they cared about was the book of regulations, and counting one's buttons, and even measuring the distance with a pocket-rule from button to button with great gravity."[4] The duke of Kent was a prime example of a general so obsessed; as the commander of the Gibraltar garrison in 1803, he wrote *Standing Orders* of three hundred pages (in fine print) that dwelled at great length on minutiae. These included commands that all officers and Other Ranks not be allowed to disembark upon their arrival in Gibraltar before getting the duke's regulation haircut, and, to attain a perfect posture for standing and listening to divine services, that officers of the various corps "are frequently to practice their men at standing in this position, in order that they may become habituated to remain in it with perfect steadiness for a length of time."[5]

The most elaborate attention was given to every aspect of outward appearance—weapons, equipment, uniform, headgear, shoes—whenever a soldier was publicly displayed, be it mounting the guard, marching, or performing in a review or parade. The goal was an immaculate appearance, ensured by a weekly inspection of every soldier's kit.[6] Regulations in effect until the end of the French wars specified that musket barrels and metal fittings were to be "as bright as a looking-glass," and all belts were to be pipeclayed a snow-white color.[7] Even the leather backpack was to be "very pretty to look at, varnished like a mirror, and without any crease or wrinkle."[8] Soldiers were under strict orders never to appear "slovenly or unsoldier-like," and were supposed to wear working clothes (worn drill order or full dress) to perform manual labor so that their best regimentals would not be dirtied or damaged.[9] Before being furloughed, they were required to appear "perfectly clean."[10]

Every aspect of the soldier's life that had to do with physical appearances received the most minute and exacting attention. For example, when the soldiers of the Second Royal North British Dragoons (Scots Grays) made their beds, they were ordered to "fold the blanket, the two sheets, and the rug, so as the colours of the rug shall appear throughout the folds of the sheets like streaks of marble. They must take the point of a knife and lay the edges of the folds straight until they look artistical to the eye."[11]

Even the most mundane and unglamorous articles of equipment could be made to serve as decoration. The list of "stores of all sorts" for the

Royal Horse Artillery was extensive and included many of the standard tools of military engineering, such as artificers' and entrenching tools, as well as separate categories of miscellaneous stores, stable necessities, and ordnance stores, in addition to soldiers' personal items and those supplies needed for a battery on campaign. One officer noted with pride that "it has always been a special care in the Royal Artillery to maintain this completeness, and to take as much pride in the appearance of the stores of all sorts as in the more ordinary and showy details."[12]

Artillery and cavalry horses were also an important part of the show, and consequently were as closely scrutinized as other equipment. One custom was to teach artillery horses to "dance or pirouette," but other practices were not so harmless.[13] Cavalry horses were actually painted ("colored") so that they would all be the same color on parade, even though this was detrimental to their health.[14] During the French wars many regiments used the curry-comb too often, which tended to deplete the oil on the horses' skin and render them more prone to catching cold. Another custom was to trim the hooves too closely, which often resulted in their becoming tender-footed.[15] Hussar saddles were sometimes placed on their backs in such a way as to make the rider uncomfortable and likely to be pitched forward and injured.[16] This was done "from the point of view of parade and appearance" and also negatively affected the animal's comfort and performance.[17]

The soldier's body and posture were also deemed important, and height and attractive mien were considered very desirable. Some uniforms were apparently designed to be worn by tall men.[18] The army sought the tallest recruits, and regimental regulations included minimum height requirements that continually changed.[19] In 1806, the Forty-third Foot was reported to have men "all of the same height."[20]

These priorities hindered recruiting efforts, especially in wartime. A contemporary noted in 1811, "We can not help observing that if mere size were less attended to . . . the recruiting branch would be considerably benefitted."[21] The preference for tall men continued, even though they were "ordinarily the first to fail under fatigues; and medical men know, from observation, that they commonly suffer from diseases in greater proportion than others."[22] This emphasis on height must have exacerbated the manpower shortages that have been the most significant problem for the British army throughout its history.

This paradox highlights the importance of appearances, since with each reduction in the army's strength, the shortest men were simply dismissed, and a regiment that had just returned from overseas service often lost its only true veterans.[23] These men were discharged as "worn out," even though they might still be fit for service, because the colonels wanted their men to look young and be active.[24] Some commanders even accepted men of bad character as long as they had "a masculine and soldierly aspect."[25] In 1795, the colonel of the Eightieth Foot, the first marquess of Anglesey, so disliked the fact that all his tall men had died on campaign that he wanted the unit to begin fighting again quickly so that the "ugly little fellows" could be killed off.[26]

There is probably a connection between this emphasis on height and the tendency for light cavalry to become too heavy during periods of peace; some colonels could not resist the temptation to enlist taller men to enhance their unit's appearance, and so larger horses were required, and light cavalry became heavy in the process. This custom hampered the cavalry's flexibility, because heavy and light units were meant for different duties and tactical situations. But the aesthetic priority also put a great strain on the horses; the total weight (including the rider) carried by Scots Grays horses in 1822 when on "actual service" was estimated at 363 lbs., 14 oz., although as dragoons they were supposed to be medium cavalry.[27] Horses died from carrying lesser burdens; a Royal Horse Guard's mount in the mid-1830s died "from overexertion and the great weight he had to carry (nearly 20 stone [280 lbs.])."[28]

Height requirements also influenced decisions on promotion. Promising or deserving soldiers were often prevented from attaining higher rank because commanders liked to promote tall, good-looking men.[29] In one instance, Sergeant Calladine of the Nineteenth Foot was recommended for promotion to pay-sergeant in 1820, but because he was not tall enough for the colonel's taste, he lost the promotion and six pence a day of extra pay until years later, when another colonel took over command.[30]

Generally, the more prestigious and exclusive the corps, the taller the height requirement. The guards had the most stringent standards, followed by the fusilier regiments and line infantry. Sometimes the desire for tall men led to conflicts within regiments. Grenadier companies in foot units, for example, were traditionally made up of the tallest men in each corps; one officer complained that this practice was designed to "gratify the vanity of the captains of those companies . . . and ruins the appearance of the regiments."[31] This often-evaded rule was not supposed to apply to hussars (or lancers and light dragoons) because of their tactical uses; hussars were in many ways the elite of the cavalry, both in the brilliance of their dress and in their combat achievements. By the end of the eighteenth century, men could not become hussars if they were tall.

The tallest cavalrymen were those in the elite heavy regiments of Household Cavalry, and the First Life Guards would take no recruit who was not a full six feet tall without his shoes.[32] To weed out the shortest soldiers, *General Orders* from 1815 stipulated that men selected as officers' servants were to be the shortest of the regiment, those from the center and rear ranks.[33] Like many other directives that were in keeping with the colonels' preferences, this had probably been practiced in many units for years.

The height of soldiers was emphasized by their posture, which for appearance' sake was to be "quite straight." Officers were advised to walk "without affectation, easy, and erect, with a frank and open front." The ideal soldier's build was "a good figure . . . broad chest, long neck, arms, back, and shoulders"; stout officers were advised to wear "military belts," or corsets.[34] In the Seventy-fourth Highlanders, the men's carriage and gait while off duty were considered important enough to require "constant attention."[35] When soldiers appeared in groups on public streets they were ordered to march together, as "this sort of practice will assist you very much in retaining the air of a soldier."[36] Men were even taught to walk in a manner peculiar to their corps, and it was sometimes possible to identify a soldier's regiment by his gait. Soldiers of the Seventh Foot (Royal Fusiliers) were expected "at all times [to] walk in that light and airy manner which distinguishes the fusilier."[37] The Prussian ideal for soldiers' coats, which called for a tight fit that constricted movement, tended to enforce this posture, though it was modified over the years.

Posture, gait, and tight-fitting clothing were not the only elements that marked a soldier—the brilliant and often gaudy uniform was a trademark of the army. The significance the soldiers accorded to the uniform as a symbol of their profession is underscored by the fact that the service itself was referred to as "the cloth."[38]

The uniforms worn by different branches of the service varied greatly; although coat colors consisted primarily of the traditional scarlet for infantry and engineers, scarlet or dark blue for cavalry, dark blue for the artillery, and dark green for rifle units, each regiment had its own coat facing colors, which consisted of a different color (originally the coat lining) for the collar, cuffs, and lapels. The facings were a wide variety of rich, brilliant, or subtle hues. Yellow or green was a favorite choice, and between 1802 and 1812 eight different shades of yellow and ten of green were used.[39] Facing colors often varied over the years with the changing taste of the colonel and the officers, which was sometimes initiated by irregularities or accidents in dyeing.[40]

Officers' coats were trimmed with gold or silver bullion lace, and white worsted lace was used for the Other Ranks. Coats carried between twenty and forty buttons, depending upon the regiment, and a button lace surrounded each buttonhole in the Other Ranks' coats. Each unit had its own button lace pattern of a rectangular or "bastion" shape, consisting of decorative "worms" (stripes) running around the lace, usually in two or three colors.[41] Officers also wore bullion epaulets, whereas the Other Ranks often wore epaulets of worsted wool.[42]

Headgear also contributed to the striking appearance of soldiers and received a good deal of attention from the army's commanders. It was often tall and imposing (especially in the cavalry) and topped by plumes, usually of white or red and white, and green for light infantry and rifle corps. Shakos were decorated with a brass plate, a hat cord—made of braid or worsted wool, depending upon rank—ending in "acorn" decorations, and chin scales of brass, leather, or cloth.

The end result was a very impressive display, with the British army providing one of the best military shows in Europe: "It was superior in show and brilliancy of appearance to any army in Europe. The dazzling colour of the uniform, the variety of facings, the contrasts of the different part of the dress, the profusion of ornaments, namely feathers, frisures, powdered locks, ponderous queues, and polished accoutrements, were singularly contrived to strike the admiring multitude . . . The size, figure, and the complexion of the men, presented a dazzling *coup d'oeil*."[43]

The uniform clearly set soldiers apart from civilians, but whereas early-eighteenth-century male dress had tended, like uniforms, to be colorful, the two gradually diverged in character. The old spirit in civilian high fashion had been aristocratic, focusing upon the wearer's individuality; the trend that would eventually become identified with the middle class and urban society tended (with some exceptions) to be more sober and restrained in color, and did not attract as much attention.

Restraint was certainly not the appropriate image for the early-nineteenth-century fighting man. The soldier embodied the heroic image of the defender of the realm, especially in wartime. Samuel Johnson observed: "They who stand forth the foremost in danger, for the community, have the respect of mankind . . . Every man thinks meanly of himself for not having been a soldier."[44] Such a man could swagger and strut, a peacock among duller, more ordinary folk.

Before the late 1830s, when soldiers were still required to wear a side arm, this swagger was enhanced by the latent threat of violence. Although the carrying of swords had ceased to be fashionable for gentlemen by the late 1780s, the bearing of weapons was traditionally considered essential for soldiers, and regulations required officers to wear swords while in uniform. In addition to its doubtful utility as a weapon, the sword served as an officer's symbol of authority. When he was too disabled or sick to carry it on parade, an orderly or servant carried it for him.[45] Some officers felt a strong attachment to their swords; John Shipp related an anecdote about a British officer in a French prison: "They should not have taken his sword; he gazed upon his empty sword-belt as a man gazes on the grave of his brother."[46] When General Sir John Moore was severely wounded at the battle of Corunna in 1808, he would not allow his aides to remove his sword, though it aggravated his wound. He feared that his sword would be lost, even knowing he would never need it again.[47] In peacetime, to ensure that passers-by would not miss the effect, many officers wore their swords low, so that the end of the scabbard, the "shoe," would make noise by dragging on the ground. Some dandy officers had small "treeks" (wheels) attached to the shoe.[48]

Enlisted men also carried weapons, and though cavalrymen wore swords, the abolition of the hanger (short sword) for heavy infantry in 1768 left the bayonet as the infantryman's side arm (rifle regiments used sword-bayonets). The triangular bayonet was more lethal than the sword, although it was less handy to use. The *General Regulations* of the Regency period stipulated that the bayonet be worn with the uniform, which meant that soldiers, who were not allowed to possess mufti (civilian clothing), were always armed when out in public.[49] Many regimental order books also required soldiers to wear side arms with their uniforms.[50] The great pride enlisted men took in being armed is illustrated in an 1835 measure added to the punishment a soldier was to receive for using his weapon in a brawl. He would be "stripped of his bayonet and bayonet belt, and proclaimed by the commanding officer as a man unworthy to be intrusted with the care of his bayonet, except in the ranks . . . and his name posted in some conspicuous place in the barrack room or elsewhere."[51]

The use of weapons off-duty was a serious and unsolvable problem. The common soldiers were notorious for their drunken quarrels, and the possession of side arms at such times led to the loss of a number of men, either by their being killed or crippled, or by the execution or imprisonment of the culprits. The regulation that soldiers always appear in arms contradicted a much older directive of 1687 from the secretary of state—that they were never to appear off-duty in public with bayonets, precisely because of their tendency to use the weapons in brawls. The Horse Guards (the office of the commander in chief) renewed this directive with a circular in 1837, and it appears that in the years before the Chartist political actions of the 1840s, there were more violent conflicts with civilians.[52] Yet it is difficult to say how effectively this order was enforced before the Crimean War. The social researcher Henry Mayhew interviewed "a soldier's woman" in the late 1850s who told him that a drunken guardsman had wounded her with a bayonet "three or four years ago."[53]

These instances of the importance of image superseding needs that were intrinsic to the army's most basic interests and functions are by no means isolated ones. General Lloyd declared that the great concern shown for appearances was sometimes pursued "even with a degree of madness." By modern standards of military efficiency, this fixation on appearances certainly seems to contain much that was absurd, given that so many elements of soldiers' clothing and equipment were uncomfortable and even dangerous.[54]

Army dress did undergo official review and direction, however, and the army's Clothing Board sat to issue opinions on newly proposed items and make recommendations on new patterns, alterations, or discontinuations in clothing and equipment. But, though it appears that a desired change might be legitimized by the board's recommendations, it lacked the power to keep poorly designed items from being adopted (see Chapter 2); especially bad ones, however, might be altered on its recommendation. The board suggested that the "Belgic" shako of the late Napoleonic era be made of leather rather than felt, because the latter could fall apart in the rain. This advice was not taken, but it seems the board's recommendation for a height reduction was adopted, and the height was reduced, but apparently to retain an imposing appearance a higher false front was attached.[55]

Military headdresses provide striking examples of equipment chosen with minimal consideration for convenience or utility. Their shade was inadequate to cool the head in hot weather, they provided no real warmth in the cold, and they gave no protection from the rain. The board reported that "the (stovepipe shako) cap at present worn by the infantry is objectionable—unsteady on the head, and [it provides] little protection from the weather."[56] The shako, bearskin, highland bonnet, lance cap, and most other types of cavalry headgear directed rainwater "in an incessant stream" down the back of the neck of anyone unfortunate enough to be wearing one in rainy weather, which was especially harmful to sentries on cold, rainy nights.[57] The shako peak (bill) was also thought to make the soldiers "unsteady" in taking aim.[58]

Although various types of headgear had oilskin covers to preserve their glittering ornaments from wet weather, the soldier's health was not considered important enough to adopt more practical designs. The bearskin cap was a terrible head covering in rainy weather, because the fur absorbed and held a great deal of water, as did hussar and fusilier busbies and dragoon helmets' large fur crests. On the march, furry hats also collected dust, which, if not present on the road, was sometimes created by the pipeclayed uniforms. The highland feather bonnet shared most of these disadvantages (although it was supposed to be equipped with an oilskin cover). After a long march, soldiers would spend hours restoring their dress and equipment to a pristine condition rather than resting: "A march will never be admitted as an excuse for dirt and slovenliness."[59]

Most models of full dress headgear, including the shako, also had the disadvantage of a "sickening weight,"[60] which placed a strain on the neck and was especially uncomfortable for the Other Ranks, whose hats were heavier than the officers'.[61] A typical "Regency" shako was described in 1830 as "a very heavy and large leather and felt abomination, with a flat top about 12 inches in diameter, and with a black horsehair plume fitted in the front so that the whole weight pressed on the forehead of the wearer."[62] In 1831, the Clothing Board recommended a reduction of only three ounces in the one-pound, fifteen-ounce shako, the most it could be decreased without weakening its design. This recommendation reveals the board's belief that the shako's height was more important than the soldier's health.[63] The weight of cavalry helmets also generated complaints. "The ponderosity of the [heavy cavalry] helmet, must, we are persuaded, generate disease. A substance which is wholly . . . composed of metal, is by no means a covering to be coveted for the head."[64] This model was made larger after 1815.

Headgear that was tall or had large fur crests could be blown off if not strapped on. In a strong wind, a horseman could actually be blown off his mount, and many soldiers complained about this: "In the commonest breeze half [a horseman's] time is taken up with keeping [his headgear] from flying off, with himself in it."[65] These huge helmets, especially when feathers were added, could also frighten the horses of a yeomanry (militia cavalry) unit when operating together with the corps of the wearer, which could be dangerous during riot duty or in battle. The officers' bullion-laced shabracques and other showy equipment could have the same effect; yeomanry horses were "especially unquiet" on active duty (which was not often) because of "the noise, glitter, and irritation of the accoutrements."[66]

Military headgear caused logistical problems, too. The headdresses took a long time to make and required a great deal of care, and it was often impossible to keep enough in store, especially for the cavalry. Grenadier bearskins caused so many problems that by the second half of the eighteenth century they were put in store for units stationed in overseas garrisons (except North America), but even this did not save them from destruction. The Clothing Board stated in 1814 that even when in store, bearskins were eaten by insects "in a very short time."[67] Moth damage was a major problem, and fur caps had to be kept in glazed cases saturated with naphthalene and camphor.

An inquiry into army headdresses at the end of the century revealed that these problems had not been solved; the bearskins worn by the Brigade of Guards were typical: "Between the time of receiving them into store, and issuing them to the battalions, I have to keep men apart combing those bearskins with the greatest care, and watching them as closely as you might watch chickens in an incubator." Brass cavalry helmets also required special care and were kept in glazed cupboards to keep the moisture off them, but even so, on a foggy day "someone has to go over them all with a chamois leather." The hussar busby was also "difficult to store."[68] The fastidious attention paid to showy headgear was also applied to other areas of the soldier's appearance; for example, hair powdering, one of the worst of the Prussian customs, was still followed in the early years of the nineteenth century. Hair was worn in a queue, which was coated with a noxious mixture of grease (sometimes rancid) or tallow and then dusted with flour. This made a neat, white appearance, especially from a distance, but was a filthy encumbrance to the wearer and apt to attract vermin, especially in extremely overcrowded and often dirty barracks. It is ironic that at a time when soldiers were not fed enough to fill their stomachs, they had to buy powdering flour out of their meager pay. In the Tenth Light Dragoons, officers were required to use a pound of powder each week.[69] Most soldiers welcomed the abolition of powdering in 1808, but, typically, the guards kept it longer.

Pipeclay was another source of superficial (but unhealthy) cleanliness that caused much bother. All white surfaces in the kit—trousers, facings (when white), button laces, drill order jackets, piping, and gaiters—were painted with pipeclay, which, until dry, made it difficult for the soldier to move about, since he had to take care not to brush against anything; this was especially annoying in an overcrowded barracks. The uniform's fabric was damaged by heavy, repeated applications of pipeclay,[70] which could also come off in clouds of dust when a regiment was on the march.[71]

This damp coating was also thought to cause rheumatism and other diseases; consequently, white trousers were replaced in the Fifteenth Hussars in 1808 when too many men became ill.[72] In 1830, white drill jackets were replaced by red ones because of this problem, but it seems that sickness caused by pipeclay was not considered significant enough for the Clothing Board to recommend its abolition, for the board stated that all regiments with white facings must pipeclay them on their red drill jackets,[73] and the summer-issue white trousers were not replaced until 1846.[74] One general referred to pipeclay as "white dirt . . . more injurious to the sight and health of the men than anything that can be conceived."[75]

Red or blue coats were also detrimental to the private soldier's health, efficiency, and comfort. Despite the decorations, these were often made of very poor quality fabric and, "though highly dressed to captivate the eye, are not in reality well manufactured for the benefit of the wearer . . . not durable: the cloth is not warm; and the material is so put together that it appears to attract rather than to repel moisture."[76] In 1830, the Clothing Board recommended that button laces be abolished and the savings used for better-quality fabric, but except for the abolition of regimental lace patterns in 1836, lace continued to be used until 1855.[77] The coat could be harmful in other ways, too; in 1815 an ensign got his coattail caught in the traces of a gig that broke while moving, and was dragged a considerable distance.[78]

Some coat details were for effect only and caused additional problems for the soldier; padding the chest to attain the appearance of a pouter pigeon was widespread, but this caused "unpleasant warmth."[79] Padding could be a few inches thick and was a torment in hot, humid weather. If soaked in rain, it became quite heavy—no minor matter for a soldier wearing a full pack. At the same time, the soldier's clothing, which was made of thin cloth, provided inadequate protection from the elements.[80]

The tight fit, so important for appearances, also caused problems. In 1810, the duke of York issued a circular complaining that the coats could not be buttoned over the waistcoat, and that they "diminish the power of action in a mode highly prejudicial to the health and vigour of the soldier, drawing the body together, and checking that freedom and alacrity of motion in the body, and arms, that are so conductive to the growth and expansion of the young, and to the comfort and health of all."[81] For the cavalry, this fit caused still more difficulties. In the Third Dragoon Guards in 1831, tight overalls with straps under the instep made it difficult to mount and dismount, necessitating a new technique whereby the trooper swung himself into the saddle without bending his knees, which "required considerable practice."[82] This clothing was no better adapted for riding; after the Crimean War, an officer wrote: "The inapplicability of the costume [of pre-Crimean cavalry dress] for cavalry movements was . . . ludicrously apparent when anything was attempted beyond the 'walk.' "[83] Yet this fit was to endure for all branches of the army. At the start of the Crimean War, the Horse Guards rejected a recommendation by the director-general of the Army and Ordnance Medical Department that soldiers' coats be tailored more loosely for campaigning.[84]

The tightness of the infantry coats, together with the cheap fabric worn by the Other Ranks, caused another problem—when soaked by rain, soldiers dared not take their coats off for fear they would shrink. The coats would be impossible to put on again, but wearing damp clothes promoted illness. The rainy night before Waterloo, an officer wrote: "If I found a difficulty in getting my jacket off, the difficulty was doubly great in getting it on. I thought I should have torn the sleeves out of it."[85] This problem had plagued the Prussians in the eighteenth century, yet the British did not deem it important enough to avoid when they copied the Prussian model.[86] The greatcoat was supposed to serve as a raincoat, but it too was poorly constructed.

The detrimental effects of the clothing were made even worse for the Other Ranks by the neckstock. This was a collar made of thick leather, usually four inches high, which showed at the neck. The stock was buckled or buttoned over the shirt and under the coat, kept the wearer's head erect in the correct martial posture, and was always worn with the uniform in peacetime. But it held the soldier's head like a vise, prevented him from turning his head to the side, and cut into his neck.

The stock had emerged as a part of military dress in the early eighteenth century, and "officers, wishing the men to appear healthy," used this sartorial instrument of cruelty to enhance both discipline and appearances by having it deliberately fit too tightly around the neck to make an underfed man's face look ruddy, thus achieving a deceptive look of health. But the stock also had the effect of "almost produc[ing] suffocation."[87]

In his order of 1810, the duke of York complained of stocks that injured the soldier "by pressing on the glands of the neck, and by that means exciting scrophulous swellings in constitutions where there is a tendency to that disorder."[88] An army doctor believed the stock would "deteriorate the sight, from the pressure of congested blood upon the optic nerve, and the stock would seem to be preserved only for the purpose of generating a tendency to all kinds of apoplectic and ophthalmic diseases . . . It would be better surely, to inflict an ulcer upon the soldier's neck."[89] The stock was the most hated article of the soldier's necessaries.[90]

The problems caused by the clothing, helmet, and stock were compounded by other items in the kit and the ways soldiers had to carry them. In 1811, the Clothing Board complained that the buttons on the infantry's tight, gray gaiters caused sores on the men's legs, and that the material used for the haversack was unsuitable.[91] The thick, pipeclayed belts that carried the heavy haversack had a horizontal chest strap that caused exceptional discomfort, as did the crossbelts, which carried the canteen on one side and the cartridge box on the other and were held in place by a brass breastplate. The total weight of the equipment was seventy pounds, including grooming articles. The full kit was normally worn at drill, at reviews, on guard duty, and on most occasions when long arms were carried; many units even went to church parades in full marching order.[92]

Frequent guard duty and drill in full kit caused health problems for many men, including diseases of the lungs and heart, and the pack strap especially was the subject of complaints. Private Waterfield of the Thirty-second Foot noted that in the 1840s, his knapsack caused great chest pain, for which he was eventually hospitalized, yet: "I looked remarkably well, for to take me by appearance, no one would have imagined that I suffered from any disease whatsoever." He added that "the frequent use of the knapsack, and the hard duty caused many a premature death."[93] James Bodell of the Fifty-ninth Foot wrote that after an eighteen-mile march in Ireland, he expected to be cut in two by the pressure of the pack strap across his chest; he felt so bad that he could not eat, and many others with him also collapsed.[94]

Performing much of their duty wearing full kit was known to cause disease among the soldiers; because of chronic manpower shortages on home service, soldiers were very often on guard duty.[95] One officer claimed that the guards regiments suffered more casualties from pulmonary diseases than did line units, adding that he believed this stemmed from their having spent more nights out of bed on sentry duty.[96] The 1865 Fort Pitt Hospital investigating committee looking into the relationship between heart and lung diseases and the soldier's uniform and kit concluded that the major problem was indeed the uniform and equipment. Of the men with less than two years service, one out of every seven was hospitalized with heart disease each year and discharged from the army, and one in every three in the same category was discharged for lung disease. Manpower shortages were thus exacerbated by the soldiers' dress, yet despite many suggested changes, very few reforms were adopted in subsequent years.[97]

Even the army's footwear was subject to the demands of appearance over practicality; the blacking used during the French wars was injurious to leather but looked better than a more water-resistant blacking.[98] Later, tight Wellington boots, which looked good on parade, were said to confine the instep and annoyed soldiers on a long march.[99] Shiny boots were deemed important, but noncommissioned officers were rarely concerned with a proper fit, even though lengthy marches were frequent and punishments could include additional marching. One soldier wrote that defaulters returned to the barracks with their boots "full of blood."[100]

Nor did weapons escape the dangerous consequences of the overriding importance of appearances. During the French wars, the emphasis on bright muskets resulted in an incessant polishing of the barrels to attain a mirror-like finish, but over a period of time this wore down the metal, making the weapons dangerous to fire. After 1815, arms delivered to the regiments had to have their barrels "browned" by regimental armorers.[101] Browning made the metal rust-resistant, but browning the locks, plates, and bayonets weakened these parts, since the process involved heating the metal before the browning was applied, which could destroy the muskets' capacity to fire.[102] An order of 1815 to cease browning locks and plates had to be repeated again in a circular letter of 1824, an indication that regiments persisted in this practice to attain a uniform color for the musket metal and bayonet.[103] Sometimes musket pins were removed to make them ring during exercises or parades, which would eventually make the weapons useless.[104]

The soldier was also obligated to buy purely decorative ornaments that did not benefit his health, movements, or work. The cavalry shoulder pouch and sabretache are two examples; the Clothing Board recommended "sabre taches" as useful to noncommissioned cavalry officers and trumpeters for carrying messages, but no comment was made on their having any useful function for privates.[105] Analogously, the cuirasses (armor breast and backplates) worn by the Household Cavalry were very impressive on parade, yet "whether this arrangement is intended as one of service, or of parade only, seems doubtful."[106] The marquess of Anglesey, a cavalry general, wrote: "I think the cuirass protects, but it also encumbers and in a melee I am sure the cuirass causes the loss of many a life."[107]

The priority given to appearances hurt the service in other ways, too. Artillery drills between Waterloo and the Crimea emphasized the speed and dash important for ceremonial occasions, but the drill was altered for these shows, and exercises necessary for combat were neglected. The laying of the guns was not practiced properly, and ammunition was not carried by the batteries as it would have been in the field. A battery sent to Cape Colony in 1847 could not even harness its horses.[108] Cavalry regiments were especially prone to the whims of their commanders. The colonel of the Sixteenth Lancers, a unit wearing red jackets, attempted in the early 1850s to recruit only red-haired men, all mounted on chestnut horses.[109] This practice added significantly to the problems and costs of recruitment and made the supply of mounts much more difficult, unless the horses were painted.

Many such customs were a matter of routine, being required by both army and unit regulations. Not all these practices were followed throughout the first half of the nineteenth century, however; nor were all of them adopted in every unit. But many complaints were made throughout this era against the seemingly endless list of problems arising from the priority given to maintaining a good show, and reform was slow.

CHAPTER TWO

Command and Design

I n Great Britain, the authority to design militaria and control its display has always been the legal prerogative of the monarchs, who sanction all patterns. The sovereign, as the lawful supreme commander of the British military forces, has consistently maintained close ties to the army.[1] But the control of martial images was a frequent cause of conflict, and those further down the chain of command, from generals even to privates, attempted to shape patterns or influence styles. This raises some questions: Why was choosing styles accorded so much importance, and what does design reveal about military command, or about the significance of militaria in the army? What insights are gained about the nature of design and its role in the elaborate panoply of state and martial spectacle?

Although British monarchs have historically been much concerned with the condition of their troops, the Hanoverians especially expressed strong interests in both the army and its dress, a tradition linked to the dynasty's German origin. When George II ascended the throne in 1727, he ordered that all patterns of regimental uniforms be submitted to him for approval.[2] When war was renewed with France in 1803, George III announced that he would personally command the army against the expected invasion, despite his own lack of military experience.[3]

The Prince of Wales (later George IV) expressed a strong desire for command at an early age and displayed an ardent martial zeal throughout his life. When he was still a young man, his father made him colonel-in-chief of the Tenth Hussars, but this honor was not enough, and in 1795 he asked for a general's rank. Even though a major war was under way, his father refused, and the prince's mortification was both deep and prolonged. After years of trying unsuccessfully to persuade his father, he wrote that this was "a subject which has given me more pain than any event of my life."[4] He felt so frustrated that, contrary to "the advice of nearly all of his more responsible friends," he published correspondence on the subject in four London papers.[5] Similarly strong feelings were expressed in 1808, when he personally directed the Tenth Hussars' embarkation for service in the Peninsula. Addressing the corps, he said: "It is one of the most painful regrets of my life, that circumstances do not admit of my accompanying you." He then presented his sword to their commander, Brigadier-General Slade, and, when taking leave of the officers, burst into tears.[6]

Although he was prevented from commanding in battle, George IV's knowledge of military affairs was extensive; he was said to have "'vast powers of recollection' the accuracy of which 'excited astonishment' even amongst experienced soldiers."[7] Later in life he fantasized about having performed brave deeds in battle (although it is unclear if he merely wished to embarrass his ministers), and in a well-known incident, he told the duke of Wellington that at the battle of Salamanca, *he* had saved the day by bringing up some cavalry "when things were looking very ill indeed."[8]

George IV's brother and successor, William IV, had strong martial interests that focused on the Royal Navy, in which he had served from a young age. Upon becoming king, however, he followed family tradition and displayed a jealous concern for his prerogatives as the head of the army, showing a strong interest in military dress and music, and attended many reviews. Although it has been asserted that William IV "loathed ceremonial and ostentation,"[9] he was so eager to redesign uniforms that he began to plan changes in military and naval dress some months before the death of his brother.[10] He was said to be "a little wild (like the rest of the family) upon dress" and changed most of the blue cavalry coats to red, which he believed was the true national color.[11] As he lay dying on June 17, 1837, he thought it so important to survive until Waterloo Day (June

18) that he asked his doctors if they could keep him alive until then, and "by will power alone he preserved a tenuous grip on life throughout the day."[12] Disraeli wrote: "The king dies like an old lion."[13]

Victoria, who attained the throne just after reaching adulthood, maintained her family's traditional martial interests. Her father took her to her first review at the age of three months,[14] and while attending another review "quite early in her reign" she expressed a longing "to lead her soldiers against her country's foes."[15] She also asserted her prerogative and reversed some of William IV's changes in uniform. Most notably, much of the cavalry clothing was converted back to blue from red (partly at the behest of officers), and in 1840 the Horse Artillery and cavalry units could again wear moustaches.[16] Victoria often appeared at military reviews wearing a female version of the Windsor uniform, and wore military-style costumes at subsequent reviews.[17] When the Crimean War broke out in 1854, the queen devoted herself to military matters; Secretary at War Lord Panmure wrote: "You never saw anybody so entirely taken up with military affairs as she is."[18] After the queen presented Victoria Crosses to soldiers in May 1855, she wrote: "Noble fellows! I own that I feel as if they were my own children; my heart beats for them as for my nearest and dearest."[19] Before her death, in 1901, she left instructions that she was to have a military funeral.[20]

Prince Albert is perhaps better known than Victoria for his strong interest in army affairs, which some officers resented because he was foreign. During the Crimean War he oversaw every detail of Lord Panmure's work and tried to solve some of the army's administrative problems. He also proposed and designed a number of items of militaria and originated the idea of the Victoria Cross.[21]

Some sovereigns became obsessed with exercising their right to oversee military dress; martial appearances were so significant to George III that in later years his mental problems included a fixation on uniforms. In 1804, when signs of instability reappeared, his physicians gave him a list of activities considered harmful to his mental health, ordering that "he should avoid [donning the] several uniforms he has [had] made up."[22]

Yet for public military displays, George III was relatively restrained, being anxious to avoid any potential conflict stemming from the traditional English fear of militarism. George IV felt no such inhibitions; as soon as he became regent in 1811, and was at last able to exercise royal prerogatives, he made himself a field marshal and frequently wore the uniform. He ordered enormous quantities of clothing and accessories throughout his life, including every variety of uniform, and could remember every article of dress he had obtained in the past fifty years.[23] His tailor's bill for a six-month period in 1829 was £10,000.[24] By the time of his death, the royal wardrobe filled a warehouse, and when sold its display occupied an entire street and fetched £15,000.[25]

The regent's obsession with military display was not limited to his own dress; his great interest in designing militaria became symbolic of his reign and made him the laughingstock of the nation. In 1819, a caricature entitled "The Dandy Taylor planing a new Hungary Dress. Pity that a good Taylor should be spoiled" ridiculed his hobby. In the cartoon, the regent sits in his "tailor's hell" sewing uniforms, while behind him on the wall hang articles of military dress and headgear, with the inscription "All my invention." The Austrian prince Esterhazy, accompanied by two Hungarian soldiers, has arrived "to teach you de proper vay to make de Hungarian soldats." All three wear Hungarian hussar uniforms, and one holds an ironing board and shears. Next to George IV stands an English officer who says, "Here's your goose, sir." The goose is labeled "The Farmer's Boy" (the farmer is George III).[26] In later years, the king became even more obsessed with militaria design, which apparently served as an escape from his woes. In late 1829, his notion to change the guards' dress was his "principal occupation; [and] he sees much more of his tailor than he does of his minister."[27] This interest continued until his health gave out in 1830.

The contribution of militaria design to the world of art may be considered minor, but for the British monarchs this royal prerogative was a personal, creative expression that constituted a significant visual stamp of their reigns. The design of military uniforms is not unlike that of civilian fashion, in that its primary goal is to present a pleasing—and appropriate—appearance. Yet the trait of individuality that is usually considered desirable in civilian modes diverges from the military's aesthetic requirement of uniformity. This appears to be part of the reason that wearing articles of a uniform out of context to achieve a very different overall effect was—and is—illegal in Britain (as well as the United States and other countries) and can be subject to criminal prosecution. In this use of the uniform, the potent, attractive motifs of power are no longer proclamations of discipline and conformity but of individuality. Their deliberate combination with other, nonmilitary dress visually declares a sharp discord in opposition to the traditional martial values; the aesthetic effect is thus turned upside down, yet much of the visual impact remains intact.

Neither is military dress "fashion" in the usual sense. Unlike civilian wear, uniforms are designed and their use controlled not by those who wear them but by those who wield authority. The wearing of military dress is a matter of discipline rather than a question of individual taste, and all aspects of the image—the arrangement of the clothing, equipment, and body posture—are subject to enforcement (there are exceptions, as we will see). As symbols of state authority, military images were not selected solely to gratify a monarch's individual taste, since they always served as advertisements of the state; indeed, they displayed the state's martial glory and power as well as the army's discipline. In this sense, military dress is a form of fashion, but it is also representative of the state it serves.

Because of the special conditions affecting the design and regulation of military dress, fashion and clothing historians have tended to avoid the subject. But this is not to say that military images do not follow many of the conventions of change in civilian fashion. Patterns are borrowed in fundamentally the same way: designers see a new look or detail that they imitate and incorporate in their own creations. In the process of borrowing styles, a pleasing aesthetic, on the one hand, and a design that is both practical in providing protection for the body and comfortable to wear, on the other, are the two basic—and usually opposing—objectives of militaria design.

During wartime, a style that was popular on campaign frequently became fashionable and inspired new trends. New styles, such as the "fore-and aft" hat, might originate from a variety of sources. This fashion began as the bicorn, or *chapeau bras*, which from the 1790s soldiers wore folded with the points extending out over their ears. The navy wore the same, but with the ends of the folds pointed forward and backward. This latter style became fashionable for army officers, who shifted their hats around navy-style when off parade, and frequently got into trouble for it. Because of the relaxation of dress regulations on active service, veterans returned home wearing hats in the naval style, "and an idea of service got to be associated with this form of wearing it, wonderfully taking, particularly with the young aspirants for glory . . . This fashion in the end has completely gained the ascendancy, and the present wearers never dream of [reverting to the old fashion]." Army dress items that were to be worn only on campaign often became fashionable because of their association with active service. In wartime, this link strongly influenced martial fashions and was noted by contemporaries.[28] Before 1802, dark-blue pantaloons were one of the few dress items officially sanctioned for campaigns, but they "began to creep in" afterward for wear at home, and officers felt "very proud of ourselves when at outquarters, [away from the view of superiors] we could thus dress, as it looked so like service." The pantaloons were officially sanctioned in a general order in 1803.[29]

Yet aesthetics were always a strong consideration, and, as seen in Chapter 1, impractical—or even dangerous—designs for clothing or equipment were often adopted. The royal Georges especially tended to put appearances before their troops' need for practical dress, although the shift toward greater practicality began in the era of transition between George IV and William IV. In an important article on the uniform reforms of 1855, Hew Strachan points out that the trend being instituted just prior to the Crimean War was toward a divergence between service and field dress, a change from the earlier, widespread practice of soldiers' wearing worn full dress for fatigue and often for field duties. The influence of foreign styles was also significant, and he concludes that "uniform changes in the nineteenth century were as much, if not more, due to the influences of foreign armies as to the experiences in battle."[30]

This practice of borrowing martial clothing styles among peoples and states is a widespread phenomenon; the dress of fighting men has always possessed a great attraction for people, even for those victimized by the wearers. This appeal would seem to be associated primarily with the exercise of ultimate power: the threat of—and wielding of—deadly force. Indeed, Arnold Toynbee has noted that military peoples, castes, and classes are more apt to win admiration from us than their peaceful neighbors who do not risk their lives to inflict violence upon other people.[31]

The borrowing of military styles has long been a common practice among European states. It has been said that the most sincere form of admiration is imitation, and both allies and foes imitated British designs. The Swedish army borrowed long feathers for military hats from the British after Swedish officers saw their counterparts accompanying Sir

John Moore's suite in the failed mission to Gothenburg in 1808.[32] In 1816, colonists of Napoleon's last major ally, Denmark, imitated a British army style; the Danish Virgin Islands' Prinsens Liv Eskadron militia regiment adopted a uniform "virtually identical" to that of a recent occupying British unit, the Ninety-fifth Rifles.[33]

British authorities frequently paid the compliment of imitating their allies' martial styles, but of all the foreign influences, German designs had the greatest impact. During the French wars, the Hanoverian monarchs adopted a number of dress items from their allies, Prussia and Austria. George IV's assistant private secretary (and later groom of the bedchamber), Sir Tomkyns Hilgrove Turner, was active in producing paintings of Austrian and Hungarian uniforms, which appear to have been used in making designs.[34] The king also had continental correspondents who sent him samples of the latest military modes; the duke of Cumberland sent samples from Germany: "Your sashes I hope to send by the first messenger and I shall send you a hat and feather from Berlin."[35] In 1843–1844, Prince Albert later designed the "Albert" shako from "types already in use in Germany."[36]

Not everyone approved of this German influence. One officer complained about "the Prussian propensity which the prince [regent] has displayed in his recent [1811] regulations about dress."[37] But this preference continued throughout the king's life; in 1828 he "closely copied" the Prussian army shako[38] (at a time when there was debate about adopting a more Prussian-style discipline), and in 1829 even took under serious consideration a notion to change the army's red coats to blue, which was said to be "the d[uke] of Cumberland's Prussian nonsense."[39]

Of the German states, Austria had an especially significant impact upon George IV, and the Household Cavalry's crested helmet was inspired by an Austrian design, as was the infantry "chako," which was said to have been introduced to the army by the Austrian Marshal Lascy, who was credited with designing the British army greatcoat.[40] Of George IV's surviving bills of dress, headgear, and accoutrements preserved in the Royal Archives, all those that include the style's origin are labeled "Austrian pattern."

Austria and other European countries were likewise influenced by more exotic designs from the "Oriental" motifs of the Ottoman Empire, together with those from the marchlands of central and southeastern

Europe bordering on the East. Orientalism[41] also influenced the British army during the Egyptian campaign of 1801, resulting in the adoption of the Mameluk sabre by some units and individual officers.[42] Highland units campaigning there also adopted black ostrich feathers (apparently from the French), which have become a fixture of the highland bonnet.[43]

The uniform of an enemy regiment was sometimes imitated if that particular unit had earned a brilliant reputation in the field. After Waterloo, the prince regent changed the dress of some light dragoon regiments into what looked like an imitation of Napoleon's famous Polish and Dutch lancers of the Imperial Guard, and possibly of the Russian Cossacks. The *Military Panorama* noted that "the achievements of the Hetman Platoff, with his gallant Cossacks, in the grand military occupances of the Continent, have called forth universal admiration and every military man is naturally desirous to learn whether a corps of cavalry armed in a similar manner could be done in Britain."[44] During the next major European war, when Britain was allied with France in the Crimea, the royal family admired Gallic efficiency and style, and a number of French patterns were imitated. When Prince Albert met the emperor Napoleon III in 1854, they discussed military caps, and in 1860 the army adopted a French-style *khepi*.[45] These foreign influences were important later, in the reign of Victoria, who admired the French "zouave" uniform (originally based on an Algerian tribal dress) worn in the Crimea. In 1858, she commanded that the Other Ranks of the West India regiments be dressed in an exotic zouave uniform, another British manifestation of oriental influence.[46]

An important factor influencing the monarch's design of—and connection to—the martial image was the state's international military reputation. This was not merely vain display, for impressing foreigners, especially rulers, with the appearance of royal troops (particularly the guards) was always a factor in international politics; this was one way rulers sized up each other's military potential. A fine appearance was a basic criterion by which the instrument of power was judged.

The Board of Officers indicated its concern for appearances in an investigation of the Household Cavalry's dress. The board reported that it "could never presume to recommend any changes, either in clothing or in equipment, which should tend to lower the appearance or the respectability of a body of troops which are constantly retained near the person of the sovereign, which brought forward on every occasion of state or parade, in or about the Royal Palace, and whose distinguishing bearing, is so presently qualified to impress every foreigner who visits the metropolis; with the splendor and efficiency of Her Majesty's Household Troops."[47] Suggestions that the more plainly dressed line regiments perform London duty were met with the objection that "their not being such fine tall, well set up, imposing-looking men as the guards; the foreign potentates and princes would not be so much electrified as they are now on visiting the metropolis . . . Their opinions of British infantry would undergo a change for the worse."[48] And electrified they were; when the prince and princess of Prussia visited London and saw the Aldershot Review of July 1856, they were "*á merveilleux* at the looks of our troops on returning from the Crimea!"[49]

The need to manifest the crown's military power and glory was thus closely linked with a monarch's personal prestige, and the splendor could be a heady encouragement to the vanity of some. George IV was certainly the most extravagant in this respect; a British diplomat compared him to a peacock displaying its feathers, and he utilized military dress in various ways to enhance his dignity.[50] In 1811, his military secretary, Colonel James Gordon, wrote in a letter marked "secret" that "the government are straining every nerve to wrest from the prince [regent] the patronage and control of the army, so that H.R.H. shall not dispose of anything military without consulting his ministers." This deeply offended the king's sense of royal duty and privilege, and Gordon added: "This is a matter of the highest importance both to the comfort and dignity of a prince."[51]

George IV's relationship with his ministers continued to be stormy, and in 1816 he designed a new uniform for them that was almost an exact copy of a French field marshal's uniform, and some flatly refused to wear it. It appears that through this design the king deliberately intended to embarrass them as revenge; a few years later when Under Foreign Secretary Planta wore this uniform to a party, the king told him that he was glad to see it, "tho' his principals did not chose to [wear] it." When Planta told him that it was not his place to find fault with them, the king replied: "I do, & very often too."[52]

George IV was ready to embarrass any officer who dared to appear before the royal presence wearing anything less than the correct uniform. In 1825, eighteen-year-old Lord Charles Russell had just been commissioned in the Blues, and by royal command was attending a full-dress ball at Carlton House with the rest of his corps. Unaccustomed to his elaborate uniform, Russell omitted to wear his aiguillette. When the king saw him, he exclaimed in "a very high voice," "Who is that damned fellow?" After being formally introduced, he said: "Good-evening sir. I suppose that you are the regimental doctor?" The mortified cornet fled and hid from view.[53] William IV was also protective of the royal prerogative over military dress and appearances; upon observing in 1834 that the First Dragoon's band (paid for by the officers, not the state) was dressed in blue, he ordered that it be changed to the regulation red, which the officers "much regretted."[54]

George IV was not the only monarch to put fine appearances above other considerations. Once when the Royal Horse Guards (Blue) were escorting the king and queen, one of the horses collapsed. A private who was present wrote that "the poor creature, from overexertion, and the great weight he had to carry, (nearly twenty stone) had ruptured a blood-vessel in the region of the heart, at least so said the veterinary surgeon." The king inquired after the uninjured trooper, but said of the horse: "It matters nothing; it could not be helped."[55] Even the duke of Wellington suffered from indignity and potentially serious injury as a result of George IV's and Victoria's passion for the martial image. As the realm's first soldier, the duke often had to wear the uniform of the units he was connected with and the military offices he held. When wearing the nearly two-foot-high regulation First Life Guards' bearskin cap with its enormous swan feather while attending a review in 1829, he was literally blown off his horse by a gust of wind in front of tens of thousands of spectators and soldiers. The incident roused considerable ridicule in print and in caricatures, and had the undesirable political effect of giving a good fillip to the strong feelings of hostility toward the duke at a time of political crisis.[56] While attending the queen on the royal navy ship *St. Vincent* in 1842, when he was seventy-three, he wrote: "The queen had repeatedly insisted upon my wearing my hat, a large cocked hat with [a] feather, and I had besides my sword." But the weapon got tangled in the rungs of the steep ship's ladder while he was climbing down, and "I was obliged to be nearly double in order to avoid touching the top deck with my hat." He missed the last step, and his fall "made some noise." Though he was unhurt, "the duke wrote that the queen "forced me to wear my hat on Tuesday, [the next day] she repeatedly warned me not to fall again!"[57]

Officers knew that even at reviews where thousands of troops performed, the members of the royal family were "noted for their quick perceptions in all matters of military uniform." In an incident just prior to the march-past before George IV (in which each unit marched by the reviewing stand), A. C. Mercer's captain noticed that his subordinate had forgotten his "dog's ears"—false shirt collars that showed two small, upturned points of white above the black neck stock. Luckily, the captain had a piece of paper in his sabretache from which fake dog's ears were quickly fashioned.[58]

The crown's power of command over the army's appearance was thus significant as a source of gratification for the monarchs, and the fact that their ministers were willing to please them in such relatively small matters allowed the sovereigns greater leeway in designing impractical military costumes. The duke of Wellington was careful to avoid offending George IV on matters of dress, opting to save his influence for greater things; he allowed himself to be used as a model for "a preposterous shako of royal design," which he wore for several hours, declaring that "it would do very well."[59]

The sovereign's sense of royal gratification from creating military designs has a child-like dimension that was noticed by contemporaries. A satire by Thomas Moore, "The New Costumes of the Ministers," portrays the prince regent dressing his ministers in the hated French style as if they were dolls, and in his mind the game is elevated to a grand affair of state:

> "Let's see," said the [regent] (like Titus perplex'd
> With the duties of empire), "Whom shall I dress next?"
> Every pucker and seam were made matters of state,
> And a Grand Household Council was held on each plait!
> So what's to be done?—there's the ministers, bless them!
> As he made the puppets, why shouldn't he dress 'em?[60]

This passage also highlights the subservient position of those in military uniform, which resembled the traditional livery worn by servants of the nobility (and imitated by better-off tradesmen) and was often called "the regimental livery."[61] Civilian "uniforms" likewise conveyed the power, grandeur, and taste of the master; from the perspective of those in command, a servant was "supposed to have no will of his own, where the master in concerned." Footmen or lackeys were thus dressed in splendid, elaborate costumes (often the clothing of the highest nobility in earlier times) to suggest their remoteness from productive labor, as well as to emphasize a glory not theirs but their master's. The splendor of their dress did not depict their real condition; they were essentially reduced to living ornaments, mere servile decorations for their employers.[62] The master might heighten the effect by dressing in simple clothing to emphasize the contrast between himself and his handsome, sharply dressed menials. This is similar to the practice of many older officers of wearing mufti whenever possible, even at reviews.[63]

The importance of the uniform as a badge of servile status was not lost on the duke of Cumberland, who went to his father asking to be made a lieutenant-general in the English army. He was refused, but he appeared again, this time wearing the "Windsor uniform," a livery that George III had created for his servants. "I will never forget his astonishment as I [stepped] into the drawing room in the costume. I only wore it once, but my father saw that I was determined, and not long afterwards I received an English post, but I will never forget my nausea and horror as I saw . . . myself in it."[64]

Soldiers sometimes reacted with scorn to the uniforms of others; a Peninsular war officer described the uniforms of "the tyrant" Napoleon's army as "the livery of the monkey."[65] Even uniformed British officers were sometimes described as resembling lower primates. Thomas Creevey thought that officers of the prince regent's Tenth Hussars at a Royal Pavilion dinner "looked [like] very ornamental monkeys in their red breeches with gold fringe and yellow boots."[66] Shelley's attack on George IV in 1820 with the play *Swellfoot the Tyrant* made a similar reference to the guards as "called from their dress and grin, the royal apes."[67] An 1824 satire on the Tenth Hussars describes their appearance in even more demeaning terms:

> But covered o'er with frogs and lace, and dandified from head
>   to face,
> They seem unto the gazing eye just fit in band-boxes to lie
> Until the moth on them sup,

And eat the Tenth unpityingly up . . .
And then their noise, their frogs and feathers, makes
  people pause,
And wonder whether they are not animated toys.[68]

These uniformed men were perceived to be, literally, the possessions of those who controlled the military machine. The uniform's connotation of servility thus expresses visually the ideal of soldiers' total subservience to the will of those in command. This dimension of military dress reveals seemingly contradictory traits—for example, the livery of the red-coated slave has a negative connotation, yet it is also the badge of martial heroism. This phenomenon highlights the uniform's multifaceted character, its capacity as an image to project different—and even sharply contradictory—values and associations. The reaction of the viewer to this ambiguous image appears to be largely dependent upon the context of the perception, either positive or negative.

The implication of servility may be a factor in the widespread occurrence of high-ranking officers usurping the crown's legal right to control the troops' appearance. The colonels' tradition of independence in regimental management and their supervision of the clothing supply tended to sanction their continued control over design, although inspections acted as a partial check on the changes they imposed. Even though maneuvers, drill, and other management matters had become much more homogeneous throughout the army in the nineteenth century, and dress designs had also become more regulated, regimental colonels still defied royal authority and often altered the designs. At a meeting of the Select Parliamentary Committee on Army and Navy Appointments of 1833, the witness Colonel Henry Beauchamp was asked: "Do not the colonels sometimes interfere, and very minutely, with the clothing?" He replied: "Always." But many went further still: "Commanding officers [not only] depart from the patterns approved by His Majesty, but even . . . introduce articles of clothing and appointments."[69] One of the few surviving Other Ranks' coats dating from the French wars, that of a battalion soldier of the Twenty-sixth Foot, provides an example of the liberty taken by officers. The regulations of 1802 state that the collar is to be three inches high, but the collar on this coat is higher by three-quarters of an inch.[70] When the Rifle Brigade was stationed in Canada in 1849, officers discussed a proposal to adopt a frock coat to replace the tail coat and a helmet to replace the Albert shako.[71] A Highland Infantry colonel in the 1840s even tried to dress his men in green.[72]

Whereas a pleasing image rather than comfortable, workmanlike clothes was a major design priority in peacetime, practical alterations were possible once a regiment was mobilized for active service. Full dress deteriorated quickly under field conditions (see Chapter 6), and, as special clothing for cold or hot climates was largely unsanctioned by the state, the colonel chose alterations at his own discretion. Most clothing was replaced every year, and any deviation detected by the inspectors merely resulted in an order that the proper dress be supplied, by which time the unit had probably transferred to another posting.

Exercising this control over the details of dress and drill was as gratifying for many officers as it was for the monarchs. Colonel William Russell, commanding the Eighth Hussars, wrote of the "unaccountable and irresistible pleasure in the pride & pomp & circumstance of war that is very delightful."[73] For some, the pleasure of expressing a personal taste in military images transcended financial considerations. In 1816, even though there was a huge surplus of accoutrements after the post-Waterloo reductions and the colonels might have saved much money by buying them, "very few or none" accepted the surplus because the patterns had changed, and in 1833 the equipment was still in store.[74]

Some colonels changed their corps' uniform frequently, having "numberless vagaries . . . in articles of dress and appointments, not only in regard to officers, but even to the men."[75] One officer wrote that his Scottish colonel was "so fond of dress, that he changed the appointments of the officers several times."[76] This practice brought many complaints from soldiers and civilians: "Nothing is so short-lived as a good uniform; it varies with the taste of a commander-in-chief, or a commander-in-chief's toady; or the fancy of some royal favorite . . . Get a new one, and the probability is that you will not show it on parade half-a-dozen times before a new regulation is out, and then more work for the tailors . . . Military costume . . . is doomed to change."[77]

But while designing was a pleasure, it was also a psychological tactic that gratified both the wearer and the viewer. A tailor noted that changing fashions "are very captivating; for things that are new raise a kind of pleasure in the fancy, [and] surprize as it were the imagination, and gratify the curiosity with things it did not possess before . . . If it were not for the unstable fluctuations of fashions, People would be too familiar with one set of objects, and wearied out with the dull repetition of the same thing [and this brings] a kind of refreshment . . . Our fancies are constantly amused, by the brilliancy of every newly engendered improvement, and our own minds become respondent for every change."[78]

As in the world of civilian fashion, change was a basic element of martial design. But the tendency to alter dress in the military was probably greater owing to the harsh, nomadic life of the soldier. More than one veteran has noted that "nothing is more agreeable to the soldier than variety—give him a change and he cares for no more."[79] A journalist noted that "in regiments, [dress] alterations are frequently beneficial, and experience and the eye best decide upon the general effect."[80] This emphasis on change also tended to reinforce the ideal of visual perfection, as "nothing strikes so forcibly upon the mind as beauty in perfection—that is the seat of satisfaction; when we once attain that, the imagination is at rest, and the faculties are in their meridian of enjoyment." But because this satisfaction was necessarily transitory, to maintain it, further changes inevitably had to follow.[81] Changing patterns periodically redirected the eye to the ideal of military imagery, refreshed its function as spectacle, and hence renewed its impact on all who saw it.

The transformation in a unit's appearance could be quite significant over a period of years, and changes in command often effected drastic alterations; this shift in the style of command, and frequently in the resulting appearances, was often accompanied by a change in spirit among All Ranks. In 1796, George Elers wrote that the Forty-third Foot was "the worst dressed regiment I ever saw," but ten years later, after the soldiers were converted to light infantry, he pronounced them "without any exception the finest body of men I ever saw, so well dressed."[82]

Frequent changes had another significant and beneficial political effect for the state: the officers' low pay, combined with the high cost of dress and equipment, strongly discouraged those lacking an outside income from entering the service, and a large amount of money was considered essential in many regiments. Dr. Gibney of the Fifteenth Hussars noted that "to shirk expense was decidedly disapproved of" in the mess.[83] Sir Ralph Abercromby wrote that his officer sons "ought, as soldiers, never to want money."[84]

During the long French wars, a considerable number of poorer men received free commissions into the officer corps (Britain was the last European country to abolish the purchase of commissions, in 1871). Although they contributed much to the British war effort, after 1815 they were viewed as politically untrustworthy. Middle- and lower-middle-class officers were less likely to be committed to the status quo, and were thus more prone to become mercenary or revolutionary in sentiment (like the French officers who had risen with the Revolution). The reactionary duke of Cumberland felt this was the case with the post–1815 Prussian army: "Many of the generals and principal officers with whom I am in daily habits agree with me, that what was good and necessary in 1813 to 1815 ought to have ceased after the war, as it was only calculated for the necessity of the times, but this was not done [and the army] was made subservient to the worst of objects . . . a class of officers who were never intended for such a profession."[85]

If the cost of continually replacing the kit was not enough to drive these poorer men out, those in command had only to alter the styles and thus increase expenses. In the years after Waterloo, the prince regent altered the dress of many corps, and in 1816 a member of the Commons complained that "the officers of some [cavalry] regiments . . . had not been yearly, but quarterly obligated to equip themselves anew."[86] The elaborate and costly dress of elite units not only indicated a high status, but also symbolized their loyalty to the state. In the Life Guards' dress regulations of 1822, three different sword patterns were to be kept by officers for "full dress," "dress," and "undress."[87]

Control over the design of military uniforms symbolized authority and power, and was thus a frequent area of conflict. Officers, who were required to report deviations from the regulation dress, often attempted to alter styles themselves. Even the duke of Wellington was jealous of his prerogative in army dress and equipment; after Quarter-Master De Lancy was killed at Waterloo, his successor, Sir Hudson Lowe, tried more than once "to teach [Wellington] how the British army ought to be accoutred, and referred to the Prussians." Wellington had the "d——d stupid fellow" sent home.[88]

Relations between a corps and an inspector-general were affected by this conflict, and disputes over authority in other contexts were often both reinforced and symbolized by the desire to control designs. After Charles

De Ainslie took command of the Seventh Dragoon Guards in 1849, he ran into difficulties with the local inspector: "From the very commencement, Sir Thomas Brotherton persistently carried on against me a system of harshness, oppression, and vexatious interference, which necessarily to a great extent paralysed my endeavors, and rendered the whole period of my being under his command one continual struggle." The animosity was so pronounced that Brotherton would not dine at the mess, as was customary, and sat in his carriage instead.[89]

Some inspectors continually harassed the corps they were sent to review. George Elers wrote of "that Brute Brigadier-General Acland," who "very often paid us visits of inspection." He "kept an orderly dragoon, who was continually galloping backwards and forwards with reports and returns."[90] The opinions of reviewing officers might differ considerably. When the Fifteenth Hussars were reviewed in May 1815, General Grant found fault with the regiment "as usual," whereas Lord Uxbridge "complimented the regiment in the most handsome way."[91]

High-ranking officers could be as particular about dress as any fastidious art connoisseur; the duke of Cumberland expressed an opinion to Sir Walter Scott's son about his unit's uniform: "He examined the 18th [Hussars'] uniform very minutely, found out a great many faults, and that it was not the exact Hungarian dress."[92] In their pursuit of perfection, many company and troop officers also sought the best-looking soldiers.[93]

Some officers were openly hostile to those among them who did not wear regulation dress. Colonel Hill was snubbed by his commander, General Whitelock, when he appeared before him out of uniform.[94] Any new detail in an officer's dress might thus be subjected to the most intense scrutiny and criticism by his fellows; when an officer appeared one Sunday evening (circa 1804?) at the Plymouth Dock promenade wearing hussar boots with a silk tassel hanging from the pointed brim, Captain Mercer wrote: "I shall not in a hurry forget the sensation caused . . . 'Oh, the puppy!' was heard on all sides. 'If he has not silk tassels to his boots! Only think! silk tassels on boots!' "[95]

New designs were often jealously guarded, and the borrowing of a design by another unit could cause a quarrel. Captain Mercer of the Horse Artillery wrote that in 1804 he and Captain Duncan designed a new forage cap for Duncan's troop based upon the French *bonnet*, and "numerous were the fancies he and I tried, some in sketches, some he actually made up, until at last we pitched upon the . . . most elegant." Duncan was "delighted" with the creation, which he contemplated "with rapture." But despite careful efforts to conceal the pattern from prying eyes, another colonel found out about it and adopted the design for his Royal Artillery Corps of Drivers. After Duncan's troop appeared for the first time wearing the new cap, the drivers issued from their barracks wearing the same pattern, "to the disgust of Duncan, whose rage I shall long remember."[96]

Although each corps' uniform was based on a common pattern, it had to be unique in at least some minor detail to differentiate that corps from every other unit. Each regiment was thus expected to preserve the individuality of its image; when it was discovered that the Seventy-third Foot's second battalion officers were wearing a uniform almost identical with that of a Foot Guard unit, the commander in chief ordered the Seventy-third "to divest themselves of two slips of gold lace, from the skirt of their regimental jackets."[97]

But imitation is also a form of flattery; some uniforms were designed as close copies of another corps' dress, or two colonels working together might create a shared design for their units (which must have created some confusion when they served together). George Elers of the Twelfth Foot believed that his commander and Colonel George Paget of the Eightieth Foot "laid their heads together to dress their regiments as alike as possible," because the corps' uniforms were only distinguished by different colored hat feathers.[98] Even lower-ranking officers might aspire to have their company or troop look like another unit. After joining the Thirteenth Light Dragoons in 1842, Captain Thomson and his lieutenant decided to replace the troop's uniform; Thomson wrote that "our ambition was to get the men to look like the 9th Lancers."[99]

Officers' wives and female friends also influenced designs, and sometimes the wife of a general or colonel decided upon a new style; Lady Chatham (the wife of Lord Chatham, Master-General of the Ordnance) was instrumental in getting the Horse Artillery light cavalry-style velvet turbans for their helmets in 1805.[100] For one hussar corps a certain Lady Fanny had "undisputed" taste in matters of dress, and made numerous suggestions that were adopted, including the style of the Austrian knot (a lace design on the pantaloons), the pelisse fur collar, the side seams, welts (cords that edged the seams), necklines, sliders, and olivets; all were said to be "lasting monuments of her refinement."[101]

But a pleasing aesthetic in dress was only one dimension of military display, which also included the soldiers' correct posture, their orderly movements and behavior, the quality of their performance at drills reviews, and so on. An attractive display of martial splendor was also evidence of good unit management. One officer praised his colonel's regimental administration, because "from confusion he produced order and beauty."[102] Simply having a new uniform was not enough, as newness itself was perceived as evidence of inexperience; in the 1820s, a hussar officer pronounced a lancer regiment "too new, and [they] have not yet acquired the polish of the hussars."[103] There were subtle details to consider; in a report of 1829 on a dragoon corps, an inspector noted that the corps was "steady and well-conducted . . . But it is by no means to be called a fine regiment—there is about it a want of that air and smartness which should always be found in a body of troops."[104] Management was thus blended with aesthetics, and in this sense "war" was literally a visual art, possessing its own aesthetic rules that were rooted in the ideal of the machine.

Command was frequently perceived as an aesthetic task; a sergeant was described inspecting a row of new recruits "with a most artistic expression of countenance."[105] General Burgoyne noted "the artistic combination and refinement of a regiment and army."[106] This art might even ascend to the exalted realm of the sublime: "The art of war . . . is only a trade to the common observer, while to genius it presents a boundless sphere for the range of human intellect. Indeed, a British regiment, in any part of the world, displays to a man fond of contemplation, a variety of subjects for the useful exercise of thought. [Among them] he may reflect with profit on the beautiful order of a well-regulated corps: what a fine chain of subordination . . . what harmony! what mutual dependence!"[107]

This notion of the art of war as being sublime tended to gratify those in control of the military display, and often inspired them to exercise their creative powers by putting a personal mark on the appearance of their soldiers. The medium for this expression of individual taste was integrally associated with power, unity, and harmony, all of which inspire, gratify, and reassure. This form of art lacked the permanency of architecture or monuments (favorite royal hobbies), but such stony enshrinements of personal taste are inert and passive. A regiment or army, by contrast, is composed of living men and is a machine of great latent strength, the most dangerous of all forces to be directed by the human will. Indeed, the sense of the sublime in this era was closely linked to the notion of power and the latent threat of armies: "It has always seemed to me more rational to refer to the source of the [concept of the] sublime [as being rooted in] power . . . such as . . . a great hostile army."[108] Edmund Burke asserted that "terror . . . is a source of the sublime; that is, it is productive of the strongest emotions which the mind is capable of feeling."[109]

Display was thus a major priority in many regiments, and it was important to the colonels that their men do well when performing in public, as any significant deviation from a fine, orderly appearance was dishonorable. In 1802, in Clonmel, Ireland, an artillery review included civilian artificers, one of whom, Mr. Wheeler Burton, was described as "a cross-grained, grumbling, chattering politician [who] loved to thwart those in authority over him." The artificers had been ordered to wait while the soldiers marched past the Commander of the Forces in Ireland. Burton "took it into his head that he was insulted in being left behind" and, in his plum-colored coat with large white buttons, marched after the soldiers, to the "horror and rage" of the commanding major: "With the emblem of his trade, his claw hammer, held erect between two fingers, and his eyes fixed with imperturbable insolence of gaze on the Commander of the Forces, who in his turn looked on with unmoved gravity, evidently taking Wheeler Burton for a legitimate part of the exhibition, whilst the major was foaming with rage, every one else bursting with laughter."[110]

But when things went well, exercising a battalion could be a great pleasure. Even Wellington enjoyed drilling troops; on one occasion at Walmar, he did so "in order to amuse himself."[111] Some colonels so enjoyed this power that they jealously guarded their right to drill their corps and never allowed subordinates to exercise the battalion, even though this was contrary to regulations,[112] and also a cause of complaints. A captain wrote to Adjutant-General Lieutenant-General Sir Herbert Taylor: "Lieut.-colonels are so jealous on this point, so anxious to impress on the men the notion that they, and they only (I believe the majors are excepted) are competent to manoeuvre, that they seldom, or never, give the junior officers an opportunity to manoeuvre battalions. The consequence is, that a junior officer, however perfect in the theory of his profession . . . when called upon to go through the actual *practice*, and in the heat of action, *cannot* have a proper and necessary confidence in the men."[113] This could have serious consequences in battle; prior to Waterloo, Colonel Stirling left the Forty-second Foot, and his successor, Lieutenant-Colonel Macara, became colonel. Although he was "a brave man, who feared no personal danger, [Macara] was not well acquainted with field manoeuvres or military tactics . . . his predecessor seldom having been absent from the regiment; so that not having the command sooner, he had not the opportunity of perfecting himself."[114]

Lower-ranking officers had to content themselves with exercising companies or troops, but for some there was still an irresistible attraction in exercising soldiers, even at ordinary drill, and especially if there was an audience. A young Scots Grays officer, who was acting adjutant for his squadron's sword drill, normally commanded through the fugleman ["pattern-man"], but because a "great number of people were looking on . . . my evil genius tempted me to give the word of command."[115] Even those of the humblest rank might aspire to a dash of glorious command. In 1802, a militia private in the Edinburgh "1st or Gentlemen's Regiment," returning home late and tipsy after a field day and a militia dinner, bribed two regular army sentries with half a crown to "do me general honors."[116]

Receiving such honors was a major gratification for those well-to-do officers who cared only for appearances and were indifferent toward other, essential aspects of duty. Such men could afford to buy commissions in peacetime, and those with a taste for the service often carried on for years in the pursuit of aesthetic perfection. They were known as "pipe-clay officers," and one soldier wrote that they delighted "in frequent, prolonged parades," and in the mess liked such "conversation (at the risk of being fined a dozen [bottles] of claret for talking shop) to such topics as the goose-step, corporal punishment, court martials, and the like."[117]

These "petty tyrants" were said to torment their men into desertion and drinking; such an officer was described as "a zealous fool, hot after unimportant minutiae, in the exact execution of which he considers the fate of the nation to depend, and in the enforcement of which he, most indiscreetly, uses his 'discretionary powers' [for severe punishment] with a vengeance."[118]

Many of these officers were known for their archreactionary opinions; though they were frequently incompetent when it came to conducting war, their views rendered them politically safe for the state, and they were thus considered reliable. The infamous Lord Cardigan is a noteworthy example; he incorporated his personal inclinations in military ritual by flogging a soldier in the regimental riding school on Easter Sunday immediately after the service, "in such a way that the punishment appeared to be a continuation of divine service."[119] It was the "unimportant minutiae" that induced such men to become officers, and their control over martial imagery gave them free reign to pursue this never-ending game of aesthetic self-gratification and punishment.

Their personal role in shaping appearances was so important to some colonels that they stoutly resisted new dress regulations, and toward the end of the French wars many old colonels strongly disapproved of the new styles. In the Twenty-ninth Foot, known for its fine turnout, the colonel in 1807 insisted that his officers continue to wear the old square-front cocked hat with the queue, and an outdated coat style. Major John Patterson noted that they "had too much of the antique about them."[120] Sometimes after an alteration, older officers refused to update their own dress and continued to wear antiquated designs; Colonel Donellan of the Fifty-eighth Foot fought in the Peninsula with his hair powdered in the old style and wearing outdated jack boots and buckskin knee breeches.[121]

A colonel might also indulge himself by running his unit in a way that was eccentric or childish; the army included many odd characters in an age noteworthy for such behavior, which was easier to get away with on remote, foreign stations. During the Eighth "Kaffir" War in the early 1850s, Colonel Sir James Dennis of the Third Foot (the Buffs) was reported to "sometimes march his regiment in a circle, while he stood in the centre, and stamping with [h]is staff on the ground as they marched round him, he would sing, 'Buffs go round, go round, Buffs go round, go roundy-da-da,' while the other troops of the garrison often stood looking on and laughing." When he was ill and thought death was near, he would take a captured colour, wrap it around himself in bed, and say: "I'll die a Buff."[122]

In an occupation where appearance was so important, privates, too, attempted to alter minor details of the uniform to suit their personal taste. The last place one would expect such boldness was in the Grenadier Guards, yet in 1830, soldiers were warned that "the cloth must not be pared away under the idea of improving the fashion of the coat, which I understand has been formerly done." In 1831, the colonel reported that "the men wear forage caps of various fanciful shapes. The regimental pattern is quite flat on the top, and this must be adhered to."[123]

Control over martial imagery was thus a means of putting a personal and artistic stamp on the appearance of soldiers. It helped to uphold the dignity of both the monarchy and the army, and was therefore a matter of considerable importance. One of the fundamental values of the military is that it is a uniform system of power, and the logic of the martial machine dictates that all its components maintain an idealized sense of solidarity of purpose. In this regard, control over imagery indicates the possession of power, whether of command over the whole or merely of one's own appearance. In Great Britain, only the personal embodiment of the state—the monarch—was supposed to control the army's appearance. Attempts to alter aspects of dress—on the part of both officers and the Other Ranks—indicate that individuals within the system retained a sense of individuality, despite the best efforts of the state to overcome such feelings.

CHAPTER THREE

Recruiting

Martial spectacle was a powerful enticement for young recruits, who were drawn by the aesthetic, social, and philosophical attraction of military imagery, which appealed to their sense of male prowess, patriotism, and idealism. The allure of display was vital not only to gain the officers and manpower needed for the Other Ranks, but also to help procure noncommissioned officers, that select group of promising young men who were absolutely essential to the army.

Many contemporary military handbooks and memoirs mention the importance of the uniform and what it symbolized about army service to potential recruits.[1] But most modern historians tend to take this appeal for granted, giving it a brief, passing reference or not mentioning it at all, perhaps because the lure of the uniform seems archaic and primordial, part of a more innocent age. Instead, they concentrate on more "serious" aspects of recruitment motivation, especially employment, and mention the glamour and excitement of military life or the "hypnotism of the recruiting party" without exploring the larger significance of such factors in the recruiting process.[2]

The importance of the imagery's appeal is highlighted by the harsh realities of military service, which the often naive recruit soon discovered. The enlistment bounty never covered the cost of clothing and necessaries, except during the French and Crimean wars, so a recruit might enter the army in debt and not receive any pay for six months or more after enlistment.[3] He might be finagled out of his bounty by noncommissioned officers (a common occurrence in the early decades of the century), but more often his barrack-mates victimized him. One soldier's bounty was almost completely spent on his new companions, who manipulated him into buying them treats: "It appeared to me that I was set up at auction to be knocked down to the highest bidder." When the first payday arrived and he asked for the money back, he was laughed at for expecting to be repaid for squandered bounty money.[4] Hazing was also a common practice among veterans, and many newcomers suffered violence at the hands of their new companions.[5]

Given the conditions of the service and the army's poor reputation, the difficulties in recruiting were substantial. These were further enhanced by the ongoing manpower shortage, which was due to the small size of the British population compared with its continental rivals. This has probably been the most significant factor affecting military operations— and policy—throughout the entire modern period, during which the army has rarely achieved the desired strength, even in peacetime.[6] In a major war, foreign mercenaries, as well as captured and purchased slaves, bad characters, and deserters, were all utilized.[7] After the disastrous campaigns of the mid-1790s, which ended in many casualties (mostly from disease), Englishmen were less eager to pursue the glories of martial valor. The ensuing shortage resulted in the enlistment of large numbers of Irishmen, induced by poverty and the ever-increasing bounties.[8]

Many who enlisted as common soldiers did so from motives of destitution and want—after all, despite the harsh conditions of army life, soldiers did not starve to death—yet a variety of other factors also influenced the decision to enlist. Restlessness and a desire to see the world or to escape from their home district were factors.[9] The lure of an extended debauch on the recruiting bounty might also induce young men to join up. Others wanted to escape parental authority or a bad master; a recruiting poster from the Fourteenth Light Dragoons appealed to "all [of] you . . . with too little wages, and a pinch-gut master . . . too much wife . . . or obstinate and unfeeling parents."[10] The state usually accommodated these recruits, since minors under the control of parents or guardians could not be legally prevented from enlisting.[11] Others wanted to escape the burden of a family, or were responsible for an illegitimate pregnancy in the parish.

Debtors had an additional incentive to enlist, for they could escape liability for debts (and prison) for amounts up to £30 by joining the service.[12] Others who committed crimes were offered enlistment as an alternative to jail, and in times of great need, even prisons were emptied to create new battalions. Prisoners were by no means the only involuntary recruits, however; during the first years of the French wars, men were still being kidnapped by "crimps," who made a trade of "man-stealing" (selling their victims to recruiters), and the forced enlistment of vagrants was traditionally a source of recruits in peacetime.[13]

Drink was essential in placating the men, given the conditions of the service, the inadequate and bad food, poor pay, and rigid discipline, together with the human material that made up the Other Ranks. Yet at the same time it added further to the army's bad reputation and often deterred recruits of good character. The rum ration was distributed every day before breakfast, and alcoholism was so widespread that those who did not drink were often ostracized by their fellows. Some men were appalled by the company they had joined. One anonymous private later wrote: "I could not associate with the common soldiers; their habits made me shudder."[14]

Despite these negative conditions and the many excellent reasons for those with any other likely prospects to avoid military service at all costs, capable young men who had alternatives still enlisted. An important factor was their youth; recruiters usually targeted fifteen-to-twenty-year-olds, but younger boys were also taken, especially if they looked older. A recruiting instruction of 1814 for the Seventh Light Dragoons states that lads of sixteen would be taken, but the sources often stipulate only that boys be "well grown."[15] Henry Metcalfe joined the Thirty-second Light Infantry in 1848 at age thirteen years, two months.[16] Although wartime saw the enlistment of older men, who tended to make up a greater percentage of the undesirable element, most recruits were adolescents. These lads were usually unsettled, unmarried, inexperienced, and not established in a trade. A veteran described this period of life as "hobble-dehoyhood," a time of pride and inexperience.[17]

In the 1790s the army was so short of men that boys "likely to grow" were taken in the belief that many would be excellent material for future noncommissioned officers. In 1797, thousands of orphan boys between the ages of ten and fifteen on parish relief were inducted into experimental units whose purpose was to teach them the basics of their future duty.[18] In 1808, ten boys per company were officially borne on the strength of certain battalions, and others served in the Royal Veteran Battalion until they became old enough for regular duty.[19] Other boys served as drummers, fifers, and buglers, and most were the sons of men in the Other Ranks who normally followed their fathers' trade.

The importance of youngsters to the service is further highlighted by the fact that in 1812, during a major war, the state went to the expense of setting up regimental schools taught by an extra sergeant to educate the children of noncommissioned officers. The purpose of the schools was to "qualify them for noncommissioned officers" (during the French wars, most soldiers who showed potential to be noncommissioned officers were illiterate).[20] The sons of deserving officers also received free educations for army careers at the Royal Military Asylum at Chelsea and the Royal Hibernian School at Dublin, which together provided the service with 2,050 graduates between 1801 and 1830.[21]

The youth and inexperience that characterized the most desirable and available recruits rendered them easy to entice. Recruiting parties visited places where young boys could be found, including fairs, markets, and public houses, and often put on an elaborate and very expensive show to entice recruits. Sometimes the recruiter organized a spectacle for the target village or neighborhood; the attraction usually consisted of a procession with at least a drummer to draw a crowd, but a larger-scale operation might feature additional musicians or even a full band, depending upon the size of the recruiting party and its needs. A large procession might include a brewer's dray or pack animals loaded with kegs of whiskey and beer, and, in one example, ready-to-eat hot food accompanied the parade, carried by pack animals and complete with knives and forks hanging by strings from the trappings. The animals bearing these tempting treats were richly decorated, and the recruiter held a bag of gold, jangling the guineas as he walked.[22] This show had a considerable effect on poor villages suffering from hard times, and the quantities of liquor distributed could be enormous. A bill was submitted to the headquarters of the Seventy-ninth Cameron Volunteers in 1793 for sixty-six gallons of whiskey, which is thought to be for the party's recruiting efforts at Fort William.[23] Sometimes additional efforts were made to gain the local community's goodwill by giving money to the poor.[24]

Convincing a young man to enlist, however, often meant easing his fears about leaving home for a substantial period of time. To increase the sense of maintaining a home-county connection and to court the local gentry's goodwill, the army in 1782 had assigned county titles to regiments according to where they were recruiting at the time: "Officers were directed to cultivate an intercourse with that part of the county, so as to create a mutual attachment between inhabitants and the regiment."[25] Some recruits found the service more attractive when they could join their "own county's" regiment. In 1847 James Bodell wanted to enlist in the artillery, marines, or cavalry, but on meeting a recruiting party from the Fifty-ninth, Second Battalion, Nottinghamshire regiment, he decided to join it because he was a Nottinghamshire man.[26] In the early 1850s, a recruiter for the First Nottinghamshire Regiment ordered to recruit in that county wrote: "The 45th, being a Nottingham regiment, numbers of recruits flocked to our rendezvous, eager to proceed to Kaffirland, and that at the time when the struggle there was at its height."[27] Some Scotsmen would enlist only in a corps in which family members had served; one Scotsman walked from Inverness to Edinburgh with the intention of enlisting in *his* regiment, the Seventy-first Foot, a highland corps.[28]

Some men were attracted to the army because they thought that as soldiers they would avoid physical labor.[29] This dovetailed neatly with the contemporary notion that because soldiers did not labor in the conventional sense, they were thus superior to civilians in the same way aristocrats were superior to commoners, and were therefore gentlemen. A military journal contributor in 1820 assured his readers that "a soldier is a gentleman, however subordinate his rank,"[30] while another officer asserted that military men possessed "every quality that ennobles men" to a greater degree than any other group of men in the land.[31] This notion of superiority over civilians, which was very widespread among soldiers of all ranks, sometimes had unfortunate results; soldiers often treated civilians with contempt, and the Other Ranks' drunken brawls and the duels fought by young officers only added to the soldiers' bad reputation.[32]

But their swagger could also be attractive; feelings of hauteur were encouraged, fostering pride among the Other Ranks, with results that were not lost on potential recruits. Inspector-General Robert Jackson noted that the erect military posture served to enhance feelings of self-consequence: "When the young soldier is brought into this position [it gives] an air of importance to the figure, and an internal sensation of consequence arising from the impression of acquired superiority."[33] This was reinforced by the uniform, for "a becoming dress tends to elevate men in their own estimation," but the appeal of the fantasy was even more elaborate.[34] One Scots veteran wrote of the effect of military splendor in the late 1820s:

> In Scotland, young men smitten with military ambition . . . talk vauntingly of [the Second Dragoons, the Scots Grays], the grey horses, their long white tails, the scarlet coats, the long swords, the high bearskin caps and the plumes of white feathers encircling them in front, the blue overalls with the broad yellow stripes on the outside, the boots and spurs, the carbines slung at the saddle side, the holster pipes and the pistols, the shoulder belts and pouches with ammunition, and, in the wet or the wintry wind, the long scarlet cloaks flowing from the riders' necks to their knees . . . Of these they talk proudly, and depicture in their inward vision the figures of themselves thus accoutred and mounted, the grey chargers pawing the earth beneath them, sniffing the battle from afar, the trumpets sounding, the squadrons charging, Napoleon's columns broken by the charge, *their* charge, with Napoleon exiled, and Europe at peace![35]

Such visions were of incalculable value in inducing enlistments; a contemporary recruiter stated that, though "sentimental chaps" were often intelligent enough to see through bombastic recruiting speeches, they were "the easiest caught after all."[36]

The fantasy of the uniform with all its associations, however, was especially appealing to those who wanted to bolster their self-esteem and sexual appeal. One young ensign traveled back to his village after receiving his uniform to try to impress a girl who had rejected him: "I wish her to know that I am not so insignificant . . . I wonder if she would have slighted me had she seen me . . . but she may look and die."[37]

This connection between the power of military imagery—and especially the uniform—and the sexual appeal of soldiers is mentioned very often in contemporary sources. A fifteen-year-old infantry ensign wrote of "all the pretty women who unblushingly stared at me."[38] Jane Austen's novels attest to the uniform's magnetic attraction; in *Pride and Prejudice,* Mr. Bennet's two younger daughters "could talk of nothing but officers; and Mr. Bingley's large fortune, the mention of which gave animation to their mother, was worthless in their eyes."[39] Women of all classes might pursue soldiers for liaisons, and though these women have frequently been referred to as prostitutes in the sources, it was often they who gave money to the men, aiding many a redcoat in his eternal quest for drink. Henry Mayhew reported: "I heard that some of the privates in the Blues [the Royal Horse Guards] and the brigade of guards often formed very reprehensible connections with the women of property, tradesmen's wives, and even ladies, who supplied them with money, and behaved with the greatest generosity to them, only stipulating for the preservation of secrecy in their intrigues."[40] Edward Leeves's diary from 1849 to 1850 also highlights the gay dimension of soldiers' sexual appeal, revealing his obsession with privates of the Royal Horse Guards (Blue) and his "romance with the gallant Blues," who were "all that I love." He gave them money and collected their regimental canes and buttons.[41]

The uniform was thus a major attraction for some recruits because it embodied the martial image and projected a powerful aesthetic appeal. A recruiting poster from the French wars mentions "highly attractive" clothing and accoutrements.[42] Recruiting spectacles put much emphasis on making the uniforms and other displays as appealing as possible, and recruiters below commissioned rank sometimes wore officers' clothing—a serious breach of the strict regimental sumptuary laws if these had been worn on any other occasion.[43] The techniques employed in 1814 by a recruiting sergeant of the Royal Sappers and Miners illustrate the significance of an especially elaborate uniform. The sergeant wore gold bullion epaulets, white breeches, a hat with a gilt frontispiece "as big as a sun-dial, and brazen scales, surmounted by a long slashing feather . . . He looked like a prince among savages." He had a crimson shoulder sash (also not regulation) overlaid with blue, scarlet, and yellow silk ribbons, and on his breast wore a ribbon-cockade, or "bang-up"—the sign of a recruiter.[44]

Another standard tactic was to use "decoys," men who were very handsome, in the recruiting party. In one example, two decoys were more than six feet tall with "ruddy countenances, bright eyes, and pleasing features." They were dressed like the sergeant, but in clothing that was not so costly; each wore a huge bow on his breast, and gaudy, colored streamers more than a yard long were fixed to their hats.[45] Recruits were given their own ribbon-cockades, which signified their new status, but they were sometimes allowed to wear one of the recruiting party's shakos or a soldier's old coat, or to carry a sword.[46]

This extravagant display was very expensive, especially in wartime; a military handbook of 1813 complained that the additional finery and "useless trappings being introduced to entice and lure the lads" cost the colonels too much.[47] Nevertheless, during the era of the French wars, "recruiting extravagances" were often considered a point of professional honor; a Sergeant-Major Cutteridge got himself £900 in debt after his recruiting efforts.[48]

During the French wars, many recruits were transferred to the regulars from the various nonprofessional militia and volunteer units.[49] Because these men had already experienced military service, they were less likely to be seduced by the recruiters' lies or drawn by the hope of escaping poverty. Yet despite their familiarity with the realities of military life, the recruiters' display was still a powerful lure for these citizen-soldiers.

Rifleman Harris of the Ninety-fifth Rifles participated in such a recruiting drive aimed at men of the East Kent Militia in 1809. The "strongest and smartest" riflemen of the regiment were chosen for the job, and while the militiamen were drawn up on parade, the recruiters "strutted up and down before their ranks arm in arm, and made no small sensation amongst them." The party had made a special effort with their appearance, and the sergeant-major wore his sword slung like an officer, with a "tremendous green feather," an officer's sash and pelisse, and a double allowance of ribbons in his cap. Harris mentions that he dressed "as smart as I dared appear," indicating that he must have donned elements of sergeants' or officers' dress. The recruiters carried on as if they were generals, the militiamen cheered them, and many enlisted. A few days later, Harris's party managed to persuade one hundred and twenty-five men and two officers of the Leicester Militia to volunteer for the Ninety-fifth Rifles—after they had already pledged themselves to the Seventh Fusiliers. He wrote that "our rifle uniform" and the sergeant's blarney convinced them.[50]

The uniform's attraction was by no means limited to potential privates, however, and some new young officers reacted enthusiastically, and often ecstatically, to the privilege of wearing it. One new ensign could not sleep until the "delightful" dress arrived.[51] Another recalled:

> Never did I behold so beautiful—so ravishing a sight! The coat like silk—scarlet silk; the pantaloons blue as the sky—ethereal blue; the epaulettes and lace as bright as the sun—or 20 suns! price! what was the price to me? . . . It would be endless to describe the evolutions, the marches, and the countermarches, which I performed before the looking-glass that day. I nearly wore out my scabbard with drawing and sheathing my sword; I absolutely tarnished my epaulette by dangling the bullion of it, and the peak of my cocked hat was very much ruffled and crushed by practicing my intended salutes to the ladies. I dined—in full uniform, and unshackled by the presence of strangers to interrupt my admiration of it . . . This was the climax of my hopes.

He spent the first day after his uniform arrived strutting around London, watching the ladies stare at him. He repeatedly walked past sentries to hear the slap of muskets as they saluted him, and ate a huge quantity of ices and jellies, not because he was hungry, but because "the lounge—the graceful halo which the discussion of an ice throws round the military figure in a pastry-cook's shop is everything!"[52]

Some quit the army when the novelty had grown stale. A "noble scion of an illustrious house" who had joined the heavy cavalry arranged to exchange his commission (doubtless at no small expense) for one of a hussar regiment after a month, because he found the riding school and drill a bore, but "above all, the helmet of the heavies [was] considerably inferior in beauty to the chaco [shako] of the hussar." After exchanging his commission, which entitled him to don the coveted headgear of the hussars, he went on leave, and was "consumed with examinations of his pelisse, dolman and sabretache, with which he found very considerable delight in bedecking his person" during leisure hours. But the new toy's appeal soon faded, for "so thoroughly did he make himself acquainted with every article of dress appertaining to the regiment, that his zeal in the new cause had considerably evaporated before he embarked to join it [He fled after three days]."[53]

The mere sight of a soldier in uniform sometimes sparked a desire to enlist; one future officer wanted to join as a private after seeing "two officers whose appearance on a market-day had first decided me in favor of the military profession." He said that he "was attracted not by the show and splendor, as some would say, but rather by the genuine elegance . . . of regimental costume."[54] One English recruit enlisted after seeing Private Edward Costello of the Ninety-fifth Rifles wearing "an old green jacket of his sergeant's" while in Dublin. Although on recruiting service, Costello was off-duty when "accosted by [this] smart young fellow."[55]

The uniform also enticed men of higher social status to volunteer for militia duty. Some of these prospective militia and other nonprofessional corps officers considered its influence to be decisive. General John Burgoyne believed that for the militia the uniform was "almost the only inducement" for young men to become officers, for among society's elite, an officer's uniform conferred social acceptability.[56] This factor was important for the regular army during the augmentations of the French wars, when officers were greatly needed, and men of modest backgrounds sought free commissions. This elevated rank and status was so important to some that after being put on half-pay when the wars ended, they clung to their acquired glory and refused to take work they considered beneath them. Many lived an eccentric hand-to-mouth existence of shabby and often obscure gentility.[57]

Another appeal was the privilege of carrying weapons, which conferred power upon the bearer through an implicit threat of violence. An officer noted that one reason young men became subalterns was to "carry a dangerous weapon."[58] This also seems to have influenced recruits for the Other Ranks before the late 1830s; a poster promised recruits that they would get to carry silver-hilted swords in the Eighty-first Foot regiment.[59]

Many young men were infected with military zeal long before joining the army; this enthusiasm was expressed in child's play, which was often the impetus for their attachment to their future profession. One colonel began his memoirs by describing a working toy cannon he had received when a small boy, which he fired on the queen's birthday;[60] another future officer caught the "red-coat mania" as a boy from seeing the guard mounted at Dublin Castle, and soon after began painting soldiers on cards and putting them through maneuvers.[61] Others were inspired by reading campaign accounts; one sergeant-major wrote: "As a youth [I] had much admired the appearance of a soldier . . . I also read with eagerness Wellington's brilliant career . . . In the early part of 1854 . . . thrilling accounts were appearing in our newspapers about the different fights at the seat of war."[62] He soon enlisted. As a child, General Sir Henry Havelock was said to have been "a great reader of all papers . . . relating to military affairs," and hearing veterans' battle accounts also stimulated his ambitions. He was inspired to seek a commission in 1815 after hearing his brother describe service with the Forty-third Foot at Waterloo.[63]

In wartime, groups of children formed "ragged regiments" and played at drill with homemade uniforms.[64] In Edinburgh in the late 1790s, "several regiments of little boys in the New Town who had flags, drums, swords, belts and military caps" imitated the continual military display of volunteer units.[65] A toymaker stated that during the invasion scare of 1803, "every child was a soldier."[66]

Boys were also seized by military fervor after seeing soldiers perform some military ceremony, hearing military music, witnessing a recruiter in action, or merely seeing soldiers perform their duties. One lad's enthusiasm was "fanned into a flame" when an English militia sergeant was quartered in his father's home in 1796 and, as a favor, drilled the fifteen-year-old and his friends in the evenings.[67] John Shipp first became enamored of military life after seeing a recruiter at work.[68] Still another boy enlisted in the Thirty-second Foot in 1844 after seeing a military band accompanying the soldiers from a church parade to the barracks. He declared: "I thought that it was the finest sight that I had ever seen." The sight was sufficient to entice him to enlist despite having "a good place, and a good master . . . We agreed very well." For an apprentice to enjoy such advantages was good fortune indeed, and highlights the powerful lure of imagery.[69] A future major described the inspiration of having local garrison troops march past his school every day: "Had they studied in what way to turn our heads, they could not have done it more effectually."[70] These last two instances illustrate the power of music in the military march, which inspired young men and boys to follow the soldiers and sometimes try to enlist.[71]

Other recruits were influenced by the regimental display of a unit's military achievements: its battle honors. Recruiting posters sometimes mentioned these,[72] and at least one fencible (militia) corps had a battle honor invented by its colonel.[73] Honors helped instill in some the desire to join what they thought were superior units, and this may have been a factor in the increased number of battle honors awarded after 1815. Other honorable decorations also attracted recruits; not all units had badges in the early part of this era, but those that did claimed that this distinction marked their corps as special. One poster proclaimed that recruits for the Fourteenth Light Dragoons would have "the exclusive right of wearing the Black or Imperial Eagle of Prussia."[74]

The message of martial glory and renown was reinforced by other inducements to enlist. Posters often emphasized military prowess and idealistic motives; one proclaimed: "Young fellows whose hearts beat high to tread the paths of glory, could not have a better opportunity than now offers."[75] Some men were greatly inspired by the idea of sharing in the honor of soldiering. Upon hearing a recruiter's harangue, John Shipp wrote: "So inspired was I by the word 'victory!' "[76]

Recruits were also motivated by the idea that they would participate in the glories of martial ceremony. A petty thief sick with consumption actually paid a bribe to join the Royal Artillery in the 1870s in order to acquire martial honors; he wanted only to die a soldier and receive a military funeral. He was immediately put in the hospital after arriving at camp, and received neither a uniform nor training, but spoke with "extraordinary animation about the military band that would play him to his earthly resting-place, and the Union-Jack that would cover his coffin, just as if these were honours that he had won by his merits." He liked to have Creasy's *Fifteen Decisive Battles of the World* read to him.[77]

Loyalty and patriotism were also standard themes in recruiting, and the appeal of serving the monarch could be very strong. One young subaltern stated: "I loved the king with a veneration which has no adequate term to express it." After his corps was shipped to France, he liked to refer to "le roi mon maitre."[78] Colonel Alan Cameron of Erracht's recruiting poster for the Seventy-ninth Foot proclaimed that he was raising the regiment "at his own private expense" for no other reason than to obtain the "pride of commanding a faithful and brave band of his warlike countrymen, in the service of a king, whose greatest happiness is to reign as the common father and protector of his people."[79]

During the French wars, the recruits' feelings of personal loyalty to George III were often intensified by his attendance at victory celebrations, military reviews, and other public events.[80] The royal magic was even evoked by official notice of a new subaltern's appointment: "There I was in print,—in absolute print; and that, too in the Gazette—by the king's royal authority!" Becoming a soldier was overwhelming to this young ensign: "I was more than a duke, more than a king, more than an emperor; I was a SUBALTERN. In idea, I was already a captain, a colonel, a general!"[81]

Scotsmen sometimes felt an especially strong sense of loyalty to Scottish corps; Alexander Somerville wrote: "Tell the young Scotchman who recites the glories of his favorite Greys while he rests on the harvest field with listening shearers all around . . . or when he listens . . . to the veteran . . . that the highland regiments were not the regiments 'always in front of Wellington's battles' . . . that the 42d Highlanders were not slain at [the battle of] Quatre Bras, on the 16th of June, through their impetuous bravery, but through the irregularity of their movements . . . and he will tell you that you are no Scotchman; that you are not worthy of having such regiments as the 'Heelant Watch' (42d Foot), or the 'Gallant Greys.' "[82]

Military spectacle thus played a vital role in the recruiting process, and an investigation of army headdresses in 1897 for the Secretary of State for War gives us some idea of the type of recruit the army hoped to attract by the show.[83] Questions were put to recruiters, adjutants, and colonels, and all but one agreed that headdress and uniform played an important role in recruiting.[84] One colonel stated that for the majority of men the uniform offered no inducement, but after further questioning, he stated that those who were attracted to "seeing a smart regiment" march through their village were the "better sort of recruits."[85] In the first half of the century, these rural recruits were even more desirable, for, as one colonel noted, "there is too much knowledge in these towns . . . The more recruits they get with a straw hat and smock frock the better . . . the more ignorant, the better soldiers."[86]

Other respondents who were asked about the importance of dress agreed that a smart headdress and uniform drew better-quality recruits: "I think the more attractive the head-dress, the better the class of men you get as a recruit, and I think that applies to uniform generally."[87] One soldier was said to have enlisted under the condition that he be allowed to wear a lance cap; he was described as an educated, well-spoken, and "well-grown" (tall) country lad, and had plenty of work in his trade (shoemaking) at the time. The question was then asked:

> "Those better class of men would calculate upon a better class of dresses, would they not?"
> "Yes."
> "Those are the men we want in the army?"
> "Yes, certainly."[88]

This better class of recruits were also valued for their moral qualities; Inspector-General Jackson noted that "moral virtue" was more important in "the permanent success of arms" than physical prowess, but ability and education were also significant factors.[89] Promising men of intelligence who were attracted primarily by the imagery were absolutely vital, because they were the ones promoted to noncommissioned officers, who were "the life and main spring of a regiment,"[90] and in wartime especially these essential men were in short supply.[91] Men like Sergeant Thomas Morris and Sergeant-Major Timothy Gowing were the best of the Other Ranks, and some who felt most inspired by the appeal of military glory, including John Shipp and James FitzGibbon, rose even further to attain the almost unreachable prize of commissioned rank.[92]

Without the enticement of military dress to help lure high-quality recruits, the state would also have been hard-pressed in wartime to find enough officers willing to serve. Inspector-General Jackson noted that "vanity often leads to acts of enterprize; that is, it entices a man to enter the field of battle with a shew of courage: it is honour, or mental pride only, which secures him from leaving it without disgrace."[93] The "vanity of dress," so crucial to the recruiting process, thus played an essential role in the nineteenth-century art of war.

CHAPTER FOUR

Discipline

Military imagery was vital to maintaining the discipline that soon brought about great changes in the life of the recruit. From his enlistment, the army's high standards required the private soldier's constant labor and attention. The upkeep of the dress and equipment and the ways in which these were worn reinforced the powerful effects of drill and training. Together these factors composed the core of the idealized martial image, and produced powerful psychological effects that strengthened discipline. They were also instrumental in molding the recruits into the kind of soldiers the commanders needed.

The idea of linking dress with authority was not confined to the military; in early-nineteenth-century Britain one's status was normally conveyed by dress. But in no other institution was rank so clearly defined by outward appearance—nor dress so complicated and varied—as in the army. Hierarchy was absolutely central to the system of discipline and command, and it was the uniform that communicated rank to soldiers.[1] The delineation of the three basic ranks—officers, noncommissioned officers, and privates—was reflected by differences in the uniform's quality and decorations, and was thoroughly understood only by soldiers and their families.

New officers visited a military tailor to be fitted for their uniforms, but the Other Ranks' coats, trousers, and other garments came in several standard sizes and almost always had to be altered or resewn after delivery.[2] The coat qualities varied, with two or three grades of fabric and dye, which were different for each basic rank. Officers' coats were a scarlet color made from cochineal, a dye imported from the Iberian Peninsula and Mexico, sergeants' coats were usually red, and privates' and corporals' coats were sometimes true red, but more often were colored with a cheap red dye (often madder) called "brick red."

Noncommissioned officers' coats were usually of better quality than the privates',[3] but in the cavalry regiments, better-quality dye was often used for the Other Ranks' coats as well.[4] High-quality wool with decorations of gold or silver bullion lace further distinguished officers' coats, while the Other Ranks usually wore coats made of blanket wool or some other cheap, woolen fabric.

Lesser amounts of metallic lace, sometimes of an inferior quality, decorated the noncommissioned officers' coats, whereas privates wore white, cotton-worsted lace (some Ordnance and cavalry units wore yellow). Rank was also marked by other decorations on the uniform; until 1830, officers were distinguished by one or two epaulets (after 1830 all officers wore two). Officers and sergeants also carried swords, which further set them apart (except in the cavalry, horse artillery, and rifles) from those of inferior rank, who carried bayonets.[5]

The basic ranks were further identified by three or sometimes four different grades of headdresses. The various items of equipment and appointments also came in two or three qualities. All these emblems were an integral reflection of hierarchy: "Experience has taught . . . that the most just mode of securing discipline in a regiment is . . . the establishment of such an exact gradation of responsibility . . . that every individual entrusted with command, knows his precise station and what is required of him."[6] These markings had long symbolized authority; noncommissioned officers' chevrons (copied from Prussia), for example, were originally thought to be an emblem of "power and royalty."[7]

These marks of hierarchy were reinforced by military ceremonies and drill, which visually replicated the array of the battlefield. On parade, privates stood in straight lines with their superiors (the cadre) standing apart—either in front, behind, or to one side of the body of men, emphasizing their superior status. Officers positioned in front of the troops symbolized leadership, whereas a station to one side or behind a formation symbolized control. This hierarchy also applied to the regiments. The oldest units had the place of honor on the right, and the most recently raised corps were on the left. Those with the highest numbers had the lowest status, and in battle the same hierarchy applied. In Egypt in 1801, the Ninety-second Highlanders and another unit of recent origin, "being the junior regiments were ordered to advance and act as riflemen, there being none of these troops with the army."[8]

But not all aspects of the image were so easy to regulate, for some colonels sought to control the design of the martial image (see Chapter 2), in violation of "the uniformity of system which it is so essential to maintain."[9] Like the colonels who altered the monarch's designs, regimental officers also deviated from their own unit's dress rules. An officer's jacket that has survived from the Seventy-ninth Highlanders does not conform to the regulations of 1802, having many additional buttons and gold loops.[10] One officer noted with some disgust that "it is impossible to specify any direct [clothing] regulations [for officers], since custom . . . has given to different regiments as many deviations . . . as convenience or caprice can dictate."[11] Grose's military satire advised officers: "The fashion of your clothes must depend on that ordered in the corps; that is to say, must be in direct opposition to it . . . Never wear your uniform in quarters, when you can avoid it. A green or brown coat shews you have other clothes beside your regimentals, and likewise that you have courage to disobey a standing order. If you have not an entire suit, at least mount a pair of black breeches, a round hat, or something unmilitary."[12]

This habit reflected in part the Whig heritage of 1688, when independent-minded Englishmen had thrown off what they considered to be tyrannical royal authority. Whereas Prussians or other continental officers might consider any deviation in dress to be a crime, British officers saw it as a sign of their political status as free-born Britons, and in the design of their uniforms many defied not only the adjutant-general's regulations but also the regimental ones. Some even dared to wear white hats, a symbol of "hostility to the government and defiance of authority."[13] These were sometimes specifically prohibited in regimental standing orders.[14] Some officers even prided themselves on their ignorance of uniform regulations, making bets in the mess about the details: "Mr. Fisher lost one bottle of wine that the regulation for [an] officer's appearance in the mess is with black belts and swords."[15]

This visual statement of independence received encouragement from another quarter; General Mercer noted that toward the end of the French wars, "women . . . learned to look on a man as a spiritless quiz, who stuck to regulation in wearing his uniform."[16] This deliberate flouting of dress regulations was also shaped by the force of the officers' collective opinion, which sometimes imposed a style upon their peers. An artillery officer found, to his embarrassment, that a hat he had ordered "according to regulations" made him a mockery, since it "was large, ungainly, and . . . the sides curled up like the gunners', whereas the droop [of the sides] had just begun to be all the go . . . The conical feather, though strictly of regimental length, etc., was like nobody else's, and hideous."[17]

But the novelty of fancy dress frequently wore off once the officers matured. When reminiscing about dress in his early days of service, General Mercer noted—as did other veterans—"what a conceited little puppy I was . . . what a jackanapes I must have been."[18]

The younger officers, who enjoyed wearing flashy uniforms, were more prone to extravagance than the older, more experienced men, who tended to prefer the comfort of looser, more casual dress. Once they had matured and become accustomed to duty and advanced in experience and rank (and often had put on more weight), the appeal of tight, heavy, confining dress gave way to a desire for more comfort and a looser, less ostentatious costume. A popular alternative to scarlet was the undress blue frock coat, which "is now more generally worn than any other dress."[19] A more subdued appearance had long been popular among fashionable British men: "It became a British characteristic [from the seventeenth century] for persons of station and authority to dress plainly, with finery reserved for special occasions."[20]

Many strongly disliked wearing any uniform; the commander in chief of the Crimea army, Lord Raglan, was often mistaken for a civilian tourist by both officers and men, and many contemporaries describe officers wearing mufti, even for reviews.[21] At a cavalry review in 1827, a German visitor saw "fifty or sixty officers in plain clothes—several generals among them."[22] Some even carried umbrellas on duty instead of swords, a practice that was often viewed with horror.[23] Officers' independence in matters of dress was thus a tradition, and some colonels were easy-going about it, adopting the attitude that a gentleman's dress was his own affair.

But the dominant opinion in many regimental messes was that dress should be uniform for the officers of the same corps, and an inspecting general might note even minor deviations with disapproval: "There appears to be a slight difference in the size of bullion [epaulets] supplied to the captains by different tradesmen."[24] Superiors could also be adamant about the disciplinary necessity of conformity to dress regulations; when officers of a cavalry unit in northern England wore mufti in quarters, this was said to cause "a serious obstruction to discipline," and the commander in chief issued a general order that "all officers commanding districts and regiments . . . take special care that no officers under their command shall ever appear at their quarters without their uniforms."[25] Captain Gronow of the First Foot Guards was threatened with arrest by the duke of Cambridge "for not having sufficient quantity of [hair] powder on my head" when on guard duty.[26] Some colonels demanded that officers always wear full regimentals when walking out of quarters.[27]

Uniformity was also a goal of those colonels who dictated from which firm regimental officers could purchase kit items. After their return from the Corunna campaign (by which time their uniforms were ragged), officers of the Twentieth Foot were instructed by their colonel to purchase their buttons only at Firman & Westalls in the Strand, "and none else will [be] permitted to be worn."[28] A colonel could also insist on the rigid enforcement of regimental dress regulations to harass officers he disliked or wanted to sell out.[29]

Another point of conflict in the struggle to control images was the practice of some officers of dressing their soldier-servants in a livery instead of the corps' uniform. After he received a commission in the Ninth Lancers in 1836, Cornet Ansthruther-Thomson's brother officers all recommended that he dress his soldier-servant in livery.[30] But in many units, including the Life Guards, liveries were contrary to the *Standing Orders*.[31]

Conflicts over this nonregulation—but uniform—dress were sometimes resolved by the regiment's agreeing on a special livery for the soldier-servants of officers. The Eighty-fifth Light Infantry's mess adopted a blue frock coat with brass buttons, a yellow waistcoat with covered buttons, and black velveteen breeches for servants. This livery was enshrined as a part of the *Standing Orders*, "as it will tend very much to the respectability of their appearance."[32]

Likewise, a regimental mess might agree on adopting for themselves a nonmilitary but uniform civilian-style costume to wear on social occasions, thus avoiding the heavy regulation uniform, as did the First Dragoons' mess in the early 1830s. One of the officers wrote of getting married in 1832 wearing a "blue evening-coat with fancy buttons, that we had adopted in the regiment." The outfit also included "a white watered-silk waistcoat and light fawn-colored trousers with boots and spurs."[33] An infantry regiment also had a "full military ball dress," separate from the dress coat, as formal evening wear.[34]

The importance of the uniform in promoting discipline is highlighted by the fact that some units clothed soldiers' children in uniform dress. In the 1840s, the Seventy-fourth Highland regiment was purchasing bulk quantities of tartan cloth "of one texture" for the "soldiers' girls [daughters] of the regiment" who were attending the regimental school.[35] "Hard regimental tartan" was later purchased to make trews and waistcoats for the boys and frocks for the girls. The children, like their fathers, were inspected.[36]

Inspection was the primary method of controlling the many deviations and conflicts over dress, and was necessary for the army to maintain some degree of order and uniformity. Observation and inspection were thus never-ending tasks, and inspections by general officers took place yearly and quarterly. But it was the many regimental inspections that were the most important; when a unit was stationed in a faraway place, the senior officers on the spot were responsible for that unit's dress. Regimental inspections took place according to the wishes of the colonel, usually at weekly intervals (or twice a week with full pack) with numerous minor daily inspections.[37] The sergeants who usually carried these out were so adept at catching any minor deviations or dodges that, in effect, inspections occurred whenever any noncommissioned officer was in the presence of a soldier. Noncommissioned officers had the primary responsibility for looking after the privates' appearance, with the sergeant-major and adjutant overseeing the whole regiment.[38] "At all inspections, which . . . he [the sergeant-major] may have occasion to perform . . . he must be pointedly exact, and never allow the most trifling article to escape him or appear unworthy of his notice."[39]

Wellington believed that soldiers should be watched "from hour to hour [and that] they should never be exempt from observation and free from controul."[40] Some colonels made a practice of holding inspections on short notice so that the soldiers would always be prepared.[41] Infractions of dress regulations by the Other Ranks could be met with severe punishment, such as a flogging or extra drill, although the degree of severity was at the colonel's discretion.

These frequent inspections and the threat of punishment for even minor infractions meant that common soldiers had to devote a great deal of their time to the upkeep of the kit. This had the effect of keeping them busy in their off-duty hours; the more time the soldiers spent cleaning their accoutrements, the less time they had to get into trouble.[42] This means of control was meant to reinforce discipline, but the coercive dimension of the system, combined with the other harsh realities of army life for the privates, generated the worst discipline problem: it drove men to drink. For most soldiers, alcohol was the only escape; it was customary in many regiments to pay the men once a month, and most would then drink until their money was gone. Many units had standing orders that officers and noncommissioned officers were to avoid drunk privates, since they often attacked their superiors.[43] This was apparently an unsolvable dilemma, for such men were essential to a unit's fighting spirit: "The most profligate fellows in a regiment die like heros at the muzzle of a gun."[44]

The authorities thus tacitly acknowledged that escapism in drink was a normal part of life in the Other Ranks, despite the fact that it was also the army's greatest discipline problem and that acute alcoholism was the downfall of the soldiers who had cost so much money to recruit and maintain.[45] Alcoholism was so pervasive that it became closely identified with the soldiers' primary visual image—the uniform. A "tailor's slang" expression has survived from the early nineteenth century in the word "tight," equating the tightness of military dress with drunkenness.[46]

So widespread was alcohol abuse by the Other Ranks that those men of sober character who did not spend all their pay in drunken dissipation were ostracized or harassed by the others, who called them "Methodists" or "misers."[47] Nevertheless, drink was an inescapable—however destructive—counterbalance to the disciplinarian army life, even though it contributed so much to the weakening of that same system and the violation of its laws. The soldiers could tolerate the most relentless discipline as long as they could get drunk once in a while, but if the authorities took away the drink, then trouble would inevitably follow.[48]

Drink was just one factor that tended to harden common soldiers in this harsh milieu, and many had little or nothing to lose in either personal property or reputation.[49] Consequently, severe punishments were not enough to control them, yet discipline was absolutely essential. The answer to this problem dovetailed neatly with the army's other management techniques; the perfect paradigm of control was expressed in a context that embodied the ideal of perfection: the machine.

From the authorities' perspective, the machine was the consummate model of control. The logic of this idealistic, mechanistic mindset renders humans mere tools with no independent will of their own, existing and acting solely for the benefit of those in authority. As a regulating principle it was thus invaluable for those in command. The machine metaphor appears frequently in the sources; the general who referred to this "mechanical discipline" and considered war to be "a practical science" was merely expressing a widely held concept.[50] The word "perfection," connected as it was with this ideal, frequently appears in reference to duty: "The whole [regiment] can never obtain the wished for perfection, unless a general anxiety that it should be so, lies in every man's breast to a certain degree, and unless his officers in particular are animated [with the same]."[51]

This mechanistic quality was most effectively displayed in the soldier's posture and movements when carrying out most of his everyday assignments, and all duties that served as spectacle also operated with a machine-like quality. When at drill or on parade, each part of the soldier's body was precisely regulated in relation to all others and to his dress: "When at attention the little finger only [is] to feel the trousers, the palm of the hand [is] turned a little outwards [with] fingers extended and the thumb close to the forefinger. Elbows [are] to be close to the sides. When with arms at the 'Order' the men are to place the right hand alongside the firelock with thumb under the sling to steady the piece. Elbows invariably [are] to be kept close together."[52]

The soldier's movements were normally regulated by music, and to keep the proper cadence in marching, the drum-major "must scrupulously observe the ordered times of march, whether ordinary or quick, and use no tunes but such as are particularly adopted to such times of march." This was so important that the drum-major was "not to be allowed to trust . . . his own ear . . . but at all times to have a plummet [metronome]."[53] Cadenced movement was important enough that it superseded the need to show a spotless dress in public, but it also increased the time-consuming labor that kept soldiers busy. When on the march, soldiers were not allowed to step out of line to avoid mud or water that might soil their dress.[54]

Ideally, the application of these principles so molded the soldiers that they would respond automatically under any circumstances, as if they were cogs in a machine (and they were frequently referred to as "machines"). Although urban recruits were more prone to disease and insubordination than rural recruits, industrial workers were thought to be better adapted to "the great machine" owing to the manual dexterity required by their work: "As artizans acquire a ready use of their hands and fingers, in the practice of their callings they learn manual exercise with great facility; and they perform it with dexterity and correctness: they also assume the military air speedily . . . for mechanistic movement . . . is the habit of their life."[55] This advantage was offset by the greater degree of savvy that urban recruits possessed; those in authority preferred soldiers to be ignorant, for they were less likely to mutiny.[56]

Drill and uniformity in appearance were considered aesthetic ideals and, theoretically, were supposed to be pursued to the point of perfection. Their importance provided a rationale for the many demanding, exacting, and seemingly pettifogging rules for minor matters of appearance: "Remember that uniformity in every thing is most indispensable for the appearance of a regiment. In the slightest article of dress, the size of a tuft, the fitting of a strap and buckle, the length of a picker and brush—even to every man having the brush or picker on the same side—wings, shoulder-straps, everything alike."[57]

A manual for noncommissioned officers emphasized the importance of perfection: "No mistake or inaccuracy, however trifling, can possibly escape the instructor's notice if he is at all attentive, seeing he has only one man, or at most, two at a time under observation."[58] Colonel Rolt also believed that attention to detail was essential, declaring that it was only through "the uniform attention to all, to the minutest circumstances of discipline, that a regiment acquires [military] habits."[59]

The more often soldiers were in the public eye, the greater was the stress put on the ideal of visual perfection. The movements of sentries, for example, had to be perfectly precise in every detail: "[If any] sentry . . . in the performance of any one of his motions, is incorrect in the slightest possible degree, [he] must be visited again and again until found perfect." The sentries' expression was to be mechanical, as they were instructed not to smile or take any notice of people who came near.[60]

Sentries were thus to appear as a living manifestation of this idealized machine image because they were always visible to the public. This was the subject of a royal order in 1832: "The king has observed to the general commanding-in-chief, that His Majesty considers the manner in which guards and sentries perform their complimentary motions of the manual exercise, a fair criterion whereby to judge the general state of discipline of the regiment to which such guards and sentries belong."[61]

The paradigm of the machine, with its "habits of regularity," was also thought to induce soldiers to behave themselves when off the parade-ground. One colonel complimented his men after a good showing at an inspection, writing that "by a continuation of their zealous exertions in carrying out the excellent system of interior economy . . . in this corps, the men will at no distant period become so confirmed in habits of regularity, that punishment will become almost unknown among them."[62] Regularity combined with strictness had the desired effect. An instruction to noncommissioned officers noted that they must take great care to enforce any assignments of extra drill, because "slight punishments of this nature, when rigidly inflicted, are generally the most effective means of preserving the young and thoughtless soldier from falling into those [crimes] which are much more serious."[63] The logic of these techniques was described by one sergeant who wrote, apparently without any trace of sarcasm, that the army's "lords and gentlemen . . . have only to devise a military system as oppressive as possible in every respect to that which the army has groaned and bled for the last half century, and they will soon have an army that neither needs the lash nor the halter; that will be feared abroad, respected and trusted at home, and upon which neither cant, corruption, nor Chartism can make an evil impression, or turn aside from its duty."[64]

This need to maintain a sense of loyalty among soldiers on anti-riot duty at home was essential (see Chapter 7). When on the march in the dangerous year 1819, the Sixth Foot's noncommissioned officers and privates were heard to use "disloyal and mischievous language," and "evil disposed persons" were thought to "be on the watch to corrupt them." Many felt that this behavior originated with men who "are unaccustomed to the habits and manners of soldiers." A major part of the remedy for this threat was "the most constant attention to . . . discipline."[65]

Such control was also vital for the army when in the field. The frightening, chaotic, and confused conditions of battle made it absolutely necessary to maintain maximum control over large numbers of ill-treated, underfed, and mostly young men, many of whom would have preferred to be elsewhere. Control was also essential for tactics that relied primarily upon the vollied firing of smooth-bore muskets, to obtain the greatest effect from their limited range and complicated loading procedure. Diligence was thus crucial. As one colonel observed, "There is nothing minute and trifling in war; any negligence in the slightest things insensibly leads to indifference in those of greater moment."[66]

The machine ideal was therefore both a disciplinary and a tactical principle, and when it could not be employed, the loss of control was always a threat. At the siege of Badajoz in 1812, when the attacking British troops were confined to a ditch before the walls, control over the soldiers was replaced by individual initiative. One officer stated: "There being no formation of troops to make them as a machine, only the bravest . . . followed their officers."[67]

The coordinated, machine-like movements were also necessary to move large numbers of men from one place to another in an orderly manner.[68] For those in command, "it is absolutely necessary that they should at all times know what space a company, or any other division of the battalion, will occupy." The most precise regulations thus governed the most minute details of any maneuver, and the length of the pace in marching and the distance between men were essential.[69]

Thus the machine ideal emphasized a basic message: systematic uniformity and implicit obedience were essential (and mutually supportive) for effective training.[70] To achieve this control, the common soldier's uniform as well as his movements was strictly regulated. The endless attention devoted to petty matters of the kit in the relentless pursuit of perfection had significant psychological effects: "The enforcement of careful habits amongst the men [is] only to be formed by the constant and minute attention of officers to details."[71]

The uniform constrained the wearer, and its tightness limited his motions, forcing him into the proper military posture. The fit was frequently even tighter than required, because most soldiers were still growing when they enlisted. After growing two inches, John Shipp complained: "My jacket had literally become a strait-jacket, for I could scarce raise my hand to my head."[72] During every waking hour of his entire military service, each man of the Other Ranks was rigidly constrained in every movement by his uniform (and equipment), to the point where a rigid posture became habitual. This was also a matter of regulation: "Soldiers should always carry themselves erect, and move like soldiers; and by constant attention a steady and upright carriage will become . . . habitual."[73] Other movements performed on duty were also proscribed, both to make them effective and to attain the correct "style."[74]

Together, the training and uniform were so effective in controlling the men's movements that a permanent influence reigned over their motions, and they would "find difficulty in standing or moving in an unsoldier-like manner."[75] Thus "the proper adjustment of clothing [has] a distinguished place in a scientific system of moral discipline."[76] Veterans were permanently marked by this posture and carried it for the rest of their lives; years later they could still be spotted walking like soldiers,[77] and descriptions of ex-soldiers often included a mention that they walked with "a military air."[78]

The neckstock added considerably to this effect, and as a means of physical control it was the most constraining part of the kit. This item of the Other Ranks' necessaries was intended to impose conformity, and in the case of men with large necks, it was more like a punishment, for it appears that all neckstocks came in a single size.[79] One sergeant wrote of "the cruelty of the stock" and called it "Calcraft's cord"—the hangman's noose.[80] Conformity was further ensured by the rule that the rigid, tight stocks were never to be made thinner by scraping or cutting away the interior leather. In some units, this rule stood even for a soldier who was injured and suffering because of it; to alter the stock might earn a severe punishment.[81] The stock is described as being an "almost iron neckband"[82] that left a permanent scar on the neck.[83] Apparently, there was a "gradual substitution" of a more pliant variety after 1845, when Wellington was "grudgingly" won over to it, but many colonels probably resisted the change.[84]

Wearing the uniform and equipment was torturous for those marching in a tropical climate; during the Second Sikh War, after a hot and fatiguing march without food, the colonel of the Thirty-first Foot reprimanded a soldier for taking his stock off: "I . . . observed a wild expression come over his worn face. For a moment I thought that he was going to shoot the colonel; then he put his forehead on the muzzle of his firelock and blew his brains out."[85] The severe tightness of the uniform and equipment, together with the rigid posture, thus served as a form of coercion as well as control. In this regard, army discipline resembles the management techniques of observation and coercion described in Michel Foucault's *Discipline and Punish*, though the problem of discipline in the military was much greater than in any other institution.[86]

Drill was also an important means of molding soldiers, but it was a source of torment for them as well. New recruits, both enlisted men and officers, spent a great deal of their time at drill for the first two or three months after joining their regiment, until they had learned it properly—and had been conditioned by it. Some colonels were more demanding than others, but a recruit who learned quickly would spend less time drilling, although one adjutant warned: "Too much attention cannot be paid to the first instruction of the soldier."[87]

Drill was a daily exercise, and some units had recruits drill four times each day, with veterans drilling three times a day. This was repeated until it became second nature, and it reinforced the constraints and controls of the uniform, for "if proper attention [to drill] be paid by the officer commanding companies, no falling off can take place in the discipline of the men."[88] The importance of drill in maintaining discipline is illustrated by the fact that whenever soldiers were away from their units on detached duty, they were given extra drill.[89] Drill was thus an integral part of the soldiers' routine, and was always central to the labor they performed.

Drill was also used as a punishment, and could be quite unpleasant in its effects.[90] In the early 1830s, the Second Dragoons punished "gross misconduct" by "saddle-bag drill," in which the soldier marched back and forth over a patch of ground carrying his full kit, including weapons, saddle, and all other equipment, from six in the morning until six at night, for a week or two.[91]

Yet the use of the uniform, posture, drill, and other elements of spectacle as a means of control was more subtle than harsh punishments, and probably more effective in conditioning the soldiers.[92] It had the effect of molding their minds by the simple application of routine rules, and the correct impressions were thus instilled "by insensible degrees."[93] Inspector-General Jackson asserted that "institutions engender habits by a continuance of mechanical routine; and may even so confirm them that they be calculated with some certainty of result." A corps was thus "united scientifically by internal power."[94] Colonel Stepney agreed, and it is revealing that his language is that of biological manipulation; he wrote that "much depends . . . on the depth with which [the soldier] has been imbued (not to say inoculated) with the proper virus."[95]

This management technique was a fundamental aspect of the army's daily routine—especially in peacetime—through the constant use of aesthetic images combined with the physical control exercised over soldiers. As such, it is closely linked with the management problem of maintaining domination over men who were cowardly, rebellious, or disorderly—over any who opposed authority and resisted the goals of the machine's operation. The system's logic also stipulated that soldiers not show any initiative and merely function as the machine's components. The soldiers would "stand sentry . . . or mount guard . . . till the mind has settled into one undeviating train of barren thought."[96] Yet this mechanistic technique had effects that, from the point of view of those in charge, were also detrimental; after years away from military service, an ex-sergeant wrote that when he became a soldier again temporarily in the colonies, he "was almost afraid to think."[97] During the Crimean War, one veteran noted that in comparison with the French, British soldiers seemed helpless, and when outside of regular quarters could not look after themselves.[98]

But in times of disorder and crisis, this management technique played a crucial role in helping to maintain or restore order. When soldiers got out of hand—fighting or abusing civilians—parades and drill could restore discipline; they could also prove useful in containing excesses during wartime. After the bloody siege of Burgos in April 1812, "many disgraceful scenes of irregularity [were] still continuing to prevail, [and] Lord Wellington ordered the troops to remain on parade under arms throughout the day."[99]

When the far more serious problem of mutiny threatened, the mental effects of the machine could be decisive. In 1818, when a mutiny among sailors broke out on board a troop ship, the veterans of an invalid corps were ordered to fall in to repress it, although they were enduring the same abuse from the captain as the sailors. An officer present wrote: "Although many of them were lame and ailing they all fell in with the greatest alacrity, and remained upright, silent, steady, as though they were so many automatons."[100]

In combat, where the men often suffered greatly, the psychological effects of the machine could mean the difference between destruction and survival. During the terrible retreat to Corunna in the winter of 1808–1809, a private of the Seventy-first Highland regiment who was tired, hungry, and cold wrote that "my mind was so confused I could not arrange my ideas. I almost think I was deranged." But when a party of Frenchmen approached, he instinctively responded as he had been drilled: "Unconscious of the action, I started upon my feet, leveled my musket . . . fired, and formed with the other stragglers."[101]

The emphasis on appearances thus helped impose order in battle, and had further effects as well.[102] Subtle and deep-rooted messages became fixed in the minds of the soldiers, both on an unconscious and a conscious level. As one officer noted, "There is a stiffness and an angularity about their movements (the result of endless drill) which seem imparted to their very ideas."[103] Inspector-General Jackson also noted that "man is an animal of imitation in all his steps and gradations; animal action assumes, through frequent repetition, a constitutional habit which becomes in some degree a second nature."[104]

The disciplinary dimension of martial imagery can thus be understood as an integral aspect of the military machine, and its ability to control and shape human perception and thought was intrinsic to the system of discipline. For those in command, responsibility for maintaining the perfectionist ideal for martial images was often very attractive, and was frequently a source of personal gratification. Because of the traditional independence of the colonels and the great control exercised daily by adjutants and sergeants, physical brutality died out only gradually. Illegal (and judicial) brutality continued in some units long after regulations formally ended such practices. This was especially true when a unit was stationed in some faraway posting; most soldiers serving in such units would not return from the deadly tropical climate, and many years might elapse before a unit returned home, making it unlikely that abuses would be reported. In any event, the soldiers could not be certain the authorities would take their complaints seriously.[105]

Officers in some regiments could beat soldiers or order beatings to be inflicted whenever they pleased, well into the early nineteenth century, and though the worst of the abuses gradually lessened in severity, such punishments were only modified to more subtle techniques.[106] These conditions thus helped render army life attractive to those officers who possessed a taste for inflicting pain on helpless victims.[107] Many sources mention officers and sergeants whose behavior and motives can only be interpreted as sadistic,[108] and the atmosphere of brutality in some units was also marked by the habitual use of profanity by superiors toward inferiors, and by the common soldiers to each other.[109]

Some commanders became so obsessed with punishment that eventually they found themselves at the center of a scandal when one of their soldiers was flogged to death for some trifle, and they were then forced to sell their commission. Others entertained preposterous expectations in their pursuit of the mechanistic ideal of perfection. In Nova Scotia during the snowy winter of 1824–1825, a rifle unit colonel reprimanded an officer for allowing his sentries to wear greatcoats, for "he had an idea that a rifleman could or should 'stand anything.' "[110]

Although not all martinets were sadistic, the "mad adjutant" was a stock figure in the army; according to one contemporary account, he "lives and wallows in pipe-clay . . . and is wretched if he cannot find something or someone to find fault with."[111] Moreover, "His love of the 'pomp, parade, and circumstance of glorious war,' is as powerful as his love of life."[112] Sometimes adjutants were promoted from the ranks, in which case they were known to be the most exacting and harshest of officers. One was described by another officer as "so full of positiveness and illiberality of sentiment, that it was difficult, at times, to hide the disgust I felt at a disposition so uncongenial to my own. He [seemed] to think the military law and discipline ought to prevail throughout the world."[113]

This phenomenon appears linked to the vast gap in social status between officers and the Other Ranks, for an officer's obsession with military discipline—which made him useful to those in authority—could also have helped him control his own behavior in the harsh environment of the ranks. One such officer of the Sixtieth Rifles serving in the Peninsula wore the same "hard leather stock and a brass clasp" as the Other Ranks, and "all his trappings were of the same coarse material as his men." He was also known never to indulge in anything beyond his rations.[114]

The behavior of these "ranker" officers helps explain why the soldiers preferred to be commanded by gentlemen rather than by those of their own class: "In our army, the men like best to be officered by gentlemen, men whose education has rendered them more kind in manners than your coarse officer, sprung from obscure origin, whose style is brutal and overbearing."[115] Privates who were bullies were often preferred for advancement; indeed, "In general the surest passport to promotion in the service, is to evince a disposition to tyrannize over your fellows, and to seem regardless of their feelings and interests."[116]

Gentleman martinet officers, however, tended to be effective mainly at parades. They disliked light infantry drill, which involved less of the showy, coercive, machine-like drill of the heavy infantry, and therefore less rigid control.[117] The adoption of Torren's *Field Exercises* in 1825 to replace the Dundas *Manoeuvres* forced such officers to learn light infantry drill, and *they* were followed around and harassed by drill sergeants while practicing the new exercises; this served to "drive many old hands upon half-pay."[118] For such martinets, however, battle was something else entirely, and they were often incompetent in the field. At the Buenos Aires disaster in 1806, General Whitelock refused to answer "silly questions" that were vital to the operation.[119] Many soldiers considered martinets as a group to be incompetents and cowards.[120] When placed in the danger of combat they were often of little use or even harmful to their units, but they were most useful in the peacetime enforcement of discipline.

The punishments these men employed might have seemed to them a moral reaffirmation of the machine and their role in it, but while the forms of castigation varied a good deal, they were often harsh and cruel, and flogging was a usual method of punishment for most of the period under discussion.[121] A flogging served both to humiliate the offender and to impress the terror of official retribution upon the Other Ranks.

All punishment ceremonies were performed with the same aesthetic movements as every other military ritual: the soldiers' motions and the linear configurations of the rituals suggested the machine, and they were always administered publicly. The offender's entire unit (and sometimes other units) were required to witness the ceremony. The men were drawn up in a square, in full-dress and arms, with the victim and the executioner at the center.[122]

The army utilized imagery and spectacle in punishments to impress soldiers with the horror of the scene. This was highly successful, for flogging was horrible in the extreme. The "cat" used for flogging was made of whipcord leather, with nine tails, each one having three knots.[123] A sadistic colonel might order that the cats be soaked in brine beforehand, even though this was against regulations, and if caught, he could be court-martialed.[124] Some units had a special "thief's cat," which had nine knots in each tail instead of three.[125] But all these instruments reduced the victim's back to gory, black rags of flesh, and it was common for soldiers witnessing the punishment to faint.[126]

Civilians who complained about crimes committed by soldiers that resulted in the culprit's being flogged were often horrified, and sometimes tried to deny that the man had committed the offense. A farmer denied that a stolen goose belonged to him after he heard that the punishment was a flogging.[127] Civilian mobs might interfere in a punishment, and sometimes succeeded in stopping it.[128] Even when no civilians were present, however, the infliction of harsh punishments was a risky business, because the soldiers often felt sympathy for a man who was condemned to the possibility of death by flogging. Until 1795, no limit at all existed for the number of lashes a regimental court-martial might "award" for whatever crime the accused was charged with.[129] But the same crime was usually thought insignificant if committed by an officer or, in the case of drunkenness, was considered normal behavior for an officer.[130]

Visual elements were intrinsic to all punishments. The bodies of deserters were permanently "branded" (tattooed) with the "deserter's escutcheon," the letter "D" on the left shoulder, to prevent men from enlisting, deserting, and repeating the process for the bounty money.[131] Another, less severe means by which soldiers might be marked and also punished was the shaving of the head.[132] Other punishments included forcing a culprit to wear his coat inside out—"turning the coat"—sometimes with the word "thief" written on the back, or to stand guard outside the barracks without his trousers.[133] One colonel had a "kind of long smock-frock, with a green cross painted on the back and front of it" that the offender was obliged to wear.[134] Sometimes reminders of the crime itself were visually incorporated into the spectacle, as at Gibraltar when a private was executed for killing a sergeant. The door of the room in the barracks where the crime had been committed was left open, and a sentry was placed on each side of it, while all the other doors of the barracks were closed.[135]

The uniform also played a role in flogging, and the culprit's loss of status was marked visually. If he was to be degraded in rank, the tokens of his previous rank were publicly removed before the punishment was administered. If he was to be "discharged with ignomy," all honorific tokens were stripped from his clothing, such as those bearing the monarch's cipher and regimental markings, including the facings, badges, cap plate, buttons, and lace.

A culprit who was to be "drummed out" of the regiment after the punishment wore a halter around his neck as a mark of ignominy.[136] He was then marched out of the barracks to a slow drum cadence or to mournful trumpet music to the center of the drill square. He was stripped to the waist and tied to a wooden triangle by his wrists, while the band played "The Dead March in Saul."[137] In some regiments—at least until the end of the French wars—the offender was stripped naked to increase his humiliation.[138] This punishment not only divested him of all dignity but symbolically removed the honorable status represented by the uniform. If the victim was to be executed, his uniform was trimmed in black.[139]

The regimental drummers (infantry), buglers (rifle regiments), or farriers (cavalry) took turns inflicting the punishment. Field musicians and farriers had low status, and thus their administering the flogging increased the degradation to the victim. If the culprit was to be expelled from the regiment, the youngest drummer or bugler always gave him a kick on the backside as he left the barracks.[140]

Sometimes courageous men would try to employ humor to spoil the solemn and awful ceremony of their punishment. In 1826, an Irish private of the Fourth Light Dragoons turned his flogging "into a farce, rather than an example" by making some absurd remark between each round of floggings.[141] A French prisoner who had volunteered into a condemned corps and was caught deserting in Canada in 1812 showed great spirit at his execution, smoking a cigar and even examining the coffin's size. The colonel "found it necessary to direct that the provost proceed with the execution as quickly as possible."[142]

The imagery was thus a vital factor in maintaining army discipline through the paradigm of the machine. By utilizing drills, dress, inspections, and punishments, those in command were able to mold—mentally and even physically—the soldiers in their charge.

Tenth (the Prince of Wales's Own) Royal Regiment of Hussars

A typical example of the elaborate—and very expensive—hussar uniform.
The Tenth was among the fanciest of the light cavalry, and in the 1820s was
often a target of attacks on military arrogance.

The Great Army Tailoring Question: or,
Who Is the Real Sufferer—the Private or the Colonel?

In the latter part of this era, questions were increasingly raised
about the fairness of the colonels' management of the dress supply.
Note the young age of the privates.

The Eighteenth (Royal Irish) Regiment of Foot
at the Storming of the Fortress of Amoy, August 26, 1841

First Opium War, 1839–1842. Chinese "tiger" uniforms illustrate a different approach in sartorial intimidation. The Chinese army imitated circus entertainment to display threat, using tumblers and fantastic costumes, whereas in Britain the circus imitated the army.

The Black Choker

The hard leather neckstock was always worn
with the uniform, and was often considered a form
of torture by the privates. Like a slave's collar, it
exerted powerful psychological effects on
the wearer and helped enforce discipline.

Striking Effect of Choking and Overloading
Our Guards at a Late Review

The absurdity of the heavy pack and neckstock is parodied.

The Sixth, or Royal First Warwickshire Regiment of Foot, 1839

The sergeant wears white lace, the officer wears gold, and both
have white gloves and the "bell shako." Note the officer in
the background wearing the looser, dark-blue frock coat.
This unit had silver facings before 1830.

Regiments of Light Infantry

The Ninetieth Light Infantry, Perthshire Regiment. The soldiers wear the "Albert shako" (1844–1855). Only the dark-green pom-pom visually distinguishes this unit as light infantry; light infantry (except rifle units) wore red, despite its disadvantages in battle.

The Dandy Taylor Planing a New Hungry Dress. What a Pity
a Good Taylor Should Be Spoiled

The prince regent (later George IV), dressed as a tailor, sits sewing military uniforms. The floor is littered with bundles of stuffing and padding. George says: "A taylor there was and he lived in a stall, which served him for palace for *kitchen* and hall. No coin in his pocket no nous in his pate, no ambition has he nor no wish to be great." George's military aide holds a tailor's iron—called a "goose"—labeled "the Farmer's Boy," a reference to the more sober reputation of the regent's father, George III. The regent is visited by the Austrian ambassador Prince Esterhazy, followed by two Hungarian tailors. Esterhazy is dressed in an elaborate hussar uniform with "false bosoms," an exaggerated example of male cross-dressing in Regency-era high fashion. He explains that they have come to "teach you de proper vay to make de Hungarian soldats." The visitors have queues and large mustaches, emphasizing their foreign origin. The parody reveals the public's disapproval of both George's obsessive interest in designing uniforms and his extravagant, continental taste in martial dress.

Rifle Brigade, First Battalion

Although the dark-green and black uniform of the Rifle Brigade was a form
of camouflage, it was based on hussar dress, and was thus very elaborate.

Charge of the Third Dragoon Guards upon Rioters in Queen Square, Bristol

October 31, 1831. This is the only fine print I know of that depicts
soldiers fighting fellow Britons, a situation the public considered most disturbing.

A Scene in Downing Street, November 9, 1830

This true incident highlights the formidable quality of the
martial appearance in riot control.

Mars in Disguise, or the Terrors of the Bear-skin

This satire from the Seven-Years-War era mocks the idea of martial headgear as a form of intimidation. The grenadier's bearskin is exaggerated, and civilians flee or mock him.

*Maj. Everard William Bouverie, Royal
Horse Guards (Blue), 1835*

In 1829 the Duke of Wellington was blown off his horse by
a gust of wind while wearing this huge cap and
swan's feather at a London review.

The King and the Duke.
Let Me Be Feared, Let Me Be Loved

The top part of this print, showing
an armed Duke of Wellington,
flips down to reveal an amiable
King William IV. Thus the two
faces of state power, coercion
and attraction, are depicted.

The Seventy-fourth Highlanders

This highland officer *(right)* wears trews and a shako instead of the kilt
and ostrich-feather bonnet. Note the dirk, the basket-hilt "Claymore"
sword, and other distinctive features of highland dress.

A Charming Young Sentinel, the Delight of His Corps

This caricature features a series of faces on a paper wheel, which revolves behind a cut-out above the uniform, showing various droll expressions. This illustrates the strong emphasis on the martial image as a visual ideal, which made it a target for humor and the object of many parodies.

CHAPTER FIVE

Morale

Discipline is vital for armies, but morale is equally important, especially in promoting *esprit*, that "animating spirit . . . essential to success in action."[1] Wise commanders therefore had compelling reasons to try to enhance morale in whatever ways they could. But this had to be done within the existing regimental system, and without interfering with other, indispensable components of management. The harsh economic realities of army life did not allow for much improvement in the soldiers' miserable existence, especially if the colonel wished to profit from their off-reckonings. But it was possible to make elements of the soldiers' dress and equipment more appealing, and thus enhance the honor and glory of the service through these trappings. The uniform was essential to this management tactic.[2]

So important was the uniform's association with honor that soldiers denounced the use of its elements by liveried civilian servants as degrading: "With regard to the cockade, it is to be lamented, that a badge, evidently intended to convey notions of purest honour, should be within the reach of every prostitute's servant. Nor does it reflect much credit upon our noblemen . . . to load the shoulders of their lackeys with epaulettes of rich bullion."[3] Generally, the more showy an army uniform, the greater the implied honor attached to it.[4] Very plain uniforms were associated with a lower status and a lesser—or absent—degree of honor.[5] Being well dressed was an important source of unit pride, and some cultivated a reputation for a fine appearance; for example, the expression "being dressed to the nines" originated in the impressive sartorial appearance of the Ninety-ninth Foot in the 1850s.[6]

A focal point for officers' sense of *esprit*, and for the dress in most regiments, was the mess, and fashionable regiments' messes were said to be laden with better tables than many noble houses in Germany; the atmosphere might be very self-indulgent, but the better regiments had strict standards of behavior.[7] Dress standards reflected the army's decorum and importance, and formal full dress was worn for many years. The Twenty-fifth Foot maintained fastidious standards. Even when officers were not on duty, they were to wear "their coats hooked up in front, facings buttoned back, and the sash (which is to be worn at all times with the uniform) tied around the body, over the coat, the knot on the left side, except flank officers, who tie theirs on the right side." Duty officers were also subject to this code, with the added requirement that they wear their appointments and gorgets.[8]

Only the great heat of the tropics stimulated the development of "mess-dress," in which the less-formal shell jacket was adopted to replace the heavier full dress, although the waistcoat, worn with the unbuttoned mess jacket, made its own statement of sartorial splendor.[9] This growing sartorial informality was accompanied by increasing ritual as regiments developed elaborate ceremonies and customs. For example, in the Twenty-ninth Foot, the "Ever-sworded," officers traditionally dined wearing their swords.[10] Such customs did much to help nurture the sense of regimental uniqueness and *esprit de corps*. For the Sixth Dragoon Guards, never drinking to the king's health in the mess was a source of pride. According to tradition, the privilege was granted by King William III, "as our loyalty was undoubted."[11]

Unlike officers, common soldiers had no institutionalized ritual and camaraderie at mealtime (although sergeants' messes were established during the Crimean War). Other factors, however, including the uniform's visual elements combined with regimental duties, proclaimed the sort of values those in authority encouraged in soldiers, and tended to enhance their loyalty and identification with the unit.

Every regiment's distinctive uniform proclaimed the corps' uniqueness, and one of the most important distinctions was the facing color. The soldiers sometimes made associations with particular regiments based at least in part upon this decoration,[12] and they made up songs about their own units with the facings as prominent elements.[13] The importance attached to facing colors is highlighted by the troubles the duke of Wellington had with his regiment, the Thirty-third Foot, over its red facings. Because they were the same color as the coat, the red facings made the uniform less showy, as if it had no facings at all. In the Peninsula, soldiers from other units accused the men of the Thirty-third of having had their facings taken away as punishment for losing their colours, an insult that led to fistfights and no end of trouble for the duke.[14]

Other aspects of the uniform could also stimulate rivalry and brawls between regiments; riflemen, who wore black belts rather than white, and black buttons that were not polished like brass ones, despised pipeclay and the button stick and "looked upon them as fitted only for men less useful than themselves."[15] This feeling of superiority over heavy infantry undoubtedly enhanced the internal cohesiveness of rifle corps, but it also led to problems.

A serious affray between Rifle Brigade soldiers and Royal Artillerymen occurred over "some dispute as to the respective merits or demerits of certain regiments" and ended in the deaths of two artillerymen, who were shot while breaking through the locked door of a public house defended by riflemen. A Rifle Brigade officer commented that "a more dangerous subject [than interunit rivalries] cannot possibly be agitated by any military man, from the drum-boy to the commandant of a regiment." Yet in the next sentence he asserted that "no man is worthy to wear the uniform of his corps, be that corps what it may, who is not as tenacious of its good name as of his own individual character, and as ready to stand forward in its defense."[16] Brawls between men of different corps were a frequent problem, yet the authorities could not help sanctioning the regimental loyalty that prompted these fights. This ambivalent attitude reveals a significant conflict between unit pride and the need for discipline, and highlights the vital importance of *esprit de corps*.

The uniform's other decorative elements were unique to each regiment, and included the button, the badge (when used), and, until 1836, the lace pattern, as well as the number designating the unit. Such seemingly minor details could touch soldiers' emotions by the unity, honor, and pride they symbolized. In 1820, a retired captain saw a drunken man in the street wearing his old corps' coat; he bought it for five shillings "rather than he should disgrace the button of the regiment."[17] This incident seems to bear out the claim of "The Hermit of London" that "time, absence and separation do not destroy the feeling which a good soldier has for [the] number of his regiment; 'the Old Greys,' 'the Old Buffs' . . . 'the Blues,' 'the Old Forty-second.' "[18]

The regimental badge—unique to each corps—was an important source of unit pride. Granted as a distinction by the sovereign, the badge was painted on the regimental colour, and during this era, it was increasingly displayed on the buttons, shako plate, forage cap, and breastplate in place of the regimental number.[19] One man felt so strongly about his former regiment, the Third Dragoon Guards, that he had its badge tattooed upon his arm. Sir Garnet Wolseley recalled that this "impressed upon me early in my career how deep is the affection men retain for their first love, the regiment in which they serve."[20]

Officers were very much aware that the soldiers' strong, positive identification with the visual symbols associated with their corps was important—if not vital—for success. Writing in the late eighteenth century, General Lloyd emphasized the importance of having a brass plate with either the number or the name of the regiment on it, to be attached to the soldiers' hats: "It is incredible how much this trifling circumstance would contribute to enforce discipline and valour."[21] Even elements of dress that proved to be of little use (or even a hindrance) were sometimes retained because they were thought to improve morale.[22] Soldiers' pride in their appearance on parade had to be reinforced continually by the endless spit-and-polish if it was to improve their performance, although submitting the men to constant drudgery could also backfire.[23]

Colonels thus made additions to the uniform and other aspects of regimental imagery as positive reinforcements, telling the soldiers that these were distinctions special to their own corps and symbolic of a superior status. Even a relatively minor decoration could instill a sense of importance in the men, as in the case of the Sixth Foot, where a white stripe down the front of the red shell jacket was considered a mark of superiority. In another instance, a captain of the Royal Horse Artillery Rocket Battery at Waterloo accented his unit's uniqueness by displaying nonregulation white and sky-blue flags on the rocket fasces.[24] Such nonregulation innovations were sometimes later adopted by the army as a whole. In 1841, for example, the colonel of the Eighty-fifth Light Infantry had red collars put on his men's white shell jackets, a forerunner of the brass collar badge, which was officially adopted in 1855.[25] Army inspectors recognized that these additional decorations were important for morale, even though they were supposed to report deviations in uniform.[26]

Even without unauthorized additions in dress or display, most corps had a number of unique elements. The guards were the army's elite, and as such were distinguished in both their tradition and their imagery.[27] The highland regiments were proud of their unique dress and traditions, associating these elements with behavior superior to the rest of the army.[28] One officer believed "that to wear [the uniform] alone appears an incentive to loyalty and good conduct."[29] Highland units were also considered "the most showy-looking troops in our service."[30] This shows a strong correlation between a superior self-image and a unique, fancy uniform,[31] although there were then (as today) Englishmen who ridiculed highland dress.[32] This uniform also cost more than that of other infantry regiments in the post-1815 era; the kit of a nonhighland corps private was three guineas at the most, whereas in a highland corps the limit was five guineas.[33]

Among other foot regiments, the light infantry and rifles were more attractive to recruits than the heavy infantry.[34] The rifle units' dark-green uniform was considered most attractive, and one soldier of a light company of the Sixty-sixth Foot wrote that he "fell in love" with the "smart, dashing, and devil-may-care appearance" of the Ninety-fifth rifles and volunteered for the unit.[35] The popularity of these corps was such that in 1816, because of disbandments, they did not need the usual recruiting methods and recruiters could be far more selective.[36]

Within individual regiments, elite companies were distinguished by special ceremonies and tokens on their uniforms. The grenadier companies were the most eminent of the line infantry, having caps adorned with white feathers or plumes.[37] The light companies were also elite, and their Other Ranks wore a green plume as a distinctive mark, whereas their officers wore the "wing epaulet," which was heavier and more elaborate than the usual pattern. Such was the superior status of light company men that they might be punished merely by being forced to do the duty of battalion company men.[38] General Mitchell believed that in the Peninsula these elite companies were "far superior to the rest of the infantry, by their *morale* alone."[39]

Regardless of the unit, military decorations were one of the more significant visual signs of honor and glory in this period. Unit commanders led the way in introducing special marks of good conduct to be worn on the Other Ranks' uniforms. Captain Robert Lawson, commanding a company of the Eighth Battalion, Royal Artillery, in the Peninsula, introduced "an order of merit" for the Corps of Drivers in the form of a "stripe of red cloth on the left arm," which was doubtless intended to encourage good behavior.[40]

Traditionally, medals had been awarded only to officers. Although no specific policy on granting medals appears to have existed for the army before 1813, medals from the Crown were awarded mostly to general officers, and from 1810 they were given to lieutenant-colonels for victories.[41] This was extended to majors in 1813,[42] although very few men of the Other Ranks got gold-lace laurels sewn on their left sleeves for participating in a "forlorn hope."[43] After 1815, when the Waterloo medal was issued to All Ranks present, there were demands for wider distribution. Like other visual elements that were increasingly used to encourage soldiers to be courageous in battle, medals provide an interesting test case of contemporary notions about the importance of such symbols. The change in policy for awarding them also exemplifies the shift toward granting more visual rewards and encouragements to the soldiers during this period.

Medals were a mark of long service, distinguished unit conduct under fire, or personal bravery and valor, and both soldiers and civilians had great respect for them.[44] But as with other visual rewards, medals were first awarded to common soldiers by certain regiments, not the army authorities. In the mid-eighteenth century, the Fifth Foot began giving medals to men of the Other Ranks, and by the time of the French wars, a few other units had adopted the practice as well.[45] Medals were granted for heroic conduct, with the corps' officers paying the cost themselves. In some units, medals were also awarded for marksmanship.[46] The distinction conferred by a medal was further enhanced by the ceremony that accompanied the award, and one sergeant recalled that such a ceremony "was well calculated to make an impression upon the mind of a youthful soldier, such as I then was."[47] Sometimes the soldiers themselves even had medals made up as mementos of some great action in which they had fought.[48]

The army's great effort in the Peninsula and the hard service and high casualties suffered there helped kindle the opinion that His Majesty's loyal soldiers deserved some reward for their hard work. These men sometimes endured insults to their pride because they had no outward mark of their achievements. Belgian civilians in 1815 did not believe that Peninsular veterans had served in Spain because they were not decorated.[49] What really galled veterans, however, was the granting of Waterloo medals to everyone who was with a unit that participated in that battle, regardless of personal involvement.[50] Many Peninsular veterans who had fought bravely for a number of years were not present at this final battle, having been sent overseas to India or America, and consequently received no special distinction despite their long service. This opened a floodgate of criticism and complaints that might otherwise have remained primarily a topic of private conversation. Some officers who received Waterloo medals refused to wear them until the Peninsula officers had been given their just reward.[51]

One case that stands out for its injustice is that of an officer whose service had not gained him a decoration, though he had fought in seven battles and volunteered for three storming parties in sieges. He was disabled and his face had been disfigured in battle. He once overheard civilians speculating that he received his commission out of favoritism, as he was obviously lame and incapable of doing duty. Two officers who were with him at the time both had Waterloo medals, but neither had fought; one was a paymaster and the other a lieutenant of the Royal Waggon Train (whose members carried the wounded off the battlefield).[52] This officer noted that Wellington was made a field marshal and a duke as rewards for his service, yet "not a vestige of a medal, cross, or ribbon, has been granted to me, not an hour's extra service." In frustration, he declared that he would beat flat the two musket balls that had wounded him and suspend them from colored ribbons on his breast.[53]

Veterans of the French wars felt so strongly about medals that disputes over them resulted in more than one serious riot between Waterloo regiments and Peninsula corps. One incident occurred in the Occupation army in France, where the men of a recently raised unit whose only action had been Waterloo told Peninsular veterans who had served in many battles that they would have gotten medals if they had deserved them.[54]

This desire to be rewarded for merit went far beyond mere vanity; often men who received decorations considered them their most prized possessions. In 1838, an officer in Canada who had escaped when his quarters caught fire reentered the burning room to save a medal: "He soon came out again into the square, holding the treasure in his hand, and calling out 'I am all right, I've got it.' " The next day he died from his burns.[55] A decorated soldier of the Eighty-eighth Foot lost his kit at sea, and when the officers raised money for him, his reaction was: "Give me another medal . . . I care not for anything else!"[56] In another case, when an old veteran was granted his request for a medal: "It was the best thing that could have been done for him. By its exhibition he lived day by day . . . a badge on the breast of a broken-down and distressed warrior, which connected him with the stern struggles of a past age, stirred into activity the most comatose sympathy."[57]

Eventually, the authorities did begin to reward soldiers for their efforts, yet it came rather late and was done in a half-hearted, grudging manner. A Peninsular medal was not authorized until 1847, with clasps for eighteen different actions; nineteen thousand men submitted claims.[58] Good conduct medals were finally awarded to soldiers—but only upon discharge—beginning in 1830.[59] Not everyone thought that medals were necessary, however, and one veteran flatly declared that "the British uniform alone is a mark of distinction."[60]

By the 1840s, campaign medals were being awarded with increasing frequency, and the Victoria Cross was instituted during the Crimean War. The debate about the granting of medals highlights the larger conflicts over army reform in this era, and the degree to which the Other Ranks felt appreciated—or neglected—by the authorities, as well as the vital factor of the army's loyalty, appear to have been decisive factors. In 1811 the *Independent Whig* denounced a proposal that the king grant medals only to officers who were lieutenant-colonels or higher, comparing this unfavorably with the practices of the French in awarding medals to all ranks. The *Military Magazine* commented on this opinion, touching upon the general concern for the Other Ranks' loyalty to the state: "No man who desired the present order in society or who regarded the liberties of his countrymen would wish to discountenance publications, when they tended to the well-being of the community. The purport of this [article], however, was to create disgust, and to sew dissention, in the minds of the soldiery; by alleging, that so material a branch of the defence of the empire, was contemned and despised by those, who as forming the executive, were bound to protect and to reward them."[61]

The *United Service Journal*, which advocated granting a Peninsular medal, later voiced this concern during an era of both continental revolution and the First Reform Bill crisis: "The elements of discord are so rapidly spreading in neighboring nations, and . . . it is impossible to say how soon they may reach our own shores, [that] it would be the height of impolicy not to remove any just cause of dissatisfaction."[62]

Fears that soldiers might be dissatisfied because they felt unappreciated may have contributed to the increase in medals awarded, but such distinctions were only one element that boosted their feelings of self-esteem and satisfaction. Public recognition after a victorious battle was also a heady stimulation to unit pride. In the First Afghan War, during a time of low morale, General Sale's army was victorious at Jallalabad, and Governor-General Ellenborough promptly awarded medals, honors, and extra pay to All Ranks: "It electrified the army . . . it went straight to the hearts of good soldiers. Old officers burst into tears . . . all declared that the 'batta' (extra pay) is nothing—It was the *honours*. This is just the point to which I wished to bring the army. They will do anything now."[63]

For a unit to be mentioned in dispatches after a battle was a treasured honor; in 1813, an artillery captain in the Peninsula believed that his regiment was slighted by not receiving mention in Wellington's dispatch during the siege of San Sebastián. He wrote: "I burn to see the corps named as they should be."[64] A Peninsular officer wrote that his division had not been present at the battle of Salamanca but had "longed eagerly for the battle." He added that "this jealousy of fame, the 'avarice of praise' is common in camps [on campaign], and I need hardly add, incalculably useful to sovereigns and commanders-in-chief."[65]

Regimental battle honors, displayed on the corps' colour and badges, were another factor promoting regimental *esprit de corps*. They were said to "proclaim to the young soldier the former laurels of the regiment,"[66] as they did for a private from the Fortieth Foot who wrote that his unit was "without exception, the most honorable one in the whole service, as it bears upon its colours, I believe, more engagements than any other regiment."[67] The prospect of earning such fame was also an incentive for the men to fight bravely; the colonel of the Fifty-first Light Infantry in

1809 pointed out to his men the battle honor "Minden" inscribed on their colours and breastplates as an exhortation to valor before battle at Walcheren.[68]

Although some battle honors were granted soon after the French wars ended, no significant number of awards were presented for that era until 1844, when the duke of Richmond raised the question in the House of Lords.[69] Officers were so grateful for his action that committees were formed in many towns and foreign stations, and a large sum of money was raised to present him with a handsome set of silver plate.[70]

Although battle honors boosted a regiment's *esprit* and feeling of uniqueness, its members cultivated a particular "style" that transcended the appearance of uniform and decorations. Because of this, other military men could often quickly identify which unit soldiers belonged to, even if they hadn't served with that regiment in years. A private who saw an officer in a Ninety-first Foot uniform doubted that he was really part of that corps because "there was something about him that did not correspond exactly with the usual style of that distinguished regiment."[71] Style could be most distinctive:

> There is something in the appearance of many corps, not easily defined; but which at once gives even to the most inexperienced eye the impression [of] a 'crack' regiment. This may be distinguished by an off-handed style of doing things—a smartness of trim—a neatness and particularity, even to the very polish of their buttons—a sharp lively step of confidence—a sort of pride in one another, expressed upon the countenance; all of which . . . breathes the very life and soul of a soldier . . . So particularly are they characteristic in this way, that even after the lapse of years . . . they still retain the impression that seems associated with their "number," in your mind, beyond the possibility of erasure.[72]

Nothing was more important for regimental pride and *esprit* than the colours (battle flag), which were a centerpiece in peacetime ceremony and ritual and the rallying point in battle. Until 1813, the most junior ensign carried them, and for a young man in his first battle, this was a duty of great importance and encouraged a sense of resolve in a time of crisis. The colours were even the object of religious veneration, as evidenced by remarks at a presentation service in 1850: "Roman soldiers considered a species of deity to be inherent in their standards . . . the cross itself was made the emblem of war . . . and colours are now made to supply its place."[73]

Many soldiers were passionately attached to the colours, as in the case of an ensign carrying a colour in the midst of combat. When sent to skirmish with the light company, he kissed the colour, "thinking this might be the last time I should ever see it."[74] The Twenty-fourth Foot lost a colour at the disastrous battle of Chillianwallah in 1848 because a mortally wounded private had wrapped it around his arm and "would not give it up to any of his comrades, though entreated to do so."[75] The colours were associated with the creation of the honorific rank of colour-sergeant during the Peninsular war in 1813, when colour-sergeants carried the colours in battle and received extra pay and a large, gold-lace badge on their right sleeves.

Loss of the colours in combat was a great disgrace, and a unit that lost theirs at Waterloo secretly made new ones to avoid the stigma.[76] Likewise, to capture an enemy colour was a great feat; a private who did so received special marks of superior status. Private Anton Lutz of the Ninety-seventh Foot received an embroidered badge on the left breast of his coat for the colour he captured from the Twenty-first Demi-brigade Légère at Alexandria, and was privileged to wear a plume larger than that allowed by regulations.[77]

The presentation of new colours was an important ritual. When the Forty-fourth Foot received theirs in 1843, after the first battalion had been wiped out in the disastrous retreat from Kabul during the First Afghan War of 1842, they were "presented with unusual form, to give the young soldiers a proper pride in their regiment."[78] Like any other sacred object, they were treated with utmost respect: "Abuse of the colours was subject to severe punishment. The colours are always to be treated with the highest respect, any non-commissioned officers or soldier ever found to fail in this particular, either in conduct or language, shall be instantly brought to a court martial, and punished, in a most exemplary and severe manner."[79]

Colours that were damaged by enemy fire, however, were considered proof of valor, even though placing the colours in the line of fire might result in needless casualties. An ensign carrying colours at the third siege of Badajoz in 1812 stood up with them so they might be shot, "and thus afford evidence of his danger," although his unit had been ordered to lie down to avoid artillery fire. He was shot twice, crippled, and ended up on half-pay.[80]

In 1816, the *Military Register* asserted that "of all military ceremonies, [the presentation of the colours] is the most important in every point of view."[81] The presentation of new colours in 1840 to the Fortieth Foot in India appears to be typical of such ceremonies; the Reverend Mr. Burnell consecrated the colours, and the men's reaction was recorded by a sergeant: "Not a member of the corps then present but felt his heart echo the fervent strain, as he dwelt upon feature after feature in the noble history of its long and noble career, and when appealing from the past to the present, and calling upon those who then composed it to emulate the conduct of those who had won for it such a splendid reputation, the burst of enthusiastic concurrence could scarcely be suppressed, and every one on the ground felt that, come when it would, the trial would not find them wanting, and that the colours, if opportunity offered, would be adorned by names as bright and glorious as any in the list the old ones bore emblazoned in their broad bright cloth."[82] This feeling often continued throughout a soldier's life; the last dying wish of the colonel of the Nineteenth Foot was that the colours be buried with him, and they were.[83]

The colours were sometimes even considered to have supernatural powers. The Fifty-first Light Infantry's colonel used them in a ceremony in 1810 to "cleanse the guilt" of a sergeant who had stolen and then deserted. The man walked twice under the colours, and after the first pass, the colonel declared him "half clean" and ordered that he be touched by the colours when passing under a second time, after which the colonel pronounced that "his crime he's blotted out for ever, he is regenerated, the new born babe is not more innocent, and woe to the first man who ever mentions this affair to him."[84]

This veneration could take different forms, and a revealing incident took place when the Second Battalion, Eighth Foot, was informed in 1815 that it would be disbanded. On hearing the bad news, the officers assumed that the colours would be sent back to the regimental agents and end up as cleaning rags. Rather than allow such sacrilege, they resolved to destroy them: "Rather let us divide them amongst us, and even though torn into a thousand fragments, they will be as much endeared to and as religiously guarded by us, as when they were displayed before the enemy." The poles were broken and burned, and the ashes collected and buried; the Officer of the Day then read a prayer over them, and a sentry was posted on the grave for the rest of the day and through the night.

The authorities' reaction to the incident is equally revealing as an example of the kind of attitude they liked to see manifested by officers. The duke of York issued an order to the army expressing official disapproval and singling out the colonel for blame. The officers then wrote to the duke, stating that they had done the deed before the colonel was aware of what had happened and taking all the blame themselves. They fully expected that they would never again receive commissions in any unit. But shortly after the disbandment, all except three or four received new postings, and the colonel got command of "a distinguished regiment in India." The narrator concludes that in reality, the duke "was far from being individually or personally displeased," and "a distinguished officer . . . holding an important office near the person of His Royal Highness, even stated that such was indeed the duke's impression."[85]

Such events could only strengthen the soldiers' loyalty to their generals. The remoteness of commanders made this loyalty more difficult to achieve, yet it was essential that the soldiers feel confidence in their leaders. The men knew when a general was competent—Wellington possessed such a reputation—but a dramatic public gesture could solidify the soldiers' loyalty. In the middle of battle in the Peninsula, when a light infantry brigade was being hard pressed by the French, General Fane shouted out: "'Well done 95th!' as he galloped up and down the line. 'Well done 43d, 52d, and well done all. I'll not forget, if I live, to report your conduct to-day. They shall hear of it in England, my lads!' A rifleman rushed up to the general and presented him with a green feather he had taken from the cap of a Frenchman he had killed, saying, 'God bless you general! . . . Wear this for the sake of the 95th.' The general then put it in his cocked hat."[86]

Soldiers often bestowed nicknames on commanders they respected as a mark of esteem: "A good-humoured by-name is often given by soldiers to their commanding officer . . . and nothing more strongly proves their esteem for him than this practice."[87] Wellington, for example, was called "Old Nosey." These nicknames and expressions of approval, which were a form of judgment and therefore a breach of discipline, were overlooked and even sanctioned on campaign. Lord Wellington was "astonished and exasperated" when he heard soldiers murmuring at a review in the Peninsula until he found out that they were talking about "Old Charley," a quaint, old-fashioned colonel who wore the powdered wig and jack boots of the 1790s. The men were saying, "There goes Old Charley," "God bless the old boy." An officer who witnessed this incident wrote: "When this was known to the commander-in-chief, he was perfectly satisfied, and all were delighted as Old Charley uncovered, and shook the powder from his cocked hat in waving a cordial salute to his worthy soldiers."[88]

Of all military leaders, the monarch had the least to do with combat, yet he was an important link between the state and its military instrument and potentially a great source of morale for the army. The monarch was vital as a focus for the soldiers' loyalty, as is shown by the central part the sovereign and the royal family played during the French wars in the public ceremonies of the day.[89]

A personal connection with the monarch was emphasized on special occasions. When the queen conferred a medal upon All Ranks present at the battle of Inkerman, the commander wrote in a general order: "The commander of the forces has the greatest satisfaction in . . . expressing the queen's entire approbation of the conduct of the troops at the battle of Inkerman . . . signifying Her Majesty's gracious intention of conferring a medal upon all officers and soldiers of the army." Her dispatch stated: "The queen desires your lordship will receive her thanks for your conduct throughout this noble and successful struggle, and that you will take measures for making known her no less warm approval of the service of all the officers, non-commissioned officers, and soldiers who have so gloriously won by their blood freely shed, fresh honours for the army of the country which sympathizes as deeply with their privations and exertions as it glories in their victories and exults in their fame. Let not any private soldier in those ranks believe that his conduct is unheeded. The queen thanks him,—his country honours him."[90] For the monarch to ignore this duty could be dangerous; it was believed in London that an abortive mutiny in the guards in 1820 was due in part to the prince regent's "never appearing amongst them [his soldiers]."[91]

Many articles of the kit, including the shako and breastplates, buttons, cartouche pouches, badges, shabracques, and sabretaches, bore the monarch's cipher, as did the king's (or queen's) colour. All weapons and most other equipment were normally stamped with the crown as an identifying mark. Thus, as John Mollo has pointed out, the soldier bore upon his body many tokens of service, and these symbols served as constant reminders of royal authority.[92]

Many regiments, such as "the 16th, or the queen's Regiment of Light Dragoons," also had a formal affiliation with the royal family. When a unit was linked with a monarch, the royal name was incorporated into the regimental title and the unit's facings altered to royal blue.[93] A sergeant whose regiment was made royal in 1821 wrote that "we are of course all proud of the distinguished honor."[94] When Victoria's cousin George, the duke of Cambridge, personally led his division into action at Inkerman, an officer present noted that his men "were proud of being commanded by a general so nearly connected to our queen."[95]

When a member of the royal family died, the whole army went into mourning, and black crepe was put over the uniforms' ornaments.[96] The monarch's and royal family members' birthdays, together with great victories, were special occasions that strengthened the royal tie through celebration. Officers received brevets for the birth of a royal heir, as in November 1841, when the Prince of Wales was born.[97] For the coronation of King George IV, the Nineteenth Foot and a Royal Artillery battery had a holiday, and the soldiers were allowed to drink their fill of ale and eat good, wholesome food, a pleasant change from the usual diet of nasty and inadequate rations and cheap gin, arak, or rum. The regiment fired a *feu de joie*, cheered "three times three," and toasted the king at dinner. One soldier recalled that it was "the only time I saw the [whole] regiment sit down together." The band later played "God Save the King," while soldiers mingled with the cheering townspeople of Daventry.[98]

The monarchs were well aware of the importance of this connection. Queen Victoria received a suggestion in 1848 that in the future she not be burdened with signing each officer's commission. She replied that "the queen does not at all object to the amount of trouble . . . entailed upon her, as she feels amply compensated by the advantage of keeping up a personal connection between the sovereign and the army, and she very much doubts whether the officers generally would not feel it a slight if . . . they were in future only to receive a certificate from the secretary-at-war."[99] This personal connection with the monarch affected many soldiers; one half-pay officer wrote: "My king and his gallant army will ever be dear to [me]."[100] Enlisted men were also deeply touched by the monarch's attentions, especially when in the field. Amid the horrors of the Crimea, Florence Nightingale noted that for the soldiers, "to be assured of the queen's sympathy was the highest pleasure . . . We [all] feel it the more because on all hands we hear of the pains & interest she takes in informing herself of all that concerns them."[101]

Personal attention from the monarch was a special treat for a unit. The Seventh Fusiliers received this mark of favor in 1836 when mounting the guard at Windsor, and King William IV became a member of the officers' mess. The king honored the regiment by removing a rule from 1745 that officers must drink to the health of the sovereign after dinner, then "a token of loyalty to the House of Hannover." They also received the privilege of not standing up when the band played "God Save the King" in the mess.[102] It was suggested that regimental efficiency encouraged this attention. After the king's visit, a major-general addressed the fusiliers, stating that "it is principally by being in this most efficient state that such magnificent and flattering attention has been paid [to you] by [your] most gracious and beloved sovereign."[103]

Sometimes there were conflicts over which regiment would have the honor of serving the sovereign's person; in the early 1840s, the colonel of the Scots Grays, General Sir Kier Grant, was "very indignant" when his regiment arrived at Brighton and found that a squadron of the unit the Grays were replacing, the Eleventh Hussars, had been left behind to escort the queen. He "hurried up to the Horse Guards" demanding to know why his corps could not perform the duty, arguing that the Grays' horses were of a "superior stamp" to those of the Eleventh. The matter was referred to the duke of Wellington, who concluded that there was no reason this custom should prevail, and allowed that henceforth both heavy and light cavalry would perform this honorable duty.[104]

The army's imagery also aided in the psychological isolation of soldiers from civilians (see Chapter 7) by promoting this strong sense of identification with the regiment and service. A man would have to be insensitive indeed to remain completely unmoved by the *esprit de corps* of the community in which he was literally a captive—the only enduring social group to which he had access.[105]

For some men, upholding their individual honor was equally critical, and being known as a well-behaved, upstanding soldier was crucial to their self-respect. Some men who feared they had broken a rule or were criticized by their superiors even went so far as to kill themselves. A corporal of the Ninety-second Foot shot himself in 1813 because he had been reprimanded for being dirty, "and as he had formerly been a very clean soldier, he could not brook the idea of being found fault with."[106] A paymaster sergeant who served with the Scots Grays at Waterloo and was mortally wounded was found with his name written in blood on his forehead. "This his comrades said, he was supposed to have done that it might not be imagined he had disappeared with the money of the troop."[107]

The powerful visual symbols instilled in soldiers great pride in being components of the machine, yet it is ironic—and most remarkable—that this process was still fundamentally coercive. The functioning of military management as a system is central to understanding this apparent dilemma. The private was forced to take part in a precisely regulated, perpetual spectacle; every waking moment of his life he wore the vibrant tokens of martial honor representing sublime values. He labored for a considerable time each day in the spit-and-polish maintenance of these tokens, and drilled and performed in an endless round of ceremony and ritual. In the context of the harsh reality of a soldier's daily life—and most would never again experience any other—this elaborate complex of visual and physical manipulation became a core feature of his identity; it literally became a part of him, both body and mind. Could any private long resist such manipulation when its omnipresent appeal constituted such a compelling—and often the primary—gratification in his bleak life?

Thus the soldier did not just acquire a new identity in the army; this process was much deeper and more profound. To a great extent, the Other Ranks' (and to a lesser extent, the officers') identity was forged anew by this manipulation of both the senses and the body within a mostly nomadic, isolated subculture. The security of the British state was largely established upon this system of martial management, whose objective was to "make the most of fear and love."[108]

CHAPTER SIX

Campaign and Combat

War is an army's acid test, and the transformation from peace to a wartime footing brought about fundamental changes in the life and imagery of a regiment. The advent of a major war also temporarily reversed the public's strongly negative attitude toward the army, and sometimes even the staunchest anti-militarists were swayed by the enthusiasm. When the Seventh Fusiliers in Manchester, a city known for its pacifism, marched to the railway station on the first leg of their journey to the Crimea in 1854, they were received by crowds "wrought up to such a pitch of excitement as almost amounted to madness."[1]

In wartime, the youngest, weakest, and least useful of the Other Ranks were kept at home to form the regimental depot,[2] and officers "who only liked pipeclaying and playing at soldiers also got out of the way by retiring upon 'urgent private affairs.' "[3] The imagery was greatly affected during the transition. Mobilization could be a rapid process, and so the colonel was expected to prepare his corps in peacetime for the possibility of a campaign.[4] In reality, however, colonels did not decide how to dress their soldiers until a unit was sent abroad. In cavalry regiments, swords were sharpened, the Other Ranks were issued a second pistol, and carbine bayonets went into store.[5] The practice of coloring the horses to make them all look the same usually ceased, and the custom of allotting them to each troop on the basis of color diminished.[6] Cavalry officers sometimes had leather patches or inserts sewn on the insides of their pants to protect them from the additional wear of active service.[7]

Other preparations were made throughout the army. Although hair powdering was not abolished for line units until 1809, long before then many ceased the practice when sent out to campaign, and the queues were cut off.[8] Certain types of headgear could also be altered; bearskin caps and highland feather bonnets were sometimes cut down in size, as was the case in the Brigade of Guards and the Ninety-third Highlanders before embarkation to the Crimea in 1854, and visors were added to highland bonnets and forage caps.[9] In the infantry, pantaloons were regulation for active service, though knee breeches were still worn on home service until 1823.[10] Soldiers might also remove their coat laces before going on active service.[11]

The degree of change in the overall uniform, however, was dictated to some extent by the climate in the theater of operations; generally, commanders expected a European campaign to be conducted in the same full dress worn at home.[12] A number of units in the Peninsula carried their tight, home-service breeches and gaiters in their knapsacks, an additional burden for those much-harassed soldiers. Dragoon regiments continued to wear the enormous jack boots "that baffle all powers of ridicule,"[13] and cavalrymen might be shipped out wearing peacetime uniforms, the jackets cut so tightly they could not use their sword arms. Some colonels (who may not have had campaign experience) insisted that these be worn in combat, often with fatal consequences. After the Napoleonic wars, a French marshal recalled seeing "the gross error [of cavalry] prisoners so tightly habited it was impossible for them to use their sabres with facility."[14]

In the kilted highland corps, regiments took the kilt or tartan trews into the field during the Peninsular war, as in past wars.[15] Replacements became such a problem, however—owing to the difficulties of obtaining the correct tartans for each unit—that most were resupplied with the standard gray infantry pantaloons instead.[16] For campaigns outside Europe, some colonels assumed a more relaxed attitude about active-service dress. When John Shipp received orders in 1816 to join the Eighty-seventh Foot in Ceylon after being promoted to ensign, he ordered an officer's coat that proved to be very different from his new corps' uniform. The colonel told him not to bother replacing it, as it would do very well for fighting, and the corps expected some hard service.[17]

The long trip from England to the scene of conflict could also bring changes in uniform, for it took months to reach faraway stations like India, and the colonel had to decide how to clothe his men for the trip. Soldiers on shipboard were normally dressed in "slop clothing," which was a cheap, crudely made dress of canvas.[18] In 1834, this dress became regulation for voyages farther than Gibraltar, though it had long been in use.[19] Slops preserved the more expensive clothes from wear and saved the men money in the long run. This coarse dress was acceptable because there was no audience to see the soldiers, yet nevertheless it had to be kept pipeclayed like other white clothing.[20]

Once at the scene of conflict, slops were usually put aside and the soldiers' appearance changed once more. A special light dress for tropical conditions had been proposed as early as the 1660s for use in the colony of Tangier in the Maghrib, but East Indian service seems to have contributed the most to its development.[21] Light gray was the usual color in the late eighteenth century, and was worn as late as the 1850s by some Crimean units for summer dress.[22] Lighter-weight clothing was also issued to troops in the West Indies in the mid-1790s, apparently as a response to the many casualties incurred from sickness.[23] The red coat might be cast aside altogether in favor of white cotton clothing, sometimes with the collar and cuffs the same as the facing color. In the later French wars, the West India regiments wore an unlined "round coat" that had been standard for British units in the West Indies since the 1790s.[24] Froberg's regiment (a foreign corps) was stationed at Malta in 1807 wearing red, but as a concession to the climate, the fabric was cotton instead of wool.[25]

Campaign dress could vary a great deal, and although the need for adaptation was especially strong in the tropics, much depended upon the circumstances surrounding a corps' departure. Colonels had the option of ordering white clothing of a lighter-weight fabric for their men, and this eventually became standard. Toward the end of the French wars, the Horse Guards officially sanctioned the option of a special tropical dress.[26] After the Napoleonic wars, white clothing was given to troops on their arrival in India, apparently as a free issue from the East India Company, an indication that the company considered the soldiers' health important.[27] By the 1820s, all ranks wore white cotton during the hot season, and scarlet with white trousers during the cool season, though scarlet was also reserved for formal occasions.[28]

Not all units sent to hot climates were able to get tropical dress; some sent to India during the Great Mutiny of 1857, for example, were rushed off with minimal preparation for the hot, humid climate. The Seventy-eighth Highlanders arrived during the hottest month of the year dressed in red wool, and fought the whole campaign in temperatures of more than one hundred degrees,[29] while the Fifty-second Light Infantry wore slops.[30]

White headdresses had been used in India from the eighteenth century, and by the era of the French wars these were regulation for regular regiments.[31] After 1800, white or light-brown shakos were often used for tropical dress,[32] although these appear to be standard issue only in the temporary units that were stationed in the tropics for the duration.[33] White helmet covers, sometimes with havelocks (white covers that hung down behind to shade the neck) were widely used in India and became standard by the 1850s, but for those unfortunate soldiers who went out wearing black shakos or helmets, the usual protection against the heat was a white handkerchief draped on the shako or helmet.[34]

Tactical considerations also influenced some uniforms in the nineteenth century. Camouflage campaign dress was first introduced in the late eighteenth century with the development of light infantry, which often had clothing that would blend in with the undergrowth in places like the American wilderness, where the soldiers did not normally stand in the traditional straight lines on an open field to deliver machine-like volleys.[35]

By the late 1790s, some army units began to experiment with dark-green clothing, largely in response to the successful and greatly increased use of light infantry tactics by the French Revolutionary armies. An interesting example, however, comes from the South African bush, where in 1799 men taken from the heavy infantry were dressed in green to form a rifle company.[36] The Fifth battalion of the Sixtieth Foot was the first regular unit to receive dark-green dress officially, in 1799.[37]

Such changes, even when based on sound principles, met with strong opposition within the army. War with France and internal British political conflicts in the 1790s had resulted in much political symbolism being attached to clothing.[38] In the army, some officers believed that training rifle corps privates to take individual initiative in battle was a threat to discipline, and thus many strongly resisted the adoption of the dark-green camouflage that symbolized this tactical freedom. Despite his alleged indifference to the army's uniform, the duke of Wellington always disliked rifle green. At the beginning of the transition from smooth-bore muskets to rifles in the 1840s, he vigorously opposed dressing the army in green, a "jack-a-dandy" uniform, lest the men think of themselves as riflemen,[39] despite evidence that "the [red] color of [some riflemen's] jackets, so unsuitable for light troops, exposed them glaringly to fire . . . while our riflemen in green, escaped with comparatively little loss."[40] The authorities refused to adopt the Clothing Board's recommendation that the light infantry receive green clothing and black belts.[41] The desire to retain maximum control over the Other Ranks was thus allowed to override this factor, which improved their safety and combat efficiency.

Green was not the only option for camouflage uniforms, and khaki, or "karkee," first appeared in 1849, when Colonel Lumsden of the Guide Corps, a recently raised East India Company unit, dressed his men in "mud-colour." He apparently preferred khaki because it blended in with the Indian terrain better than green, or possibly because the regiment had dressed in clothes dyed that color before it had an official uniform.[42] By the time of the Great Mutiny of 1857, army regiments were unofficially adopting the same color by dyeing their white clothes.

The concerns expressed by officers for their troops' appearance on campaign were not necessarily the result of mere fancy or frivolity, for the quality and condition of a unit were conveyed by its appearance. In the field, maintaining the soldiers' appearance was as vital to discipline as in peacetime. An official report stressed that "the very essence of discipline, depends on the officer and soldier taking care of his appointments [especially cavalry] when in the field."[43] General Cavalié Mercer noted that following Waterloo, the Sixth Dragoons "presented a sad spectacle of disorganization and bad discipline" because they had lost half their appointments.[44]

One way a general could show the efficiency of his command—whether to his superiors or foreign allies—was to have a field day. Wellington staged a grand cavalry review in Flanders in May 1815, when there was great concern for the coming battle and Allied cooperation was vital for success. The units arrived before the review and immediately set to brushing and scrubbing, having brought brushes and even straw to wisp over their horses. Mercer noted with some conceit: "Need I say that the foreigners (generals) were loud in praise of the martial air, fine persons, and complete equipment of the men and horses, and of the strength and beauty of the latter."[45] This was a favorite practice of Wellington's, and on one occasion, in July 1815, when he was commander in chief of the Allied army in France, he held a two-hour grand review of 200,000 men in heavy marching order.[46] On another occasion, he ordered a review of 30,000 to 40,000 men on less than twenty-four hours' notice to impress the Allies with his staff work.[47]

As in peacetime, reviews, drill, pipeclay, and other elements of spectacle helped keep idle soldiers busy and out of trouble.[48] If a unit was on a long march, the appointments would be shined once a week for a parade, or whenever the commander thought it necessary. Reviews also reinforced the idea that presenting a proper appearance was part of an officer's duty, and the duke of Wellington reportedly declared many times that well-dressed officers were among his best. Some contemporaries emphasized that careful attention to dress on campaign was a duty, and not mere foppery.[49]

Attention to dress did not necessarily mean uniformity, however; in the Peninsula it became fashionable for the officers to keep their uniforms as unique as possible, just as they did in peacetime. Yet, lacking peacetime social amenities and diversions for months on end, many officers on campaign became obsessed with dress to alleviate the boredom.[50] This alone cannot explain the sartorial magnificence of many, however, and the dandy fashion so prevalent in Regency England had a significant effect on many Peninsular war officers.[51] In classic dandy tradition, some seemed to think that the sole purpose of their existence was to maintain a pristine personal appearance, and for many, cavalry dress was the fashion regardless of their unit. Among the popular styles were braided hussar pelisses in a variety of colors, brass spurs that screwed into boots, "mustachioes," and long hair.[52] Anything that was *outre* was the fashion, but lavish amounts of bullion lace were especially popular for younger officers who could afford them. One ensign was so elaborately decked out in gold braid that Portuguese riflemen captured him, thinking he was a French marshal. One officer tried to downplay the undeniable obsession with appearances: "Dress . . . with its attractions, by no means engrossed all our thoughts."[53]

The pleasure of dress was more cultivated on European campaigns, where a larger "society" of officers was formed, with a greater number having wealth and a high social position. During the horrible retreat to Corunna, a soldier remembered with amazement a lieutenant who had managed to maintain his "spotless and meticulous clothing [He was] the very quintessence of an exquisite [who] seemed on all occasions as if he had emerged from the limits of a band box." But replacement costs were also a factor; an officer whose arm was fractured at the battle of Vitoria was much more concerned about his bloodied coat than his wound.[54]

Generally, wealthy officers preferred to stay in Britain, where they could swagger and strut in their splendid costumes without being exposed to the unpleasantness of a campaign in some faraway, unhealthy, and unpleasantly hot and inconvenient country. Officers who fought in these places were looked down upon as "India officers" and were not socially acceptable to the high-society officers of Mayfair.[55] Nevertheless, some dandies did go on colonial campaigns. An officer of the Seventh Dragoon Guards wanted starch in his shirts when engaged in bush warfare at Cape Colony, where material conditions and especially shortages were as harsh as anywhere else the army had fought.[56]

Rich dress was not only of questionable utility; it could be a disadvantage or even a danger in the field. Bullion lace had value as booty,[57] and wounded officers' lace made them targets of battlefield looters, who sometimes killed their victims, although the lace might also be bartered for food in a pinch.[58] Even off the battlefield, the demand for the formalities of full dress could be dangerous for any soldier: "How many a fine enduring soldier in the Tropics have not a defective head and body dress caused the death!"[59] Throughout the first half of the nineteenth century, officers on official business were obligated to wear buttoned-up full dress with a sword even in the hot season.[60] A colonel stationed in Calcutta had to report to the governor general, a visit for which he was required to wear full dress even though it was the hottest month of the year. He recalled his fear that he would die, for men similarly clad had been found dead from the heat.[61] Yet despite such incidents, some colonels insisted that their corps maintain the pristine peacetime appearance to as great an extent as possible; some believed that wearing a buttoned-up scarlet coat and white gloves in combat was necessary for the proper image, because scarlet symbolized British power to the "natives."[62]

The desire of some colonels to uphold peacetime spit-and-polish could be detrimental to the health of the Other Ranks, and could also sap their energy and morale. On a long, miserable march in India, one cavalry unit held a field day after a particularly violent storm during the monsoon season, even though "arms and accoutrements [that were] mixed pell mell with the debris of the demolished tents and [were] scarcely distinguishable from the mud in which they are embedded, must be . . . restored to the usual pipe-clay order."[63] General Napier warned against keeping men standing too long under arms "in hot, cold, or wet climates."[64] But so important were appearances to some officers that they lost touch with reality in their single-minded pursuit of perfection; during the dreadful, muddy siege of Sebastopol in 1855, when many soldiers were in rags, one colonel "abhorred anything like soiled or shabby clothes."[65] At besieged Kabul in 1841, severe shortages and the prohibitively high cost of pipeclay led three soldiers to dig deposits of the stuff (probably chalk) in the nearby, enemy-occupied hills, where they were killed.[66]

The ability to maintain a fine appearance would naturally depend upon the scene of the campaign, yet there were many ways in which the ideal of the immaculate image could be pursued. A colonel might require his men to wear shakos or even neckstocks in battle, despite the discomfort, inconvenience, and possible danger such orders posed.[67] Hence the uniform and other elements of imagery in battle were mixed blessings at best; some officers felt disgust at the army's "idiotic pride in dressing in India as nearly as possible in the same clothing they wore at home."[68]

Although the uniform was supposed to help identify soldiers in battle, this function was not always effective. The troops were often obscured by smoke, dust, fog, or darkness, though they might be identified by their silhouettes.[69] The uniforms were frequently dirtied and discolored, and there were sometimes so many different colors used—especially if units from more than one nation were present—that identification was difficult. Many times troops fired at allied soldiers and men from other British regiments; in one case in India, an infantry colonel was accidentally shot by a cavalry colonel.[70]

In the right circumstances, though, a uniform coat color did aid in identification, both on and off the battlefield, but maintaining the uniform as a source of national identification is only part of the reason soldiers' appearances were emphasized during a campaign. Indeed, had national identification been considered the most important factor, all British troops could have been clothed in red. The cavalry wore blue for the most part (except during William IV's reign), as did the artillery. In 1812, red was adopted for other Ordnance troops (the Royal Engineers, the Royal Sappers and Miners, and the Royal Military Artificers) because in the trenches, the French tended to fire most often at those men in blue who looked different from red-coated infantry working parties.[71]

Despite the desire to maintain the army's appearance in the field, however, the realities of campaigning made the peacetime ideal of immaculate uniforms "fatal or simply impossible."[72] On campaign, uniforms could look reasonably good for some months, provided that the army had good billets and did not undergo long marches. Comfortable conditions were rare, however, and hard marching and campaigning were typical. Soldiers usually lived and slept in the open, under all extremes of weather, amid dust, mud, and a pervasive atmosphere of death. The roads (where they existed) were usually deep in either mud or dust, and especially on the vast plains of India, weeks of marching and living in the field, together with the harsh conditions of violent dust and rainstorms, swollen rivers, and dense forest and jungle, took a rapid toll on an army's appearance. A private wrote of marching in India in 1848 on a road "knee deep in sand and dust," stating that his unit looked more like chimney sweeps than soldiers, owing to the "immensity of dust that would settle upon us which is quite black."[73] Some units wore red until it was tattered, patched, and barely recognizable, as did the Sixth Foot in the bush warfare of South Africa in the early 1850s.[74]

The transition from peace to war made supply more precarious, and regiments might not be resupplied with clothing for years.[75] The army encountered serious problems in sending out fresh supplies: ships sank and supply trains were captured or destroyed.[76] Even under the best conditions resupply took months, and the government's reluctance to institute change further prevented any improvement in the system. Only the controversy caused by the Crimean War finally brought about fundamental changes in the way the army was supplied, and resulted in more competent management.[77]

For some campaigns, merely supplying the army was itself a task the East India Company's commissariat or that of the Peninsular or the Crimean army would not have been able to accomplish, even if they had been efficient. Sometimes clothiers sent shoddy, inferior, and worthless clothes, accoutrements, and shoes, so that even a resupply of clothing and equipment might not provide much improvement in the soldier's lot.[78] Poor-quality material was either worthless or wore out so quickly that soldiers might be in rags and go barefoot for months.[79] In 1801, the Twenty-second Foot at Cape Colony wore white trousers that were patched so often that the men looked like spotted leopards after marching 1,500 miles.[80] Supply problems could result in starvation and exposure for the soldiers, and heroic efforts had to be made just to stay alive.

During the Peninsular and Crimean wars, some resupply came from the state through free issues or "donations," because the kit wore out more rapidly in the field.[81] Cavalry clothing and appointments in the Peninsula wore out at a rate one-third faster than at home, and it was risky for the army to use the men's meager pay to purchase new equipment once fighting had begun.[82] This problem resulted in extra expenses to the regiments "beyond any precedent," and the most expensive war in British history up to that time temporarily made sartorial concerns a lesser priority for the state.[83]

Sometimes supplies could be made up locally. Shoes were cobbled in Portugal for an Irish regiment in 1811, and in 1812 the Twenty-eighth Foot had sandals made from the hide of a bullock that had run amuck and was killed.[84] Sources closer to the theater of operations sometimes furnished supplies, as when Italian-made clothing was shipped to the Crimean army, but like similar shipments sent from Britain, some of the bales were short.[85] Nonregulation items were also sent at times; for example, British-made sheepskin coats were received in the Crimea in early 1855.[86]

Men of all ranks picked up whatever was at hand to try to keep dry, warm, or cool; loosely made clothing was better suited to campaigning, as was local dress. Thus in India soldiers sometimes wore turbans, although these were not regulation, and many recommended them as vastly superior to any regulation headgear. The Second Battalion, Military Train, wore turbans during the Indian Mutiny after the unit was converted into cavalry; the turban kept the head cooler and provided protection from sword cuts.[87]

Indeed, regulation articles were sometimes thrown away or intentionally destroyed "for fear of future accidents, in the shape of being ordered to wear them again, [we] played football for a short time with the shakos, and threw both stocks and gloves away as useless."[88]

Sometimes a particular item might even become fashionable among the officers, or unconventional clothing would be adopted, either because of shortages, or as a makeshift tropical dress to suit local conditions.[89] The Nineteenth Foot was provided with flannel clothing for the Kandy campaign.[90] Shoes and socks were put aside, and officers donned pajamas in the steaming jungles of the First Burmese War of 1824–1826, but these were considered unsuitable for wearing in the sight of the women of the regiment, and were confined to the invasion stage of the campaign.[91]

Even where climatic conditions or supply problems did not cause changes in uniform or equipment, a number of independent-minded officers—who did not share the concerns for proper uniform that so occupied some of their peers—often rid themselves of cumbersome clothing, headgear, or equipment. Having a number of full dress jackets, some wore out their older garments on campaign, thus preserving the newest items to reduce the high replacement costs.[92] Other officers, owing to their poverty, a strong sense of duty or indifference, wore their uniforms until they were shabby.[93] Many brought practical clothing on campaign rather than be burdened with what they considered to be useless garments; instead of scarlet, some wore shooting coats, quilted jackets, or the blue frock coat.[94]

Although some officers were heedless of appearances on campaign—especially outside Europe—the imagery still became irrevocably associated for many with the deep emotions evoked by combat. A major at Corunna saved his best uniform for battle. In the retreat that preceded the battle, made without any rations and in the dead of winter, most soldiers threw away everything that was not essential, and many died of exhaustion and exposure while being pursued by superior enemy forces. Yet this officer burdened himself with a new coat and silver epaulets, which he preserved for combat.[95] Such men believed that their best uniform was the only appropriate dress for the gravity and glory of the occasion, and many of them possessed a reputation for great bravery. Other symbols of honor could also inspire acts of valor during the heady excitement of a battle; two privates in Cadiz, Spain, both tried to assume the post of a dead artilleryman, "equally ambitious for what they considered the post of honour," and were both killed when a shell burst between them.[96]

Such symbolism, together with the fancy uniforms and martial glitter, might even outshine and obscure the ugly horrors of war. At the battle of Leipzig, amid a heap of amputated arms and legs, Lord George Aberdeen noted the effect of the "pomp and circumstance" of the five armies. "The emperors and princes assembled give a lustre which might prevent many from seeing anything else."[97] An Indian veteran wrote: "What a happy thing it is that the many deformities of war are disguised by such gaudy trappings and such heart-stirring accomplishments!"[98]

Yet the same imagery that masked the harsh realities of war diminished as the campaign progressed. In addition to the wear on clothing and equipment, practical difficulties could affect the army's official attitude toward some aspects of combat dress. Although wearing a full dress coat might represent glory to some officers, it could be a significant disadvantage. Elaborate uniforms were popular targets because they attracted attention, as did any dress that stood out from the others.[99] Even civilian dress that looked vaguely military could put the wearer in danger if it attracted attention; while watching the battle of Vitoria, an assistant-commissary and a civilian wearing a hat with a huge black feather were almost captured by French dragoons, who were "attracted by the importance attached to feathers of such large proportions."[100]

Because fancy dress made officers easy targets in battle, the Clothing Board suggested in 1811 that their uniforms "be assimilated with the patterns of the men, and particularly the cap and jackets."[101] This view was shared by many officers. One wrote that in the Peninsula it was often impossible to tell officers from soldiers by the uniform alone; only their swords set them apart.[102] By 1810, clothing sent from Britain was "very practical . . . and as loose as sacks."[103]

Combat also tended to level the rigid military hierarchy and affect discipline. Wellington noted this in the Peninsula: "The discipline of every army after a long and active campaign becomes in some degree relaxed and requires the utmost attention on the part of the generals and other officers to bring it back."[104] Generally, the more dangerous and lengthy the campaign, the greater the tendency for even arrogant officers to treat their men like fellow creatures,[105] and in extreme circumstances, the "ball stoppers" even tasted something like equality.[106] An officer captured at Waterloo was beaten and then turned loose by the French. He wandered for many hours in the company of a wounded private, "for in such a state of misery, I threw off my superior rank and treated my suffering companion like a brother."[107]

All sorts of practices were allowed on campaign that never would have been tolerated in peacetime; talking, for example, was often permitted on the march.[108] The army's imagery could also change drastically, inverting the usual norms of behavior. After the plundering that followed the Peninsula sieges, soldiers often changed their clothes and put on just about anything that caught their eye: priests' robes, court dress, enemy uniforms, even silk and velvet gowns.[109] They obtained permission to sell these spoils of war, then got leave in which to do it.[110] A needy common soldier might even loot the coat of a British sergeant.[111]

Such behavior was unavoidable, and battle plunder was considered an important motivation for common soldiers to fight, although officers sometimes tried to curb the worst of the excesses that accompanied these drunken sprees.[112] The soldiers felt that they had earned the right to extra compensation owing to the numerous casualties among their comrades from disease and combat, and the suffering caused by privations and shortages that were all too typical in the early-nineteenth-century army, especially during sieges. Alexis de Tocqueville noted this tendency in "aristocratic armies" for discipline to become more relaxed in wartime, "because that discipline is founded upon habits, and war disturbs those habits."[113]

Most young soldiers, however, had also achieved something that many had desired from the start: they had fulfilled their adolescent visions of glory, which their uniform and appearance symbolized. This is reflected in a practice of the Fifteenth Hussars dating from 1818; if a veteran private returning to Britain from the Peninsula saw that a soldier who was not a veteran was equipped with a better sword and scabbard than he, the veteran could complain and the officers would make the two men exchange weapons.[114] Such veterans had proved that they could meet their country's enemies in deadly strife and win. But in the process they had matured and even grown old with the slaughter, and were witnesses to horrors they never could have dreamed of as civilians. Changes in their dress reflected these experiences.

The pristine, full dress uniform that had attracted many young men to the army became worn or disintegrated into rags during the campaign, despite efforts by some commanders to maintain the idealized image. The emotional and psychological impact of battle made clear to many soldiers that the spotless, full dress uniform was merely the outward image of honor, and that true glory was the attribute of the man himself—not of the shell. Veterans who donned the uniform felt they deserved it, yet they often preferred their campaign uniform, which had lost its glossy newness. It became fashionable among officers to wear uniforms that looked a bit worn, though not shabby, because this was the image of a veteran. For these men, uniforms worn on campaign were preferable to new ones.[115] Facial scars were also coveted by some as a sign of valor, similar to a dueling scar.[116]

New uniforms became associated with the untried officers sent out from Britain. These men were usually inexperienced, and sometimes full of vanity, ignorance, pomposity, and pretension. Militia units that landed in Southern France immediately after the peace was signed in 1814 "took care to impress upon the inhabitants of Bordeaux their value as soldiers, by parading their battalions with all the pomp and circumstance of war. [They] appeared but a sorry sight in comparison with British veterans who had [fought] a hundred battles."[117]

In this sense, the "coat of glory" did not confer genuine valor, but was only its outward image, and might be worn by men who did not deserve the status and achievement the coat was supposed to confer. Those who claimed the character of a true soldier knew that a gaudy uniform was not the point: "I am a soldier at heart, not for a name, or the sake of an idle life, or a gay coat."[118] One ex-commissary and officer declared: "I received no recognition [for years of service], nor was I disposed to solicit any. Nevertheless, I am comforted by the thought that the duty I performed for my king under the strain of all manner of exertions and privations, forms a star which now glows indelibly on my naked breast, whereas the official orders and medals only hang on the combatant's tunic."[119] Others might share this view and yet cherish old, battle-worn garments, reminders of heroic deeds of valor and symbols of a special time in a man's life.[120]

Veterans who experienced a campaign together also grew closer as a unit, and formed the vital core of each regiment. The symbolism of the dress and the equipment was essential in stimulating and maintaining their loyalty. This core of old hands—the minority who could be counted on to remain both obedient and brave to the end—often ensured a unit's reliability in a crisis. The *Times* noted this important factor: "An army can never be relied upon unless a certain proportion of it consists of well-trained men with that certain fellow-feeling and . . . professional spirit."[121]

These men were of the greatest value to the service, these old veterans of many campaigns and survivors of the era's primitive medical care, seasoned by exposure to a variety of deadly diseases brought on or exacerbated by conditions in the army. Such men were the core of a regiment's fighting spirit, and included most of the noncommissioned officers, although many tended to lose their rank after a drunken binge or an assault charge involving alcohol. Yet they felt a deep sense of pride in being soldiers, which was manifested and symbolized by their appearance.

This feeling was so strong that they might prefer to wear uncomfortable and even painful items of dress if their appearance was thereby enhanced. Soldiers were said to prefer boots to shoes, even though boots confined the instep, "because they look better."[122] General Wolseley noted that in steaming jungles during the Second Burmese War of 1852, after being told that they could take off their "great stiff leathern stocks . . . most of the old soldiers clung to theirs, asserting that the stock protected the back of the neck from the sun and kept them cool." General Bell emphasized the danger of the stock in these conditions when he commented that "under a broiling sun . . . many a stout man has been lost to the service, and will be lost in the very hour of need, from the red-tape system of choking the soldier with a stiff leather collar about his neck."[123] Wolseley assumed "that it was force of habit that made them think [it was necessary],"[124] and some men were even convinced that the stock was essential to their health. A hospitalized Crimean War soldier with a sore neck, back, and arm believed that the pain was the result of *not* wearing his stock on parade.[125]

The emotions that underlay these remarkable examples were expressed in a manner that tended to maximize soldiers' usefulness to authority; they would literally perform their duty until they collapsed or died. In the Crimea, "men died at their posts from sheer exhaustion or starvation rather than complain . . . A bright but melancholy proof was then given of what Britons will endure before giving up."[126] An army report asserted that men "will bear and suffer much, rather than incur the imputation of being 'soft'—some, to my knowledge have walked on through a field-day, and have died rather than give in."[127]

These were the kind of men the army needed. They were dedicated components of the machine and literally allowed themselves to be destroyed while attempting to live up to the perfectionist martial ideal, even if their deaths were a senseless waste, or caused by inadequate material conditions or a superior's incompetence. Regiments containing many such men were formidable units, distinctive for their tenacity and fighting spirit. These were the finest and best managed—the crack regiments—and were said to be "handed down as an heirloom from one clever fellow to another."[128]

Such units were essential to the state's foreign policy, especially in light of Parliament's strong criticisms of the army and the frequent demands for reductions in military spending in this period—the latter being a major factor in keeping the soldiers' material condition at a sub-standard level, although this has been used to excuse administrative incompetence. Indeed, the imagery and its symbolism could aid considerably in preventing disasters; G. M. Trevelyan noted that "the splendid regimental traditions" saved the Crimean army from disintegration and defeat.[129]

Military imagery thus functioned as a very effective and powerful cultural and psychological instrument, both on campaign and in battle. Although it affected individual soldiers to varying degrees, it was an integral component of management, an essential means by which the state achieved a maximum degree of control over armed men who were underpaid and often ill used, yet whose work was to wield deadly force. Thus the imagery and its symbolism helped preserve the army's political dependability—so vital to the survival and power of the state—considerably enhancing the effectiveness of this inadequately supplied machine.

Upon their return from overseas service, the regiments would be detained on dirty, overcrowded troopships, waiting for new clothing and equipment to be delivered. The authorities thought that this seemingly insensitive treatment of veterans was necessary to reestablish the pristine home service image, allowing the soldiers to appear once again in a "more gentleman-like condition."[130] It also symbolizes the shift back to peacetime discipline, highlighting the importance of presenting a proper military image to civilians.

CHAPTER SEVEN

Civil Disorder

Britain was an expanding industrial society with a growing urban population in the first half of the nineteenth century. Political activity, like other forms of the assertion of power, occurred on an increasingly large scale, involving ever greater numbers of people, and organized labor and political groups acting in opposition to the state frequently took to the streets in protest. In this era the army was still the main vehicle to maintain and restore order, and it was successful in fulfilling these duties in large part because of the power of military spectacle to awe and intimidate the rioters. But ironically, organized groups of protesters adopted these same images for their own use.[1] The imagery was as important for them in a managerial sense as it was for the army, helping to preserve discipline and order, promote *esprit de corps*, and thus enhance their overall effectiveness in confrontations.

The containment of organized and sometimes violent civil opposition was the most difficult duty for the home service army. Soldiers did not relish being policemen: "Of all the services which a soldier is called upon to perform, there is none so unpalatable to him as that of waging war against a domestic enemy."[2] Unlike foreign combat, no glory, booty, or prize money was to be gained. Many noble officers found the task of protecting industrialists from strikers unpalatable and beneath their dignity.[3] Many believed that the masters were simply greedy and had no sense of the traditional paternal obligation to protect and care for their men.

Moreover, factory owners often used the presence of troops to exact greater concessions from desperate workers, for strikes were illegal, and the military's role in disputes thus tended to benefit the masters.[4]

Police duty was never easy. Major Macksworth, who commanded the Fourteenth Light Dragoons during the Bristol riots of 1831, wrote that the use of military force against a mob backed by public opinion "becomes a delicate and hazardous undertaking."[5] One of the era's foremost soldiers called this duty "the most arduous and difficult task for a British soldier."[6] A Royal Horse Guards officer described some of these dangers during the Queen Caroline riots of 1820: "We knew that among the mob were men of desperate character, bent on stabbing or laming the troop horses, cutting our reins, and trampling down any dismounted men . . . Innocent men, women, and children, from idle curiosity, formed part of the throng, all of whom would suffer if an order to fire upon or charge the mob was given."[7]

Anti-riot duty in the countryside presented its own problems. Rioters usually adopted tactics of guerrilla warfare, making it necessary to disperse the troops into small groups. Tactically this was dangerous, for it not only weakened each unit but also tended to undermine discipline, and made desertion easier.[8]

The army's size was never adequate for its police role; during the Luddite riots of 1812, General Maitland was forced to disperse his men using classic antiguerrilla tactics. He wrote that there were not enough army troops stationed in England to meet the demands of the West Riding of Yorkshire alone.[9] The situation had not improved a decade later, when the regular forces stationed in the British Isles numbered fewer than 45,000 men; of these, 30,000 were quartered in Ireland and a good many were garrison troops stationed in permanent posts.[10] An officer serving in troubled Ireland in 1825 believed that, though the forces there were "considerable," the Catholic Association could have massacred half of them, together with the Protestants, because the troops were so scattered.[11] In 1831–1832, only 11,000 troops were stationed in England, the majority in and around London, and one historian has speculated that an organized uprising during the reform bill riots would have completely overwhelmed the army.[12] During the French invasion scare of 1846, the Master-General of the Ordnance reported that after finding men for fortresses and posts, only five to ten thousand were left for a field army.[13]

Certain laws governing the maintenance of public order hindered the army's effectiveness. Under existing law, a justice of the peace or a magistrate had to read the Riot Act publicly during a disturbance, and then an hour had to pass before any action could be taken. By that time the mob had usually gone elsewhere, and the whole process would be have to be repeated.[14] Local courts sometimes successfully prosecuted soldiers for murder or other felonies when death or injury resulted from their actions, despite the fact that they were acting legally.[15] Many civilians believed that soldiers, like ordinary citizens, were obligated to repress any open violation of the law.[16] Consequently, civilians sometimes tried to convince them to disobey orders, arguing that they had two duties to perform—as both soldiers and civilians—and that it was for them to decide how far and in what manner those duties were compatible, including the option of refusing to obey illegal orders.[17]

Local magistrates did not always cooperate with the military, because they either feared the rioters or sympathized with them. Such was the conclusion of a study of the Luddite agitation of 1811–1816, asserting that local law officers were the most serious obstacle to law enforcement.[18] Cooperation between soldiers and the police—notorious for their corruption and inefficiency—was often difficult and sometimes caused serious problems. In Clare, Ireland, in 1833, soldiers and policemen fought over an attempt to arrest a drunken soldier; the matter ended when the soldiers chased the police out of town.[19] In another instance, soldiers of the Seventieth Foot stationed at Leeds in 1840 believed they had been abused by the police. They assembled in a mob and beat up all the policemen they could find, cheered on by the populace.[20] So disliked were the police that even army officers sometimes insulted them.[21]

One of the most serious obstacles to the army's effectiveness as a police force, however, was the soldiers' tendency to sympathize with the rioters, who were often from the same impoverished background as the Other Ranks. This sympathy, combined with some recruits' general disgust for army life, resulted in cases of disaffection and desertion.[22] The most serious case occurred in mid-June 1820, when battalions of the Brigade of Guards were in a state of semirebellion. Led by sergeants and encouraged by some of their women, soldiers of the Third Battalion, Scots Fusilier Guards, refused to hand over live ammunition, a most serious act. The abortive mutiny caused a significant scare in London, but the most frightening aspect for the authorities was that the soldiers had acted in the name of Queen Caroline, who was then a focal point for political agitation against the king and his Tory government. The idea of upholding the queen's cause gave strong support to claims that the mutiny did not violate the soldiers' oath to defend the throne. Wellington wrote of the Brigade of Guards at the time: "Nobody knows who is on or off duty . . . and the duty is ill done."[23] During the summer and autumn of 1820, a number of other incidents occurred in which the men of the guards and other regiments denounced the king and proclaimed their support for the queen.[24]

There were other mutinies in this era, but in many cases the motives are difficult to pinpoint. The harsh conditions of the service, coupled with political considerations, appear to have incited some disturbances, and these were the mutinies the army's leaders most feared.[25] In late September 1820, an officer actually wrote an appeal to the common soldiers in a military periodical, pleading with them not to overthrow the British state in the name of Queen Caroline: "You and I know that though Serjeant Toms, or Corporal Johns, are very good men in their duty, as directors of the state they would make but a poor figure."[26]

In many cases, the cause of disaffection was clearly political. In 1832 in Birmingham, Private Alexander Somerville of the Scots Grays was flogged two hundred lashes and dismissed from the army for writing in the *Weekly Dispatch* that his corps would not become "the tools of despotism," and he was not alone in his sentiments.[27] When soldiers refused to help quell a St. Patrick's Day riot in Dublin in 1832, the authorities were afraid to treat the affair as a mutiny, and pretended that it was only a drunken brawl.[28] The South Wales rebellion of 1839 had even more serious overtones; when the Twenty-ninth and the Forty-fifth Foot were stationed there on police duty, one hundred and thirteen soldiers deserted over a ten-month period (though not all joined the rebels). Having veterans among them, the rebels understood the power of army discipline, and especially the uniform's psychological influence. Men of the Forty-fifth were said to have been "made drunk," after which they changed clothes with the rebels, and "considerable difficulty is felt in keeping up the proper state of discipline." Some received help in deserting and others joined the Newport rising. A sergeant became the rebels' "drill sergeant and fugleman" and led the attack on the Westgate Hotel, where he was killed. Local magistrates had asked that barracks be erected to isolate the soldiers more effectively, and the Twenty-ninth was removed from that area before the rising, probably because it was thought to be too unreliable.[29]

The Chartist movement was an even greater threat to the soldiers' loyalty. General Napier discovered that many men from at least three of his units that were deployed to oppose Midlands Chartism in 1839 were either Chartists or sympathizers. He received an anonymous letter—which he believed to be genuine—stating that discharged soldiers would be the first to be hurt by the new Poor Law.[30] Three years later, thirty soldiers were sent to the Tower "very heavily ironed" for refusing to fire on Chartists.[31]

The authorities were alarmed at the prospect of soldiers' joining with or refusing to repress rioters, indicating the degree to which they believed the Other Ranks were tempted to mutiny. In 1817 and 1833, military and government officials at the highest level were notified of the presence of a single suspected radical in the Brigade of Guards.[32] An indication of the First Dragoon Guards' sympathies may have been expressed when they adopted "The Trades Union" as their regimental nickname in the late 1820s.[33]

Problems of disaffection were compounded by the arrangements for quartering soldiers; an unnamed Home Office official wrote in 1819 that "the necessity of avoiding easy communication between soldiers and the mob, which occurs in quarters, must be obvious."[34] Commanders considered billeting in public houses especially dangerous because the soldiers could become friendly with their potential foes. Consequently, they attempted to isolate soldiers from civilians, and officers appealed to the men's sense of pride to maintain a safe distance between them and the people.[35]

Military imagery was important in achieving this psychological isolation because it promoted a strong sense of identification with the regiment and the service. An artillery captain in the Peninsula stated that the sense of solidarity the uniform conveyed was itself a mark of the soldiers' superiority over civilians: "Uniformity in dress . . . ought to imbue him [the soldier] with feelings of pride, and place him upon a level above ordinary folk."[36]

But the importance of isolating soldiers and instilling a sense of superiority in them was often taken to extremes. When the earl of Cardigan brought Captain Wathen of the Fifteenth Hussars to a general court-martial in 1833, one of the charges was that when Wathen addressed his troop after a six-month inspection to tell them of the inspector's approval, he had added "that some strangers or civilians had particularly remarked [on] the soldier-like appearance of his troop."[37] Units were often kept on the move to prevent them from establishing ties with the local population, and frequently two units merely exchanged quarters.[38]

Despite these efforts, radicals sometimes attempted to win the common soldiers' sympathy (although violence occurred between soldiers and civilians, especially in pubs). A broadside from 1821 warned: "Everything in the shape of a quarrel with the regular military should be carefully avoided, as our rulers, and their dependents, studiously seek to foment those quarrels between the soldiers and the people."[39]

Ironically, the army's composition made the prevention of disaffection in the ranks more difficult. Privates stationed in the British Isles were mostly young recruits who had more recent ties to civilian life than veterans, and were more inclined to be unsteady in confrontations. Compounding this was the fact that the majority of men in the ranks were Celtic, and thus employing them to repress civil disorders in Celtic countries was very dangerous.[40]

In an attempt to counteract this, the authorities tried to station regiments with significant numbers of men of a particular nationality outside their own country.[41] In a notable instance, General Napier wanted regiments with the greatest number of Irishmen to quell Chartist riots, believing that "the difference in religion and country offers additional safeguards for the soldier's fidelity."[42] But the usual troop shortages made this tactic difficult to maintain, especially in an emergency. The Seventy-eighth Highlanders were employed to enforce the bitter eviction of their countrymen from the Isle of Skye in 1840, a dangerous move that can only be explained by a desperate shortage of men.[43]

In Ireland, discipline and isolation were the only effective defenses against disaffection by Irish-Catholic soldiers.[44] Concerned authorities sent a circular to all units in 1825, ordering that each regiment provide an exact count of the men of each religious persuasion in the monthly returns.[45] This was clearly an attempt to head off potential conflicts involving units to be stationed in Ireland, for despite all efforts to keep them isolated from the locals, animosity existed between Catholic and Protestant soldiers, and the fear of conflict was certainly justified.[46] In 1828, the lord lieutenant of Ireland, Lord Anglesey, "made almost public [a statement] that the Catholic soldiers are not to be trusted."[47]

An even more serious situation occurred when religious hostility erupted between Irish-Protestant and Irish-Catholic soldiers of the same corps, which could cause serious breaches in discipline. A number of "Orange lodges" (an Irish-Protestant Orangemen's fraternal order) were military, and a sergeant of the Nineteenth Foot in Ireland in 1825 was invited to join one, but refused for fear of disrupting the regiment, which was half Catholic at the time.[48] That a sergeant was even invited to participate in a group so disruptive to discipline while he was working to restore civil order indicates just how much things had gotten out of hand.[49] Thirty-one units held "Orange warrants," and in 1835, 20 percent of all Orange lodges were "military lodges."[50]

Soldiers were given extra pay, or "riot money," for police duty, apparently in order to secure their loyalty at critical moments.[51] That this money was intended to buy soldiers' loyalty is indicated by the contrast between this unusual generosity and the extreme miserliness of the government in almost every other aspect of their lives. Still-hunting in Ireland, which was "very unpleasant,"[52] also paid extra money, as did aiding the Excise service, but for these tasks soldiers could prove unreliable.[53]

Soldiers' lack of enthusiasm for police duty was reinforced by the unreliability of their weapons. The bayonet was poorly made and had a tendency to bend, and the mechanism for attaching it to the Brown Bess musket was often defective; rioters sometimes pulled bayonets off the end of muskets.[54] The musket also had some major design problems. One supply of arms that had been stored for nearly thirty years was useless owing to its inferior iron work and rotten stocks. This was a common problem that, an officer acidly noted in 1834, "every infantry officer commanding a company knows."[55] In a report of 1846, the Royal Engineers harshly criticized the Brown Bess.[56] Even the cavalry sword was not exempt from defect, as the Heavy Brigade's troopers learned at the battle of Balaclava, when their swords "all bent and would not go into a man's body."[57]

Because of all these factors making police work difficult for the army, the authorities desperately needed any advantage that could help to counteract the problems of riot control. Discipline was absolutely essential for this process, and the imagery was one of its basic components, but the spectacle possessed another advantage for the army in police work: it made soldiers appear intimidating in confrontations, just as it did on conventional battlefields.

Many sources mention the effect of the soldiers' appearance in confronting civil disorders. For example, a quartermaster-sergeant of the Royal Sappers and Miners described a confrontation with a Chartist mob: "Our martial bearing, bold looks, cold steel, and apparent resolution, no doubt, had the effect of curbing the spirit of the rebels and restraining their excesses." He also mentioned "showing them a cool and defiant front." After this incident passed, the corps was said to be "ready at a moments notice to turn out in all the pomp and circumstances of glorious war," an indication that the author believed the unit's appearance played a role in repressing civil disorder.[58]

There were other incidents in which spectacle helped curb civil disturbances. A historian of the Luddite riots mentions that artillery and a rocket troop of the Royal Regiment of Artillery were employed in 1812 against Luddite rioters "as a show of force, the aim being to awe the rioters into submission by parading the units around the disturbed parts of the region."[59] In 1839, a colonel opposing Chartists at Manchester "displayed troops in order to prevent and deter any outbreak."[60]

Soldiers were sometimes issued blank cartridges for riot duty in addition to live ammunition, highlighting the major aim of such operations: to prevent and minimize violence and restore order rather than seek armed confrontation.[61] Intimidating display was a common tactic that often worked, and mounted cavalry charges and orders to open fire were, for good reason, "relatively rare."[62] When troops were sent to Wisbeck in 1827 to quell disorders by canal workers, the Home Office stated that "these troops were to be stationed there only for effect, and not to be resorted to except in 'urgent necessity,' when the Civil Authority is manifestly unequal to put down [the] disturbance."[63]

In this era, the extravagant styles of male fashion influenced the basic designs of both military and civilian dress, which were similar in many respects. A characteristic of male fashion was its tendency to make the wearer appear imposing and, in the right circumstances, intimidating. One London dandy exemplified this threatening image: "King" Allen (formerly of the Forty-eighth Foot) was "tall, stout, and pompous-looking," and "remarkably well got up, with an invariably new-looking hat and well-polished boots." During a visit to Ireland when "Peel and the Tory government were very unpopular," his driver ran over an old village woman. A threatening mob quickly surrounded the open carriage, at which point "the 'king,' with a coolness and self-possession worthy of Brummell, rose up, displaying an acre of white waistcoat, and called out, 'Now postboy, go on, and don't drive over any more old women.' The mob, awe-struck by 'King' Allen's majestic deportment, retired."[64]

Civilian men at this time also wore headgear that could be perceived as intimidating.[65] Even the advertisements for such fashions were imposing; in the 1830s and 1840s, an early form of advertising displayed huge mock-ups of commodities that were paraded around the streets in carts. Thomas Carlyle described a seven-foot hat advertisement that was driven around London.[66]

But military dress was perceived as potentially more threatening than civilian fashion. In 1820, a political pamphlet asserted (with mocking exaggeration): "Dress a parcel of children in red coats, and they will put to flight ten thousand of the Cockney's!! . . . When a red coat appears, it is immediately 'the devil take the hindmost.' "[67]

Martial headgear has frequently been described as intimidating in terms of both height and decorations. For example, Major-General Mitchell wrote of "the threatening horse-hair,"[68] and another officer called the bearskin "war-like."[69] Headgear worn at a rakish angle was also linked to threat, though it could mask a quaking heart: "The hat *à la militaire*, cocked fiercely to one side intending doubtless to represent outwardly that recklessness and resolution which the wearer, perhaps, by no way inwardly feels."[70] The Scottish kilt was also considered threatening and "very imposing."[71] It is possible that the kilt was intimidating because it resembled women's clothing—with the implication of male cross-dressing. The lord lieutenant of Ireland, the marquess of Anglesey, wrote to Lord Melbourne in 1831 what many generations of Irishmen have known, that "those petticoats have a marvelous effect on Pat."[72] Men's dressing as women to carry out illegal political activities was an old tradition, and was manifested in this era by the Welsh "Rebecca" rioters of the 1840s.

The brightness of the uniforms also tended to elicit strong public responses, as is illustrated by an episode from the life of Lord Palmerston.

As a young man at Cambridge, Palmerston, along with other undergraduates, joined a university volunteer corps in 1803. Instead of choosing the traditional red, the "University Rangers" chose "a grave uniform" consisting of a dark-blue jacket, black stock, gray trousers, and black gaiters. These were adopted "to give as little offence as possible," despite the fact that martial enthusiasm was then at its height, as huge numbers of men (and some women too) were clamoring to join the volunteers to fight the threatened invasion.[73]

The colorful military marching bands were also very effective, and their brilliant, impressive performances appear to have been a factor in the army's policing duties. The Twenty-ninth Foot's black drummers were described in 1807 as having "a fierce and remarkable appearance, while hammering away on their brass drums."[74] Bandsmen also wore swords—always a latent image of threat—as a standard part of their uniform.

Other forms of martial display might also provoke hostile reactions, yet ironically, they were intended to elicit pleasure from spectators. In one example, at the Leatherhead Fair in 1803, soldiers of the Tenth Light Dragoons "began to display their address in performing the sword exercise . . . and drew on them the displeasure of the crowd, who attacked them with stones. The soldiers charged the people with drawn swords, but the crowd stood firm, and proved victorious."[75]

The mechanistic aesthetic, which was intrinsic to the flavor and character of all these forms of martial spectacle, further enhanced these imposing qualities, especially when the military confronted civilians as opposed to other soldiers. One of the foremost poets of the day, Lord Byron, observed this effect: "What makes a regiment of soldiers a more noble object of view than the same mass of mob? Their arms, their dress, their banners and their art and artificial symmetry of their position and movements."[76] Lewis Mumford noted for the Early Modern era, when standing regiments first appeared in European cities, that "the aesthetic effect of the regular ranks and the straight line of soldiers . . . greatly contributes to the display of power, and a regiment moving thus gives the impression that it would break through a solid wall without losing a beat. That, of course, is exactly the belief that the soldiers and the prince desire to inculcate in the populace; it helps keep them in order without coming to an actual trial of strength."[77] The visual effects of the machine paradigm thus conferred a psychological advantage on the military when it confronted civilians, an advantage that was not lost upon organized rioters and workers.

As the primary symbol of this martial machine, the uniform was especially disliked by the citizens of London, who had long feared armies, and the appearance of uniformed soldiers sometimes resulted in fistfights between soldiers and civilians. In an incident from 1809, a newly commissioned ensign was annoyed by people grabbing at parts of his clothing and was later abused by "ruffians." When he complained to a watchman, he was seized and told that he had no right to give orders outside of barracks; the watchman then referred to the "greasy ruffians" as "respecatable." The ensign later recounted the watchman's response as an inclusion of local color, but perhaps with the authentic voice of a common Londoner: "I'll larn him, that he sha'n't come out of a night with his feathers, and his flipper-flappers, and his red coat, to kick up a bobbery with the people. Ve don't vant soders in London—that God! ve can do without 'em. Ve vant no miilientary govament here, my lad; and if you come amongst us, vy you must leave off your implements 'o var, and behave like a spectacle abitont. The soders, I say, ought to be pulled up, for they are a d——d imputant set; tickerly the guards: they try to come it over us venever they have a tunity; but I'll let them know vhat's vhat, and larn them how to bemean themselves."[78]

But during the long French wars, Londoners' distaste for uniform diminished. An officer wrote that in 1809 it was not "the thing" for off-duty officers to wear their uniforms in London, but after returning from abroad in 1811, he found that "people had become more used to officers wearing uniform."[79] This was probably due to the large size of the wartime army (350,000) and greater numbers of uniformed servicemen. It would seem that the uniform's appeal had increased during the sustained patriotic atmosphere of two decades of war. This was a factor in the adoption of styles *à la militaire* in men's fashion during the Regency period. William Cobbett called this the era of "the gorget and the sash."[80]

People from most levels of British society took offense at the sight of the military: the poor, the working class, the lower-middle and middle classes, and even the nobility might object to the red coats. Civilians could sometimes show a great deal of hostility toward uniformed men; indeed, this was so common that one soldier observed: "There exists, amongst the inhabitants of many towns a strong disposition to insult the military."[81]

This was due in part to the soldiers' behavior, which was particularly offensive to middle-class moral sensibilities. The poor and working classes resented the army's policing duties, as well as the fact that soldiers were allowed to work at civilian jobs, thus undercutting local wages.

William Maginn believed that the "disposition to insult the military . . . is wholly confined to the lowest order of people," but some groups seemed to dislike uniform and military display particularly.[82] In the early 1850s, some Lowland Scots Christians (probably Presbyterian) strongly objected to highland soldiers' wearing the kilt. A petition to Parliament from Stirling in 1850 called for the abolition of the kilt, referring to it as "an exceedingly indecent and inconvenient dress" whose wearers were reduced to "a state of comparative nudity and discomfort." The petitioners also denounced it as "conducive to the development of bodily infirmity and disease, promotion of vice and immorality, and painful to the feelings of all men imbued with a correct sense of the principles of propriety, morality and religion."[83] The hostility some Christians felt toward the army is further reflected in the fact that so few men of nonconformist beliefs were present in the ranks.[84]

The civilians' hostility was leavened by their feelings of attraction for the martial show, however, and the people were alternately attracted or repelled by the spectacle. This reaction depended on the context in which the martial image was displayed. For example, soldiers seen on duty— guarding a post, marching in column, or performing at a review—were viewed much more positively than off-duty uniformed men on the street, especially if the latter were drunk and rowdy. Large groups of soldiers under the control of noncommissioned officers were not seriously harassed, unless they were engaged in riot duty. Clearly, the sight of a large body of men in uniform was more aesthetically pleasing—and more appropriate to the ideal of rigid discipline that the uniform symbolized— than the sight of privates who had temporarily escaped from the watchful eyes of their superiors.

This phenomenon was evident at the coronation of George IV, where "privy councillors who were not peers wore Elizabethan fancy dress of white and blue satin with trunk hose." Sir Walter Scott observed: "Separately so gay a garb had an odd effect on the persons of elderly or ill-made men; but when the whole was thrown into one general body all these discrepancies disappeared, and you no more observed the particular manner or appearance of an individual, than you do of a soldier in the battalion that marches past you. The whole was so completely harmonized in actual coloring, as well as in association with the general mass of gay, and gorgeous, and antique dress, which floated before the eye, that it was next to impossible to attend to the effect of individual figures."[85] This might be the reason some units ordered their men to march in step when walking out of barracks in groups—thus projecting an aspect of the rigid, formalized display onto the street. The imposing quality of large bodies of uniformly dressed men was apparently greater than the sum of its parts, and this appears to have influenced the varied reactions of civilians.

Even apart from armed confrontations, military spectacle thus elicited strong responses from the state's enemies; stock themes in Chartist speeches denounced "military glory" and "corrupting and brutalizing spectacles."[86] William Lovett, the publisher of the radical periodical the *Poor Man's Guardian*, also denounced "the power and monopoly of the few [that] have enabled them to set their thousand schemes in action, to brutalize and stultify the people—war, glory, splendour, fame, spectacles, songs, and every other brutalizing and degrading means the demon of evil could suggest."[87]

Leaving aside one of these "schemes"—war—one might ask whether "glory, splendour, fame, spectacles, [and] songs" could be considered "brutalizing and degrading means" suggested by His Satanic Majesty. Whether martial dress was attractive or intimidating depended upon the context of its presentation; indeed, a display of military finery and pomp that was very appealing—or at worst seemed impressive but unattractive—could be quite threatening to the viewer when displayed in a hostile context. The public's reaction to this imagery, which was strongly positive in some contexts, could therefore be very negative in others.[88] The ability of the martial image to threaten and attract spectators rendered it most formidable, and thus considerably enhanced the army's power. The effects of this phenomenon on the public thus mirrored the image's function to both discipline and punish yet also inspire the soldiers who were participants as well as spectators of the martial show.[89]

For the enemies of the state, ridicule was the most effective weapon against the army's spectacular image aside from defeat in battle. The radical journalist Douglas Jerrold, for example, ridiculed the finery as "gauds and trinkets; fripperies." Many such slang words were used to demean martial appearance in this era.[90] For example, common soldiers often suffered from lice, and a number of terms with military connotations were used to describe these parasites: "Scots Grays," "light troops," "silver laced," and "full march" all referred to a man with a head full of lice. A braying ass was a "trumpeter," and "the curse of God" was a cockade.[91]

Yet the powerful tactical advantage that the image and its accompanying managerial elements conferred upon its users was not lost on the army's opponents in civil disturbances, and many elements of military imagery—especially those that aided organization and control—were adopted by organized protesters. For civilians who challenged the power of the state and its laws, the basic problems of engaging in civil conflict—organization, discipline and tactics—were essentially the same as those faced by the military. In public demonstrations, the crowd's leaders were anxious to maintain order and show the peaceable respectability of the group. Yet in a confrontation, events could easily become confused, volatile, and violent, especially if firearms were discharged.

The difficulty of managing large numbers of people in such cases thus led to the adoption of elements that conferred the "strength which arises from order," and the state's opponents employed the same techniques the army itself used.[92] Their adoption in part resulted from the fact that many veterans of the regular army and nonprofessional corps belonged to such groups. After the long French wars in particular, there was an especially large number of ex-soldiers among the laboring classes, when it was said that at least one member of every British family had served.[93]

The literature of organized civil disorders and popular protests contains many references to the adoption of military formations and drilling by protesters, and it was this deliberate show of organization and decorum that frightened the authorities, for organized groups were more difficult to deal with militarily and politically. Drill was important for a large-scale organization to be effective in confrontations, and for this reason was prohibited in the first provision of the Six Acts of 1819. Samuel Bamford mentions drilling's significance at Peterloo: "There was no hyperbole in the statement which a magistrate afterwards made on oath, that 'the party with the blue and green banners came upon the field in beautiful order!' adding, I think, that 'not until then did he become alarmed.' "[94]

Other elements of military spectacle also accompanied protest parades, and banners, drums and fifes, marching bands, uniforms, and martial titles of rank were all utilized as a martial panoply. The paramilitary Catholic Association in the 1820s and 1830s marched to the music of drums and fifes, and formations of thousands of men, both mounted and on foot, paraded in makeshift uniforms.[95] Even organized thieves adopted characteristics of military organization; a gang of forty Somerset turnip-stealers was led by a captain who shouted military commands during a raid on a field.[96]

Trade unions and associations taking part in demonstrations utilized ribbon cockades and "signs," such as a sprig of laurel worn in the hats of all those attending, similar to the traditional field signs worn by armies.[97] The mayor of Leeds in 1819 described 2,500 to 3,000 colliers who "paraded the streets of Leeds in military array and [were] attended by bands of music."[98] Sir Harry Smith noted that radicals employed regimental organization in 1819 in Glasgow, forming sixteen battalions commanded by a general.[99] An organization of spinners in the Manchester strike of 1818 was described by an informer in these terms: "One man from [each] shop is chose by the people and he commands them, he forms them in ranks and . . . they obey him as strickley as the army do their colonel and [there is] as little talking as in a regiment."[100] A contemporary soldier similarly described a Catholic political procession in Ireland in 1843: "A column as close as ever soldiers formed, moved along to the music of many bands, all the latter in full uniform with a flashy drum-major at the head of each; in fact, it was a military movement in civilian dress, even for the masses of the people, for they kept the step; there was no talking, no laughing, nor levity of any kind, and there was a look of cool, dangerous determination in the countenances of the people."[101]

The use of such tactics could evoke strong emotional enthusiasm and loyalty among participants. In 1832, the *Poor Man's Guardian* lauded Irish political activists after a successful attempt to stop the sale of confiscated cattle. It mentioned "the music of the popular bands, and flags and banners rousing the fiercest and most latent feelings of the people . . . the Catholic priests alone preserving law, and restraining the temper of the infuriated multitude."[102]

The martial images utilized by such groups could also elicit a reaction from enemies who perceived them as threatening. A woman who was present at Peterloo made a flag out of the black silk petticoat and green liberty cap she wore that day, and displayed this emblem on every anniversary of the massacre. In 1839, local authorities became so fearful that this token would incite Chartist revolution that they sent constables and a troop of the Sixth Dragoon Guards to seize "these terrible and terrifying emblems of sedition."[103] The old woman with her petticoat was not the only female to participate in the imagery of opposition. The "handsomest girls" were placed at the front of political processions, because it was thought that forcing the soldiers to fight against women might weaken their resolve.[104]

Those participating in demonstrations often wore their best clothes, motivated by a concern to display cleanliness, sobriety, and decorum.[105] The idea was not only to create a brave show, but also to display the protesters' respectability and moral legitimacy.

A spectacular example of the power of the show can be found in the case of "Sir" William Courtenay, who led Kentish peasants in battle against soldiers in 1838. The flamboyant Courtenay had murdered a villager, and when two companies of the Forty-fifth Foot came to apprehend him, a participant wrote, "we found there one hundred men in military line awaiting us, with guns, pistols, scythes, pitchforks, and all sorts of weapons."[106] The major commanding the company declared that he had never seen such fanatical courage in battle as that displayed by Courtenay's band, and the affray resulted in some twenty casualties. Part of Courtenay's appeal was the image he projected, having a flamboyant style and fancy costume; his dress was of crimson velvet, trimmed with gold lace, including epaulets, a sword, two pistols, and a laced and tasseled cap.[107]

The civilian use of military-style display raises some questions about the meaning of organization and appearance in organized civil disobedience. The adoption of elements of military imagery and spectacle by those involved in political protest against the government indicates more than the need to maintain order and discipline among protesters. Although the fact that they wore their "best clothes" helps to show the desirable "order and decorum," it is also typical of the world of carnival in traditional Europe, the time of "the world turned upside down," and indicates an attempt to legitimize protest.[108] In "the inversion of the normal rules of culture [and in] the adoption of [special] costume . . . carnival was the ultimate symbolic inversion of the social hierarchy." Chartists also adopted elements of carnival in their attempt to mobilize support.[109]

The tradition of Guy Fawkes Day drew upon these notions and featured military imagery in this manner. On the night of Guy Fawkes Day in southern England, effigies of people the "Guys" perceived as enemies (foreign and domestic, including policemen, employers, and the clergy) were burned, and serious property damage was sometimes inflicted upon local targets. The riotous "Guys" dressed in showy, grotesque, and fantastic disguises, usually all alike and thus similar to uniforms. Military clothing was a desirable part of the costume; a Kentish man noted that the "Guys" of his village liked to wear old soldiers' caps and carry swords.[110]

Protesters used banners, bands, and other forms of display for the same reasons the army did: to uphold morale and attract attention to the cause. For example, Bamford writes of a Rochdale association that considered preservation of their colours a point of honor "worth any sacrifice."[111] But further questions arise about the meaning of these displays.

Modern scholars have argued that the adoption of an enemy's clothing or equipment acts as a symbolic transference of the enemy's power. At Peterloo, a green banner captured from the crowd was afterward worn by a yeomanry trooper (who had probably taken it himself) as a sash.[112] This symbolic assumption of a foe's power and claim to legitimacy appears to have been a major factor in the adoption of military images by early-nineteenth-century organizations that challenged the law in the streets.[113] Their use of banners bearing messages, and drums, fifes, bands, and the like can be interpreted as an assertion of moral legitimacy in opposition to the state's claim to uphold justice.

This is so even if some of the features adopted were those of the government itself; the military uniform symbolized service to the state as the livery of the crown, and is one of the most important symbols of the power and legitimacy of the state. By using elements of this uniform in their protests, opponents of the state thus asserted a notion of justice different from the rule of law they considered unjust. This claim encompassed the notion of "the world turned upside down."[114]

Military spectacle was also blended with carnival or charivari when labor and political organizations publicly ridiculed their enemies through demonstrations and parades. For many years after Peterloo, the Manchester and Salford Union ridiculed Major Birley, the hated commander of the Manchester and Salford Yeomanry Regiment, by reversing their banners and flags when marching past his house. Their bands would play "The Dead March in Saul," accompanied by groans and catcalls.[115]

E. P. Thompson suggests that charivari processions in early-nineteenth-century Britain, in which marchers banged pots and pans and hooted at the door of a perceived moral transgressor, were "anti-processions" that mocked army ceremonies, the church, and the justice system. The object of these processions was always to call attention to what the marchers saw as a moral transgression or injustice. These were not the pranks of adolescents and wild young men, but serious assemblies at which adults were present "apparaissaient comme les instigateurs; et souvent en grand nombre."[116] Hence the organized rioters' adoption of the trappings of authority and legitimacy—in the reversed form of mock marching bands and parades—conferred on their demands for justice a claim to moral validity in the same way as was visually asserted by martial parades and spectacle.

An example of this can be found in a Guy Fawkes Day celebration of 1833 at Bethnal Green. An effigy of a police spy was paraded through the town by huge crowds, who sang, "Sneak, a tyrant's will to please—Sells his soul for bread and cheese/To the tyrants, who enslave us from the cradle to the grave." The effigy was beheaded, the body burnt, and the head impaled upon a stick; the crowd then sang "Rule Britannia."[117] Even though they were breaking the law and the symbolic victim was a servant of the state, the crowd sang a patriotic song, thus proclaiming a true moral legitimacy, regardless of the song's praises for the military power of the British state. This phenomenon, in which the radical political opponents of the status quo perceived themselves as British patriots, was common in the first half of the nineteenth century.[118] For example, in 1838 Richard Oastler told the Chartists to arm themselves in the name of the Church and the throne.[119]

But ironically, the popularity of the military spectacle as a form of entertainment attracted many of those very people who, in case of civil unrest, would face the army as opponents. After an inspection of the South Nottingham Hussars Yeomanry in 1846, the *Nottingham Journal* rather condescendingly commented: "Being such decided advocates as we are of holidays for the people, we should be sorry to see the Yeomanry Corps disbanded, even if they proved to be of no earthly use, because such an occurrence would deprive our townsmen of a day's enjoyment."[120]

The people of Nottingham had experienced the spectacle of the South Nottingham Hussars Yeomanry before, but in street conflicts. Chartism was very strong in Nottingham, and the regiment had been active in quelling Chartist riots, a duty it had carried out a number of times previous to this inspection.[121] The popularity of the regiment's public reviews is especially significant considering that rioters hated the yeomanry soldiers involved in repressing riots much more than they did regular troops.[122] This is a striking example of how military imagery could be alternately attractive and threatening, depending upon the context in which it was displayed.

This paradox appears to have been the cause of occasional hostile behavior on the part of spectators at reviews and on field days. During the tense summer of 1830, crowds in Hyde Park attending a review for William IV's accession, amid the tensions of the First Great Reform Bill, "behaved in the most disgraceful manner, by pulling up the young trees and dismantling the great mortar of its chevaux-de-frise."[123]

There were also those who dismissed martial imagery as a transparent illusion that beguiled the weak, including children, overly sentimental young women, and the foolish. Thomas Carlyle saw it as both a facade and a shield, "a huge scarlet-colored, iron-fastened apron, wherein society [the elite] works guarding itself from . . . the world."[124] Although it is difficult to gauge the extent to which military imagery influenced civilians, the fact that this spectacle was a popular form of entertainment despite the fears of militarism that were so strong in the first half of the nineteenth century, indicates that the imagery influenced enough of its audience to counteract, contradict, or at least soften public dislike of the army.

Entertainment, Power, and Paradigm

Military spectacle was an important entertainment genre that exerted a deep, sustained impact on British society far beyond both Waterloo and the Crimean War. The spectacular quality of the show was so pervasive in martial life that even routine tasks such as sentry and escort duty, marching, Sunday church parades, off-duty soldiers walking in the street with the correct manner and "military air," and the endless public drills elicited great interest and excitement from onlookers.[1]

The most popular and entertaining public manifestation of the spectacle was the review, which usually included more than one corps performing together. Reviews consisted of evolutions of drill, musket volleys with blanks, and cannon salutes. Often a sham battle or mock-siege was staged between two opposing corps, or a bayonet or cavalry charge was featured. Reviews could last for three to six hours, and even more elaborate, grand reviews were held on special occasions.[2]

Many parade-ground evolutions were staged purely for entertainment. Captain Grose's satire advised adjutants that "maneuvers performed by a regiment are merely intended to shew the skill of the adjutant . . . All maneuvers should therefore be calculated to astonish the spectators, and the more confused and intricate they are, the better."[3] A colonel wrote of Torren's 1828 drill book that in a battle "those fancy movements are dangerous. If you attempted one-half of the present manoeuvres in the battlefield, you would get into such a tangle with the enemy you could not escape nor re-form before the cavalry would cut you down and disperse all before them, with little danger or loss on their side." The "pretty" drills were thus useful only "in Phoenix Park, or in London."[4]

The spectacle, which was always accompanied by martial music, was enhanced at the mass rituals and ceremonies in which entire corps participated. These shows included the presentation of new colours to a regiment, the changing of the guard, trooping the colors, field days, the quarterly and yearly inspections, funerals, and so on, all of which were normally played out before an audience composed of crowds of civilians.[5]

In wartime, the review boosted morale at home and strengthened loyalty to the crown. Military spectacles took place regularly during the French wars, and in 1798, 1803, and 1815, when war excitement was at a fever pitch, some martial ceremony, such as presenting regiments with new colors, took place almost every week.[6] The spectacle of war was a craze. An Edinburgh lawyer recalled that in 1803 "we were all soldiers, one way or another . . . The parade and the review formed the staple of men's talk and thoughts . . . and similar scenes were familiar in every town and every shire of the kingdom."[7] Yet this surge of patriotism and loyalty during wartime cannot entirely explain the public clamor for military spectacle.

The situation of British volunteer regiments during the French wars is a case in point. These units appeared throughout Britain, and though many had no weapons, this did not deter them from performing at reviews, which the public eagerly attended. So great was the martial enthusiasm that the government was besieged by an "insurrection of loyalty." Charles James Fox believed that these units had little to do with war, however, calling them "theatrical, ostentatious foppery," fit only for the top of a hill, where they could be admired from afar.[8] Their excesses highlight the fact that martial display transcended the purposes of war and suggest that spectacle was for many Britons—both participants and spectators—the most important element in these shows.

Grand reviews were an awesome sight. In 1811, when the prince regent held a Royal Review at Wimbledon Common to celebrate his accession to the Regency, 20,000 soldiers performed, drawn up in two parallel lines that extended for two miles. The number of spectators was reported to be a "full 200,000," and their carts and wagons "formed a circle [a] full six or eight miles in circumference."[9] The prince regent, who always made a great presence in public, outdid himself; he was accompanied by a "vast retinue," and his saddle alone was reported to have cost nearly 500 guineas. "Military tellegraphs" (heliographs), then a novelty, were used to convey orders along the line of troops.[10]

Grand reviews were usually held in conjunction with some major event, such as the anniversary of a battle, a royal accession or birthday, or some other royal celebration, and they often involved great numbers of soldiers and spectators. At least one member of the royal family, or occasionally the commander in chief, would attend, and programs were printed up for the public.[11]

Yet it would be a mistake to interpret such events only as wartime efforts to raise morale or to inspire civilians with patriotic fervor, for reviews were extremely popular in peacetime as well. A review held in July 1817 at Hounslow Heath caused an immense traffic jam: "The road to Hounslow [from London] was, at a very early hour, crowded with vehicles of all kinds, and every horse was put in requisition long previous to the day appointed for the review."[12] In 1830, during the first week of King William IV's reign, at least three grand reviews took place.[13] It was reported that at the first of these "the number of persons assembled was immense. The top of the Horse Guards, Admiralty, Treasury, and all the adjacent buildings were completely covered, and presented but one mass of both sexes. The park was so full it was nearly impossible to move along."[14] Four days later at another London review, an entire regiment of cavalry and six hundred policemen were required to cordon off the ground,[15] and the crowd was described as "immense beyond description."[16] Two days later William IV was officially proclaimed king at another review, which one-fourth of the entire population of greater London reportedly attended.[17]

A fascination with royalty probably accounts for part of the attraction, but smaller-scale shows held throughout the realm—and not attended by royalty—also drew large numbers of civilian spectators, indicating that the military imagery provided much of the appeal for these occasions. A military gymnastics event held in 1828 by the Fiftieth Foot at Manchester "attracted an immense concourse of spectators."[18] A similar crowd was reported in 1831 when new colors were presented to the Thirtieth Foot at Ashton-under-Lyme.[19]

Although the poor constituted the majority of spectators, wealthier people also found military displays compelling, and fashionable people held social events in conjunction with reviews. Mary Anne Wyndham Lewis (the future wife of Benjamin Disraeli) held a party in 1829 for ninety guests, half of them lords and ladies, to watch a review in Hyde Park.[20] In Ireland, the presentation of new colors to the Thirty-second Foot in 1845 attracted "the elite of Dublin."[21] Perhaps the most famous review spectator was Charles Dickens's character Mr. Pickwick, a typical middle-class early Victorian who was "an enthusiastic admirer of the army." In *The Pickwick Papers*, he attends a grand review, together with "the whole population of Rochester and the adjoining towns . . . in a state of utmost bustle and excitement."[22]

The powerful appeal of these shows—whether large or small—is in part explained by their context; in the nineteenth century, a gratis public spectacle that involved hundreds or thousands of splendidly dressed performers, complete with "fireworks," was quite a treat for all. But an important added dimension was the military music that accompanied the soldiers' movements. The bandsmen's brilliant uniforms were especially colorful, and one veteran asked "whether it was the splendor of their uniforms, or the beauty of their music, that at all times attracted so great a crowd about them."[23]

Military music was inspiring. In 1856, one contemporary noted that "the strains of martial music cause the pulse to pound and fire the imagination."[24] In the earlier decades of the nineteenth century, one or more black musicians often performed in each band, usually as drummers, drum-majors, or cymbalists dressed in rich, splendid costumes that were a cross between Middle Eastern ("Turkish") and European military dress. They wore silk turbans with brilliant, brightly colored uniforms decorated with lavish quantities of bullion lace, adding a dash of the exotic oriental to the show.[25] Military bands often performed at private social functions such as parties or weddings, as well as at nonmilitary public events, including the dedication of new churches, buildings, and canals, and they drew large crowds.[26] The fancy Eleventh Hussars' band frequently played for "crowds of a thousand or more" at the fashionable seaside resort of Brighton during summer evenings when the regiment was quartered there in 1840. Its popularity was said to be equal to that of the famous actor Charles Kean, who was performing Shakespeare at the nearby Theatre Royale.[27]

The bands were so popular that Britons apparently considered the show a right. In 1829, the editor of the *United Services Journal* pointed out that this seemed to be the public perception after he received a letter from a civilian who complained "rather angrily" of the late exclusion of the public from the Sunday performances of the Coldstream Guards' band at the Tower of London.[28] Reviews were also seen as a public right, and in 1816, after the public was misled into believing that one would be held at Wimbledon to commemorate Waterloo, the angry crowd set Combe Wood heath on fire. They at last got to see the guards when a detachment was sent to disperse the riot.[29]

Reviews were popular despite some disadvantages and disappointments. Bad weather could force a cancellation, and an unexpected rain shower might damage the uniforms; in 1845, *Punch* humorously suggested that the troops be equipped with umbrellas.[30] The fact that so many people attended these events also meant that many could not see the show or hope to enjoy much more than the music and the firing of the guns. Despite problems, however, the shows' great popularity was encouraged by army commanders, including Colonel Vandeleur and the officers of the Tenth Hussars, who "were ever ready to promote the pleasure of the citizens by the presence of their band on all public occasions."[31]

The extent of the show's appeal is also reflected by the inclusion of military themes in civilian culture. The spectacle influenced a wide variety of genres—popular entertainments, pastimes, and amusements, as well as reading, art, literature, folk songs, and fashion. The impressions made upon children were especially strong; one boy bribed sentries to allow him past the barrack gate, where he watched and imitated the platoon drill.[32] An especially imposing ritual might also remain stamped upon a child's memory for the rest of its life. A six-year-old who saw a military funeral in 1846 talked about it until his death in 1935 at the age of ninety-five.[33]

Children imitated soldiers in their play, and many of their toys manifested images of war. By the mid-1780s, "soldiers and forts of every variety" were sold in London. Paper toy soldiers were available in the growing toy market after 1815, with colorful, interchangeable clothes.[34] Male dolls dressed as officers were popular for small girls.[35] Educational toys could also have martial themes; during the Crimean War, an ABC book featured a military theme for every letter: "Ensign, who ne'er would his colours forsake" (depicting an infantry ensign with the colors fighting two Russian soldiers); "F for the fort they determined to take" (depicting Sebastopol).[36] Children, together with the rest of the family, were also charmed by the miniature "toy theater" developed in 1813; the inventor's best-selling play was the *Battle of Waterloo*, of which "nearly 10,000" copies were printed, and others imitated his success.[37]

The incorporation of military imagery into theatrical productions was a part of legitimate theater as well, and sometimes plays used contemporary military dress in the show. Productions of Shakespeare and other period plays featured characters in military roles wearing regimentals, as a blending of historical styles was typical of the time.[38] Sometimes theater managers enhanced the visual impact by hiring soldiers in uniform to perform, but many units forbade their men to appear in uniform on stage, possibly because commanders feared that the military spectacle might be ridiculed and thus rendered less imposing.[39] It appears that these performances were useful as wartime propaganda, however, and guardsmen "were allowed by the authorities" to take part in a London production that staged the battle of Inkermann in August 1855.[40]

Musicals were also influenced by military images, and not long after the first marching bands appeared in British regiments, around 1720, the performances began to include military marches as part of the repertoire.[41] A variety of now archaic stage shows that were popular in the early nineteenth century—including pantomimes, extravaganzas, comic operas, and burlettas—might feature martial music and drill.[42] The opera also utilized military themes, especially in wartime; in 1815 a London opera featured "a wonderful piece of music . . . descriptive of the sounds peculiar to a field of battle."[43] During the Crimean War, two military bands played at a state opera performance attended by the queen, Prince Albert, and the emperor and empress of France.[44]

Modest entrepreneurs also profited from the public's taste for productions incorporating martial images. Street entertainers staged battles with magic lantern shows, shadow-boxes, and other "exhibitions." These were the most significant—and often the only visual—accounts many Britons received of particular battles.[45]

But the most spectacular manifestation of martial themes in the nineteenth century was equestrian drama, and elaborate productions were staged with hundreds of horses and uniformed actors. Like the military spectacle they copied, these shows were, in the words of one scholar, "naive, colourful, melodramatic and, above all, popular."[46] They were also well attended by the burgeoning working class.[47] The greatest of the hippodromes was Astley's Amphitheater, and after the successful production of *Harlequin Mamluke, or the British in Egypt*, battles became a stock theme. The action was realistic, as an officer who attended wrote: "I was amazed at the accuracy with which the military evolutions were executed."[48] Ninety horses performed during one scene in a production of 1831, and elephants were featured in *The Afghanistan War; or, The Revolt at Cabul and British Triumphs in India*, produced in 1843.[49]

Astley's most popular piece was *The Battle of Waterloo*, which capitalized on the public's great fascination with this battle. One officer who fought there wrote: "I shall not be far wrong in asserting that there exists not in the United Kingdom, man, woman, or child, who has not either seen pictures or panoramas of Waterloo, heard songs on Waterloo, read books on Waterloo, talked for weeks about Waterloo, and [a] full two-thirds of the adult population could not rest until they journeyed forth to have a look at Waterloo."[50] The production was called "gargantuan in everything except dullness." One of the greatest and most frequently performed dramas in the entire history of Astley's, it was an "overwhelming success." It ran for 144 consecutive performances (the whole season) on its first run in 1824, and was revived every year for many decades. At the first run of *Waterloo*, the hippodrome was honored by the presence of the duke of Wellington, who returned to see it again in 1829.[51]

During the Crimean War these shows were the most popular theater productions in London.[52] But the continued appeal of the shows between 1815 and 1856—and beyond—illustrates the sustained public enthusiasm for martial spectacle. In 1850, for example, three separate military productions were being performed in the greater London area.[53] Recent battles were normally produced as soon as the news of them arrived; *The Battle of the Alma* (with four hundred extras) was performed only thirty-three days after the event.[54]

The martial origin of these equestrian shows is underscored by the life of the founder, Philip Astley, a retired sergeant-major from the Fifteenth Light Dragoons who gained invaluable experience in training army horses, from which these equestrian productions developed.[55] But his influence is broader still, for these productions were a significant factor in the later evolution of the modern circus, which utilized numerous martial images, including military-style brass bands (sometimes mounted) with uniformed performers, ringmasters dressed like cavalry officers, a fashion set by Astley's famous ringmaster Widdecombe, who also adopted the machine-like, superior military mien.[56]

Nonperformance elements in early-nineteenth-century British circuses and other places of entertainment also included military images. For example, paintings displayed in a series of canvases, known as "panoramas," often featured dramatic events, including military subjects. The first of many nineteenth-century battle panoramas was "The Storming of Seringapatam" by Robert Ker Porter, displayed on 2,550 square feet of canvas for an admission of one shilling.[57] Its London exhibition (April 17, 1800–January 10, 1801) netted Porter a "clear profit of £1,202.14s. 7 1/2d." This amounts to more than 24,000 admissions, not including the admissions that would have covered his expenses, and it later toured in both Britain and America.[58] Panoramas brought art to the more isolated parts of the British Isles and were seriously reviewed by the critics.[59] Battle painting also had a significant effect upon the production of military prints at the cheaper end of the art market, which constituted a portion of nineteenth-century print production, attracting patrons who might have scorned battle painting.[60]

Other forms of entertainment involving physical skills also utilized military elements. A famous gymnast astonished his public "by throwing a [somersault] over a dozen grenadiers, standing at 'present arms,' with fixed bayonets."[61] The world of British sport adopted martial dress too; the Royal Company of Archers wore military-style coats with lace, cross-belts, and breastplates, and officers bore military rank.[62]

Military themes were also popular in music. Martial illustrations decorated nineteenth-century sheet-music covers, especially from the 1840s, when the price of the piano was lowered, placing it within the reach of the middle classes. Nearly five hundred pre-1914 illustrated sheet-music covers are known to have incorporated military motifs.[63] Folk songs held a prominent place in the lives of common people, and they too featured military themes. In the long wars with France, military music was a familiar feature that readily became incorporated into the folk music of the day. A contemporary wrote that in 1803 "every town was a sort of garrison . . . In one place [people heard the music] of some youth learning to play the drum, at another place some march or national air [was] being practiced on the fife."[64] A collector of Scottish folk songs noted that "the twenty years that ended with Waterloo have left more traces on our popular minstrelsy than any other period of our history."[65]

The ballad-singer was another important source of music for the poor, and during the French wars he provided "historical abridgements to his country's glory [and] no battle was fought, no vessel taken or sunken, that the triumph was not published, proclaimed in the national gazette of our ballad-singer . . . It was he who made them yearn towards their country, albeit to them so rough and niggard a mother."[66] The authorities appreciated this influence, and during the French wars, the government paid the balladeer Charles Dibdin to "keep up the national feeling against the French."[67] Military themes were also of major interest in story-telling, and were doubtless no less popular when embellished. An early Victorian novel included this scene: "As it was known that Sandy had been a soldier, the people about the [village] smithy expressed an anxiety to hear some stories of the wars."[68]

This theme also flourished in literature, and a large body of martial memoirs was published after 1800, some of which went into three printings. A satirist noted that "there are few messes which cannot boast of a considerable number of authors—historians, novelists, and memoir writers."[69] The popular novels of "Harry Lorrequer" (Charles Lever) on the Peninsular wars were best-sellers from the 1830s, and were issued as cheap "railway novels" well beyond the Crimean War.[70]

Although it might appear that memoirs and accounts of campaigns (which sometimes contained detailed descriptions of the army's harsh conditions) could undermine the glory and glamour of the imagery's appeal by injecting a large dose of reality, this does not seem to have been the case. Indeed, public interest in martial literature—with its emphasis on heroic action and exotic foreign places—tended to complement the charms of the spectacle rather than contradict its appeal. One scholar has noted that "the impact of newspapers, journals, cheap book printing, ballad sheets and prints [was] vital in the process of manufacturing an heroic image."[71]

This image stimulated a desire among civilians to imitate the martial appearance itself, and military uniforms greatly influenced civilian fashion in the first half of the nineteenth century and beyond. During the long

French Wars, this influence increased significantly, building on the impact of George III's creation of the "Windsor uniform" in 1778, which was said to have originated in the uniform of the Berkshire Volunteer Cavalry.[72] Likewise, the nobility adopted military elements such as epaulets, cocked hats, shell jackets with brass buttons, and other motifs in clothing their male servants.[73]

By the very end of the eighteenth century, the uniform had come to replace the *habit habille*, the European elite's formal wear in this era. But some fashionable trends worked against this style, most notably those represented by George "Beau" Brummell, whose notions of proper dress came to epitomize the tone of male fashion during the 1790s. Brummell had tried and rejected military uniform in 1798 as an officer in the Prince of Wale's Own regiment, the Tenth Light Dragoons.[74] Most of his sartorial values were quite different in character from those of the military and included restraint, naturalness, and simplicity, using subdued colors such as dark blue, buff, brown, and white. He maintained that a gentleman should never dress so as to attract attention in the street.

Nothing could have been more contrary to this notion than the effect of military uniform, yet both approaches shared the emphasis on a tight fit, which was probably a major factor in the subsequent merging of these two styles of male fashion.[75] British military uniforms had been tight since 1768, an aesthetic that was derived from the Prussian army, and late in the French wars this fit became even tighter in both military and civilian dress. The tailoring, together with the flamboyance of hussar and other extravagant military dress, combined with some of Brummell's notions to create a variant on the "dandy" fashion image that lasted from the Regency period until the 1830s, an extreme mode sometimes called the "Butterfly dandy."[76] The following satirical poem describes this new style:

> My pigeon breasts and padded sleeves,
> Made my whole front en militaire . . .
> By their aid youth receives
> The approbation of the fair.[77]

The chief influence for male dandy dress *en militaire* was the fancy hussar uniform. This very tight and elaborate light cavalry dress was most often the target of attacks on both "military foppery" and arrogance in the press and in caricatures from the Regency through the reign of

William IV. A civilian commentator links this dandyism with hussars in denouncing the moustache, which was regulation in hussar regiments: "The dandyism of the moustache [is] incongruous and coxcombish when pasted on an English countenance."[78] In attacking this style as "finery and frippery," an officer identified the principal influence as the "degenerate taste [of] the French."[79]

But this style did not sufficiently capture the uniform's appeal for some young civilians of modest means who wished to cut a dashing figure, and they bought secondhand officers' uniforms to wear for strutting around in public. In 1819 in Scotland, highland regimental dress was said to be "now universally looked upon as the holy-day uniform of all the writers' clerks in Edinburgh," and the masquerade continued for years.[80]

After the dandy image declined in popularity (although it never completely disappeared), male fashion became less ornate, reflecting the developing image of middle-class respectability. After 1815, the wartime fashion of civilians' wearing military or quasi-military dress declined,[81] but in the long run, its appealing associations have made a considerable impact, for many military motifs have been adopted for civilian dress, including lapels, cuffs, straps, pocket flaps, extra buttons, buckles, ties, and so on.[82] The overall impact of military design on civilian dress has thus been most significant, and gentlemen's fashions in Britain (and Europe as a whole) have been fundamentally influenced by the clothing of officers or huntsmen.[83]

Women's clothing also borrowed military motifs. The custom of officers' wives' wearing female versions of their husbands' uniforms was a precursor of styles inspired by uniform from the late eighteenth century.[84] The wife of a general who was the governor of Jamaica wore "a full lieutenant-general's uniform" as a "dress of ceremony" on the ship voyage back to Britain.[85] Fashionable women wore clothes derived from the popular rifle regiments' uniforms, such as green-velvet rifle dresses and hats, and from hussar uniforms and headgear, of which the pelisse (originally the hussars' braided outer jacket, richly laced and lined and faced in fur) is now a much-altered survival.[86] This trend continued into the Regency, and in Scotland noblewomen reflected the pride taken in the highland regiments' performance at Waterloo by wearing highland jackets and plumed bonnets;[87] a new color, "Waterloo blue," was also adopted for high fashion.[88] The Crimean War later inspired another new color, "Alma brown,"[89] and in 1856, leather belts, thick military heels, and jackets modeled on dragoons' dress became fashionable.[90] The cardigan sweater and raglan sleeve proved to be more enduring contributions to ladies' fashions.

Military dress also influenced children's clothes in wartime, and girls, like their mothers, dressed in fashionable hussar jackets, epaulets, and feathered shakos.[91] Boys were sometimes dressed as soldiers or highlanders from the end of the eighteenth century,[92] and by the time of Waterloo military dress for children had become "quite a vogue."[93] A Berkshire lad in the 1820s seems to have imbibed some of the martial mentality associated with his hussar cap and jacket, and was described as "the youngest piece of gravity and dignity I ever encountered . . . He stalks about . . . like a piece of machinery."[94]

The public's attraction to military imagery rendered it useful to the state; when war broke out martial spectacle was intrinsic to mobilizing both the army and public support, and Britons were much more positive and enthusiastic about the armed forces than they were in peacetime, especially if they believed the country was threatened. But though antimilitary feelings were temporarily eclipsed, they persisted under the surface, and this latent hostility often reemerged with greater vigor after the war ended—as it did in 1815, when an enormous war debt had accumulated and large numbers of unemployed veterans returned to seek work in a weak economy.

Thus the appeal of the peacetime military spectacle was an important concern of military leaders, and some commanders devoted careful attention to crowd pleasing. The *York Herald* recorded Colonel Vandeleur's successful promotion of the Tenth Hussars on their departure from the city in 1846: "An immense mass of people assembled at the railway station on the morning of [the Tenth's] departure and relieved their friendly feeling to the regiment by loud and repeated cheers."[95]

This enthusiasm had political overtones, for the spectacle helped override the traditional dislike many Britons felt toward the military (just as positive appeals helped counteract the harsh discipline within the army). At times, the authorities encouraged spectators to such an extent that the army's entertainment role interfered with training for war. In 1853, after heightened fears of a French invasion, much-needed large-scale maneuvers were held at the experimental Chobham Camp, where "the good

Sixth Dragoon Guards (Carabiniers), Officer

The honorific title "guards" was bestowed on dragoon regiments in the
eighteenth century as compensation for a reduction in their pay.

Frontispiece of a pamphlet advertising a play at Pollock's Toy Theatre.

Up the Alma's Height, or the Fusilier

Illustrated music sheet cover. These illustrated music
sheets appealed to buyers and sold as much for
the cover as for the music.

The Victory Polka

Illustrated music sheet cover. The far-off battle of Inkermann (in the Crimea)
invades the Victorian parlor in this panorama-like scene.

First Regiment, Grenadier Guards, Drummer

Blacks added an exotic "oriental" touch to the military's
marching bands in this era. Note the turban, the
elaborate bullion-lace design on the arms, and
the oriental-style scimitar.

Militaria *(clockwise from top left):* coatee of a private volunteer of the Grenadier Company, Loyal London Volunteers, *c.* 1805 (the dress of volunteer units was patterned on the army, but for fancy units like this one, better-quality cloth and gold lace were often adopted, even for the Other Ranks); drum major's mace, Scots Fusilier Guards, *c.* 1840; officer's cuirass and helmet, Household Cavalry, *c.* 1830; officer's levee sword, Fifteenth (the King's) Hussars, *c.* 1850; officer's shoulder pouch, Eleventh (Prince Albert's Own) Hussars, *c.* 1850; officer's cocked hat, Yeomen of the Guards, *c.* 1845; officer's dirk, Seventy-eighth Highlanders, *c.* 1850.

Appointments and Militaria *(clockwise from top left):* officer's epaulets, Royal Company of Archers (Queen's Bodyguard for Scotland), *c.* 1850; officer's shoulder pouch, Second Royal North British Dragoons (Scots Grays), *c.* 1850; officer's Albert shako, Twenty-third Foot (Royal Welch Fusiliers), 1844–1855; officer's 1812 model shako plate, Seventh Foot (Royal Fusiliers); Other Ranks' cartridge box plate, Grenadier Guards, *c.* 1850; officer's breastplate, Fifty-seventh Foot (West Middlesex), *c.* 1850; medals: Waterloo, 1815, Punjab, 1848–1849, and Military General Service with Peninsula campaign bars; infantry officer's model 1822 presentation sword, 1823; officer's gorget (middle), line infantry, *c.* 1820.

Making a Lancer

Two women assist a third in dressing in a lancer
costume (which might have been made especially for a
woman, since it is not correctly tailored), complete with
false moustache. Two soldiers watch the scene through a
window, and the joke is emphasized by a print on the wall
depicting the Isle of Man (its badge is three legs joined
together). This highlights the appeal of martial dress
in female high fashion despite the
illegality of cross-dressing.

Col. Sir Wm. Payne Bart

The Twelfth (Prince of Wales's) Lancers. The prince regent converted
some light dragoon units into lancers after 1815 in imitation of Napoleon's
Lancers of the Imperial Guard. The uniforms were based
on Polish light cavalry dress.

British Royal Horse Artillery, No. 2, Review Order

This print shows a field battery in review order, wearing the braided hussar-style uniform with shako. This extra-fancy light cavalry dress was adopted by horse artillery, who were equipped with guns light enough to be pulled by horses at cavalry speed.

*Pall Mall; Wellington's Funeral Procession Passing
the Senior United Service Club*

The duke's riderless horse leads this 1852 parade. Military funerals attracted
extraordinary attention from the public in this era.

Officer's shoulder belt plate, Thirty-first Foot
(Huntingdonshire Regiment), *c.* 1850. Battle honors and the
corps' number are the primary decorative features
of this gilt brass plate.

The Review in the Park at Windsor

A Crimean-era review, featuring the Household Cavalry; the trumpeters on the left
wear livery-style state dress. The guards were the most visible units in London's
many military spectacles, as well as in its civil conflicts.

*Officer, Royal Horse Artillery
(Horse Brigade) Review Order*

The sabretache bears the cipher of King William IV.

His Royal Highness the Prince Regent and Duke of Wellington's . . . First Visit to Waterloo Bridge, on June 18, 1817

The martial spectacle was a standard feature at most large public ceremonies in the early nineteenth century, especially in London.

*Officer, Review Order, Second [Royal North British] Dragoons
(Scots Grays), 1833–1836*

The Scots Grays were the only Scottish cavalry unit, and the only
line cavalry to wear the distinctive bearskin cap.

effect" was said to have pervaded the whole population, and the public was allowed "the most liberal freedom of the camp, to make it as popular as the [Great] Exhibition," even though this policy interfered with the maneuvers. Commanders believed that the long-term benefits would outweigh these short-term disadvantages, and by encouraging civilians to view the training they hoped to induce members of Parliament to vote for more military spending.[96]

Punch hinted at the camp's priority of spectacle over training, remarking that the aides-de-camp at Chobham were "flying about in all directions . . . delivering 'property' dispatches, similar to those 'gallant officers at Astley's [who] are in the habit of prancing over the platformed planes of Waterloo.'"[97] But despite Mr. Punch's many lampoons directed at the army, he was still won over by the show, publishing a poem at the end of the summer entitled "Farewell to the Camp," which concluded with the lines: "And we'll mark the M.P. for a short-sighted scamp / Who grudges one mil for the Chobhamite Camp."[98]

Those who opposed the state's policies also recognized this seductive appeal. The radical journalist Douglas Jerrold believed that Britain's rulers used the show to counteract the army's negative image: "When nations . . . cut each others throats . . . we must have red coats and muskets and sabres; but seeing that the duty of their bearers squares neither with our innate good sense, nor our notions of what ought to be—we are fain to gild the matter over—to try to conceal, from ourselves, the butchering nature of the business we are sometimes forced to undertake, and so spring up military spectacle—military finery—military music . . . Clothe war therefore in gayer colours than peace . . . let the steel which cuts glitter like valued gems; the evolutions which destroy, be graceful as the motions of dancing girls!"[99]

The state's supporters realized that the spectacle was more than mere entertainment, and would help the army retain its appeal to the public despite radical propaganda. One officer wrote during the crisis of the Great Reform Bill:

The radical and leveling press . . . has for years directed [its] fiercest attacks against the British army, but has not yet been able to destroy, or even to weaken its popularity: the failure may seem strange to some but . . . there is yet an honest manliness of feeling about the people of Britain that makes them delight even in the contemplation of deeds of hardihood and danger; and makes them proud of the unrivaled achievements of their sons, brothers and countrymen, as well as of the country that produced, and of the institutions that fostered, such men, because it enables the most peaceful citizens to say with inward satisfaction—Even such would have been my conduct had chance placed me in the ranks of war, instead of casting my lot in a happier and more peaceful sphere![100]

While the spectacle thus achieved a measure of success in counteracting the army's negative reputation, it exerted another, deeper influence on British life that transcended the army's image-building and funding problems. This impact, which continues into the twentieth century, stems from the values that have been documented in previous chapters: discipline and order, hierarchy, conformity, efficiency, solidarity, and *esprit de corps*. These values were especially influential in the first half of the nineteenth century, when contemporaries saw them as useful—and even vital—in coping with a proliferating set of social problems.

The rise in population, rapid urban growth, and, to an increasing extent, the new techniques of industrial production promoted a multitude of social problems that were generating chaotic and disturbing trends in British society. These consisted of a vast array of serious urban, health, political, economic, domestic, spiritual, and other social pathologies, all of which have been described in detail by a number of contemporaries and historians, and many of which had not then—nor subsequently—been satisfactorily resolved. Many "felt that something evil had intruded itself into British life, something not only avaricious and cruel, but dangerously reckless and unreliable as well."[101] In a sermon of 1839, Thomas Arnold spoke of "our monstrous society—absolutely without . . . parallel in the history of the world." Thomas Carlyle wrote that "the intellectual lightships had broken from their moorings [leaving] the lights all drifting, the compasses all awry."[102] In this often confusing and disturbing environment, Britons felt they had lost many of the certainties of traditional life.

Under these conditions, the idea of organizing society to ensure order and stability possessed a strong appeal for many. In an age increasingly influenced by machines and the interests of their masters, it was the martial spectacle's ideal of mechanical regularity and predictability that made it especially attractive. As a visual image, it echoed and reinforced the new and essential values and needs of the growing industrial revolution—discipline, hierarchy, conformity, uniformity, and efficiency—which were both symbolized and manifested by the machine. "In the Victorian mind, the ideal of strength is a combination of force and firmness [and] there is enormous admiration for the power of machines."[103]

But this machine constructed for violence was unlike any other. It was no heartless, lifeless engine of destruction; its components were human—Britannia's sons, a bulwark of both British rights and independence, and of the majesty, dignity, and glory of the British monarchy and state. The charismatic appeal of the military machine's brilliant panoply was enhanced by these human components, who were not performers or actors, but real soldiers whose profession was associated in the public's mind with glory, self-sacrifice, the defense of the realm, and victory over powerful and dangerous foreign foes. Yet the spectacle was presented in a carefully controlled context, with the troops normally isolated from the public. The effect was that martial values were presented in an idealized manner—or as advertisement.[104] Color, tradition, and pageantry thus united with the latent threat of deadly force, rendering the martial show fascinating and even compelling.

For those who commanded the industrial machines, this vision's manifestation of solidarity of purpose, order, conformity, and enthusiasm for duty made it a model for operations, suggesting how they *ought* to run, especially in light of the new—but highly unpopular—pattern of work discipline. The larger scale of operations rendered such management a formidable task, which Thomas Carlyle described as "the immense problem of organizing labour, and the first stance of managing the working classes."[105] The army seemed especially appropriate as a model for this task, being one of the few—and perhaps the best—examples of a large-scale, complex organization in this era.

As work became more impersonal, laborers tended to be less loyal to the new management, giving the businessman much to admire in the operations of his military counterpart. John Ruskin noted that "it is easy to imagine an enthusiastic affection existing among soldiers for the colonel. [It is] not so easy to imagine an enthusiastic affection among cotton-spinners for the proprietor of the mill."[106]

The impersonal tone and larger scale of the ways of work in the era of the industrial machine made an utter necessity of a new pattern of factory discipline the workers resented. As a manual for cotton-spinning management noted: "It is absolutely necessary to maintain a proper authority, and keep uniform good order, as the end of all government is order."[107]

G. M. Young noted the resulting dilemma from the perspective of the era's elite, stating that "as the country became more and more dependent on machines, its stability turned more and more on the subordination and goodwill of the savage masses which tended them."[108] From management's perspective, the necessity of this new discipline rendered the military paradigm even more appropriate. Ruskin thought that one of the most simple and clear "example[s] of [a] relation between a master and operative is that which exists between the commander of a regiment and his men."[109]

Pioneer industrialists were thus fascinated by the idealized military image, and even adopted some of its trappings. Josiah Wedgwood thought of himself as a general commanding his worker troops. He used military metaphors in instructions to subordinates, aiming "to make such machines of the men as cannot err," adding that "it is glorious to conquer so great an empire [making ordinary workers into artists] with raw, undisciplined recruits." He also awarded clothing to workers, both as a reward and as a badge of good behavior.[110]

Robert Owen was also impressed with the military spectacle and imitated some of its features. Although famous for his "benevolent" approach to management, he demanded military-style discipline from underlings. His factories were compared to barracks with him as commander in chief. Workers marched between jobs "in strict military order" at the Queenwood, Hampshire, community,[111] and at New Lanark, workers' children were organized into "regular companies and divisions" and drilled every day in military formations with fife and drum bands, "with [a] precision equal, as many officers of the army stated, to some regiments of the line," wearing Roman-style uniforms of his design.[112] He wrote that the "execution of combined movements" was "calculated to produce regularity and order," appealing to children "through their amusements."[113] He also used military "emblems" to teach them grammar, with each part of speech personified by military rank; examples include General Noun "in his cocked hat, sword and double epaulettes," Colonel Verb, Corporal Adverb, and so on.[114]

But the mentality promoted by this vision proved to be its greatest influence on industry. Thomas Carlyle wrote of the industrial "regiments," noting that "'captains of industry' are the true fighters . . . and lead mankind in that great, and alone true, and universal warfare," whereas laborers were "noble workers, warriors."[115] Early railway executives and managers of large ports also adopted martial titles.[116] Karl Marx and Friedrich Engels noted this phenomenon, describing the condition of factory workers as that of "privates in the industrial army."[117]

The spirit of the martial paradigm—and especially of discipline—was also applied to other institutions in this era. The military model for police organizations is well known,[118] and from the end of the French wars, prisons also adopted a distinctively martial tone.[119] Other institutions likewise derived inspiration from the paradigm; for example, a private madhouse proprietor thought his attendants' sense of duty should be like that of soldiers.[120]

Individuals were also attracted by the military paradigm as a method for promoting social order and personal discipline in a troubling era; the most widespread use of this model was found in the gospel of self-help.[121] Samuel Smiles, that extremely influential, "do-it-yourself" Victorian educator, perceived military virtues as a major source of inspiration for the "correct" understanding of one's obligations in life, noting that "we often connect the idea of duty with a soldier's trust." Smiles included almost seventy pages of exemplary military and naval heroes in *Duty*, and gave many examples in his other books, such as *Character* and *Self-Help*.[122] For Smiles, too, this vision's power was infectious, and its echo reverberates in his prose: "These soldiers—who are ready to march steadily against volleyed fire, belching cannon—or to beat their heads against bristling bayonets . . . were once tailors, shoemakers, mechanics, weavers and ploughmen; with mouths gaping, shoulders stooping, feet straggling, arms and hands like great fins hanging by their sides; but now their gait is firm and martial, their figures are erect and they march along to the sound of music, with a tread that makes the earth to shake."[123]

For him the truest duty was purely mechanical, and, ideally, individuals were to give no thought to their own interests: "Duty in its purest form is so constraining that one never thinks, in performing it, of ones self at all . . . It has to be done without any thought of self-sacrifice . . . The truest source of enjoyment is found in the paths of duty alone."[124] Thus

155

underlings were not to allow themselves the luxury of claiming any credit for their work, and labor was to be so innately satisfying that it would constitute a worker's greatest source of pleasure. In this view, any dispute over workplace conditions or wages would be nothing less than disloyalty toward the sanctity of labor itself, as well as treason against the quest for victory in the momentous economic battles of the industrial revolution.

But the influence of the military model was broader still, being applied in other, less combative contexts, and its echoes are to be found in some rather unexpected places. After Waterloo, Sunday schools were inspired to use military titles for participants, with superintendent "colonels," inspector "majors," teacher "captains," and monitor "sergeants"; the best pupils were "corporals." Often the "sets of rules were extraordinarily extensive."[125] Military discipline was idealized and imitated by the entertainment world, too; an opera conductor was called by his musicians "a duke of Wellington amongst us, and I believe perfectly aware of the fact, for he always called us his *troops;* and under admirable discipline we were."[126]

Even domestic life was touched with this spirit. In the most popular of the nineteenth-century housekeeping advice books, Mrs. Beeton informs her readers that "as with the commander of an army, or the leader of any enterprize, so it is with a house." Her next book mentioned "standing orders," "inspections," "orders for the day," and stressed "regularity and order."[127]

This ideal provided a model for Britons in a variety of other contexts, too, and applied equally to different duties, such as church-going, paying taxes, philanthropy, or family obligations. Progress in resolving social problems was slow at best, and individuals had little control over such concerns (however optimistic the spirit of the age). This mindset encouraged people to believe that they could exert some command over their confusing and disturbing surroundings.

Although the adoption of martial terminology suggests that the military paradigm was used to repress unproductive or undutiful behavior, by the time of the Crimean War, the martial model appears to have represented for some a vision for coping with life's problems. It could promote feelings of honor, or enthusiasm for trying to overcome difficulties, with positive reinforcement provided by the vision's charisma. This reinforcement value did not diminish after 1856; indeed, the "glamour of uniform and weapons and so on only multiplied from the post-Crimean reforms."[128] But it appears that the vision was most effective when its inspirational and entertainment features were present.

The military virtues were stressed by organizations in which participation was not only a duty but a pleasure. A noteworthy example for the period after 1859 is the amateur soldiers of the volunteer movement. To attract potential recruits, the volunteers relied on the appeal of participating in the military spectacle, for its "reviews and parades were as much a public spectacle and pageant as a military exercise."[129]

But the volunteers show how military discipline affected the participants' attitudes and behavior in civilian life. "The world of the factory was reproduced on the parade ground"[130] and inspired these amateurs "with habits of order, silence, obedience, cleanliness, punctuality and courtesy," in the hope that "the toils of the countinghouse, the warehouse and the shop would be undertaken in a new spirit of dutiful delight."[131]

The new values could also instill political obedience, as the *Times* pointed out: "The man who enters a volunteer regiment cannot, even if he would, escape the influence of *esprit de corps*. He is enlisted at once on the side of 'order'; he may have been inclined to disorder, or even to sedition, but when he becomes a soldier, a citizen soldier, he feels that he has ranged himself on the opposite side to all disturbers of society."[132] Thus martial values served not only to curb actions and ideas considered undesirable by the state and the status quo—and encourage acceptance of the new work ethic—but also to foster allegiance to the political system promoting these images.

Likewise, the military drill adopted by British schools in the 1870s was also thought to have beneficial economic effects by enhancing productivity. Edwin Chadwick believed that "with such training . . . three might eventually do the work of five," and school boards liked the fact that drill enhanced discipline.[133] The inspirational nature of the example must have been of incalculable value as well; though the duke of Wellington did not actually say that Waterloo was won on the playing fields of Eton, people believed that he had. It is also significant that military heroes in this era were sometimes said to have been more accomplished athletes at school than had actually been the case, and fallen soldiers are still venerated in the public schools today, with inscriptions that echo the values of martial virtue.[134]

These military values were also perceived as useful in combating the "chaos and irreligion" of the great cities, and many saw them as a model of organization designed to protect the young from moral contamination. "A strong belief in the abstract value of regular military drill and military organization," which was thought to promote high moral standards and protect the young from the corruption of city life, was a direct inspiration for the creation of the Boys' Brigade of the 1880s.[135]

Martial management techniques were employed to help those who needed reformation from their evil ways, and the idea of boot-camp "shock" treatment administered to incarcerated juvenile offenders is not new. *Punch* noted in 1863 that the "young thieves" undergoing reformation at the Middlesex Industrial School at Feltham were "marshalled by word of command, and marched to their bread and cocoa with the precision of [the Brigade of] Guards. They . . . sang grace to the sharp orders of the master." Corporal punishments were "administered by a tall muscular drill-master, who has, I believe, been in the army."[136]

William Booth's Salvation Army is a better-known example of the power of the martial inspiration as a weapon in the war against moral decay. Booth adopted most of the panoply of the spectacle, including uniforms, a system of ranks, flags, and marching bands, and organized parades that drew as many as fifty thousand marchers.[137] This was merely a later version of Carlyle's vision that the army provided an admirable model for confronting and solving a variety of difficult social problems: "O Heavens, if we saw an army ninety-thousand strong, maintained and fully equipt, in continual real action and battle against human starvation, against chaos, necessity, stupidity, and our real 'natural enemies,' what a business it were! Fighting and molesting not 'the French' . . . but fighting and incessantly spearing down and destroying falsehood, nescience, delusion, disorder, and the devil and his angels!"[138]

Inherent in these visions was the belief that British society suffered from a growing social divisiveness that was dangerous to the status quo. One of the greatest appeals of the military image was that it could help one triumph over evil or one's enemies, because it promoted harmony and unity of purpose, qualities that were more appealing than ever before. These attractions seized Dickens's Mr. Pickwick when he was watching the review, for "nothing could have . . . harmonized so well with the particular feeling of each of his companions as this sight," whereas Mr.

Snodgrass felt moved by deep-seated emotions that found lyrical expression: "In [his] bosom a blaze of poetry was rapidly bursting forth."[139]

Admiration of this harmonious vision drew a much more serious response from the poet and writer Rudyard Kipling, inspiring a short story in which unity is forged from the sharp discords of early-twentieth-century British society. "The Army of a Dream" (1904) presented the notion that an idealized, English national unity could be created through the acceptance of military service for all young men, with encouragement from a rule that only those who had served could vote. In the story, military drill was taught in school from the first years, and as Kipling's biographer points out, it "shows army organization deliberately used to alter the social structure by encouragement of the efficient and the officer type." But he also points out that the utilization of military spectacle was the most effective part of this social manipulation, for "nothing has done more . . . to reconcile the ordinary city-dwellers to the new national life than the privilege of free military funerals for all and the free spectacle of seeing so many cortèges pass in the streets." Thus in this "ideal state . . . all classes pull together," and the powerful have lost their exalted status.[140]

This vision of harmony, in which society was free of discord, everyone had his own place, and the whole moved and functioned with efficiency, precision, and order, constituted a denial of conflict, doubt, and defeat.[141] This was a potent attraction in an age beset by many bitter and destructive conflicts: between labor and management, the poor and the rich, country and city, and the old and the new. The use of the martial model by those who desired social harmony was not solely based on the order, discipline, and stability inherent in military institutions, however; the army was also noted for a tradition of heroic self-sacrifice in the defense of the realm.

This ideal, in which hardship was endured for higher goals than mere profit, was particularly attractive for those who felt that the traditional aristocratic virtues of generosity and disdain for money-grubbing were being ignored by the growing entrepreneurial interests. Critics such as Carlyle believed that disregard for traditional values highlighted the pettiness of the all-consuming goal of personal gain and explained why society was so "painfully decadent": "With our present system of individual mammonism, and government by laissez-faire, this nation cannot live." Carlyle condemned the state's civilian supporters as "an empty semblance"; the "highest king's-cloaks, mere chimeras . . . getting unsightly, almost offensive, like a costlier kind of scare-crow's blanket." The horse-hair wig-wearing jurist was "a sort of failure; no substance," and from "the shovel-hat (minister) who comes forward professing that he will save my soul" Carlyle wanted only "absolute silence." He contrasted these institutional failures with the army: "In such universal down-rushing and wrecked impotence of almost all old institutions, this oldest fighting institution is still so young!"[142]

The seductive attraction of the martial vision, and the political and economic conditions that had helped to generate this appeal, thus tended to encourage the adoption of the image and its values by many who wished to create a more just, equitable, and humane alternative to the economic and political status quo. It would be a mistake to assume that only those who supported the status quo admired and were influenced by the values the imagery represented, for the utility of the management dimension fostered by the paradigm cannot easily be separated from the values that were advertised. The army veteran Robert Blatchford, the editor of the early-twentieth-century socialist periodical *Clarion*, admired the army as a model for society, writing that "the drilling of masses of men together makes a community of thought and feeling; makes a crowd into a regiment, makes a rabble into a nation."[143]

The spectacle's compelling power could sometimes even delude its viewers, convincing fervent admirers that it embodied traits quite different from those actually seen. Dickens noted this power to instill self-delusion in enthusiastic spectators by Mr. Snodgrass's reaction to the review; he convinced himself that the soldiers' faces were "beaming—not with warlike ferocity, but with civilized gentleness: their eyes flashing—not with the rude fire of rapine or revenge, but with the soft light of humanity and intelligence." Although Mr. Pickwick "entered into the spirit of this eulogium," he could not quite agree, observing that "the soft light of intelligence burned rather feebly in the eyes of the warriors, inasmuch as the command 'eyes front' had been given; and all the spectator saw before him was several pairs of optics staring straight forward, wholly divested of any expression whatsoever."[144]

Smiles cultivated a similar delusion when he wrote that the discipline of army service would render the British people more "sober"—a most dubious claim in light of the soldiers' reputation for drunkenness. Similarly, he mistook the mechanistic, psychological imprinting of drill for "education": "Wonderful is the magic of drill! Drill means . . . education." Yet in the army itself, education was considered suspect and even dangerous.[145] More remarkable still is that for the socialist Robert Blatchford, this innately dehumanizing aspect of the martial image was transformed into something very different: "The drilling of masses of men together . . . develops in men a new faculty of humanism."[146] That this technique of domination and dehumanization could be equated with "humanism" highlights the image's facility for delusion, obscuring the actual substance that lay behind the carefully regulated facade. Much of this influence is explained by the facility of drill to reinforce powerfully the sense of solidarity.[147] This was the most important influence of the military paradigm on civilian life. This new management tool fostered a sense of empowerment, a feeling of strength through unity and *esprit de corps*, while obscuring the fact that in reality this sense of solidarity was directed not by its members but by the state. Here is a magic of great and subtle power.

This magic is a management art, to impress the "ruder sort of men [with] some attraction which seems to transcend reality, which aspires to elevate men by an interest higher, deeper, wider than that of ordinary life." This was the aspect of state power that Walter Bagehot described as "theatrical . . . that which is mystic in its claims; that which is occult in its mode of action; that which is brilliant to the eye; that which is seen vividly for a moment, and then is seen no more; that which is hidden and unhidden; that which is specious, and yet interesting."[148] Linda Colley, in discussing the transformation of the British monarchy's spectacle in the eighteenth and early nineteenth centuries, mentions "the evolution of a new kind of royal magic and mystique [requiring] romance, glamour, irrationality, and unconditional devotion."[149]

Although such management techniques have existed in various forms at least as long as the state itself, Carlyle noted that in the nineteenth century, the emergence of "Huge Democracy, walking the streets everywhere in its sack coat" created new difficulties in this ancient management art, for "no man is, or can henceforth be, the brass-collar thrall of any man." He thus advised those who ruled: "You will have to bind him by other far nobler and cunninger methods. Once [and] for all, he is to be loose of the brass-collar, to have a scope as wide as his facilities are." In the long run, this would be beneficial for those who ruled; Carlyle asked rhetorically: "Will he not be all the usefuler to you, in that new state? Let him go abroad as a trusted one, as a free one; and return home to you with rich earnings at night! [He] will build cities, [and] conquer waste worlds."[150]

And conquer he did, bringing the martial model with him to the Third World, where its organizational advantages were utilized, perhaps to an even greater extent than at home. The military paradigm was frequently applied in the colonies by administrators (often ex-soldiers) and missionaries. But the remarkable extent of its pervasive and appealing character in imperialist circumstances is highlighted by its voluntary adoption by some of the victims of imperialism, whose social, spiritual, and political institutions were severely damaged or destroyed by colonialism.

In colonial British Trinidad in 1808, slaves in predominantly French districts organized themselves into *convois*, such as the Convoi de St. George, and "regiments," including the "Regiment Danois" (composed of slaves from the Danish West Indies), that imitated state and martial organization. Each group had adopted the concept of a state structure, with a king, a queen, and high officials, as well as soldiers and police. The colonial governing council held a special meeting to investigate these groups as a revolutionary threat.[151] In colonial Kenya, a black church adopted a system of uniforms and ranks, reportedly "without any instruction or intervention from any white man."[152] Thus, as in the case of those organized Britons who opposed the policies of the state, centralizing economic and political forces tended strongly to encourage such groups to adopt the organizational techniques and appearance of their enemies.[153] The necessity of this model of military organization for conventional warfare in fighting a modern, state-sponsored army is shown by the fate of the United Irishmen of 1798. Many sources stress the rebels' poor discipline; William Maginn believed their defeat was due in large part to poor organization and serious discipline problems.[154] A private of the Ninety-second Highlanders noted of the Catholic peasantry (witnesses to the particularly harsh military discipline in the British army): "When they had been persuaded by those who stirred them up to rebellion, that they were slaves, and that they would obtain freedom by rising in arms, they could not see the consistency of this, without submitting to the slavery of being drilled like the soldiers. 'We are a sovereign people—we are free—

we will not be drilled like those slaves of [the] government, the red coats.' After the French landed, the majority who were equipped with arms, accoutrements and clothing, deserted as soon as the French began to drill them."[155]

When imperialism became a significant theme in British popular culture in the late nineteenth century, the influence of the military imagery's symbolisms broadened in scope. These were reflected on the stage, in literature, children's playthings, and advertising, and have been well documented.[156] In the realm of dress, military uniforms had primarily influenced high fashion in the early 1800s, but by the late nineteenth century many of the traditional occupational costumes signifying a worker's job and status were transformed into uniforms and subtly changed into an image of duty. This was especially true for workers who labored under the auspices of an institution or large-scale enterprise, or who had to uphold a public image. Examples include railway employees, messenger boys, undertakers, lift-boys, and mad-house attendants.[157]

The Boy Scouts (a successor to the Boy's Brigade) utilized uniforms and the martial model, but in the group's creation there was a close identification with the values of militarism. This was merely a further development of the mid-Victorian concept of "Muscular Christianity."[158] Tom Hughes, the author of *Tom Brown's Schooldays*, wrote: "From cradle to the grave, fighting, rightly understood, is the business, the real, highest, honestest business of every son of man."[159]

By the early twentieth century, the notion of never-ending war was implicit in the mind of the Boy Scouts' founder, General Robert Baden-Powell, and his book *Scouting for Boys* (1908) was based upon a militaristic view of life: "War . . . constitutes the central metaphoric conception of the vision of human life implicit in the book . . . and a set of assumptions that place struggle and violence of all kinds squarely at the heart of things." Smiles's ideas about dedication to work also appear in the book, but in the context of war: "Be prepared to die for your country . . . not caring whether you are going to be killed or not."[160]

One strand of this can be found in Carlyle's visions, but the issue for him was much broader than the proper training of the empire's youth—he wanted to resolve the agony of his age, and to reconcile democracy with authority. For him, the central question was: "How, in conjunction with inevitable democracy, indispensable sovereignty is to exist." Carlyle be-

lieved this was "certainly . . . the hugest question ever heretofore pro-
pounded to mankind!" He predicted "organisms enough in the dim huge
future; and 'United Services' quite other than the redcoat one; and much,
even in these years, struggling to be born!" What Carlyle foresaw in his
redcoat vision was for him "interesting," yet its dark side was also clear:
"Strange . . . most mournful . . . was this then, of all the things mankind
had some talent for, the one thing important to learn well, and bring to
perfection; this of successfully killing one other?"

Perhaps it was also the idea of human beings' working like machines
that led him to assert that "the soldier is perhaps one of the most difficult
things to realize."[161] By the latter part of his life, Carlyle believed that he
had finally found the answer for the society he so criticized; this included
his belief in the importance of the heroic leader, the "man of genius," part
of a concept that one scholar has described as "a kind of totalitarian and
fascist program."[162]

As a political philosophy, the twentieth-century cult of fascism com-
bines the worship of both the state and the machine-rooted values of the
military. This belief system is inconceivable without its panoply of images—broadened from the martial paradigm—in which great importance
is accorded to the visual messages communicated by uniforms, mass ral-
lies, and parades. Indeed, fascism can be seen as the application of the
military machine paradigm to all society: to economic, cultural, political,
artistic, social, intellectual, and educational endeavors.[163]

Yet despite the fact that display has always been impressive and imposing in the British army, fascism has had a rather limited appeal in Britain,
where the traditional suspicion of armies and soldiers has by no means
disappeared (although fascism appears to be growing in the youth culture
of the Western world). The significance of military imagery as a cultural
phenomenon and managerial paradigm in the British case is thus to a
degree ironic. That the former army officer and Labour MP Sir Oswald
Mosely and his British Union of Fascists were unsuccessful in appealing
to Britons highlights the irony of the British case, but also reemphasizes
the universality of the military paradigm as a means of organization and
control.

In this respect, the military paradigm in Britain has been shaped with
an eye toward accommodating the traditional fear and dislike that Britons
have felt toward standing armies, protected as they were from a sea-borne

invasion by the strength of the Royal Navy. The British army's image has thus tended to be less coercive and more appealing than that of its continental counterparts, especially Germany and Russia, where the political systems have traditionally been more authoritarian, the potential for invasion greater, and the public belief in the absolute necessity of maintaining large armies stronger. The influence of the military paradigm in British life, the experience of two world wars, and improved material conditions for the working class and the poor since 1914, however, have forged closer ties between the British people and the army than perhaps at any time since the standing army first emerged in the seventeenth century.

In 1800 Britons, like their American cousins, hated and feared the sight of soldiers, but since the nineteenth century, the world has witnessed much economic and political change. In the process, this pervasive organizational paradigm has endured—and even proliferated—as a machine-rooted vision of reality.

Conclusion:
The Martial Vision

T he imagery and spectacle of the British army is a symbolic vision that has elicited a fascination from Britons and significantly influenced the values and attitudes of both soldiers and civilians in the nineteenth century. For the military, this influence was pervasive. Beguiled by the spectacle, young recruits entered into the harsh and coercive environment of the army, where imagery became intrinsic to every aspect of their lives. They experienced it in the clothing and equipment they wore every day, in the rituals and ceremonies in which they participated, in how they addressed other soldiers, and even in the way they carried themselves.

The spectacle was decisive in army management. With so many reasons for common soldiers to loathe their situation, to mutiny, to sympathize with rioters at home, or to flee from battle, the imagery was essential for maintaining order and discipline. The British army was very successful in this period; it fought an almost uninterrupted series of campaigns between 1800 and 1856, expanding and policing an empire that became the largest the world had ever seen. Despite occasional defeats by well-organized and formidable enemies, vast areas of territory were brought under British authority. At the same time, in spite of frequent civil disorders at home and occasional minor mutinies and insubordination, the army neither suffered any great disaster nor caused the government any major problems.

This achievement is all the greater considering that the army was always kept to a minimal number, often fewer than were necessary to ensure the safety of the state. Moreover, its administration was noted for inefficiency, complexity, and sometimes disorganization. Given the conditions of the service, the successful management of this military machine would have been considerably more difficult—if not impossible—without the visual and physical influence of the imagery.

The martial management art combined drill and discipline with other factors, and was then embellished and enhanced by the style of the dress and equipment to make a colorful, visually arresting image. This art was a fundamental dimension of all military routines, and the display was designed to make the maximum impact upon viewers and participants. Those in authority made continual adjustments through the medium of military fashion, using the artistic strokes of form and color to maintain an aesthetic effect that would elicit the desired response.[1]

This was a game played by those in military authority as a dimension of governing, a tactic of control that was intrinsic to the wielding of power over this deadly institution. Success was gauged by the reactions the images elicited, by the degree to which they influenced emotion, implanted the desired thoughts and fantasies, and generated a favorable response from the audience. Although the art involved in creating this spectacle may seem superficial or even childish in its appeal, the show's conspicuous character masked effects that could be subtle, and even those who at once saw through it might still be affected by its power.

Like the royal ritual and ceremony of which it was a part, military spectacle made "the greatest impression by appealing to some vague dream of glory, or empire, or nationality. [Some men] will sacrifice all they hope for, all they have, themselves, for what is called an idea—for some attraction which seems to transcend reality, which aspires to elevate men by an interest higher, deeper, wider than that of ordinary life [for images] which appeal to the senses, which claim to be embodiments of the greatest human ideas."[2] This connection highlights what C. Wright Mills has called the "master symbol," which is "rarely simple" and includes "complex combinations of many elements, each with a different emotional and intellectual charge, appealing in different ways to different kinds of people, and often imperfectly. Hence 'their use to justify . . . the arrangement of power in a society.'"[3]

Raymond Firth points out that Kingsley Martin's analysis of the British monarchy in *The Crown and the Establishment* harmonizes well with this notion, but the "master symbol" concept applies equally well to the army, which was both created and influenced by the monarchy. Firth's description of the British monarchy as a "master symbol" reads like an analysis of army spectacle: "The manipulation of this master symbol by the power hierarchy . . . had the effect, with many people, of reconciling them with an existing power structure to a greater degree. Yet some people were alienated, by what seemed to them needless waste of resources, or mystic jargon, or pandering to public sensationalism. The symbolic relevance of the ceremony was not exhausted by interpreting it simply in power terms; it had aesthetic and moral interest even for many who rejected the assumptions of power distribution built into it."[4]

Like the royal show, this military version of the master symbol was intended for everyone. To many ordinary citizens, the army symbolized Britain's power and greatness, appealing to deep-seated emotions about the ultimate superiority of the British people and state. By viewing the spectacle, civilians shared in the feelings of glory symbolized by the imagery. This effect was surprisingly pervasive; many a radical was just as proud of the army's many victories—especially Waterloo—as those Britons who were horrified at the idea of changing the economic and political status quo.

But the spectacle's impact transcends its capacity to stir patriotic emotions. Indeed, the appeal influenced culture and institutional organization, emphasizing qualities such as discipline and order, hierarchy, conformity, efficiency, solidarity, and *esprit de corps*, which were much admired in this realm with its growing population, overcrowded and burgeoning cities, and an expanding industrial economy. These values were straightforward and simple yet powerful and compelling. The soldiers who advertised them through their dress and their posture represented—and literally embodied—the notion of power, for the purpose of the army was to threaten or destroy human life and property with the most dangerous weapons available.[5]

These values possessed less appeal in pre-industrial British societies, where the ancient, smaller-scale patterns of family and community life had provided great incentives for voluntary cooperation. But as the ubiquitous functions of these older groups were gradually reduced and superseded by economic and political centralization, and the population increased, a larger-scale organizational method that could dominate, direct, and coordinate the labor of great numbers of people replaced the ancient ways of work and life.

It therefore became essential for those who wielded power to do their utmost to ensure that the human components in the new, proliferating institutions worked efficiently. To achieve success for the new masters of business, they had to adapt to new patterns of labor, which would maximize workers' effectiveness on the job and attempt to counteract any feelings of alienation and discontent.

But most workers were not taken in, and this vision by no means succeeded to the extent that its admirers would have liked. As Eric Hobsbawm has noted, the new, bigger scale of industry "tended to fall back on the only available models of large-scale management, the military and bureaucratic . . . Yet it did not solve the problem of keeping labour itself at work, loyally, diligently, and modestly."[6]

The fundamental conflict between workers and owners and the accompanying social problems that arose have been called the growing pains of industrialization, as if this period was simply a transition to a better world. But these dilemmas of modernization have continued to plague humanity; such are the effects and consequences of the centralization of economic and political power. For this fundamental change in work, culture, belief, and mentality, the problems of organization and management have been—and remain—a major challenge. In this predicament, the values displayed by the military machine advertised an inspiring model of order and organization directed by an elite.

Not everyone embraced or even liked the martial show, and there were always critics who condemned the spectacle as both a base form of indoctrination and a waste of money. But as the patterns of modernization continued to develop, and wars continued periodically to reemphasize and reinvigorate the martial example, people began to apply the spirit of this vision, and the mentality it fostered, to their attempt to solve the multiplying social problems of their age. Its ability to inspire participants and spectators transcended the vision's negative effects, and ordinary people were influenced by it and sometimes persuaded to accept voluntarily the values and ideas embedded in the martial paradigm—despite the fact that it condemned the overwhelming majority of them to positions of subservience.

Perhaps it was the forceful yet artful combination of orderly and mechanistic values that rendered the martial paradigm so attractive, even to the state's domestic opponents. The martial model's associations with strength, organization, solidarity, and discipline were not only useful but essential for any group attempting to challenge the power of the British state. But in adopting the military paradigm these groups were tacitly admitting that they were compelled to utilize a system of control and organization that, though unique in certain respects, used the same organizing principle as the army.[7]

The spirit of the paradigm is merely one manifestation, however spectacular, of Mumford's larger megamachine.[8] Other inspirations for the megamachine's values have derived from a wide variety of sources that have proliferated over the centuries, and these have appeared in many contexts, including the worlds of government, science, art, architecture, leisure, belief, and religion. Not the least of these was—and is—the industrial machine itself and the ways it has operated. In one example of such an application, the disapproval voiced by respectable middle-class critics of disorderly, rough-and-tumble, traditional English sports emphasized the Puritan values of "regularity, orderliness, sobriety, providence and dutifulness [reflecting] a general regard for individual and social discipline" that aided the needs of "industry . . . the linchpin of English progress."[9]

Such examples thus advertised the same powerful message embedded in the paradigm of the megamachine. From the nineteenth century, this force has intensified and eventually become of primordial importance, profoundly influencing and shaping human culture, belief, experience, and action. As Marx and Engels observed as early as 1847, bourgeois culture "is for the enormous majority, a mere training to act as a machine."[10]

In his analysis of the megamachine and armies, Mumford noted some of the developments pioneered by the military in the early modern era: "The regimentation and mass production of soldiers, to the end of turning out a cheap, standardized, and replaceable product, was the great contribution of the military mind to the machine process." But though he stated that "the first important by-product of this transformation was the military uniform itself," he overlooked the symbolic and charismatic role of the uniform and other elements of military spectacle as aesthetic factors promoting the logic and values of the megamachine.[11]

The hierarchical and fundamentally authoritarian political structure intrinsic to the megamachine appears to be essential for all large-scale institutions, and has often been manipulated to promote—and disguise—the aims and values of those in power. Although such powerbrokers may claim to uphold egalitarian principles, this ideal is difficult to achieve and maintain because hierarchy and discipline are inherent in such institutions.

In this regard, the significance of the military model extends far beyond Britain and its empire. With the expansion of Western economic and political systems in the last few centuries, this vision of management and control has become a major factor in the mentality of the modern world, and central to the structure and organization of institutions in virtually every country, and intrinsic to the organization of power in all modern states.

All state-sponsored armies utilize these principles and are organized and displayed in fundamentally the same way, regardless of political, ethnic, or ideological circumstances. The westernization of non-European states has also been characterized first and foremost by the necessity to upgrade military strength, as in Russia, the Ottoman Empire, Egypt, and Japan, and the adoption of the outward image of the European art of war has always been a significant factor.[12]

Thus the values symbolized by the martial machine have triumphed. Although such details as the styles of dress featured in the martial show have continually evolved, the fundamental principles advertised by the larger megamachine remain essentially the same, exerting their impact by advertising a set of values that constitute both a mechanistic, organizational metaphor and a paradigm with an importance that is nothing short of primordial in its impact upon the modern world.

Because the paradigm has the ability to foster loyalty, it can be of vital importance in a crisis. When conflict in the workplace or great political instability looms, and there is widespread stress and mass suffering, if a large enough segment of the workforce or public remains loyal to the economic and political status quo, due in part to their acceptance of the paradigm's symbolic values, then successful large-scale upheaval may be thwarted by the economic and political elite, in a manner similar to the paradigm's impressive capacity to induce soldiers to stay loyal at critical moments.

The ability of the military model to promote a particular set of values has thus become even more relevant in the twentieth century. The public is now presented—or rather, constantly bombarded—with carefully crafted images of reality as a fundamental dimension of both economic and political life. This manipulation of public opinion has intensified with the emergence and proliferation of broadcast media as a primary source of public information.

This is a significant factor in modern politics. As society becomes more complex, the importance of such images—especially symbols—in the political context is enhanced. As David Kertzer has observed, "Living in a society that extends well beyond our direct observation, we can relate to the larger political entity only through abstract symbolic means. We are, indeed, ruled by power holders whom we never encounter except in highly symbolic presentations."[13]

Such images may seem far afield from the martial show, yet the military spectacle, too, was intended to convince people to accept and embrace that which may not have been in their best interests. Much of political image-making consists of manipulating the public's perceptions of politicians or policies. In this process, the presentation of these images is also a form of advertising in which the images are carefully crafted to depict only those factors intended for the public to absorb and accept. The presentation of more complete terms—of different sides of an issue—is carefully avoided, because the public may perceive additional information as in some way detrimental to their own best interests, and might thus reject and resist adopting the intended response.

In the context of modern politics, the manipulation of such images finds its purest form in fascism. This political philosophy might well be considered the touchstone of all modern, mass-scale political management, regardless of ideological content. The origin of the modern concept of citizenship is here relevant; Charles Tilly in *Popular Contention in Great Britain, 1758–1834*, quotes Linda Colley: "In Great Britain, as in other major European powers, it was training in arms, under the auspices of the state that was the most common collective working-class experience in the late eighteenth and nineteenth centuries, not labour in a factory, or membership of a radical political organization or an illegal trade union." Tilly continues: "Through the increasingly visible presence of the tax collector, the recruiting sergeant, the militia commander, the press gang, and the Member of Parliament, ordinary British people acquired much more extensive direct contact with the state than they had experienced since the revolutionary period of 1640–1660. This time it lasted."[14] This military dimension to the origins of the modern British concept of citizenship and organization, and the increased contact of ordinary Britons with the state, are significant. They raise further questions about the degree to which militarization and martial culture are intrinsic factors that have shaped—and continue to shape—modern life.

The political factor is thus linked with the martial paradigm in the context of management, and I interpret this form of state influence as a kind of "magic," but in a particular sense. One definition of "magic" in the Oxford English Dictionary states: "a secret and overmastering influence resembling magic in its effects."[15] Indeed, one of the earliest functions of the monarch—the human embodiment and focal point of the state—was that of magician, and this ancient role has, like so many aspects of monarchy, not entirely disappeared. It remains in the altered form of royal ritual and ceremony, together with the other trappings of majesty.[16]

In the modern context, this much older form of magic, this persuasion (or propaganda), has transmuted, or been modernized, into a technique of rule and management essential for political and economic elites wishing to retain their power in a democratic polity. In the contemporary United States, this technique is especially important for presidential politics and the shaping of foreign policy.

Martial values thus continue to both represent and advertise an instructive vision for the organization and management—and especially discipline—of any hierarchical group or institution. Since the Middle Ages this has only intensified, as have the complexities of interconnection and interdependency in the world, and wealth has become concentrated in fewer hands. These trends have affected Britain, Europe, and now the entire world, and it does not appear that their influence will diminish in the immediate, foreseeable future. As long as they continue, the machine-rooted paradigm for war, statecraft, disciplinary organization, and domination will continue to be useful—and essential—to those who wield power.

BIBLIOGRAPHY

NOTES

ACKNOWLEDGMENTS

INDEX

BIBLIOGRAPHY

Sources for this study have included both visual and historical material, but the most important sources by far have been soldiers' memoirs, recollections, collected letters, and autobiographies and autobiographical novels. This large body of primary material has been supplemented by a variety of additional sources, including civilians' letters and memoirs, military and civilian journals, military handbooks, polemics on martial subjects, and novels, poems, and stories. War Office and regimental *Standing Orders*, orderly books, unpublished letters by soldiers, and both army and Parliamentary reports have also been included. The *Journal of the Society for Army Historical Research* (hereafter *JSAHR*) has been a valuable source of information. All titles cited in the Bibliography and the Notes retain their original spelling and punctuation.

ARCHIVAL SOURCES
British Library

BL ADD MSS 27,597, *Sir D. Dundas' Report on Army Clothing, Etc.*, 1810/11
BL ADD MSS 32,468, "Journal of the Campaign in Portugal, by John Westcott, late Master of the Band, 1st Battalion, 26th or Cameron Regiment of Foot; 1811–12," ff. 120
BL ADD MSS 35,060, Rowland Hill Papers
BL ADD MSS 37,878, Windham Papers
The Francis Place Newspaper Collection

Henry E. Huntington Library

HEH MS ST 151, John Foster, "The Private Soldier's Monitor, or Pocket Companion in Three Parts"
HEH MS, *2nd Regt. Buckinghamshire Hussars Regimental Order Book*, Print Box 216/60

Home Office Papers

H.O. 41/5/274, 41/5/298-9, 41/7/416, 50/11

National Army Museum

NAM MSS 7,309-53, Orderly Book of Captain William Russel, 20th Regiment of Foot, February 17–May 12, 1809

NAM 7,311-6-1, *Standing Orders of the 15th Regiment of Foot* (1813-45)

NAM MSS 7,311-6-2, Orderly Book owned by John Humphreys, 15th Regiment of Foot, November 1, 1813–December 1830

NAM 8,301-81, Paybook of Private John Hurd, 19th Lancers, September 1816–December 1819

National Library of Scotland

NLS MSS Brown Correspondence, 1,863, 1,866-1,868, *Standing Orders and Regulations for the 85th Light Infantry* (London, 1813)

NLS MSS 2,869, 2,873-2,875, Regimental Orders, 2nd Battalion, Rifle Brigade (1824-1841)

William Wilson Papers MSS 9,667-9,669

Parliamentary Papers

Hansard's Parliamentary Debates

"Report of the Select Committee on Army and Navy Appointments: with Minutes of Evidence and Appendix" (London, 1833). Reprint ed.: Irish University Press Series of British Parliamentary Papers. *Report from the Select Committee on the Establishment of the Garrisons and on the Pay and Emoluments of Army and Naval Officers with Minutes of Evidence and Appendix: Military and Naval*, 2 vols. (London, 1833; reprint ed., Shannon: Irish University Press, 1969)

The Royal Archives

Accounts of King George IV, GEO ADD. 15 Box, nos. 1,697-1,779

MSS 29,518, 29,524-5, 29,535, 29,540-1, 29,543, 29,545-6, 29,548, 29,560, 29,568-71, 29,578, 29,612-3, 29,615, 29,619-20, 2,622, 29,640

Royal Fusiliers Archive

Files G/18, H/6, P/15, P/Powley, S/13

Standing Orders of the 4th Battalion The Royal Regiment of Fusiliers (Dublin, 1906)

Scottish Record Office

Orders for the Assistance and Guidance of Non-commissioned Officers of the 1st Battalion, the 79th Regiment (Colchester, n.d.), GD/174/2315

Royal Scottish United Services Museum Archive

RSUSM MSS q 355.486 * 213.2, "Scots Greys Regimental Papers . . . Waterloo and Crimean Campaigns." DRESS .826.1, Box no. 35, MSS Notes on the Evolution of Uniform, 47th Regiment, S. M. Milne, 1891, 01.812.1 Box no. 10, File F.G. 856.1
Standing Orders of the Seventy-Fourth Highlanders (London, 1850)

War Office Papers

General papers, correspondence, orders:
W.O. 3/20, 3/365, 3/376, 3/611, 5/1, 5/56, 27/193, 33/68, 33/210, 34/103, 43/739, 43/741, 44/608, 50/11
Special reports on clothing and accoutrements:
W.O. 7/56–59, Clothing Board Reports: Board of General Officers and the Cavalry Board
W.O. 33/15, Report of the Committee Appointed to Inquire Into the Present System of Carrying the Accoutrements, Ammunition and Kit of Infantry Soldiers and Drill Etc., of Recruits

MILITARY PERIODICALS

Cavalry Journal
Colburn's United Service Magazine
Military Magazine
Military Panorama
Military Register
Naval and Military Magazine
United Services Journal/Journal of the Royal United Services Organization

CIVILIAN PERIODICALS

Annual Register
Athenaeum
Blackwood's Magazine
Chamber's London Journal
Douglas Jerrold's Shilling Magazine
Douglas Jerrold's Weekly Newspaper

Fraser's Magazine
Gentleman's Magazine
John Bull
London Packet and Lloyd's Evening Post
New Monthly Magazine and Literary Journal
Poor Man's Guardian
Punch
Times

PRINTED PRIMARY SOURCES

Adams, Buck. *The Narrative of Private Buck Adams, 7th (Princess Royal's) Dragoon Guards on the Eastern Frontier of the Cape of Good Hope, 1843–48*. Edited by A. Gordon Brown. Cape Town: W. J. Van Riebeeck Society Publications, 1941.

The Adjutant. *Memoranda for the Officers of the Scots Fusilier Guards*. [1836].

———. *Life As I have Found It*. Edinburgh, 1883.

Aitchison, Lt. John. *An Ensign in the Peninsular War: The Letters of John Aitchison*. Edited by W. F. K. Thompson. London: Michael Joseph, 1981.

Alexander, James E[dward]. *Narrative of a Voyage of Observation Among the Colonies of Western Africa . . . and of a Campaign in Kaffir-land . . . in 1835*. 2 vols. London, 1837.

———. *Passages in the Life of a Soldier; or Military Service in the East and West*. 2 vols. London, 1857.

Anderson, Lt.-Colonel Joseph [Jocelyn]. *Recollections of a Peninsular Veteran, by the late Lt.-Colonel Joseph Anderson, C.B., Knight of Hanover, of the 78th, 24th, and 50th regiments (1805–1848)*. London: Edward Arnold, 1913.

Anstruther-Thomson, Colonel [John]. *Eighty Years' Reminiscences*. 2 vols. London: Longmans, Green and Co., 1904.

Anton, James. *Retrospect of a Military Life, during the most eventful periods of the Last War*. Edinburgh, 1841.

Arbuthnot, Harriet. *The Journal of Mrs. Arbuthnot, 1820–1832*. 2 vols. Edited by Francis Bamford and the Duke of Wellington. London: Macmillan, 1950.

Armstrong, William. *Observations upon Corporal Punishments in the British Army*. London, 1834.

Army and Navy ABC. Dean's Movable Books, n.p., n.d.

Austin, Harry. *Guards Hussars and Infantry. Adventures of Harry Austin*. 3 vols. London, 1838.

Austin, Jane. *The Complete Novels of Jane Austin*. Vol. 1: *Pride and Prejudice*. New York: Vintage, 1976.

Aytoun, Pvt. James. *Redcoats in the Caribbean*. Lancashire: Blackburn Recreation Services Department (U.K.), 1984.

Bamford, Samuel. *Passages in the Life of a Radical.* Oxford: Oxford University Press, 1984.

Bayly, Colonel [Richard]. *Diary of Colonel Bayly, 12th Regiment, 1796–1830.* London, 1896.

Beeton, Mrs. [Isabella]. *Beeton's Every-Day Cookery and Housekeeping Book.* London, 1865; facsimile ed., London: Gallery Books, 1984.

———. *The Book of Household Management.* London, 1861; facsimile edition, London: Jonathan Cape Ltd., 1968.

[Bell, Major-General George]. *Rough Notes by an Old Soldier, during Fifty Years of Service.* 2 vols. London, 1867.

Best, Abel D. W. *The Journal of Ensign Best: 1837–1843.* Wellington, New Zealand: R. E. Owen, Government Printer, 1966.

Betting Book of the Second Battalion (78th) Seaforth Highlanders, 1822–1908. N.p.: By the [Officers'] Mess, 1909.

Blake, Alice Elizabeth. *Memoirs of a Vanished Generation: 1813–1855.* New York: J. Lane, 1909.

Blatchford, Serg. Robert. *My Life in the Army.* London: The Clarion Press, 1910.

Bodell, Serg. James. *A Soldier's View of Empire: The Reminiscences of James Bodell.* Edited by Keith Sinclair. Toronto: The Bodley Head, 1982.

Boswell, James. *The Life of Samuel Johnson.* 2 vols. New York: J. M. Dent, 1925.

Brock, William. *A Biographical Sketch of Sir Henry Havelock, K.C.B.* London, 1857.

Browne, Captain Thomas Henry. *The Napoleonic War Journal of Captain Thomas Henry Brown, 1807–1816.* Edited by Roger Norman Buckley. London: The Bodley Head, 1987.

Bulwer, Edward Lytton. *England and the English.* London, 1833. Reprint ed.: New York: University of Chicago Press, 1970.

Bunbury, Colonel Thomas. *Reminiscences of a Veteran.* 3 vols. London, 1861.

Bunbury, Lt-General Henry E. *Memoir and literary remains of Lieutenant-General Sir Henry Edward Bunbury, Bart.* Edited by Charles J. F. Bunbury. Privately Printed. London, 1868.

Burgoyne, General Sir John Fox. *Aide-Mémoire to the Military Sciences. Framed from Contributions from Officers of the Different Services, and Edited by a Committee of the Corps of Royal Engineers.* London, 1853.

———. *Life and Correspondence of Sir John Burgoyne, Bart.* 2 vols. Edited by Lieutenant-General Sir George Wrottesley. London, 1873.

———. *The Military Opinions of General Sir John Burgoyne.* Edited by Capt. George Wrottesley. London, 1859.

Burke, Edmund. *Edmund Burke on Taste, on the Sublime and Beautiful, Reflections of the French Revolution, A Letter to a Noble Lord.* Edited by Charles W. Eliot. New York: Collier, 1909.

Bustin, W. R. *A Militia; Its Relation to the Regular Army. The Unjust, Partial, and Oppressive Nature of the Old System. A New System Developed, and Its Tendencies.* London, 1847.

Butler, Serg. Robert. *Narrative of the Life and Times of Serjeant Butler.* Edinburgh, 1854.

Byfield, Pvt. Shadrack. "A Common Soldier's Account." In *Recollections of the War of 1812: Three Eyewitness Accounts.* Toronto: Baxter Publishing Co., 1964.

Byron, George Gordon. *Byron: Poetical Works.* Edited by Frederick Page. New ed. Oxford: Oxford University Press, 1970.

———. *Byron's Letters and Journals.* Edited by Leslie A. Marchand. 8 vols. Cambridge, Mass.: Harvard University Press, 1971–1978.

Cadell, Lt.-Colonel Charles. *Narrative of the Campaigns of the 28th Regiment since their return from Egypt in 1802.* London, 1835.

Calladine, Serg. George. *The Diary of Colour-Sergeant George Calladine, 19th Foot, 1793–1837.* Edited by M. L. Ferrar. London: E. Fisher & Co., 1922.

Campbell, Colonel James. *The British Army as It Was, Is, and Ought to Be.* London, 1840.

Capadose, [Lt.-Colonel] John. *Sixteen Years in the West Indies.* 2 vols. London, 1845.

Capel, Caroline. *The Capel Letters: Being the Correspondence of Lady Caroline Capel and her daughters with the Dowager Countess of Uxbridge from Brussels and Switzerland, 1814–1817.* Edited by the marquess of Anglesey. London: Jonathan Cape, 1955.

Carey, "Tupper." "Reminiscences of a Commissariat Officer." Reprinted from *The Scabbard: Journal of the Military Miniature Society of Illinois.* March 1991.

Carlile, Richard. "A New Years Address to the Reformers of Great Britain." In *Address to the Reformers of Great Britain.* London, 1821.

Carlylye, Thomas. *Past and Present.* Edited by Richard Altick. New York: New York University Press, 1977.

———. *Sartor Resartus.* London, 1831. Reprint ed.: New York: Chelsea House, 1983.

Cathcart, Lt-General Sir George. *Correspondence of Lieut.-General The Hon. Sir George Cathcart, K.C.B., Relative to the Military Operations in Kaffraria, until the Termination of the Kafir War, and to His Measures for the Final Maintenance of the Protection and Welfare of the People of South Africa.* London, 1856. Reprint ed.: New York: Negro Universities Presses, 1969.

Cavalry Officer. *The Whole Art of Dress or, The Road to Elegance and Fashion at the Enormous Savings of 30%!!! Being a Treatise Upon that Essential and Much Cultivated Requisite of the Present Day, Gentlemen's Costume.* London, 1830.

Chelsea Pensioner [sergeant, Fifteenth Hussars]. *Jottings from My Sabretache.* London, 1847.

Cockburn, Henry. *Memorials of His Time.* Edited by Karl F. C. Miller. London: University of Chicago Press, 1974.

Connolly, Serg. T[homas] J. W. *The Romance of the Ranks, or Anecdotes, Episodes and Social Incidents of Military Life.* 2 vols. London, 1859.

Conway, Derwent [H. D. Inglis]. *Personal Narrative of a Journey through Norway, Part of Sweden, and the Islands and States of Denmark.* Edinburgh, 1829.

Cooper, Captain T[homas] H. *A Practical Guide for the Infantry Officer.* Reprint eds., London, 1806; London: Redwood Press Ltd., 1970.

Cooper, Thomas. *The Life of Thomas Cooper.* Edited by John Saville. London, 1872. Reprint ed.: New York: Leicester University Press, 1971.

Costello, Edward. *Edward Costello: The Peninsular and Waterloo Campaigns.* Edited by Anthony Brett-James. Hamden, Conn.: Archon Books, 1968.

Cozens, Cpl. Charles. *Adventures of a Guardsman.* London, 1848.

Cree, Dr. Edward H. *The Voyages of Dr. Edward H. Cree, Royal Navy, as Related in His Private Journals, 1837–1856.* Edited by Michael Levian. New York: E. P. Dutton, 1982.

Creevey, Thomas. *The Creevey Papers.* Edited by John Gore. London: J. Murray, 1970.

————. *The Creevey Papers: A Selection from the Correspondence & Diaries of the Late Thomas Creevey, M.P.* 2 vols. Edited by Sir Herbert Maxwell. New York: J. Murray, 1903.

————. *Creevey's Life and Letters: A Further Selection from the Correspondence of Thomas Creevey.* Edited by John Gore. London: J. Murray, 1934.

Cumming, Lt. James Slator. *A Six Years Diary.* London, 1847.

Davenport, Major H. M. *The Life and Recollections of E. M. Davenport.* London, 1869.

De Ainslie, Colonel C[harles] P[hillip]. *The Cavalry Manual.* 3d ed. London, 1858.

de Ros, Colonel Lord W. L. L. *The Young Officer's Companion; or, Essays on Military Duties and Qualities.* London, 1851.

de Vigny, Alfred. *The Military Condition.* Translated by Marguerite Barnette. London: Oxford University Press, 1962.

Dickens, Charles. *The Posthumous Papers of the Pickwick Club.* London, 1849. Reprint ed.: New York: A. I. Burt & Co., n.d.

————. *Sketches By Boz.* London: Oxford University Press, 1957.

Dickson, Major-General Sir Alexander. *The Dickson Manuscripts: Being Letters, Maps, Account Books, with various Other Papers.* 5 vols. Edited by Maj. John Leslie. Woolich: Royal Artillery Institute, 1905–1908. Reprint ed.: Cambridge: Ken Trotman, 1987–1991.

Documents Relating to the Invasion of Canada and the Surrender of Detroit, 1812. Edited by Ernest A. Cruikshank. Ottawa, 1912. Reprint ed.: Arno Press, 1971.

[Donaldson, Joseph]. *Recollections of an Eventful Life, Chiefly passed in the Army.* Glasgow, 1824.

Douglas, Pvt. William. *Soldiering in Sunshine and Storm.* Edinburgh, 1865.

Doveton, Captain Frederick B[rickdale]. *Reminiscences of the Burmese War in 1824–5–6.* London, 1852.

Dunlop, William. *Tiger Dunlop's Upper Canada [Recollections of the American War, 1812–1814].* Edited by Carl F. Klink. Toronto: McClelland and Stewart, 1967.

Dupin, Major Charles. *View of the History and Actual State of the Military Force of Great Britain.* 2 vols. London, 1822.

D'Urban, General Sir Benjamin. *The Peninsular War Journal of Major-General Sir Benjamin D'Urban . . . 1808–17.* Edited by I[zac] J. Rousseau. London: Longman, 1930.

Dyneley, Lt-General Thomas. *Letters Written by Lieut.-General Thomas Dyneley C. B., R. A., While on Active Service Between the Years 1806 and 1815.* Arranged by Col. F. A. Whinyates. Reprint ed.: London: Ken Trotman, 1984.

Dyott, General William. *Dyott's Diary, 1781–1845, a selection from the journal of William Dyott, sometime general in the British army and aide-de-camp to His Majesty King George III.* Edited by Reginald W. Jeffery. 2 vols. London: Archibald Constable Ltd., 1907.

Elers, Captain George. *Memoirs of George Elers, Captain in the 12th Regiment of Foot.* New York: D. Appleton and Co., 1903.

[Farmer, George]. *The Light Dragoon.* Edited by George Gleig. 2 vols. London, 1844.

Fergusson, James. *Notes and Recollections from a Professional Life.* London, 1846.

Fernyhough, Captain [Thomas]. *Military Memoirs of Four Brothers, natives of Staffordshire, engaged in the service of their Country, as well as in the New World and Africa, as on the Continent of Europe.* Rev. ed. London, 1838.

Finan, P[atrick]. *Journal of a Voyage to Quebec, in the year 1825, with Recollections of Canada during the late American War, in the Years 1812–13.* Newry, 1828.

[Fletcher, Sergeant John]. *Advice to the British Soldier, by a non-commissioned officer.* London, 1839.

Gawler, Lt.-Colonel George. *The Essentials of Good Skirmishing.* 2nd ed. London, 1852.

George III. *The Later Correspondence of George III.* Edited by A. Aspinall. 5 vols. Cambridge, England: Cambridge University Press, 1962–1970.

George IV. *The Correspondence of George, Prince of Wales 1770–1812.* Edited by A. Aspinall. 8 vols. Oxford: Oxford University Press, 1970.

———. *The Letters of King George IV 1812–1830.* 3 vols. Cambridge: Cambridge University Press, 1938.

Gibney, [William]. *Eighty Years Ago or The Recollections of an Old Army Doctor: His Adventures on the Field of Quatre Bras and Waterloo and During the Occupation of Paris in 1815.* Edited by Maj. R[obert] D. Gibney. London, 1896.

Gleig, Chaplain-General George [Robert]. *A Subaltern in America.* Philadelphia, 1833.

————. *The Subaltern: a Chronicle of the Peninsular War.* London, 1825. Reprint ed.: London: Leo Cooper, 1970.

Godman, Captain Richard Temple. *The Fields of War: A Young Cavalryman's Crimea Campaign.* Edited by Philip Warner. London: John Murray, 1977.

Gordon, Lt. Hugh. *The Journal of Lieutenant Hugh Gordon . . . April 26, 1814– February 20, 1816.* Edited by John M. Bulloch. Aberdeen, 1912.

Gough, John B. *Autobiography and Personal Recollections of John B. Gough.* Springfield, Mass., 1870.

Gowing, Serg-Major Timothy. *A Voice from the Ranks: A Personal Narrative of the Crimean Campaign by a Sergeant of the Royal Fusiliers.* Edited by Kenneth Fenwick. London: The Folio Society, 1954.

Graham, William. *Travels Through Portugal and Spain, During the Peninsular War.* London, 1820.

Grant, General Sir Hope. *Life of General Sir Hope Grant with Selections from his Correspondence.* Edited by Henry Knollys. 2 vols. Edinburgh, 1894.

Grattan, Lt. William. *The Duke of Wellington and the Peninsular Medal.* London, 1845.

Great Britain, Adjutant-General's Office. *Addendum to the General Regulations and Orders for the Army: Being a Continuation of the Collective Orders Dated 12th August, 1811.*

————. *Addendum to the Orders and Regulations of His Majesty's Army . . . January, 1820–1830.*

————. *General Regulations and Orders for the Army.* London, 1811.

————. *General Regulations and Orders for the Army.* London, 1811, with added Regulations to January 1, 1816.

————. *Rules and Regulations for the Formation, Field-Exercise, and Movements of His Majesty's Forces.* London, 1798.

————. *A Series of Figures shewing all the Motions in the Manual and Platoon Exercises, and the Different Firings, According to His Majesty's Regulations.* London, 1828. Reprint ed.: Bloomfield, Ontario: Museum Restoration Service, 1965.

————. *Sixth Report of the Commissioners of Military Enquiry.* London, 1808.

Great Britain, Horse Guards. *Abridgement for His Majesty's Regulations for Yeomanry Cavalry.* London, 1838.

————. *Instructions to Officers Employed on the Recruiting Service.* 1806.

Great Britain, House of Commons. Select Committee on Army and Navy Appointments. Chapter 2, no. 54.

Great Britain, War Office. *A Collection of Orders, Regulations, and Instructions for the Army on Matters of Finance and Points of Discipline.* London, 1807.

————. *Historical Record of the Eleventh, or The North Devon Regiment of Foot; Containing an Account of the Formation of the Regiment in 1685, and its Subsequent Services to 1845.* London, 1845.

Green, John. *The Vicissitudes of a Soldier's Life, or a Series of Occurrences from 1806 to 1815 . . . the Whole Containing a Concise Account of the War in the Peninsula.* Louth, 1827.

Grenadier Guards Regimental Orders for Battalions and Detachments, when on the March on Home Service. London, 1830.

Greville, Charles C[avendish] F[ulke]. *The Greville Memoirs, 1814–1860.* Edited by R. Fulford and L[ytton] Strachey. 8 vols. London: Macmillan & Co., 1938.

————. *The Greville Memoirs: A Journal of The Reigns of King George IV and King William IV.* 3 vols. Edited by Henry Reeve. 5th ed. London: Longmans, Green & Co., 1875.

[Grenville-Murray, E. C.]. *Six Months in the Ranks, or the Gentleman Private.* London, 1883.

Earl Henry Grey, ed. *The Reform Act, 1832: The Correspondence of the late Earl Grey with His Majesty King William IV and with Sir Herbert Taylor.* 2 vols. London, 1867.

Gronow, [Captain Rees Howell]. *The Reminiscences and Recollections of Captain Gronow: Being Anecdotes of the Camp, Court, Clubs and Society, 1810–1860.* 2 vols. London: John C. Nimmo, 1900.

[Grose, Captain Francis]. *The Mirror's Image: Advice to the Officers of the British Army.* 6th ed. London, 1867.

————, compiler. *Dictionary of the Vulgar Tongue. A Dictionary of Buckish Slang, University Wit, and Pickpocket Eloquence.* London, 1811; facsimile ed., London: Bibliophile Books, 1984.

The Guards: A Novel. 3 vols. London, 1827.

Hall, J. H. W. *Scenes in a Soldier's Life.* Montreal, 1848.

Hanger, Colonel George. *Reflections on the Menaced Invasion.* London, 1804. Facsimile ed., London: Paul P. B. Minet, 1972.

Hardbargain, Henry [pseud.]. *Hints to the Subalterns of the British Army.* N. p., 1843.

Hardy, Serg. John. *Statement of the Services of Sergeant John Hardy 7th Royal Fusiliers.* London, 1865.

Hardy, Thomas. *The Trumpet-Major.* London, 1880. Reprint ed.: Harmondsworth, Middlesex, 1984.

Harley, Captain John. *The Veteran, or Forty Years in the British Service: comprising adventures in Egypt, Spain, Portugal, Belgium, Holland and Prussia.* 2 vols. London, 1838.

Harness, Captain William. *Trusty and Well Beloved: The Letters of William Harness, an Officer of George III.* Edited by Caroline M. Duncan-Jones. London: S. P. C. K., 1957.

Harris, James Howard, Earl of Malmsbury. *Memoirs of an Ex-Minister: an Autobiography.* 2 vols. London, 1884.

Harris, Pvt. John. *The Recollections of Rifleman Harris, as told to Henry Curling.* Edited by Christopher Hibbert. London: Century, 1985.

Henegan, Sir Richard [D.]. *Seven Years Campaigning in the Peninsula and the Netherlands, from 1808 to 1815.* 2 vols. London, 1846.

Hennell, Lt. George. *A Gentleman Volunteer: The Letters of George Hennell from the Peninsular War, 1812–1813.* Edited by Michael Glover. London: Heinemann, 1979.

Henry, Walter. *Events of a Military Life: Being Recollections after Service in the Peninsular War, Invasion of France, the East Indies, St. Helena, Canada, and Elsewhere.* Revised ed. 2 vols. London, 1843.

Hill, Captain Benson Earle. *Home Service; or, Scenes and Characters from Life, at Out and Headquarters.* 2 vols. London, 1839.

————. *Playing about; or, Theatrical Anecdotes and Adventures, with Scenes of General Nature, from the Life; in England, Scotland, and Ireland.* 2 vols. London, 1840.

————. *Recollections of an Artillery Officer: including Scenes and Adventures in Ireland, America, Flanders and France.* 2 vols. London, 1836.

Hints to Aspirants for the Army, and Young officers on Appointment. London, 1840.

A Hit at the Tenth. London, 1824.

Hobhouse, John Cam (Lord Broughton). *Recollections of a Long Life, by Lord Broughton, with additional extracts from his private diaries.* Edited by Lady Dorchester. 6 vols. London: J. Murray, 1909–1911.

Hodge, Colonel Edward Cooper. *'Little Hodge'. Being Extracts from the diaries and letters of Edward Cooper Hodge, written during the Crimean war, 1854–1856.* Edited by George C. H. V. Paget, marquess of Anglesey. London: Leo Cooper, 1971.

Huish, Robert. *An Authentic History of the Coronation of His Majesty, King George the Fourth: with a Full and Authentic Detail of the August Solemnity; an Account of all the Interesting Proceedings; the Adjudication of the Court of Claims, and an Historical Account of the Origin of the Court; A Full and Original Detail of the Regalia, and Other Important Particulars connected with that Magnificent Ceremony.* London, 1821.

Hume, Maj.-General John R[ichard]. *Reminiscences of the Crimean Campaign with the 55th Regiment.* London, 1894.

"Inventor of Military Figures for Elucidation of Cavalry Movements." *Remarks on the Proper Regulations for the Instruction, Formation and Movement of Cavalry.* London, 1832.

Jackson, Inspector-General Sir Robert. *An Outline of Hints for the Political Organization and Moral Training of the Human Race.* Edinburgh, 1823.

————. *A View of the Formation, Discipline and Economy of Armies.* 3rd ed., revised. London, 1845.

Jackson, Lt.-Colonel Basil. *Notes and Reminiscences of a Staff Officer, chiefly relating to the Waterloo Campaign and to St. Helena matters during the captivity of Napoleon.* London: J. Murray, 1903.

Jackson, Thomas. *Recollections of My Own Life and Times.* Edited by B. Frankland. London, 1847.

James, Major Charles. *A New and Enlarged Military Dictionary*. London, 1810.

————. *The Regimental Companion, containing the Pay, Allowances and Relative Duties of Every Officer in the British Service*. 4 vols., 7th ed. London, 1811–1813.

James, Sir Alexander. *Passages in the Life of a Soldier*. 2 vols. London, 1857.

Jefferies, Serg. Julius. *The British Army in India: Its Preservation*. London, 1858.

Jerdan, William. *The Autobiography of William Jerdan . . . with his literary, political and social reminiscences and correspondence during the last fifty years*. 4 vols. London, 1852–1860.

[Jones, Lt. Charles]. *Cavalry in the Corunna Campaign (as told in the diary of the adjutant of the 15th Hussars)*. Edited by Maj. Lord Carnock [Frederick A. Nicolson]. *JSAHR* Special publication no. 4. London, 1936.

Jones, Lt. Rice. *An Engineer Officer under Wellington in the Peninsula*. Edited by H. V. Shore. Reprint ed.: Cambridge, England: Ken Trotman Ltd., 1986.

Jones, Maj.-General Sir John T[homas]. *A Journal of the Sieges Carried on by the Army under the Duke of Wellington in Spain: 1811–14*. 3rd ed. 3 vols. London, 1846.

King, Captain William Ross. *Campaigning in Kaffirland; or Scenes and Adventures In The Kaffir War of 1851–2*. London, 1853.

Knight, Charles. *Passages of a Working Life during half a century: with a prelude of Early Reminiscences*. 3 vols. London, 1864–1865.

Law, Edward [Lord Ellenborough]. *A Political Diary, 1828–1830*. Edited by Lord Colchester. 2 vols. London, 1881.

Lawrence, Sgt. William. *The Autobiography of Sergeant William Lawrence, A Hero of the Peninsular and Waterloo Campaigns*. London, 1886. Reprint ed.: Cambridge: Ken Trotman Ltd., 1987.

Lawson, George. *Surgeon in the Crimea: The Experiences of George Lawson Recorded in Letters to his Family, 1854–1855*. Edited by Victor Bonham-Carter. London: Military Book Society, 1968.

Leach, Lt-Colonel J[ohnathan]. *Rambles Along the Banks of the Styx*. London, 1847.

————. *Rough Sketches of the Life of an Old Soldier*. London, 1831.

Le Couteur, Lt. John. *Merry Hearts Make Light Days: The War of 1812 Journal of John Le Couteur, 104th Foot*. Edited by Donald E. Graves. Ottawa: Carleton University Press, 1994.

Leeves, John. *Leaves from a Victorian Diary*. London: Secker & Warburg, 1985.

Lennox, Lord William Pitt. *My Recollections from 1806 to 1873*. 2 vols. London, 1874.

"Letter to *Lord Castlereagh*, Found Near His Lordship's House, in St. James's Square." London, 1820.

[Lewin, Maj. Henry Ross]. *Life of a Soldier. A Narrative of Twenty-Seven Years' Service . . . By a Field Officer*. 3 vols. New ed. London, 1834.

Lighton, Pvt. William B. *Narrative of the Life and Sufferings of Rev. William B.*

Lighton; Containing an Interesting and Faithful Account of His early Life, and Enlistment into the British Army. Rev. ed. Boston, 1844.

Lloyd, General Henry. *A Political and Military Rhapsody, on the Invasion and Defence of Great Britain and Ireland.* 6th ed. London, 1803.

Long, Lt.-General Robert Ballard. *Peninsular Cavalry General, 1811–13. The Correspondence of Lieutenant General Robert Ballard Long.* Edited by T. H. McGuffie. London: Harrap, 1951.

Lovett, William. *The Life and Struggles of William Lovett in His Pursuit of Bread, Knowledge, and Freedom; with some Short Account of the Different Associations He Belonged to, and of the Opinions He Entertained.* London, 1876.

Lysons, General Daniel. *Early Reminiscences . . . With Illustrations From the Author's Sketches.* London, 1896.

Macaulay, Lord [Thomas Babington]. *The Life and Letters of Lord Macaulay.* Edited by Sir George Otto Trevelyan. Oxford: Oxford University Press, 1978.

Mackenzie, K. S. *Narrative of the Second Campaign in China.* London, 1842.

[MacMullin, Serg. John Mercer]. *Camp and Barrack-Room; or, The British Army as It Is.* London, 1846.

Macnamara, Ulysses. *The British Army: Condition at the Close of the Eighteenth Century, Compared with Its Present State and Prospects.* London, 1839.

[Maginn, William]. *The Military Sketch-Book. Reminiscences of Seventeen Years in the Service abroad and at Home.* 2 vols. London, 1827.

——. *Tales of Military Life.* 3 vols. London, 1829.

Marx, Karl, and Freidrich Engels. *The Communist Manifesto.* Translated by Samuel Moore. London, 1888. Reprint ed.: Baltimore: Penguin Books, 1967.

Mayhew, Henry. *London Labour and the London Poor.* 4 vols. New York: Dover Books, 1968.

——. *The Unknown Mayhew.* Edited by Eileen Yeo and E. P. Thompson. New York: Schocken Books, 1972.

McKay, Serg. James. *Reminiscences of the Last Kafir War.* 2nd ed. Cape Town: C. Struik (PTY) Ltd., 1970.

Menzies, Serg. John. *Reminiscences of an Old Soldier.* Edinburgh, 1883.

Mercer, General [Alexander] Cavalié. *Journal of the Waterloo Campaign, kept throughout the Campaign of 1815 by the late General Cavalié Mercer.* London: Praeger, 1970.

Metcalfe, Pvt. Henry. *The Chronicle of Private Henry Metcalfe, H.M. 32nd Regiment of Foot.* Edited by Francis Tuker. London: Cassell, 1953.

Mills, Ensign John. *For King and Country: The Letters of John Mills, Coldstream Guards, 1811–1814.* Edited by Ian Fletcher. Staplehurst, Kent: Spellmont, Ltd., 1995.

Mitchell, Maj.-General John. *Thoughts on Tactics and Military Organization: Together with an Enquiry into the Power and Position of Russia.* London, 1838.

Mitford, Mary Russel. *Our Village*. London, 1824. Reprint ed.: Philadelphia: Rogers Co., 190–?.

Montgomery, James. *The Carding and Spinning Master's Assistant: Or the Theory and Practice of Cotton Spinning*. Glasgow, 1832. Reprinted in Alfred D. Chanler, ed., *Precursors to Modern Management*. New York: Arno Press, 1979.

Moore, Thomas. *Memoirs, Journals and Correspondence of T. Moore*. Edited by Lord John Russel. 8 vols. London, 1853.

———. *The Works of T. Moore, Esq. Accurately Painted from the Last Original Editions*. Leipzig, 1826.

Morris, Serg. Thomas. *Recollections of Military Service in 1813, 1814, and 1815, through Germany, Holland and France, including Details of the Battles of Quatre Bras and Waterloo*. London, 1845.

[Morley, Serg. Stephen]. *Memoirs of a Sergeant of the 5th Regt. of Foot, Containing an Account of his Service in Hanover, South America, and the Peninsula*. Ashford, Kent, 1842.

Mountain, Colonel S. H. Armine. *Memoirs and Letters of the Late Colonel Armine S. H. Mountain*. Edited by Mrs. A. S. H. Mountain. London, 1858.

Napier, General Sir Charles J. *Remarks on Military Law and the Punishment of Flogging*. London, 1837.

Napier, General Sir William F. *A History of the War in the Peninsula and the South of France*. 5 vols. London, 1832.

———. *The Life and Opinions of General Sir Charles Napier*. 4 vols. London, 1857.

———. *Memorandum on the Government Plan for Monopolizing the Clothing, Accoutreing, Etc., of the Army*. London, 1856.

Narrative of a Private Soldier in His Majesty's 92nd Regiment of Foot, Written by Himself. 2nd ed. Glasgow, 1820.

Nightingale, Florence. *"I have done my duty": Florence Nightingale in the Crimean War, 1854–56*. Edited by Sue M. Goldie. Iowa City, Iowa: University of Iowa Press, 1987.

Nolan, Captain L. E. *Cavalry; Its History and Tactics*. London, 1853.

Nugent, Lady Maria. *Lady Nugent's Journal of Her Residence in Jamaica from 1801 to 1805*. Rev. ed. Edited by Philip Wright. Kingston: Institute of Jamaica, 1966.

O'Doodle, Sir Phelim [pseud.]. *The Subaltern's Check-Book*. London, 1848.

An Officer [Lt.-Colonel David Roberts]. *The Military Adventures of Johnny Newcome*. London, 1816. Reprint ed.: Methuen Co., 1904.

An Officer. *Observations on the Army, in which Its Embodying is Detailed, its Present State Described, and Sundry Practical Improvements Suggested*. London, 1825.

Officer of Hussars. *Cavalry: Remarks on Its Organization . . . Equipment and Instruction*. London, 1819.

The Officer's Manual in the Field; or, a Series of Military Plans, Representing the

Principal Operations of a Campaign. 2nd ed., 1800. Reprint ed.: New York: Greenwood Press, 1968.

One Who Has Kept A Diary [George William Erskine Russell]. *Collections and Recollections*. London, 1898.

Owen, Robert. *Essays on the Formation of Human Character*. London, 1840.

———. *A New View of Society and other Writings, by Robert Owen*. London: J. M. Dent & Sons, 1927.

Paget, Henry, First Marquess of Anglesey. *One-Leg: The Life and Letters of Henry William Paget, First Marquess of Anglesey, K.G., 1768–1854*. Edited by Henry Paget, Seventh Marquess of Anglesey. New York, 1961.

Lady Palmerston (Emily Lamb Cowper Temple). *The Letters of Lady Palmerston*. Edited by Tresham Lever. London, 1957.

Panmure, Lord (Fox Maule). *Panmure Papers*. Edited by Sir G. Douglas and Sir G. D. Ramsay. London: Hodder & Stoughton, 1908.

Parry, S[ydney] H[enry] Jones. *An Old Soldier's Memories*. London, 1897.

Patterson, Major John. *The Adventures of Captain John Patterson, with notices of the officers, etc., of the 50th . . . Regiment, from 1807 to 1821*. N.p., 1837.

———. *Camp and Quarters: Scenes and Impressions of Military Life*. 2 vols. London, 1840.

Pearman, Sgt. John. *The Radical Soldier's Tale: John Pearman, 1819–1908*. Introduced by Carolyn Steedman. New York: Routledge, 1988.

Pearson, Andrew. *The Soldier Who Walked Away: Autobiography of Andrew Pearson A Peninsular War Veteran*. Edited by Arthur Haley. Woolton, Liverpool: Bullfinch Pub., n.d.

Phillips, Henry. *Musical Recollections during Half a Century*. 2 vols. London, 1864.

Picton, Lt.-General Sir Thomas. *Memoirs of Lieutenant-General Sir Thomas Picton, G.C.B. etc.* Edited by H[eaton] B[owstead] Robinson. 2nd revised ed. 2 vols. London, 1836.

Plummer, Pvt. Samuel. *The Journal of Samuel Plummer, a Private in the 22nd Regiment of Foot*. Edited by John Riles. London, 1821.

Proceedings of the General Court Martial on the Trial of Captain Wathen, Fifteenth Hussars. London, 1834. Reprint ed.: London: Frederick Muller Ltd., 1970.

Proctor, Lt. G. *Lucubrations of Henry Ravelin, Esq.* London, 1823.

Pückler-Muskau, Prince Hermann. *A Regency Visitor: The English Tour of Prince Pückler-Muskau Described in his letters, 1826–1828*. New York: E. P. Dutton, 1958.

Ramsay, Lt.-Colonel Balcarres D. Wardlaw. *Rough Recollections of Military Service and Society*. 2 vols. Edinburgh, 1882.

Regimental Standing Orders of the Grenadier Guards. London, 1830–1.

Regulation for the Clothing of the Embodied Militia. London, 1803.

Reid, Douglas O. *Soldier-Surgeon: The Crimean War Letters of Dr. Douglas O. Reid,*

1855–1856. Edited by Joseph O. Baylen and Alan Conway. Knoxville, Tenn.: University of Tennessee Press, 1968.

Ridout, Thomas. *Ten Years of Upper Canada in Peace and War (the Thomas Ridout Captivity)*. Edited by Matilda Edgar. Toronto, 1890. Reprint ed.: Toronto: Coles Publishing Co., 1970.

Robertson, Colonel James P[eter]. *Personal Adventures and Anecdotes of an Old Officer, by Colonel James Robertson*. London: E. Arnold, 1906.

Robertson, Serg. D[avid]. *The Journal of Sergeant D. Robertson, late 92nd Foot: comprising the different campaigns, between the Years 1797 and 1818, in Egypt, Walcheren, Denmark, Sweden, Portugal, Spain, France and Belgium*. Perth, 1842.

Rolt, Colonel John. *On Moral Command*. London, 1842.

Rolt, Lt-Colonel Richard. *The Days When We had Tails on Us*. London, 1849.

———. *The Guards and the Bearskin Caps*. London, 1854.

———. *The Two Mounted Sentries*. London, 1850.

Rush, Richard. *Memoranda of a Residence at the Court of London, Comprising Incidents Official and Personal from 1819 to 1825*. Philadelphia, 1845.

———. *A Residence at the Court of London*. 1833. Reprint ed.: London: Century, 1987.

Ruskin, John. *Selections and Essays*. New York: Charles Scribners' Sons, 1946.

Russell, W[illiam] H. *The War: from the Landing at Gallipoli to the Death of Lord Raglan*. London, 1855.

Ryder, John. *Four Years' Service in India*. 2nd ed. Leicester, 1854.

[S., Tom]. *A Soldier of the Seventy-First: The Journal of a Soldier of the Highland Light Infantry, 1806–1815*. Edited by Christopher Hibbert. London, 1819. Reprint ed.: London: Leo Cooper, 1975.

Schaumann, August Ludolf Friedrich. *On the Road With Wellington: The Diary of a War Commissary in the Peninsular Campaigns*. Edited and Translated by Anthony Ludovici. New York: Alfred A. Knopf, 1924.

Scott, Sir Walter. *The Private Letter Books of Sir Walter Scott*. Edited by Wilfred Partington. London: Hodder & Stoughton, 1930.

Shelley, Percy Bysshe. *Shelley: Poetical Works*. Edited by Thomas Hutchinson. Oxford: Oxford University Press, 1970.

[Sherer, Captain Joseph Moyle]. *Recollections of the Peninsula*. 4th ed. London, 1825.

Shipp, Captain John. *The Military Bijou, or the Contents of a Soldier's Knapsack: Being Gleanings from Thirty-Three Years of Active Service*. 2 vols. London, 1831.

———. *The Path of Glory: Being the Extraordinary Military Career of John Shipp*. Edited by C. J. Stranks. London, 1829. Reprint ed.: London: Chatto & Windus, 1969.

Siborne, William. *Waterloo Letters*. London, 1891. Reprint ed.: Cassel & Co., 1983.

Simond, Louis. *An American in Regency England: The Journal of a Tour in 1810–1811.* Edited by Christopher Hibbert. London: History Book Club, 1968.

Sinnott, Lt. John. *A Manual of Light Infantry and Other Duties. Originally Compiled for the use of the Non-commissioned Officers of the Forty-seventh or Lancashire Regiment.* 2nd ed. London, 1851.

———. *A Military Catechism, Designed for the Use of the Non-Commissioned Officers and Others of the Infantry, and Adapted to the Revised System of The Field Exercises and Evolutions of the Army.* 6th ed. Portsmouth, n.d.

Smiles, Samuel. *Character.* New York, n.d.

———. *Duty, With Illustrations of Courage, Patience, and Endurance.* New York, 1881.

———. *Self-Help.* New York, n.d.

———. *Thrift.* New York, 1876.

Smith, Lt.-Gen. Sir Harry. *Autobiography of Lieutenant-General Sir Harry Smith, Baronet of Aliwal on the Sutlej, G.C.B.* 2 vols. New York: E. P. Dutton & Co., 1902.

The Soldier's Companion, or, Martial Recorder. London, 1824.

Somerville, Pvt. Alexander. *The Autobiography of a Working Man.* N.p., 1848. Reprint ed.: London: MacGibbon & Kee, 1967.

St. Clair, Colonel [Thomas Stoughton]. *A Soldier's Recollections of the West Indies and America, with a Narrative of the Expedition to the Island of Walcheren.* 2 vols. London, 1834.

Standing Orders as Given Out and Enforced by the Late General Robert Craufurd, for the Use of the Light Division During the Year 1809, 10 and 11. Corfu, n.d.

Standing Orders of the 4th Battalion The Royal Regiment of Fusiliers. Dublin, 1906.

Standing Orders of the Grenadier Guards for 1831. London, 1831.

Standing Orders of His Majesty's 1st Regiment of Life Guards. London, 1814 and 1827.

Standing Orders of His Majesty's 3d (or Prince of Wales's) Regiment of Dragoon Guards. Doncaster, 1818.

Standing Orders and Internal Regulations of the 3d Regiment of Guards. London, 1822.

Standing Orders and Maneuvers for the 2nd Battalion of His Majesty's 56th Regiment, Under the Command of Lieutenant Colonel Kingscote. Bombay, 1812.

Standing Orders, for the Seventh Light Dragoons. Ipswich, 1808.

Stanhope, Philip Henry, 5th Earl. *Notes of Conversations with the Duke of Wellington, 1831–1851.* London, 1888.

Steevens, Charles. *Reminiscences of My Military Life from 1795 to 1818.* Edited by Nathaniel Steevens. Winchester, 1878.

Stepney, Lt-Colonel Stepney Cowell. *Leaves from the Diary of an Officer of the Guards.* London, 1854.

Stevens, Charles. *Reminiscences of My Military Life from 1795 to 1818.* Edited by Nathaniel Steevens. Winchester, Hampshire, 1878.

Stockmar, Baron. *Memoirs.* London, 1872.

The Subaltern's Log-Book: Including Anecdotes of Well-Known Characters. 2 vols. Ridgeway, 1828.

Surtees, William. *Twenty-Five Years in the Rifle Brigade.* Edited by John Surtees. London: Muller, 1973.

Swabey, Lt. William. *Diary of Campaigns in the Peninsula, for the Years 1811, 12, and 13.* London: Ken Trotman, 1984.

Swanston, Serg. Paul. *Memoirs of Serjeant Paul Swanston; A Narrative of a Soldier's Life, in Barracks, Ships, Camps, Battles, and Captivity on Sea and Land; with Notices of the Most Adventurous of His Comrades.* London, 1840.

The Tailor's Complete Guide; or A Complete Analysis of Beauty and Elegance in Dress. London, 1796.

Taylor, Lt.-General Sir Herbert. *The Taylor Papers: Being a Record of Certain Reminiscences, Letters, and Journals in the Life of Lieut.-Gen. Sir Herbert Taylor G.C.B., G.C.H..* Arranged by Ernst Taylor. London: Longmans, Green and Co., 1913.

Taylor, Serg.-Major William. *Life in the Ranks.* London, 1843.

Thackeray, William Makepeace. *The Book of Snobs.* Garden City, N.Y.: Dolphin Books, 1961.

Thomas, George, Earl of Albemarle. *Fifty Years of My Life.* 2 vols. London, 1876.

Thompson, Lt.-Colonel T. Perronet. *Exercises, Political and Others.* 6 vols. London, 1842.

Thornton, James. *Your Most Obedient Servant: Cook to the Duke of Wellington.* Exeter: Webb & Bower, 1985.

Tocqueville, Alexis de. *Democracy in America.* vol. 1. New York: Vintage Books, 1954.

Tomkinson, Lt.-Colonel William. *The Diary of a Cavalry Officer in the Peninsular and Waterloo Campaigns, 1809–1815.* Edited by James Tomkinson. London, 1894.

Torrens, Colonel Arthur W. *Six Familiar Lectures for the Use of Young Military Officers.* London, 1851.

Tucker, John G. P. *Hints to Young Officers.* London, 1826.

Tulloch, Maj.-General Sir Alexander Bruce. *Recollections of Forty Years Service.* London: William Blackwood and Sons, 1903.

Vandeleur, Colonel John. *Letters of Colonel John Vandeleur, 1810–1846.* London, 1846.

Verner, William. *Reminiscences of William Verner (1782–1871), 7th Hussars. An Account of Service . . . Including the Battle of Waterloo.* Edited by Ruth W. Verner. *JSAHR* Special publication no. 8. London, 1965.

Victoria. *The Letters of Queen Victoria: A Selection of Her Majesty's Correspondence Between the Years 1837 and 1861.* Edited by Christopher Benson and Viscount Esher. 3 vols. London: J. Murray, 1908.

———. *Queen Victoria's Early Letters.* Rev. ed. Edited by John Raymond. New York: Macmillan, 1963.

[Wallace, Captain Robert C.]. *Forty Years in the World; or Sketches and Tales of a Soldier's Life.* 3 vols. London, 1825.

Warre, Gen. Sir William. *Letters from the Peninsula, 1808–1812.* Edited by Edmond Warre. London: J. Murray, 1909.

Waterfield, Pvt. Robert. *The Memoirs of Private Waterfield, Soldier in Her Majesty's 32nd Regiment of Foot (Duke of Cornwall's Light Infantry) 1842–57.* Edited by Arthur Swinson and Donald Scott. London: Cassell, 1968.

Wellington, Duke of (Arthur Wellesley). *The Despatches, Correspondence, and Memoranda of Field Marshal Arthur, the Duke of Wellington, K.G.* Edited by his son, the Duke of Wellington. 12 vols. London, 1834–1838.

———. *The Prime Minister's Papers: Wellington, Political Correspondence I: 1833— November 1834.* Edited by John Brooke and Julia Gandy. London: Her Majesty's Stationery Office, 1975.

———. *Supplementary Despatches and Memoranda of Field Marshall Arthur, Duke of Wellington.* Edited by his son, the Duke of Wellington. London, 1858–1872.

———. *Wellington and His Friends: Letters of the First Duke of Wellington to the Rt. Hon. Charles and Mrs. Arbuthnot, the Earl and Countess of Wilton, Princess Lieven, and Miss Burdett-Coutts.* Selected and Edited by the Seventh Duke of Wellington. London: Macmillan, 1965.

Wheatley, Edmund. *The Wheatley Diary.* Edited by Christopher Hibbert. London: Longmans, Green & Co., 1964.

Wheeler, Pvt. William. *The Letters of Private Wheeler, 1809–1828.* Edited by Capt. Sir B. H. Liddell Hart. Boston: Houghton Mifflin Co., 1951.

White, James. *Adventures of Sir Pumpkin Frizzle; Nights in the Mess and Other Tales.* Edinburgh, 1836.

Wolseley, General Sir Garnet. *The Story of a Soldier's Life.* 2 vols. London: A. Constable & Co. Ltd., 1903.

Wood, Captain George. *The Subaltern Officer: A Narrative.* London, 1825. Facsimile ed., Cambridge: Ken Trotman Ltd., 1986.

NOTES

Introduction: Army Life

1. Robert Blatchford, *My Life in the Army* (London: n.p., 1910), p. 140.
2. "An Officer," *Observations on the Army, in which Its Embodying is Detailed, its Present State Described, and Sundry Practical Improvements Suggested* (London, 1825), p. 26.
3. Sir John Fortescue, *A History of the British Army*, 13 vols. (London: Macmillan, 1921–1927), vol. 11, p. 34.
4. The guards did not usually serve outside Europe, but line officers with enough money could buy exchanges into another unit when theirs was posted to a deadly climate. There were also elitist prejudices against serving in places like India, and men of high social standing were often expected to avoid deadly climates unless they wanted to see action. Lord Cardigan's hounding "India officers" out of the Eleventh Hussars is a notorious example of this attitude. See Cecil Woodham-Smith, *The Reason Why* (New York: Dutton Books, 1960), Chapter 4.
5. Ensigns got 5s./3d. per day. *Report From The Select Committee on the Establishment of The Garrisons and on the Pay and Emoluments of Army and Naval Officers with Minutes of Evidence and Appendix: Military and Naval*, 2 vols. (London, 1833; reprint ed., Shannon: Irish University Press, 1969), vol. 1, p. 274.
6. "British Cavalry in the Peninsula," *United Services Journal* 2 (1833), p. 70.
7. Douglas O. Reid, *Soldier-Surgeon: The Crimean War Letters of Dr. Douglas O. Reid, 1855–56*, ed. Joseph O. Baylen and Alan Conway (Knoxville, Tenn.: University of Tennessee, 1968), p. 2. Surgeons wore less expensive dress than other officers, but cavalry dress could be very expensive. For a full discussion of the officers' conditions see Fortescue, *British Army*, vol. 11, pp. 30–43.
8. W. R. Bustin, *A Militia; Its Relation to the Regular Army. The Unjust, Partial, and Oppressive Nature of the Old System. A New System Developed, and Its Tendencies* (London, 1847), p. 16.

9. Quoted from the duke of Wellington, *The Dispatches, Correspondence, and Memoranda of Field Marshall Arthur, Duke of Wellington K.G.*, edited by his son, 12 vols. (London, 1834–1838), vol. 6, p. 575. Elie Halevy, *A History of the English People in 1815*, trans. E. I. Watkin (London, 1924; reprint ed., New York: Ark Paperbacks, 1987), p. 75. "Repeatedly [Wellington] castigated 'the habitual inattention of the officers of the regiments to their duty' and 'the utter incapacity of some officers at the head of regiments to perform the duties of their situation.'" Michael Howard, *Studies in War and Peace* (New York: The Viking Press, 1970), p. 54. In all fairness to the army, Wellington's scathing remarks were made after years of war had inevitably resulted in the relaxation of discipline.

10. An army term affirms this: "Covering Serjeants" stood behind officers during battalion exercises to prompt them on the correct words of command. J. H. Stocqueler, *Military Encyclopedia* (1853), cited by H. F. J. Burn, "Replies," *JSAHR* 17 (1938), p. 185. The satirical glossary in Henry Hardbargain, *Hints to the Subalterns of the British Army* (n.p., 1843), defines a noncomissioned officer as "a person whose duty it is to furnish the captains with the word of command on field-days." John Keegan's *Face of Battle* (New York: Vintage Books, 1983) devotes more than six pages to the importance of officers at Waterloo and rightly emphasizes their bravery, yet makes no mention of the widespread incompetence and indifference to duty that characterized many off the battlefield. Keegan also overlooks the vital role of the noncommissioned officers, who have been—and remain—the backbone of most armies.

11. Philip Henry, Fifth Earl of Stanhope, *Notes of Conversations with the Duke of Wellington, 1831–1851* (London, 1888), p. 18. Six wives per company traveled with the units, and most were married to noncommissioned officers. They received half-rations and their children received quarter-rations.

12. Wellington, *Dispatches*, vol. 11, p. 141.

13. T. H. McGuffie, "Recruiting the Ranks of the Regular British Army During the French Wars," *JSAHR* 34 (1956), p. 50. "Other Ranks" meant all below officer rank, and will be so used in this book.

14. During a long stint of service in India, a unit could be destroyed by sickness. In 1844, the Seventy-eighth Highlanders lost some seven hundred soldiers to fever while billeted at Karachi, and "scarcely one hundred men were able to march . . . and every one had suffered more or less from fever." [Serg. John MacMullin], *Camp and Barrack-Room: The British Army as It Is* (London, 1846), p. 243. Other dangerous postings were the West Indies, West and South Africa, and China. When Lord Cardigan purchased the Eleventh Hussars in 1835 they had been in India for sixteen years, by no means an unusually long posting. Donald Thomas, *Cardigan* (New York: The Viking Press, 1974), p. 63.

15. A typical parental reaction is recorded by a Scotsman who wrote that after telling his mother he had enlisted, she exclaimed: "Poor infatuated boy! . . . Now you are lost to us and to yourself." [Joseph Donaldson], *Recollections of an Eventful Life, Chiefly passed in the Army* (Glasgow, 1824), pp. 66–67. Yet service for Scotsmen was generally considered more respectable among poor but decent families, a holdover from the mercenary tradition. Scottish units were often run in a more humane fashion, and much of their distinguished reputation stems from the survival of aspects of the old clan tradition, a late European variation of a pre-state social system.

16. Fortescue, *British Army*, vol. 11, p. 13. Some soldiers' acute alcoholism was such that they might become indifferent even to these inadequate quantities of food; in one case, men were confined to barracks out of fear that they would sell their meager rations to buy drink and then starve. Donaldson, *Recollections*, p. 89. Perhaps no other example can show as forcefully just how bad a choice military service really was.

17. As late as the 1890s, men complained of perpetual hunger. See Alan Ramsay Skelley, *The Victorian Army at Home, The Recruitment and Terms and Conditions of the British Regular, 1859–1899* (Montreal: McGill-Queens, 1977), p. 65.

18. When the Rifle Brigade was stationed at Bermuda in 1841, coffee, milk, and sugar were provided with the bread for breakfast, the dinner of meat and bread was supplemented with onions, potatoes, salt and pepper, and a third meal, "coffee," included sugar, milk, and bread. NLS MSS 2,875, St. George, November 18, 1841.

19. Alexander Somerville writes of tasting roast beef for the first time at an inn while on the march. Pvt. Alexander Somerville, *The Autobiography of a Working Man* (n.p., 1848; reprint ed., London: MacGibbon and Kee, 1967), p. 139.

20. "The Bad Accommodation of Soldiers Billeted on Inns," *Military Panorama* (February 1813), p. 462. Yet when stationed at home repressing civil disorders after 1815, at which time they were usually on the road, many units were better accommodated. Loyalty was essential, and they were subject to many temptations to desert or mutiny. See Chapter 7.

21. Harry Hopkins, *The Strange Death of Private White* (London: Weidenfield and Nicolson, 1977), pp. 27–28. Contributing to the overcrowding was the fact that during the French wars the size of the army greatly increased and never returned to its pre-1793 level. The government was under great pressure to economize, and the disorders that accompanied the harsh conditions of industrialization forced the army to continue building barracks as cheaply as possible.

22. *Times*, February 6, 1858, cited in Skelley, *Victorian Army*, p. 33.

23. Edward M. Spiers, *The Army and Society, 1815–1914* (London: Longman, 1980), p. 56. Fortescue describes the sanitary arrangements in barracks as

"unspeakable." *British Army*, vol. 11, p. 10. Private Buck Adams of the Seventh Dragoon Guards wrote of barracks in South Africa in 1844 at the end of the army's "dark ages"; a water shortage resulted in "15 to 20 men in succession trying to wash their flesh in less than a half gallon of water which had the appearance of (HMS) *Rodney* pea soup." Buck Adams, *The Narrative of Private Buck Adams, 7th (Princess Royal's) Dragoon Guards on the Eastern Frontier of the Cape of Good Hope, 1843–48*, ed. A. Gordon Brown (Cape Town: W. J. Van Riebeeck Society Publications, 1941), p. 35.

24. Skelley, *Victorian Army*, p. 27.

25. Correlli Barnett, *Britain and Her Army, 1509–1970: A Military, Political and Social Survey* (Harmondsworth, Middlesex: Penguin Books, 1974), p. 241. This list of disadvantages is by no means exhaustive; only the worst examples are mentioned.

26. "Each man lost about 125 rations, which at five pence per ration would amount to £2 12s 1d, the whole sum (for the force) amounting to £13,020 16s 8d." Adams, *Narrative*, pp. 178, 258. "Necessaries" were those items needed for the upkeep of the kit, including brushes, pipeclay, underclothing, and so on.

27. Robert Waterfield, *The Memoirs of Private Waterfield*, ed. Arthur Swinson and Donald Scott (London: Cassell, 1968), pp. 143–144.

28. [Capt. Francis Grose], *The Mirror's Image: Advice to the Officers of the British Army*, 6th ed. (London, 1867), p. 75. First published in 1782, this went through a great many reprints and new editions into the 1870s, showing its continued relevance.

29. Donaldson, *Recollections*, p. 85.

30. Corporal Charles Cozens, *Adventures of a Guardsman* (London, 1848), pp. 44–64.

31. P.R.O., W.O. 25/1132–1144, cited in Philip Dwight Jones, "The British Army in the Age of Reform, 1830–1854" (Ph.D. thesis, Duke University, 1968), p. 26.

32. Most of these regulations are discussed in Fortescue, *British Army*, vol. 11, pp. 9–45.

33. Charles James, *The Regimental Companion*, 4 vols., 7th ed. (London, 1811–1813), vol. 1, p. xiii.

34. BL ADD MSS 27,597, "Sir David Dundus's Report of Army Clothing, Etc.," 1810–11, doc. 1, para. 23.

35. Ibid., doc. 2, Minutes of April 18, 1811, ff.28–29.

36. Colonel John Rolt, *On Moral Command* (London, 1842), p. 135.

37. Inspector-General Sir Robert Jackson, *A View of the Formation, Discipline and Economy of Armies* (London, 1845), p. 185.

38. This happened despite the fact that the War Office specifically forbade it: "No soldier shall be put under stoppages to pay for articles of clothing not

ordered by this warrant." W.O. 43/741 (May 1844), article no. 23, p. 22, Very Old Series, Secretary-at-War's Office, Miscellaneous Correspondence, Infantry Clothing Warrant. As will be shown, such attempts to prevent these practices in this era were largely futile.

39. The men's uniforms were made by his personal tailor. Thomas, *Cardigan*, p. 77.

40. A sergeant wrote: "I shall never forget the kindness of the old colonel (of the 13th Light Infantry) towards the sick . . . he brought them his own tea, addressed them in the most soothing terms, and did everything in his power to ameliorate their condition." Macmullin, *Camp and Barrack-Room*, p. 116.

41. James Fitzgibbon, *A Veteran of 1812, The Life of James Fitzgibbon*, ed. Mary Agnes Fitzgibbon (Montreal, 1894; fac. ed., Toronto: Coles, 1970), p. 47. While a private in the Third Dragoon Guards, John Pearman wrote of the colonel of the Tenth Foot: "I think there was not a man or [an] officer who knew Colonel White that did not love him." Sgt. John Pearman, *The Radical Soldier's Tale: John Pearman, 1819–1908*, introduction by Carolyn Steedman (New York: Routledge, 1988), p. 172.

42. "The commanding officer . . . is the source from which should proceed the life and energy of the whole." Horse-Guards, Adjutant-General's Office, *General Regulations and Orders for the Army* (1811 and 1816), p. 85.

43. *Standing Orders . . . 56th Regiment*, p. 99. Reformers often stressed this point. For example, one advocated that schools should be provided, and "everything possible done, so as to make the soldiers feel that their regiments are their homes." Colonel James Campbell, *The British Army as It Was, Is, and Ought to Be* (London, 1840), p. 183.

44. [Captain Joseph Moyle Sherer], *Recollections of the Peninsula*, 4th ed. (London, 1825), p. 104.

45. "The Hermit of London," "The Disbanding of a Regiment," *Naval and Military Magazine* 3 (1828), pp. 42–43.

46. Many recruits from respectable families were appalled by the behavior of their fellows: "If a man ventured to speak in a style more refined than the herd around him, he was told that 'Every one did not read the dictionar like him.'" Donaldson, *Recollections*, pp. 84–85.

47. Whereas the term "imagery" is normally utilized in connection with literary motifs or purely visual phenomena, martial objects designed to have a visual impact frequently exerted physical effects as well, which were sometimes an important part of their overall impact. The physical dimension of images is thus included in my use of the terms "image" and "imagery."

48. This includes other contexts as well. Amateur theatricals were very popular in the army at home and abroad both before and after this era, and both officers and enlisted men acted on the professional stage.

49. A few of the best are: Philip J. Haythornthwaite, *British Infantry of the*

Napoleonic Wars (London: Arms and Armour Press, 1987); Michael Barthorp, *British Cavalry Uniforms Since 1660* (Poole, Dorset: Blandford Press, 1984), and *British Infantry Uniforms Since 1660* (Poole, Dorset: Blandford Press, 1982); and B. K. Fosten, *The Thin Red Line: Uniforms of the British Army between 1751 and 1914* (London: Windrow and Green, 1989).

50. The earlier history of the notion of uniformity is ancient; no work to my knowledge has analyzed the origin of the concept of the uniform. It probably began with tribal dress, suggesting the notion of unity that early warlords and heads of state continued by dressing alike their retainers who were not already tied by kinship bonds.

51. The literature on state spectacle is vast; a few examples for Britain are David M. Bergeron, *English Civic Pageantry, 1558–1642* (Columbia, S.C.: University of South Carolina Press, 1971); and Jeffrey L. Lant, *Insubstantial Pageant: Ceremony and Confusion at Queen Victoria's Court* (New York: Taplinger Publishing Co., 1980).

52. For example, in 1590 in Bristol, the queen and her subjects watched a three-day mock-siege and defeat of the "Fort of Feeble Policy." The lord mayor of London's show of 1609 included four emblems "which make any commonwealth truly happy," one of which was "military discipline." Bergeron, *English Civic Pageantry*, p. 300.

53. See Robert Ergang, *The Potsdam Führer: Frederick William I, Father of Prussian Militarism* (New York: Columbia University Press, 1941). As soon as his father was buried in 1713, the new king abolished court state dress and replaced it with military uniform. He seldom wore anything else for the rest of his life, and on his deathbed, when his chaplain sang the hymn "Naked shall I, too, appear before Thy stern countenance," the king shouted: "That is not so, I shall be buried in my uniform" (pp. 53–54). Quoted from Reinhold Koser, "Aus den letzten Tagen König Friedrich Wilhelms I," *Hohenzollern-Jahrbuch* VIII (1904), p. 25.

54. The Royal Navy will not be treated here, but a comparison of its images with those of the army would be useful to gain a better understanding of how military images function, especially in regard to public opinion.

55. "The discipline of well-trained armies [has had] lasting effects upon the political and social order." Max Weber, *From Max Weber: Essays in Sociology*, ed. and trans. H. H. Gerth and C. Wright Mills (New York: Oxford University Press, 1946), p. 257. An abridged version of this part of the argument can be found in my article "'The Eye Must Entrap the Mind': Army Spectacle and Paradigm in Nineteenth-Century Britain," *Journal of Social History* 26 (Fall 1992), pp. 105–131.

56. The important subject of martial music, which deserves its own study, is largely excluded, and will only be addressed where directly relevant.

57. Lewis Mumford, *The Myth of the Machine: Technics and Human Development*

(New York: Harcourt, Brace, and World, 1967), p. 192, and Mumford, *The Myth of the Machine: The Pentagon of Power* (New York: Harcourt, Brace, Jovanovich, Inc., 1970), p. 150. Also see *Technics and Civilization* (New York: Harcourt, Brace, and Company, 1934).

1. THE SPECTACULAR IMAGE

1. The ideal of perfection was mentioned very often in regimental orders: "We shall not presume to enter into any recommendation of the following orders. The perfection to which the division was brought [will] be sufficient to justify their publication." *Standing Orders as Given Out and Enforced by the Late General Robert Craufurd, for the Use of the Light Division During the Year 1809, 10 and 11* (Corfu, n.d.), p. 3.

2. Major-General John Mitchell, *Thoughts on Tactics and Military Organization: Together with an Enquiry into the Power and Position of Russia* (London, 1838), p. 224.

3. General Henry Lloyd, *Continuation of the History of the Late War in Germany Between the King of Prussia and the Empress of Germany and Her Allies* (1781), cited in Capt. Basil Liddell Hart, "Some Extracts from a Military Work of the 18th Century," *JSAHR* 12 (1933), pp. 140–141. The Welshman Lloyd was an unusual eighteenth-century officer; he was widely respected abroad yet less known—or remembered—in his own country. Liddell Hart wrote that he "was better known in other countries during the 18th century than any British soldier save perhaps Marlborough." Napoleon recommended reading his campaigns, while omitting Marlborough's.

4. [Major-General George Bell], *Rough Notes by an Old Soldier, during Fifty Years of Service*, 2 vols. (London, 1867), vol. 2, pp. 38–39.

5. The duke's hairdresser was the first person to board each newly arrived vessel. General H. R. H. The Duke of Kent, "Extracts From the Standing Orders in the Garrison of Gibraltar, 1803," *JSAHR* 2 (1923), p. 181. Parade-ground minutiae will be discussed in Chapter 4.

6. "It is expected from the soldier, that his arms and accoutrements are at all times in the highest order, that they be not only clean but highly polished." Charles James, *The Regimental Companion, Containing the Pay, Allowances, and Relative Duties of Every Officer in the British Service*, 4 vols., 7th ed. (London, 1813), vol. 3, p. 13.

7. General John Mitchell [Bombardino], "On Military Promotion," *Fraser's Magazine* 8 (1833), p. 313. By the end of the French wars, regulations stipulated that muskets were to be "browned."

8. Major John Patterson, *Camp and Quarters: Scenes and Impressions of Military Life* (London, 1840), p. 37.

9. NAM 7,311–6–1, *Standing Orders of the 15th Regiment of Foot* (1813–1845), p. 57.

10. NAM 7,309–53, "Royal Order of 13 March, 1809." Orderly Book of Captain William Russel, 20th Regiment of Foot. H.Q., Colchester.

11. Alexander Somerville, *The Autobiography of a Working Man* (n.p., 1848; reprint ed., London: MacGibbon and Kee, 1967), p. 146.

12. Colonel Francis Arthur Whinyates, *Corunna to Sebastopol: A History of "C" Battery, "A" Brigade Royal Horse Artillery* (London, 1881), p. 12.

13. James, *Regimental Companion*, vol. 1, p. lxxvii.

14. This was supposed to be prohibited by a *General Order* in 1811. Percy Sumner, "Uniforms and Equipment of the 15th Light Dragoons (Hussars) 1800 to 1813; Extracts From the Adjutant's Journals," *JSAHR* 16 (1937), p. 168.

15. James, *Regimental Companion*, vol. 3, pp. 468–469.

16. "By an Inventor of Military Figures for Elucidation of Cavalry Movements," *Remarks on the Proper Regulations of the Instruction, Formation and Movement of Cavalry* (London, 1832), p. 26.

17. Capt. George Arthur, *The Story of the Household Cavalry*, 2 vols. (London: Archibald Constable and Co., 1909), vol. 2, p. 627.

18. One example is the First Dragoons' uniform of 1835. Colonel C. P. [Charles Phillip] De Ainslie, *Life As I have Found It* (Edinburgh, 1883), pp. 89–90.

19. In 1827, "regiments within 50 men of their establishment are not to enlist men under 5'8", and [those over] 50, not less than 5'7" until they reached within 50 [men of their authorized establishment]." NAM 7,311–6–2, Orderly Book owned by Lt. John Humphreys, 15th Foot, November 1, 1813–December 1830, "Adopted for the Garrison of St Ann's, Barbados."

20. Capt. George Elers, *Memoirs of George Elers, Captain in the 12th Regiment of Foot* (New York: D. Appleton and Co., 1903), p. 200.

21. James, *Regimental Companion*, vol. 3, footnote, p. 487.

22. Inspector-General Sir Robert Jackson, *A View of the Formation, Discipline and Economy of Armies*, 3rd ed., revised (London, 1845), p. 21. The higher disease rate might well be due in part to the inadequate diet, which resulted in a weakened constitution in larger men, who required more nourishment. Many veterans noted that tall men were the first to falter under physical strain.

23. The Nineteenth Foot did this in 1820 after returning from seven years of service in Ceylon. Serg. George Calladine, *The Diary of Colour-Sergeant George Calladine, 19th Foot, 1793–1837*, ed. M. L. Ferrar (London: E. Fisher and Co., 1922), p. 90.

24. W.O. 42/42, Letter from Gen. Hardinge to Gen. Hill, December 30, 1828, cited in Philip Dwight Jones, "The British Army in the Age of Reform, 1830–1854" (Ph.D diss., Duke University, 1968), p. 27.

25. Serg. T. J. W. Connelly, *The Romance of the Ranks, or Anecdotes, Episodes and Social Incidents of Military Life*, 2 vols. (London, 1859), vol. 1, p. 289. This refers to the reductions after Waterloo.

26. Henry Paget, First Marquess of Anglesey, *One-Leg: The Life and Letters of Henry William Paget, First Marquess of Anglesey, K.G., 1768–1854*, ed. Henry Paget, Seventh Marquess of Anglesey (New York: William Morrow and Co., 1961), pp. 47–48. When he later commanded the Seventh Hussars, Anglesey "set an immensely high sartorial standard" (p. 62). Such feelings were not unusual in the aristocracy and middle classes; there were always people who looked upon the poor as significant only in their usefulness to the rich and powerful.

27. RSUSM MSS q.A.213.2, "Weight that a Horse of the 2nd/ or Royal North British Dragoons Carries in Field Order on the March." March 1, 1822. The weight "on actual service" in 1813 was only reduced by 7 lb., 11 oz. Scots Greys Regimental Papers Chiefly Relating to the Waterloo and Crimean Campaigns, "The Dragoon's Weight in the Field, March, and Service order ascertained 5th June, 1813."

28. Corporal Charles Cozens, *Adventures of a Guardsman* (London, 1848), pp. 33–34.

29. Colonel James Campbell, *The British Army as It Was, Is, and Ought to Be* (London, 1840), p. 288.

30. Calladine, *Diary*, p. 103.

31. Campbell, *British Army*, p. 66. In late-seventeenth-century siege warfare, grenadiers had to be tall because they could throw grenades farther than short men, but like many other army customs, this later became more important as a tradition than as a practical consideration.

32. General Orders, Sec. 19, Art. 36, *Standing Orders of His Majesty's 1st Regiment of Life Guards* (London, 1814 and 1827), p. 63.

33. Great Britain, Adjutant-General's Office, Horse Guards, *Addendum to the General Regulations and Orders for the Army: Being a Continuation of the Collective Orders Dated [from] 12th August, 1811 [to January 1, 1816]*, 2nd ed. (1816), *General Order*, November 16, 1815, p. 431, cited in *Scots Guards Regimental Orderly Book*.

34. Cavalry Officer, *The Whole Art of Dress or, The Road to Elegance and Fashion at the Enormous Savings of 30%!!! Being a Treatise Upon that Essential and Much Cultivated Requisite of the Present Day, Gentlemen's Costume* (London, 1830), pp. 73–76. As will be shown, this rule was not designed to protect the soldiers' health.

35. *Standing Orders of the 74th Highlanders* (London, 1850), p. 94.

36. HEH MS ST 151, John Foster, "The Private Soldier's Pocket Companion in Three Parts," p. 6. This practice also made them more secure from attacks by angry civilians, which were by no means rare occurrences.

37. *Standing Orders of the 4th Battalion The Royal Regiment of Fusiliers* (Dublin:

By the Regiment, 1906), p. 16. These *Standing Orders* are based upon those of 1834.

38. [William Maginn], *The Military Sketch-Book: Reminiscences of Seventeen Years in the Service Abroad and at Home*, 2 vols. (London, 1827), vol. 2, p. 237.

39. These were yellow, deep yellow, bright yellow, philemot yellow, pale yellow, yellowish buff, and yolk. The greens were green, gosling green, dark green, deep green, very deep green, pea green, yellowish green, full green, popinjay green, and willow green. Philip J. Haythornthwaite, *British Infantry in the Napoleonic Wars* (London: Arms and Armour Press, 1987), pp. 98–102, citing De Bosset, *A View of the British Army on the Peace Establishment in the Year 1803* (1803), Charles Hamilton Smith, *Costume of the Army of the British Empire* (1812), and the *Clothing Regulations* of 1802.

40. One can see this by examining color prints of the grenade exercise used in the First Foot Guards in 1735. These show facings of a medium/light blue, but the Brigade of Guards now wear dark blue. The same tendency toward a darker shade also affected "French Gray," which was almost white in the eighteenth century, but by 1900 had become dark gray, as in the facings of the Twenty-first Lancers. Some clue to this aesthetic shift might be gained by a comparison with the Danish army, in which the light-blue facings of the early eighteenth century have been preserved to the present.

41. These apparently were changed often, for two variations are shown for most regimental patterns. Haythornthwaite, *British Infantry*, pp. 98–102. Officers' and Other Ranks' lace was bought from specialist firms, of which there were dozens in the early nineteenth century; worms were abolished (on paper) in 1836.

42. The details of uniform—particularly in this era—are endless, and much is still unknown about regimental distinctions and the minor variations that occurred from year to year; these might depend upon the colonels' whims, mistakes or shoddy quality from the clothiers, or shortages of the various materials.

43. Jackson, *A View*, p. 185.

44. James Boswell, *The Life of Samuel Johnson*, 2 vols. (New York: J. M. Dutton, 1925), 2:10, 191.

45. Lt.-Colonel Joseph [Jocelyn] Anderson, *Recollections of a Peninsular Veteran* (London: Edward Arnold, 1913), p. 253.

46. Shipp's anecdotes, which he claimed were based upon true incidents, might sound overly dramatized, but his stories were typical of the period, and, whether accurate, exaggerated, or completely fictional, they were doubtless taken literally by many Britons. John Shipp, *The Military Bijou, Gleanings from Thirty-Three Years of Active Service*, 2 vols. (London, 1831), vol. 1, p. 207.

47. General Sir William F. Napier, *The Life and Opinions of General Sir Charles Napier*, 4 vols. (London, 1857), vol. 1, p. 96.
48. The shoe was also called a "drag." If the scabbard was made of leather this was usually made of brass.
49. Great Britain, Adjutant-General's Office, *General Regulations and Orders for the British Army* (August 12, 1811), "to which are added such *Regulations* as have been issued to the 1st January, 1816," p. 83.
50. NAM 7,309–53. Orderly Book of Captain William Russel, 20th Foot, February 17–May 12, 1809: "No non-commissioned officer or soldier is to quit the barracks without [his] side-arms."
51. He would also be stripped of his side arms by the pioneers, who had a much lower status, "in order to enhance his degradation." Great Britain, Adjutant-General's Office, Horse Guards, *Addendum to the General Regulations and Orders for the Army: January 1830—31 March, 1835*, "Gen. Order no. 520, 18th June, 1835," p. 892. Pioneers performed menial labor, which was despised in the army, and were not supposed to fight.
52. Charles M. Clode, *The Military Forces of the Crown; Their Administration and Government*, 2 vols. (London, 1869), vol. 2, pp. 597–598.
53. Bracebridge Hemyng, "Prostitution in London," quoted in Henry Mayhew, *London Labour and the London Poor*, 4 vols. (New York: Dover Books, 1968), vol. 4, p. 236.
54. Major-General Lloyd, quoted in Liddell Hart, "Some Extracts from a Military Work of the 18th Century," *JSAHR* 12 (1933), p. 141.
55. W.O. 7/56, Clothing Board, Miscellaneous Reports.
56. W.O. 7/56, undated letter of 1811, p. 96. In 1833, the board complained that the heavy cavalry helmet was "cumbersome, inconvenient from its weight, and especially from its height." W.O. 7/58, Report of July 31, 1833, p. 10.
57. Connelly, *Romance*, vol. 2, p. 121.
58. An Officer, *Observations on the Army, in which Its Embodying is Detailed, Its Present State Described, and Sundry Improvements Suggested* (London, 1825), pp. 24–25. Only some shakos had neck flaps.
59. NAM 7,311–6–1, *Standing Orders . . . 15th Regiment*, pp. 120–121.
60. Benson Freeman and Charles Stoneham, *Historical Records . . . of the Middlesex Yeomanry, 1797–1927* (Chelsea: Regimental Committee, Duke of York's Headquarters, 1930), p. 18.
61. Alexander R. Cattley, "The British Infantry Shako," *JSAHR* 15 (1936), p. 207.
62. Freeman and Stoneham, *Middlesex Yeomanry*, p. 19. Although this description is for a yeomanry (nonprofessional) cavalry corps, such units took the regular army as their model, and in this era the colonels still exercised a great deal of control over the designs (see Chapter 2).

63. Rather pathetically, the board recommended that the brass chin scales be removed in hot climates, eliminating another four ounces, "except in [full] dress and parades." W.O. 7/57, Report of March 16, 1831. The board might well have been told beforehand just what limits existed to their recommendations.

64. "New Accoutrements," *Military Magazine* 1 (November 1811).

65. "Military Uniforms," *Blackwood's Magazine* 22 (January 1828), p. 92.

66. A Field Officer of Yeomanry, "Yeomanry Cavalry," *United Services Journal* 2 (1831), p. 395. Yeomanry regulations also mention this: Great Britain, Horse Guards, *Abridgement for His Majesty's Regulations for Yeomanry Cavalry* (London, 1838), p. 10.

67. W.O. 7/56, Report of April 15, 1814, p. 503.

68. W.O. 33/68, statement no. 585, from Mr. G. D. A. Fleetwood, Director of Army Clothing, "Minutes of Evidence," *Report of the Committee Appointed by the Secretary of State for War to Consider the Various Patterns of Headdresses now in Use in the Army* (London, 1897), p. 38, and statement no. 112. Furry fusilier caps were probably no less difficult to store. It is important to bear in mind that these problems were certainly worse in the early nineteenth century, because all the full dress headdresses were larger and more elaborate than in later decades. In 1855, the army took over from regiments the job of issuing clothing, equipment, and headdresses.

69. Willard Connely, *The Reign of Beau Brummell* (New York: Greystone Press, 1940), p. 44.

70. W.O. 7/57, Report of August 12, 1829.

71. W.O. 7/57, Report of December 3, 1830.

72. Sumner, "Uniforms," p. 164.

73. Michael Angelo Hays, *The Costume of the 46th Regiment* (London: National Army Museum, 1972), p. 18. W.O. 7/57, Report of March 2, 1830.

74. Philip J. Haythornthwaite, *World Uniforms and Battles: 1815–50* (New York: Hippocrene Books, 1976), p. 113.

75. Mitchell, *Thoughts*, p. 225. The general claimed that the Prussian cavalry could not march more than a few hundred yards without being enveloped in clouds of pipeclay dust, but this seems exaggerated.

76. Jackson, *A View*, p. 354.

77. W.O. 7/57, Report of December 3, 1830.

78. *The Subaltern's Log-Book; Including Anecdotes of Well-Known Characters*, 2 vols. (Ridgeway, 1828), vol. 1, p. 42.

79. Ibid., vol. 1, p. 198.

80. Jackson, *A View*, p. 354.

81. Horse Guards, By the Order of Harry Calvert, Adjutant-General, April 28, 1810. Quoted in James, *Regimental Companion*, vol. 2, p. 295.

82. Colonel Lewis Oattes, *I Serve: A Regimental History of the 3d Carabiniers* (Chester, U.K.: Third Carabiniers, 1966), p. 130.

83. Item, *United Services Journal*, pt. 1 (May 1866), p. 35.
84. Percival R. Kirby, *Sir Andrew Smith. His Life, Letters and Works* (Amsterdam: A. A. Balkema, 1965), p. 123. This recommendation had also been made—and rejected—in earlier colonial campaigns; at the start of the 1851 "Kaffir War," Lieutenant-Colonel Edward Napier had made this recommendation, but "the military authorities were unwilling to sacrifice appearances for comfort." Ibid., p. 296.
85. William Verner, *Reminiscences of William Verner, (1782–1871), 7th Hussars, an Account of Service . . . Including the Battle of Waterloo*, ed. Ruth W. Verner, *JSAHR* special publication no. 8 (London, 1965), p. 43.
86. "On Prussia," *United Services Journal* 1 (1829), pp. 18–19.
87. Officers had their soldiers wear neckstocks "instead of allowing them more nourishing food, or treating them with more kindness." The author notes that "stocks have lately much improved." I suspect that the worst abuses of this nasty leather collar occurred before 1810. H. LeBlanc, *The Art of Tying the Cravat*, 2nd ed. (London, 1828); reprinted in *Late Georgian Costume: The Tailor's Friendly Instructor (1822) by J. Wyatt, and The Art of Tying the Cravat (1828) by H. LeBlanc* (Mendocino: R. L. Shep, 1991); "Stocks," n.p.
88. James, *Regimental Companion*, vol. 2, p. 296. Officers usually wore stocks of a soft material, such as velvet.
89. Dr. William Fergusson, *Notes and Recollections of a Professional Life*, quoted in Capt. L. E. Nolan, *Cavalry; Its History and Tactics* (London, 1853), p. 117.
90. The stock may originally have been intended in part as protection from sword cuts. General Henry Lloyd claimed this in *A Political and Military Rhapsody, on the Invasion and Defence of Great Britain and Ireland*, 6th ed. (London, 1803), p. 277. Officer George Gleig's "stout leathern stock" prevented a sword cut he suffered at the Battle of New Orleans from being fatal. Chaplain-General George [Robert] Gleig, *A Subaltern in America; comprising His Narrative of the Campaigns of the British Army at Baltimore, Washington, etc. During the Late War* (Philadelphia, 1833), p. 225. "Necessaries" refer to items other than the coat and trousers: the metal badges and fittings, shirts, socks, gaiters, shoes or boots, and articles for cleaning and grooming.
91. W.O. 7/56, Miscellaneous Reports, 1811, pp. 97, 99.
92. [Joseph Donaldson], *Recollections of an Eventful Life, Chiefly Passed in the Army* (Glasgow, 1824), p. 197. One such unit was the Ninety-fourth Foot.
93. Robert Waterfield, *The Memoirs of Private Waterfield, Soldier in Her Majesty's 32nd Regiment of Foot (Duke of Cornwall's Light Infantry) 1842–57*, ed. Arthur Swinson and Donald Scott (London: Cassell, 1968), pp. 7, 8, and 12.
94. Serg. James Bodell, *A Soldier's View of Empire: The Reminiscences of James Bodell, 1831–92*, ed. Keith Sinclair (Toronto: The Bodley Head, 1982), p. 31.

95. Before the augmentations of 1846, Royal Artillerymen had guard duty every third day. Hew Strachan, *From Waterloo to Balaclava: Tactics, Technology, and the British Army, 1815–1854* (Cambridge, England: Cambridge University Press, 1985), p. 107.

96. Campbell, *British Army*, p. 45.

97. W.O. 33/15, *Report of the Committee Appointed to Inquire Into the Effect On Health of the Present System of Carrying the Accoutrements, Ammunition, and Kit of Infantry Soldiers and Drill, Etc., of Recruits* (London, 1865), p. 12. The debilitating effect of hard duty and the kit upon health tended to be worse in the era before 1865. I am indebted to Alan Ramsay Skelley's *The Victorian Army at Home: The Recruitment and Terms and Conditions of the British Regular, 1859–1899* (Montreal: McGill-Queens, 1977), p. 61, for this information.

98. Campbell, *British Army*, p. 102.

99. Mitchell, *Thoughts*, p. 235. W. W., "Inconvenience of Wellington Boots on a March," *United Services Journal* 3 (1836), p. 407.

100. Waterfield, *Memoirs*, p. 16.

101. Howard L. Blackmore, *British Military Firearms, 1650–1850* (London: Herbert Jenkins, 1961), p. 158.

102. Only the necks of bayonets and not the locks and plates were to be browned; *Scots Guards Orderly Book*, repeating the Order of December 30, 1815, from the *Addendum* to the *Army Regulations* of August 12, 1812.

103. Circular Letter of March 24, 1824, Horse Guards, Adjutant-General, *Addendum . . . Regulations . . . 1830.*

104. James, *Regimental Companion*, vol. 1, p. 265.

105. W.O. 7/56, Report of June 6, 1815, p. 523. These might carry paper, pencils, tobacco, or even an ink-pot, but the pocket could not hold much, and they were abolished for cavalry other than hussars in the 1830s; mounted artillery officers kept them until 1901.

106. Major Charles Dupin, *View of the History and Actual State of the Military Force of Great Britain*, 2 vols. (London, 1822), vol. 1, p. 112. Many units carried ornamental or nonfunctional equipment long after 1856; J. F. C. Fuller recalled that prior to 1914, the cavalry carried so much useless equipment that they "look like mounted pedlars," and gunners "appear as if they had looted an optician's store." Major-General J. F. C. Fuller, *The Army in My Time* (London: Rich & Cowan, 1935), p. 7.

107. Undated post-Waterloo memo from Gen. the Marquess of Anglesey, in Herbert T. Siborne, ed., *Waterloo Letters* (London, 1891; reprint ed., London: Castle and Co., 1983), p. 11.

108. Strachan, *Waterloo to Balaclava*, p. 107.

109. Joseph H. Lehmann, *All Sir Garnet: A Life of Field-Marshal Lord Wolseley* (London: Jonathan Cape, 1964), p. 18.

2. COMMAND AND DESIGN

1. Charles M. Clode, *The Military Forces of the Crown; Their Administration and Government*, 2 vols. (London, 1869), vol. 1, p. 33. This power is circumscribed by Parliament's annual vote on army spending.

2. P.R.O., W.O. 71/6; cited in *The King's Own: The Story of a Royal Regiment*, ed. Col. L. I. Cowper, vol. 1 (1680–1814) (Oxford: The King's Own Regiment, 1939), p. 535.

3. Christopher Hibbert, *George IV, Prince of Wales, 1762–1811* (London: Longman, 1972), p. 181.

4. Letter no. 1795, the Prince of Wales to the King, January 17, 1804, George, Prince of Wales, *The Correspondence of George, Prince of Wales, 1770–1812*, ed. A. Aspinall, 8 vols. (Oxford: Oxford University Press, 1970), vol. 4, p. 483.

5. The *Times* declined due to "the delicacy of the subject." Hibbert, *George IV, Prince of Wales*, p. 182.

6. William Wallace, *George IV* (n.p., 1830), p. 93.

7. Sir Nathaniel Wraxall, *The Historical and Posthumous Papers of Sir Nathaniel William Wraxall, 1772–1784*, ed. Henry B. Wheatley, 5 vols. (1884), vol. 5, p. 360; cited in Hibbert, *George IV, Prince of Wales*, p. 235.

8. Thomas Creevey, *Creevey's Life and Letters: A Further Selection from the Correspondence of Thomas Creevey*, ed. John Gore (London: John Murray, 1934), p. 313, entry of November 14, 1829. He also claimed to have led a cavalry charge at Waterloo.

9. David Cannadine, "The Context, Performance and Meaning of Ritual: The British Monarchy and the 'Invention of Tradition' c. 1820–1977," in *The Invention of Tradition*, ed. Eric Hobsbawm and Terence Ranger (Cambridge, England: Cambridge University Press, 1983), p. 118. It is not true that the king despised martial spectacle, although he avoided wearing military—as opposed to naval—uniforms. He attended a series of grand reviews after his accession in 1830, and was not only the star attraction, but showed a great interest in the proceedings: "His Majesty walked up and down the ranks, paying the most minute attention to the military and clean appearance of the men." *Times*, July 23, 1830. A private in the Royal Horse Guards (Blue) wrote: "Our late lamented sovereign . . . during the latter years of his life, was particularly partial to military shows." Corporal Charles Cozens, *Adventures of a Guardsman* (London, 1848), p. 32.

10. Entry of April 16, 1830. Lord Ellenborough [Edward Law], *A Political Diary, 1828–1830*, ed. Lord Colchester, 2 vols. (London, 1881), vol. 2, p. 222.

11. Harriet Arbuthnot, *The Journal of Mrs. Arbuthnot, 1820–1832*, ed. Francis Bamford and the Duke of Wellington, 2 vols. (London: Macmillan and Co.,

1950), vol. 2, p. 370. Phillip Ziegler calls this interest "almost obsessive." *King William IV* (Bungay, Suffolk: Fontana, 1971), p. 160.

12. Ziegler, *William IV*, p. 289.

13. Benjamin Disraeli, Lord Beaconsfield, *Correspondence with His Sister* (London, 1886), p. 66, cited in ibid., p. 289. William IV died early on the morning of June 20.

14. Mollie Gillen, *The Prince and His Lady: The Love Story of the Duke of Kent and Madame de St. Laurent* (London: Sidgwick & Jackson, 1970), n. 428, p. 300.

15. E. F. Benson, *Queen Victoria* (London: Longmans, Green and Co., 1935), p. 170.

16. [Charles Phillip] De Ainslie, *Life As I have Found It* (Edinburgh, 1883), pp. 108 and 114.

17. Elizabeth Longford, *Queen Victoria: Born to Succeed* (New York: Harper and Row, 1965), p. 76.

18. Panmure to Raglan, March 26, 1855. Lord Panmure (Fox Maule), *Panmure Papers*, ed. Sir. George Douglas and Sir George Dalhousie Ramsay, 2 vols. (London: Hodder and Stoughton, 1908), vol. 1, p. 126.

19. Victoria to Leopold, King of the Belgians, May 22, 1855. Queen Victoria, *The Letters of Queen Victoria: A Selection of Her Majesty's Correspondence Between the Years 1837 and 1861*, ed. Christopher Benson and Viscount Esher, 3 vols. (London: J. Murray, 1908), vol. 3, p. 127.

20. Giles St. Aubyn, *Edward VII, Prince and King* (New York: Athenaeum, 1979), p. 306.

21. Daphne Bennett, *King Without a Crown: Albert Prince Consort of England, 1819–1861*, 1st American ed. (Philadelphia: Lippincott, 1977), pp. 262 and 259.

22. Letter 1937, Col. McMahon to the Duke of Northumberland, Carlton House, August 25, 1804. George, Prince of Wales, *Correspondence*, vol. 5, p. 91.

23. Many of his letters were destroyed immediately after his death, and the great ridicule that his design interests generated suggests that very few tailor's bills were allowed to survive. "His profusion in these articles was unbounded, because he never paid for them." Charles C[avendish] F[ulke] Greville, entry of August 3, 1830, *The Greville Memoirs: A Journal of The Reigns of King George IV and King William IV*, ed. Henry Reeve, 3 vols. (London, 1875), vol. 2, p. 23. Having the king as a patron was a great advertisement for any tradesman.

24. Greville, *Memoirs*, vol. 1, p. 253, entry of December 5, 1829. Thackeray claims that the king spent £10,000 on coats per year. William Makepeace Thackeray, *The Four Georges*, (reprint ed., London: Falcon Press, 1948), p. 103.

25. Anon., "Wardrobe of George IV," *Athenaeum*, August 14, 1830, p. 510.

26. The "goose" is a tailor's iron. See illustration.

27. Greville, *Memoirs*, vol. 1, p. 250, entry of December 1, 1829.

28. C. Marcuard, "Review of *The Uniform of the Officers of the British Army according to the Last Regulations, from Drawings Exhibited for the Prince Regent*," in *Military Register* 195 (September 1, 1819), p. 1134.

29. [General A. Cavalie Mercer], "Military Reminiscences of [the] Latter End of the Eighteenth and Beginning of Nineteenth Centuries," in R. J. Mac-Donald, *The History of the Dress of the Royal Regiment of Artillery, 1625–1897* (reprint ed., Bristol: Crécy Books, 1985), p. 49. This section reprints "the MS notes and thumb-nail sketches written and drawn in 1840 by the late General A. C[avalie] Mercer" (p. 36). The sabre is merely a variant of the much older Arabian/Persian scimitar.

30. Hew Strachan, "The Origins of the 1855 Uniform Changes—An Example of Pre-Crimean Reform," *JSAHR* 55 (1977), pp. 116–117. This highlights the ongoing and decisive influence of aesthetics for this era, as opposed to the importance of battle experience.

31. Arnold J. Toynbee, *War and Civilization*, ed. Albert V. Fowler (Oxford: Oxford University Press, 1950), pp. 12–13. China's traditional dress was greatly influenced by the dress of enemies, although the Chinese despised them as inferior barbarians. As early as 307 B.C. they adopted the "loose upper garment, long skirt and low shoes" that were worn by the mounted nomads who attacked China; by the ninth century at the latest, the nomadic "belted tunic, trousers and boots" were adopted, and noblemen wore a large hat that was derived from the nomads. L. Carrington Goodrich, *A Short History of the Chinese People*, 3rd ed. (New York: Harper Torchbooks, 1959), pp. 83–84. The influence of martial dress on British fashion is discussed in Chapter 8.

32. Lieutenant-General Sir George Wrottesley, *Life and Correspondence of Sir John Burgoyne*, 2 vols. (London, 1873), vol. 1, pp. 25–26.

33. Philip Haythornthwaite, *World Uniforms and Battles: 1815–50* (New York: Hippocrene Books, 1976), pp. 151–152.

34. See Arthur F. Loveday, *Sir Hilgrove Turner: 1764–1843, Soldier and Courtier under the Georges* (Alkham, Kent: The Alkham Press, 1964).

35. Cumberland to the Regent, June 18, 1813. George IV, *The Letters of King George IV, 1812–1830*, ed. A. Aspinall, 3 vols. (Cambridge: Cambridge University Press, 1938), vol. 1, p. 261.

36. Colonel Lewis Oattes, *I Serve: A Regimental History of the 3d Carabiniers* (Chester, U.K.: Third Carabiniers, 1966), p. 314.

37. "Better would His Royal Highness's time and strength be employed in rousing the spirit of his countrymen and thereby preserving the materials to dress his enemies." Lieutenant-General Robert Ballard Long, *Peninsular*

Cavalry General, 1811–13. The Correspondence of Lieutenant General Robert Ballard Long, ed. T[om] H. McGuffie (London: Harrap, 1951), pp. 127–128.

38. RSUSM MSS, "Notes on the Uniform . . . of the 47th Regiment," S. M. Milne (1891), p. 9.

39. Sir Walter Scott, *The Private Letter Books of Sir Walter Scott*, ed. Wilfred Partington (London: Hodder and Stoughton, 1930), p. 158. This sartorial statement might have expressed royal anger after the Catholic emancipation controversy, which occurred when Cumberland last visited the king; he was so mortified that he threatened abdication. "True Blue" had a traditional symbolism: "Religious conviction could influence the choice of colours in certain armies . . . Protestant countries . . . favored a predominance of blue." Paul Martin, *European Military Uniforms: A Short History* (London: Spring Books, 1967), p. 38. Dark blue was worn by the armies of Prussia, the Netherlands, and the post-1814 Dual Monarchy of Sweden and Norway, although it was used by some Catholic armies; the only other European state using red as the basic coat color was Denmark. Considering how strongly many soldiers felt about dress, it is perhaps worthwhile to speculate whether the army would have mutinied had the blue been adopted. Such an act was by no means unlikely; the Eighty-seventh Foot mutinied after regimental music was no longer played on their march to church. Subsequent chapters will clarify such attitudes.

40. Major-General John Mitchell, *Thoughts on Tactics and Military Organization: Together with an Enquiry into the Power and Position of Russia* (London, 1838), p. 229.

41. Orientalism had a strong impact upon the military dress not only of Britain, but also of all European (and American) armies of the era, including uniforms, equipment, headgear, and weapons, although this dimension of the subject was not discussed in Edward W. Said's *Orientalism* (New York: Vintage Books, 1978).

42. Mercer, "Reminiscences," p. 54.

43. Sergeant [David] Robertson, *The Journal of Sergeant D. Robertson, late 92nd Foot: comprising the different campaigns, between the Years 1797 and 1818, in Egypt, Walcheren, Denmark, Sweden, Portugal, Spain, France and Belgium* (Perth, 1842), p. 16. Before the British arrived in Egypt, "almost the entire [French] army . . . wore ostrich plumes in their hats." J. Christopher Herold, *Bonaparte in Egypt* (New York: Harper and Row, 1962), p. 159.

44. *Military Panorama*, supp. to vol. 3 (March 1814), pp. 659–662. Lancers were an exception to the regent's emphasis on a tight fit, because Egyptian "Mameluk" trousers were cut loosely, following the French rage for this style after the Egyptian campaign. By 1900 there were six lancer regiments in the British army.

45. Letter from the Prince Consort to the Queen, September 5, 1854. Sir

Theodore Martin, *Life of His Royal Highness The Prince Consort*, 2nd ed., 5 vols. (London, 1875–1880), vol. 3, p. 104.

46. Major G. Tylden, "The West India Regiments, 1795 to 1927 and from 1958," *JSAHR* 40 (March 1962), p. 47. Officers' uniforms were not changed, in contrast to British officers in Indian sepoy units, who wore the same "Eastern-influenced" dress as the Indian soldiers. This might well reveal differences in the way the queen and other Britons viewed Africans and Indians. Zouave dress was popular during the American Civil War, and was also worn by papal troops in Rome. The West India regiments were disbanded in 1926.

47. W.O. 43/741, "Report and Opinion," *Proceedings of a Board of Officers, assembled by the Order of the Duke of Wellington, Commander-in-Chief, on the 17th of August, 1842 and continuing . . . until the 21st of September . . . to investigate every article of Clothing and appointments in Her Majesty's Regiments of Life Guards and Royal Horse Guards, etc.*

48. "And other twaddle of the same kind." Yet the author believed that "a fair portion" of the guards should be near the sovereign "for stage effect." Lt-Colonel Jonathan Leach, *Rambles Along the Banks of the Styx* (London, 1847), p. 119.

49. Queen Victoria to the King of the Belgians, July 21, 1856. Victoria, *Letters*, vol. 3, p. 200. Britons observed foreign troops too; in 1856 Queen Victoria wanted some officers to "attend all large foreign reviews for the purpose of instruction, and in order to report upon other armies." Duke of Cambridge to Lord Panmure, August 5, 1856. Panmure, *Papers*, vol. 2, p. 283. Cambridge wrote: "I approve highly of the idea."

50. Entry of June 28, 1820. Richard Rush, *Memoranda of a Residence at the Court of London, Comprising Incidents Official and Personal from 1819 to 1825* (Philadelphia, 1845), pp. 310–311.

51. Colonel J. W. Gordon to Colonel McMahon, March 10, 1811, George, Prince of Wales, *Correspondence*, vol. 7, p. 269.

52. Entry of May 11, 1821. Arbuthnot, *Journal*, vol. 1, p. 94. The uniform was the model for British court dress and diplomatic corps throughout the world. This was not the first time that a monarch used formal dress as a means of humiliation; in the eighteenth century, Ottoman sultans presented European ambassadors with caftans. These were cheaply made and so heavy that their wearers had to be lifted up and carried into the sultan's presence, and then were jerked to their knees at intervals, and dragged away backward at the end of the interview. The caftans were then sold to dealers, who resold them to the Porte. "All the foreign envoys agreed that it was a mortifying experience." These "gifts" were worth much less than those the sultan received. Lavender Cassels, *The Struggle for the Ottoman Empire, 1717–1740* (London: Murray, 1966), pp. 59–60 and 68–69.

53. Doctors had a lower status than other officers, especially in the Royal Horse

Guards (Blue). One Who Has Kept A Diary [George William Erskine Russell], *Collections and Recollections* (London, 1898), p. 211.

54. De Ainslie, *Life*, p. 95. Their regret may have been due in part to the greater durability of the blue cloth, which was replaced only every other year instead of annually. The king probably felt strongly about this because the corps was a royal regiment; he also exercised personal approval over the Household Cavalry's clothing accounts. House of Commons, "Report of the Select Committee on Army and Navy Appointments: with Minutes of Evidence and Appendix," *Report From The Select Committee on the Establishment of The Garrisons and on the Pay and Emoluments of Army and Naval Officers with Minutes of Evidence and Appendix: Military and Naval,* 2 vols. (London, 1833; reprint ed., Shannon: Irish University Press Series of British Parliamentary Papers, 1969), vol. 1, p. 127.

55. Cozens, *Adventures*, p. 34.

56. *Times*, May 29, 1829.

57. Letter 86, March 6, 1842. Arthur Wellesley, 1st Duke of Wellington, *Wellington and His Friends: Letters of the First Duke of Wellington to the Rt. Hon. Charles and Mrs. Arbuthnot, the Earl and Countess of Wilton, Princess Lieven, and Miss Burdett-Coutts,* ed. the Seventh Duke of Wellington (London: Macmillan, 1965), pp. 179–180.

58. Mercer, "Reminiscences," p. 53.

59. Sir John Fortescue, *Wellington*, 3rd ed. (London: Ernest Benn Ltd., 1960), p. 232.

60. Moore, *Works*, vol. 3, p. 250.

61. Apothecaries kept liveried boys to deliver medicines and wait at table, "and [he] thus thinks himself on par with a gentleman who has a footman." Anon., "Rank," *New Monthly Magazine and Literary Journal* 25 (1829), p. 407.

62. *Twenty Sermons upon Social Duties and Their Opposite Vices* (1743), p. 182. Cited in J. Jean Hecht, *The Domestic Servant in Eighteenth-Century England* (reprint ed., London: Routledge and Kegan Paul, 1980), pp. 73, 12–13, 53–55, and 179. There are other similarities between liveried servants and soldiers; ideally, footmen were to be very tall and imposing.

63. See Chapter 4. This was done by Napoleon I, who preferred the modest "undress" uniform of a colonel of *chasseurs á cheval*, whereas the marshals and kings that he had raised wore the finery. Of them he said: "Les généraux ne sont rien." Liliane and Fred Funcken, *L'uniforms et les armes des soldats du premier empire: des regiments de ligne français aux troupes britanniques prussiens et espagnoles* (Tournai: Casterman, 1968), p. 14. This practice seems to have been widespread; in 1847 in Egypt, a princess was "not very gaudily attired herself, but her slave girls, of whom there was a host, were arrayed in magnificent shawls and jewels." Mountain, *Memoirs*, pp. 235–236.

64. He was already a lieutenant-general in the Hanoverian army. Quoted from an unnamed document in the Windsor Archive, May 14, 1798. G. M. Willis, *Ernest Augustus, Duke of Cumberland and King of Hannover* (London: A. Barker, 1954), p. 55.

65. British uniforms were called "leopard's skin." Lt.-General Long, *Cavalry General*, p. 165.

66. Entry of November 1, 1811. Thomas Creevey, *The Creevey Papers: A Selection from the Correspondence & Diaries of the Late Thomas Creevey, M.P.*, ed. Sir Herbert Maxwell, 2 vols. (New York: E. P. Dutton, 1903), vol. 1, p. 148.

67. Percy Bysshe Shelley, *Shelley: Poetical Works*, ed. Thomas Hutchinson (Oxford: Oxford University Press, 1970), p. 398. George Cruikshank's *My Sketch Book* (London, 1834–1836) depicts an organ-grinder's monkey dressed as a general in a scarlet, laced uniform and plumed hat. Reproduced in Dorothy Constance Peel, *The Stream of Time: Social and Domestic Life in England, 1805–1861* (New York: Scribners, 1932), p. 99.

68. *A Hit at the Tenth* (London, 1824), pp. 9 and 37.

69. Committee on Army and Navy Appointments, vol. 1, p. 131, and Circ. of October 23, 1828.

70. G. A. Steppler, "Redcoat: The Regimental Coat of the British Infantrymen, c. 1808–15" *Uniform* 8 (September 1989), p. 21. The coat is in the Musée de l'Emperi, Salon de Provence, France.

71. NLS MS no. 1,863, Brown Papers, Montreal, James Edward Alexander to Maj. John Alexander Henderson, October 5, 1849. The headgear proposal is a bit unusual, but both suggestions were probably made because of the intense cold of the approaching Canadian winter.

72. Captain I. H. Mackay Scobie, "The 'Government' or 'Black Watch' Tartan," *JSAHR* 1 (1921), p. 54.

73. He added: "But the details are tiresome & disgusting." Lord William Russell to Lady William Russell, Newbridge, August 2, 1828, Georgiana Blakiston, *Lord William Russell and his Wife, 1815–1846* (Wilmington: Scholarly Resources Inc., Delaware, 1973), p. 169.

74. "Report of the Select Committee on Army and Navy Appointments," vol. 1, pp. 112 and 111.

75. "An Officer," *Observations*, p. 26.

76. [Capt. Robert C. Wallace], *Forty Years in the World; or Sketches and Tales of a Soldier's Life*, 3 vols. (London, 1825), vol. 1, p. 196. This may have been the Fifty-ninth Foot.

77. "Aesthetics of Dress. Military Costume," *Blackwood's* 59 (1846), p. 115.

78. *The Tailor's Complete Guide; or A Complete Analysis of Beauty and Elegance in Dress* (London, 1796), pp. 9–10 and 6.

79. Hall, *Scenes*, p. 118. "Novelty is everything to a soldier." Lieutenant G. Proctor, *Lucubrations of Henry Ravelin, Esq.* (London, 1823), p. 129.

80. *John Bull* (December 16, 1827), p. 396.

81. *Tailor's Guide*, p. 10. This seems to have been the reason for the bewildering variety of uniforms in Nazi Germany. See Brian Leigh Davis and Pierre Turner, *German Uniforms of the Third Reich, 1933–1945* (New York: Arco Publishing, 1980). These frequent, superficial changes in uniform are significant as a cultural characteristic of modern fascism.

82. "In short, they were light infantry, and the officers all superb." Captain George Elers, *Memoirs of George Elers, Captain in the 12th Regiment of Foot* (New York: Appleton and Co., 1903), p. 200. Light troops were then fashionable, and were often dressy.

83. One night he was feeling ill and declined wine; his messmates assumed that "I was feigning ill health by way of avoiding expense." [William] Gibney, *Eighty Years Ago or The Recollections of an Old Army Doctor: His Adventures on the Field of Quatre Bras and Waterloo and During the Occupation of Paris in 1815*, ed. Major R[obert] D. Gibney (London, 1896), p. 104.

84. Edwin Sidney, *The Life of Lord Hill, Commander of the Forces* (London, 1845), p. 27.

85. Letter 798, Cumberland to the King, March 31, 1820. George IV, *Letters of George IV*, vol. 2, p. 317.

86. Army Estimates Debate, Mr. Wynn, March 8, 1816. *Hansard's Parliamentary Debates* 33 (1816), p. 91. Officers were obliged to buy new uniform items whenever a pattern changed, unlike the Other Ranks, who got new coats and trousers annually. If an officer allowed his dress to become too shabby, the mess would inform him that his appearance was unacceptable.

87. Michael Barthorp, *British Cavalry Uniforms Since 1660* (Poole, Dorset: Blandford Press, 1984), p. 90. These included a small sword, a pallasch (a straight-bladed heavy cavalry model used in Germany and Scandinavia), and a "slightly curved" sword.

88. The informant is Thomas Creevey, who heard it from Wellington in 1818. John Cam Hobhouse (Lord Broughton), *Recollections of a Long Life, by Lord Broughton, with additional extracts from his private diaries*, ed. Lady Dorchester, 6 vols. (London: J. Murray, 1909–1911), vol. 2, p. 153.

89. De Ainslie, *Life*, pp. 151–152.

90. "His way of conducting himself was extremely similar to that pursued some years before by General Whitelock . . . who was afterwards broke for cowardice." Elers, *Memoirs*, p. 266. Whitelock's attack plan there "must be the most inept in the whole history of war." Michael Glover, *Wellington as Military Commander* (London: Sphere Books Ltd., 1968), p. 49.

91. Gibney, *Eighty Years*, pp. 172–173.

92. Cornet Walter Scott to Sir Walter Scott, February 22, 1822. Scott, *Private Letter Books*, p. 33.

93. In the Thirty-first Foot, the grenadier company got the tallest men and the light infantry company got the best-looking ones. Col. James P[eter]

Robertson, *Personal Adventures and Anecdotes of an Old Officer, by Colonel James Robertson* (London: E. Arnold, 1906), p. 140.

94. Sidney, *Lord Hill*, p. 32.

95. Mercer, "Reminiscences," p. 51. Like many new styles that were hated at first, the boot's popularity lasted for years; some had gold bullion tassels.

96. Ibid., pp. 46–47. The drivers were despised as noncombatants, so their wearing the style was especially mortifying.

97. Serg. Thomas Morris, *Recollections of Military Service, in 1813, 1814, & 1815, through Germany, Holland and France, including Details of the Battles of Quatre Bras and Waterloo* (London, 1845), pp. 143–144.

98. The Eightieth wore white feathers, and the Twelfth, red and black ostrich feathers. Elers, *Memoirs*, pp. 53–54.

99. Thomson, *Eighty Years*, p. 87. He had just transferred from the Ninth Lancers and thought the Thirteenth's shako "abominable" (p. 85).

100. Mercer, "Reminiscences," p. 45.

101. [Maginn], *Military Sketch-Book*, vol. 1, p. 118. Many such obscure terms were then used for military dress.

102. Wallace, *Forty Years*, vol. 1, pp. 197–198.

103. Maginn, *Military Sketch-Book*, vol. 1, p. 119.

104. W.O. 27/193, Confidential Reports, 1st or Royal Dragoons, R. H. Vivian, Maj.-Gen., October 16, 1829.

105. Anon., "Scenes and Sketches of Military Life. Patrick O'Neil—The Irish Grenadier," *Chamber's London Journal* (June 5, 1841), p. 13. The author identifies himself as a veteran private.

106. Wrottesley, *Life and Correspondence*, vol. 2, p. 92.

107. Wallace, *Forty Years*, vol. 1., pp. 132–133.

108. Derwent Conway [H. D. Inglis], *Personal Narrative of a Journey through Norway, Part of Sweden, and the Islands and States of Denmark* (Edinburgh, 1829), p. 85.

109. Edmund Burke, *Edmund Burke on Taste, on the Sublime and Beautiful, Reflections of the French Revolution, a Letter to a Noble Lord*, ed. Charles W. Eliot (New York: Collier, 1909), p. 36.

110. Mercer, "Reminiscences," p. 57.

111. G[eorge] R. Gleig, *The Life of Arthur Duke of Wellington* (London: J. M. Dent, n.d.), p. 341.

112. "Commanding officers of regiments are at their discretion to take frequent opportunities of directing the inferior field officers and captains of the regiment to take the command of the parade, without any regard to their respective ranks." Adjutant-General, *General Regulations . . . of the Army* (London, 1811 and 1816), p. 86.

113. Letter from Captain J. Burke to Sir H. Taylor, June 10, 1828, Lieutenant-General Sir Herbert Taylor, *The Taylor Papers*, arr. Ernst Taylor (London: Longmans, Green and Co., 1913), p. 308. This was doubtless one of the

reasons officers needed "covering-sergeants" to tell them the correct words of command at a review.

114. James Anton, *Retrospect of a Military Life, during the most Eventful Periods of the Last War* (Edinburgh, 1841), p. 56. The sergeant-major was the ablest advisor in such cases, yet the moment of crisis might be rendered more dangerous if the colonel was unaccustomed to maneuvering.

115. He paid for his vanity when exercising the points of the drill; he ordered the fourth point and, after no one moved, was told that there was no fourth point. Lieutenant-Colonel Balcarres D. Wardlaw Ramsay, *Rough Recollections of Military Service and Society*, 2 vols. (Edinburgh, 1882), vol. 2, pp. 45–46.

116. They were much surprised when the commander in chief appeared; the regulars were sent to the guard house, but after using every connection he had, Private Jerdan prevailed upon the general to release the men and pardon him. He was called "Marshal Jourdan" (a French marshal) ever after, "to my no small annoyance." William Jerdan, *The Autobiography of William Jerdan*, 4 vols. (London, 1852–1860), vol. 1, pp. 61–62.

117. Henry Hardbargain, *Hints to the Subalterns of the British Army* (n.p., 1843), pp. 26–27. The goose-step was widely used in the British army during this era.

118. General Sir Charles J. Napier, *Remarks on Military Law and the Punishment of Flogging* (London, 1837), p. 143. Napier believed that such colonels commanded two of every ten regiments.

119. Cecil Woodham-Smith, *The Reason Why* (New York: E. P. Dutton, 1960), pp. 57–83.

120. Patterson, *Adventures*, p. 6.

121. An Officer of the Line, "The Military Sketch-Book—Reminiscences of Seventeen Years in the Service Abroad and at Home," *Naval and Military Magazine* 1 (1827), p. 491. After 1815, some officers still wore hair powder, coat styles of the 1790s, and so on.

122. "The Horse-Guards had at last to give him a major-generalship to get him out of the regiment." Sergeant James McKay, *Reminiscences of the Last Kafir War*, 2nd ed. (Cape Town: C. Struik (PTY) Ltd., 1970), pp. 200–201. Norman Dixon linked such behavior to the heavy responsibilities of command. But he may have understated the importance of the fact that those in command can get away with such behavior because they are in charge. See *The Psychology of Military Incompetence* (London: Futura, 1976).

123. Order of J. Woodward, Colonel, December 31, 1830, and March 30, 1831. *Standing Orders of the Grenadier Guards for 1831* (London, 1831), pp. 37 and 53. Soldiers in the Seventy-ninth also altered caps against orders by removing the peaks. NLS, Brown Papers, MS 2,875, Windsor, Order of April 25, 1840.

3. RECRUITING

1. Inspector-General Jackson wrote of the influence of "the tinsel of dress" in recruiting. Inspector-General Sir Robert Jackson, *A View of the Formation, Discipline and Economy of Armies* (London, 1845), p. 189. This is one of the best analytical works on the early-nineteenth-century army, yet Jackson has remained "a neglected figure." Richard L. Blanco, *Wellington's Surgeon General: Sir James McGrigor* (Durham, N.C.: Duke University Press, 1974), p. 225. His obscurity might be the result of his quasi-military status as inspector-general of military hospitals, yet Jackson's works are intelligent and insightful. Jay Luvaas, *The Education of an Army* (Chicago: University of Chicago Press, 1964) does not mention him.

2. Edward Spiers, *The Army and Society, 1815–1914* (London: Longman, 1980), p. 45; and T. H. McGuffie, "Recruiting the Ranks of the Regular British Army During the French Wars: Recruiting, Recruits and Methods of Recruitment," *JSAHR* 34 (1956), pp. 50–58, 123–132. Hew Strachan's *Wellington's Legacy: The Reform of the British Army, 1830–54* (Manchester: Manchester University Press, 1984), pp. 51–57, and William Patrick Phenix's "Splendid Anachronism: British Horse Cavalry in the Victorian Age" (Ph.D. diss., University of Michigan, 1975), pp. 78–80, have both cited the phenomenon, although the latter work covers 1854–1901. McGuffie's article is a good discussion of recruiting.

3. Sir John Fortescue, *A History of the British Army*, 13 vols. (London: Macmillan, 1899–1930), vol. 11, pp. 9–10.

4. [Joseph Donaldson], *Recollections of an Eventful Life, Chiefly passed in the Army* (Glasgow, 1824), pp. 72, 79.

5. A new recruit was "buffeted about by the old soldiers, and in fact, driven from post to pillar,—he seems without one friend to cheer his spirits under the great change which he has lately experienced." Colonel John Rolt, *On Moral Command* (London, 1842), p. 57. Somerville claims that this was the major cause of desertion; see Alexander Somerville, *The Autobiography of a Working Man* (n.p., 1848; reprint ed., London: MacGibbon and Kee, 1967), p. 143.

6. Spiers, *Army and Society*, p. 37.

7. See C. C. Bayley, *Mercenaries for the Crimea: The German, Swiss, and Italian Legions in the British Service, 1854–1856* (Montreal: McGill-Queens, 1977). Chapter 1 of Bayley's book covers recruiting and manpower problems to 1854. For the period 1859–1899, Alan Ramsay Skelley states that recruiting was "one of the biggest problems." *The Victorian Army at Home: The Recruitment and Terms and Conditions of the British Regular, 1859–1899* (Montreal: McGill-Queens, 1977), p. 235. Foreign prisoners were used during the French wars, and most deserted at the first chance. Until 1826, "bad char-

acters" were drafted from their units into the Royal African Corps, serving in West and South Africa—and very few returned. Blacks from captured slave ships were inducted at Freetown, Sierra Leone, for the West India regiments. See Roger Norman Buckley, *Slaves in Red Coats: The British West Indian Regiments, 1795–1815* (New Haven: Yale University Press, 1979).

8. Statistics on the nationality of the Other Ranks were kept from 1830, when 42.2 percent were Irish, and 13.6 percent Scottish. Although the English then constituted 58.2 percent of the population of the British Isles, they provided only 43.7 percent of All Ranks in the army. But the number of Celts was greater overall, since Welshmen, Manxmen, and Cornishmen were grouped together with the English, and the Celtic portion of the army was probably even larger from 1800 to 1830. It seems likely that the decision to compile these statistics in 1829–1830 was at least in part motivated by concern for the high percentage of Celts in the army. Subsequently, the number of Celtic soldiers diminished at a fairly regular rate until the First World War, when together the two major Celtic groups constituted only 9.1 and 7.8 percent of the army respectively. Spiers, *Army and Society*, p. 50, Table 2.6; this information comes from a table in Parliamentary Paper no. 307 (1841).

9. "By inlisting I would get out of Glasgow, and to me that was everything." Donaldson, *Recollections*, p. 66.

10. This poster dates "between 1803 and 1812." Lieutenant-Colonel Sir Arthur Leetham, "Old Recruiting Posters," *JSAHR* 1 (1921), p. 120.

11. "A minor shall be at liberty to contract engagement to serve the state [as a soldier]." Opinion by Mr. Justice Best, cited in Charles M. Clode, *The Military Forces of the Crown; Their Administration and Government*, 2 vols. (London, 1869), vol. 2, p. 34. Units were not supposed to take apprentices, but whether they did or not depended upon the circumstances, as was the case in other areas of army life.

12. "No character was, as a rule, required of him [the recruit] though the practice of regiments varied in this respect . . . There were too many men enlisted who were of the criminal class or mentally deficient." Sir John Fortescue, *A History of the British Army*, 13 vols. (London, 1899–1930), vol. 11, p. 8.

13. Clode, *Military Forces*, vol. 2, p. 48. In the eyes of the authorities, the fact that many of the enlisted were vagrants probably justified the soldiers' harsh treatment.

14. [Tom S.], *A Soldier of the Seventy-First: The Journal of a Soldier of the Highland Light Infantry, 1806–1815*, ed. Christopher Hibbert (London, 1819; reprint ed., London: Leo Cooper, 1975), p. xiii.

15. Leetham, "Recruiting Posters," p. 119. Twenty-one is often mentioned as the preferred maximum age.

16. Private Henry Metcalfe, *The Chronicle of Private Henry Metcalfe, H.M. 32nd Regiment of Foot*, ed. Francis Tuker (London: Cassells, 1953), p. 5.

17. Sir Phelim O'Doodle [pseud.], *The Subaltern's Check-Book* (London, 1848), p. 7. A Fourth Light Dragoons veteran wrote of his 1823 enlistment: "I was then a young, and like most persons at that age, a foolish and inexperienced lad." Sergeant-Major William Taylor, *Life in the Ranks* (London, 1843), p. 3.

18. A Suffolk workhouse boy who rose to captain joined one of these units. John Shipp, *The Path of Glory: Being the Extraordinary Military Career of John Shipp*, ed. C. J. Stranks (London, 1829; reprint ed., London: Chatto and Windus, 1969), p. 10. These units were abolished in 1802, but most of these lads were soldiers for life, and thus the units' significance continued for decades.

19. W.O. 40/24. This was ended at the conclusion of the war.

20. Adjutant-General, *General Regulations . . . Addendum . . . 1816*. The *General Order* of November 14, 1811, states that the government proposed these schools. McGuffie, "Recruiting the Ranks," p. 124. From the eighteenth century, many units already had their own schools to give promising men and boys a basic education.

21. Spiers, *Army and Society*, p. 45. The pupils drilled and paraded in military trappings, a practice that was attacked in Parliament as "absurd." "Proceedings in Parliament—Army Estimates," *Naval and Military Magazine* 4 (1828), p. xiv.

22. This description is from an Irish village in 1814. T[homas] J. W. Connolly, *The Romance of the Ranks, or Anecdotes, Episodes and Social Incidents of Military Life*, 2 vols. (London, 1859), vol. 2, pp. 216–227. Another strategy was to give a free dinner and ball for the recruits.

23. Cited from manuscript accounts at the Cameron Highlanders Museum, in Loraine MacLean of Dochgarroch, *The Raising of the 79th Highlanders* (Inverness: Society of West Highland & Island Historical Research, 1980), p. 11. A recruit wrote of the "extraordinary" drinking powers of a recruiting sergeant, but observed that he was no worse than many others, for "drinking is part of their professional work." [E. C. Grenville-Murray], *Six Months in the Ranks, or The Gentleman Private*, new ed. (London, 1883), p. 12.

24. Alan Cameron of Erracht instructed his recruiters to distribute £20 to the poor of Stirling, Aberdeen, Inverness, and Paisley. MacLean, *Raising the 79th*, p. 10.

25. Great Britain, War Office, *Historical Record of the Eleventh, or The North Devon Regiment of Foot; Containing an Account of the Formation of the Regiment in 1685, and its Subsequent Services to 1845* (London, 1845), p. 41.

26. Serg. James Bodell, *A Soldier's View of Empire: The Reminiscences of James Bodell*, ed. Keith Sinclair (Toronto: The Bodley Head, 1982), p. 19.

27. Sergeant John Menzies, *Reminiscences of an Old Soldier* (Edinburgh, 1883),

p. 24. This unit may have been an exception, since most corps in this period were relatively indifferent about the territorial connection. Recruits would usually know little about their unit when enlisting, just as they usually knew little of the army beyond its show. Most buttons of this era bore the unit's number, not its county title. New county designations were assigned to some units during the Cardwell reforms of 1871.

28. [Tom S.], *A Soldier*, p. 13. This was rare outside Scotland, and those Britons from south of the Tweed who did so were usually the sons of noncommissioned officers.

29. The need for soldiers to labor at siege works in the Peninsular war led in 1811 to an extraordinary request, in light of the commander's immense authority and power: "The commander of the forces begs the soldiers . . . to be employed in making facines and gabions and pickets." They received extra pay for this work. Major-General Sir John T[homas] Jones, *A Journal of the Sieges Carried on by the Army under the Duke of Wellington in Spain: 1811–14*, 3rd ed., 3 vols. (London, 1846), vol. 1, p. 89. By the Crimean War era this had changed, and soldiers at Sebastopol were dismayed when set to roadmaking: "Our youths had not bargained for this when they assumed the red coat." James [Edward] Alexander, *Passages in the Life of a Soldier*, 2 vols. (London, 1857), vol. 2, p. 232.

30. "Military Forbearance," *Military Register* 9 (July 1820). A *JSAHR* contributor asserts that the term "private" originated in the seventeenth century; soldiers resented being called "common soldiers," so "private soldiers" was used. Another writer claims it came from the "growing insolence of the Parliamentary army," whose soldiers would not allow themselves to be called "common." G. E. B., "Replies," *JSAHR* 1 (1921), p. 233.

31. Lieutenant-Colonel Stepney Cowell Stepney, *Leaves from the Diary of an Officer of the Guards* (London, 1854), p. 251.

32. An anonymous pamphlet from 1756 mentions that soldiers believed themselves entitled to the vices of gentlemen. *An Enquiry Concerning the Nature and End of a National Militia* (London, 1756), pp. 57–59; cited by J. R. Western, *The English Militia in the Eighteenth Century* (London: Routledge and Kegan Paul, 1965), p. 110.

33. Jackson, *A View*, p. 247, note.

34. J. M., "Tactics, no. IV—How Should Infantry be trained and Armed?" *United Services Journal* 2 (1834), p. 317.

35. Somerville, *Autobiography*, p. 125.

36. Donaldson, *Recollections*, p. 170.

37. *The Subaltern's Log-Book: Including Anecdotes of Well-known Characters*, 2 vols. (Ridgeway, 1828), vol. 1, p. 108. Unfortunately for the newly made hero, she was not in church that day.

38. Lt.-Colonel Joseph Anderson, *Recollections of a Peninsular Veteran* (London: Edward Arnold, 1913), p. 3.

39. Jane Austen, *Pride and Prejudice*, in *The Complete Novels of Jane Austen*, vol. 1 (New York: Vintage Books, 1976), p. 298.

40. Henry Mayhew, *London Labour and the London Poor*, 4 vols. (New York: Dover Books, 1968), vol. 4, p. 235.

41. Edward Leeves, *Leaves from a Victorian Diary* (London: Secker & Warburg, 1985), pp. 112 and 106. The Brigade of Guards were a special case, having an elite status and brilliant appearance, and were normally stationed in a single area, centered on London and Windsor, so liaisons were probably easier for them to arrange than for line troops.

42. Leetham, "Old Recruiting Posters," p. 120. These posters mention uniforms only occasionally; the appeal's impact was primarily visual, and the recruiting process provided plenty to see.

43. Recruiting instructions for 1806 mention that uniforms are to be worn "constantly," and this rule was to be enforced by the regimental field officers. Great Britain, Horse Guards, *Instructions to Officers Employed on the Recruiting Service* (1806) p. 7.

44. Connolly, *Romance*, vol. 2, pp. 216–217. Only officers (excluding surgeons) wore epaulets in 1814. The Horse Guards' 1806 *Instructions to Officers* forbade deviations from regulation dress, but this rule was widely ignored. The "bang-up" consisted of a satin rosette from which streamed colored ribbons; it was also called "colors."

45. *Subaltern's Log-Book*, vol. 1, p. 94.

46. Sergeant William Lawrence, *The Autobiography of Sergeant William Lawrence, A Hero of the Peninsular and Waterloo Campaigns* (London, 1886; reprint ed., Cambridge, England: Ken Trotman, 1987), p. 11.

47. Charles James, *The Regimental Companion*, 4 vols. (London, 1813), vol. 4, pp. 293–294.

48. Connolly, *Romance*, vol. 1, pp. 218–219.

49. An officer wrote that reinforcements sent to the Peninsula in 1813 were "chiefly volunteers from the militia." [Major-General George Bell], *Rough Notes by an Old Soldier, during Fifty Years of Service*, 2 vols. (London, 1867), vol. 1, p. 79.

50. Private John Harris, *The Recollections of Rifleman Harris, as told to Henry Curling*, ed. Christopher Hibbert (London: Century, 1985), pp. 108–110. By the latter French wars, the dark-green rifle uniform was considered extremely smart, giving Harris's party an advantage. Militiamen were more representative of a cross-section of the population than the army, but they were also much more prone to join a regular unit than were civilians. They were often poor, since anyone with money who was unlucky enough to draw a ballot could buy a replacement. Because they could not legally be compelled to serve abroad unless they agreed, the acceptance of compulsory service, which in the past had caused riots, was eased. This system has often been criticized for taking away potential army recruits, but many militiamen

were eventually drawn to the service because they grew to like their dress and martial status in the militia and were eager to join the regulars. Although relentless drill was used to force men to volunteer, Harris's experience shows that some militiamen were fascinated by the idea of becoming "real soldiers"; Sergeant Morris wrote that as a volunteer he was "almost ashamed for being only half a soldier." Serg. Thomas Morris, *Recollections of Military Service in 1813, 1814 and 1815, through Germany, Holland and France, including Details of the Battles of Quatre Bras and Waterloo* (London, 1845), p. 9.

51. *Subaltern's Log-Book*, vol. 1, p. 5.

52. [William Maginn], *The Military Sketch-Book: Reminiscences of Seventeen Years in the Service abroad and at Home*, 2 vols. (London, 1827), vol. 1, pp. 20–22 and 39–40. This sort of excess generated many criticisms: typical is that of a Tenth Foot officer who thought young men should join for a love of the service rather than for foolish vanity. W. R. Bustin, *A Militia; Its Relation to the Regular Army. The Unjust, Partial, and Oppressive Nature of the Old System. A New System Developed, and Its Tendencies* (London, 1847), p. 16.

53. Still-hunting on rainy Irish nights was too much for this hero, who exclaimed, "No man could have remained longer and lived." Harry Austin, *Guards Hussars and Infantry. Adventures of Harry Austin*, 3 vols. (London, 1838), vol. 1, pp. 187–189.

54. *Subaltern's Log-Book*, vol. 1, p. 24.

55. Edward Costello, *Edward Costello: The Peninsular and Waterloo Campaigns*, ed. Anthony Brett-James (Hamden, Conn.: Connen Books, 1968), p. 2.

56. General John Fox Burgoyne, *Life and Correspondence of Field Marshal Sir John Burgoyne, Bart.*, 2 vols., ed. Lieutenant-General Sir George Wrottesley (London, 1873), vol. 2, p. 99.

57. A number of short articles by "The Hermit of London" in the pages of the *Naval and Military Magazine* in the final years of the 1820s treat different aspects of this theme. The author writes: "I consider the discharged officer . . . a solitary wanderer in the vale of obscurity: his occupation lost, and he is zero in the wide world." The Hermit of London, "The Disbanding of a Regiment," vol. 3 (1828), p. 43.

58. O'Doodle, *Subaltern's Check-Book*, p. 8.

59. Seventeen ninety-three is the earliest possible date for this poster—long after the hanger/short sword was supposed to be abolished for infantry—but the actual date is uncertain. Leetham, "Old Recruiting Posters," p. 132.

60. "All the boys had them in those days." Colonel James P[eter] Robertson, *Personal Adventures and Anecdotes of an Old Officer* (London: E. Arnold, 1906), p. viii.

61. "Twelve Years' Military Adventure in Three Quarters of the Globe," seri-

alized in *United Service Journal and Naval and Military Magazine* 1 (1829), p. 96.

62. Sergeant-Major Timothy Gowing, *A Voice from the Ranks: A Personal Narrative of the Crimean Campaign by a Sergeant of the Royal Fusiliers*, ed. Kenneth Fenwick (London: Folio Society, 1954), p. 1.

63. William Brock, *A Biographical Sketch of Sir Henry Havelock, K.C.B.* (London, 1857), p. 10, and John Clark Marshman, *Memoirs of Major-General Sir Henry Havelock*, new ed. (London, 1885), p. 8.

64. The artist George Cruikshank described this. See Blanchard Jerrold, *Life of Cruikshank*, 2 vols. (New York, 1882), vol. 1, pp. 50–51; "Twelve Years' Military Adventure," p. 96.

65. Robert Butler, *Narrative of the Life and Times of Serjeant Butler*, 3rd ed. (n.p., 1854), p. 24.

66. Letter xxxix—February 28, 1850, "A gun toy-maker." Henry Mayhew, *The Unknown Mayhew*, ed. Eileen Yeo and E. P. Thompson (New York: Schocken Books, 1972), p. 293.

67. Mary Agnes FitzGibbon, *A Veteran of 1812, The Life of James FitzGibbon* (Toronto, 1894; reprint ed., Toronto: Coles Publishing Co., 1970), p. 17. FitzGibbon rose from militiaman to line officer and ended his career as an inspector-general of Canadian militia.

68. Shipp, *Path of Glory*, p. 4.

69. [Corporal John Ryder], *Four Years Service in India*, ed. James Thompson, 2nd ed. (Leicester, 1854), p. 1. It is worth questioning whether a significant proportion of recruits who described other reasons for enlisting did not wish to betray what was usually perceived later to have been a childish, foolish, and vain decision, or the fact that they had been duped by the recruiter. Colour-Sergeant Calladine wrote that "no apprentice could have wished for a better place," but that he was restless. Serg. George Calladine, *The Diary of Colour-Sergeant George Calladine, 19th Foot, 1793–1837*, ed. M. L. Ferrar (London: E. Fisher and Co., 1922), p. 3. Sea service might have been a better option if this was his only reason for joining the service, but the fact that his book's cover is the same green shade as the facings of his unit, the Nineteenth Foot, may be an indication of his feelings.

70. Major John Patterson, *Camp and Quarters: Scenes and Impressions of Military Life* (London, 1840), p. 39.

71. Rolt, *Moral Command*, pp. 67–68. The availability of recruits and the presence of soldiers would vary considerably from place to place, depending upon a number of factors. Display also tended to elicit a desire among recruits to become musicians, which was often encouraged—contrary to *Standing Orders*—by recruiters. The Horse Guards' 1806 *Instructions to Officers* states that "lads and boys" are not to be enlisted with the promise of being made bandsmen or drummers (p. 17). The extent to which this

was followed is difficult to calculate, but since bold lies and fraud were a normal part of recruiting (mitigated by reforms in the 1840s), the prohibition of this practice gives an indication of the extent to which it was successfully used.

72. For example, "Recruiting Poster, 92d Highlanders, *c.* 1811," *JSAHR* 32 (1954), p. 38.

73. The colonel of the Caithness Fencibles (local militia) had "Flodden" inscribed upon their belt buckles on the pretext that the Caithness men had not been embodied for service since the battle of Flodden Field (1513). Major I. H. MacKay Scobie, "The Caithness Fencibles, and a Recruiting Card of 1799," *JSAHR* 6 (1927), p. 99.

74. Leetham, "Old Recruiting Posters," p. 120. This poster's date is said to have been between 1803 and 1812.

75. Seventh Light Dragoons poster from 1814. Ibid., p. 119.

76. Shipp, *Path of Glory*, p. 3.

77. Grenville-Murray, *Six Months in the Ranks*, pp. 117, 120.

78. "My First Regimental Coat," *Naval and Military Gazette* 4, vol. 3 (September 1828), p. 51.

79. MacLean, *Raising the 79th*. The poster is reproduced on the back of this pamphlet.

80. See Linda Colley, "The Apotheosis of George III: Loyalty, Royalty and the British Nation, 1760–1820," *Past and Present* 102 (1984), pp. 118–119. The effect of the royal family's appearance at a review during the invasion scare of 1803 is described in Thomas Hardy's novel *The Trumpet-Major*.

81. [Maginn], *Military Sketch-Book*, pp. 2–3.

82. But he added: "Still there was the charm of the Greys being Scottish, with their fame for deeds of gallantry." When out of work, Somerville and a friend enlisted despite his belief that he would have a better chance of promotion in a non-Scottish regiment because of his literacy. He also noted that "an entire troop of them, shortly before Waterloo, had been raised from among the farming men in my native parish, and parishes adjoining." Somerville, *Autobiography*, pp. 125–126.

83. W.O. 33/68, *Report of the Commission Appointed by the Secretary of State For War to Consider the Various Patterns of Headdresses Now in Use in the Army* (London, 1897). The title is a bit misleading, as uniforms were also discussed. The great degree of continuity in the role of the imagery and the evidence's pertinent nature render it significant for the earlier era.

84. Only one officer stated that he did not think the uniform and headdress were significant factors, believing instead that a lack of work was the main inducement. Ibid., "Minutes of Evidence," Question 398 to Colonel G. S. Burton, comm. 9th Reg't District, Norwich, p. 27. Yet the Adjutant-General, Sir Redvers Buller, pointed out that "while many starve who enlist, many starve who don't enlist." Question 433, p. 29.

85. W.O. 33/68, question 132, put to Colonel J. B. B. Dickerson, p. 17.
86. Arthur Wellesley, First Duke of Wellington, *The Prime Minister's Papers: Wellington, Political Correspondence I: 1833—November 1834*, ed. John Brooke and Julia Gandy (London: Her Majesty's Stationery Office, 1975), p. 22. The colonel also decided that no more recruiting was to be done in the towns for his corps, the Grenadier Guards, because "it will appear that a committee of the Grenadier Guards are members of a revolutionary club," p. 21.
87. W.O. 33/68, question 190, put to F. M. Roberts, p. 19.
88. Ibid., questions 485–490, put to Colonel A. Maclean, commanding the 48th Reg't District at Northampton, p. 31.
89. Jackson, *A View*, p. 291.
90. Colonel George Hanger, *Reflections on the Menaced Invasion* (London, 1804; fac. ed., London: Paul P. B. Minet, 1972), p. 156.
91. Sir Charles W. C. Oman, *Wellington's Army* (London: E. Arnold, 1912), p. 216.
92. Gowing was offered a commission in 1862 but refused because he had a large family and could not afford to become an officer. Gowing, *Voice from the Ranks*, p. xiii.
93. Jackson, *A View*, p. 353.

4. Discipline

1. The importance of rank is highlighted by the reaction of the authorities to an address the sergeants of the Seventh Foot delivered to their adjutant upon his promotion to captain for having "very commendably conducted himself with kindness to them without departing from that strictness of discipline which was indispensable." The commander in chief did not ascribe any improper motive to the address, but it was "an act of great insubordination" because it implied that they could pass judgment upon a superior. Royal Fusiliers Archive, file G/18, General Order 543, Horse Guards, October 16, 1839.
2. W.O. 7/57, Report 28 (1829), p. 11. The ready-made coats tended to be too small. G. A. Steppler, "The Regimental Coat of the British Infantryman, *c.* 1808–15," *Uniform* 8 (September 1989), p. 21.
3. Sergeant William Lawrence, *The Autobiography of Sergeant William Lawrence, A Hero of the Peninsular and Waterloo Campaigns* (London, 1886; reprint ed., Cambridge, England: Ken Trotman, 1987), p. 167. After 1871, the coats for All Ranks were dyed scarlet, but the different fabric qualities continued. The gray watchcoats used by the Other Ranks for foul weather were normally made in two qualities: the sergeants' coats with colored facings, the privates without.
4. In 1846, the Sixteenth Lancers wore "scarlet, not dull red like the infantry."

Percy Sumner, "The Aliwal Dress of the 16th Lancers," *JSAHR* 21 (1942), p. 187.

5. The sergeant's halberd was abolished in 1830 and muskets adopted instead. The sergeant's sword was abolished in 1852 for all but staff-sergeants.

6. "The General Principle of Regimental Discipline, 1st Article," *Standing Orders of the 56th Regiment*, p. 1.

7. *United Services Journal*, pt. 3 (June 1866), p. 178.

8. Sergeant [David] Robertson, *The Journal of Sergeant D. Robertson, late 92nd Foot: comprising the different campaigns, between the Years 1797 and 1818, in Egypt, Walcheren, Denmark, Sweden, Portugal, Spain, France and Belgium* (Perth, 1842), p. 11. This seems to indicate that light troops had not yet acquired an elite status; see Chapter 5.

9. Circular of October 23, 1828, Great Britain, Adjutant-General's Office, Horse Guards' *Addendum to the Orders and Regulations of His Majesty's Army . . . Jan. 1820–1830*.

10. Donald S. V. Fosten and Bryan K. Fosten, *The Thin Red Line: Uniforms of the British Army between 1751 and 1914* (London: Windrow & Green, 1989), p. 29.

11. Charles James, *The Regimental Companion*, 4 vols. (London, 1811–1813), vol. 1, pp. 97–98.

12. Francis Grose, *The Mirror's Image: Advice to the Officers of the British Army*, 6th ed. (London, 1867), pp. 53–54.

13. Thomas Jackson, *Recollections of My own Life and Times*, ed. B. Franklin (London, 1847), p. 176. The white topper was the trademark of radical Henry "Orator" Hunt; this may also be the origin of a stock symbol in early cowboy films, where "the good guy always wears a white hat."

14. "No white hats or jockey caps, [are] ever to be worn with any part of the uniform." *Standing Orders . . . 56th Regiment*, p. 192. These orders were issued in Bombay—where tropical white was used by many units—highlighting the political symbolism of the white hat.

15. May 5, 1830, *Betting Book of the Second Battalion (78th) Seaforth Highlanders, 1822–1908* (By the Mess, 1909), p. 50. A bet was also made on how many buttons were on one of their coats.

16. [General A. Cavalié Mercer], "Military Reminiscences of the Latter End of the Eighteenth and Beginning of Nineteenth Centuries," in R. J. MacDonald, *The History of the Dress of the Royal Regiment of Artillery, 1625–1897* (London, 1897; reprint ed., Bristol: Crécy Books, 1985), p. 43. A quiz was "a strange-looking fellow, an odd dog." [Francis Grose], comp., *Dictionary of the Vulgar Tongue. A Dictionary of Buckish Slang, University Wit, and Pickpocket Eloquence* (London, 1811; fac. ed., London: Bibliophile Books, 1984).

17. Mercer, "Reminiscences," p. 42.

18. Ibid., p. 43.

19. An Infantry Officer, "Changes in Uniform," *United Services Journal* 3 (1831), p. 400. The frock was replaced in 1848 by the shell jacket.

20. Diana de Marley, *Fashion For Men: An Illustrated History* (London: Batsford, 1976), p. 59. This image would seem to have been appropriate, owing to the middle class's greater ease of assimilation into the nobility, in contrast to French gentlemen, who continued to wear the old regime-style brocaded coat until the Revolution.

21. Christopher Hibbert, *The Destruction of Lord Raglan* (Baltimore, Md.: Penguin Books, 1963), p. 257–258.

22. Letter of June 16, 1827, Prince Herman Pückler-Muskau, *A Regency Visitor: The English Tour of Prince Pückler-Muskau Described in his Letters* (New York: E. P. Dutton, 1958), p. 219.

23. Arthur W. Uniform [pseud.], "Uniform," *United Services Journal* 3 (1831), p. 550.

24. W.O. 27/193, Inspection Report of Maj-Gen. C. Campbell, October 14, 1829.

25. *London Packet and Lloyd's Evening Post* (July 26, 1820).

26. This occurred in 1813. The officers required the hairdresser every morning and before parades or field days, or if they were dining out. Captain [Rees Howell] Gronow, *The Reminiscences amd Recollections of Captain Gronow: Being Anecdotes of the Camp, Court, Clubs and Society, 1810–1860*, 2 vols. (London: John C. Nimmo, 1900), vol. 1, pp. 273–274.

27. [Capt. Robert C. Wallace], *Forty Years in the World; or Sketches and Tales of a Soldier's Life*, 3 vols. (London, 1825), vol. 1, p. 196. This would depend upon the unit's station.

28. NAM 7,309–53, Orderly Book of Capt. William Russel, 20th Foot, Reg't Order of February 18, 1809. The regimental officers as a group usually decided upon the dress of the regimental "music" (band), since they paid for it with the "band subscription" (except in the Ordnance Corps).

29. An officer of the Fifteenth Hussars was court-marshaled for being out of uniform at Chatham. *Naval and Military Magazine* 2 (1828), p. 666.

30. Colonel [John] Anstruther-Thomson, *Eighty Years' Reminiscences*, 2 vols. (London: Longmans, Green and Co., 1904), vol. 1, p. 38.

31. *Standing Orders of the 1st Life Guards* (London, 1827), p. 7. This is a repeated order from 1814.

32. NLS MSS 2,869, *Standing Orders of the 85th Regiment*, p. 143.

33. Colonel C. P. [Charles Phillip] De Ainslie, *Life As I have Found It* (Edinburgh, 1883), pp. 84–85. This sounds like hunting dress.

34. *The Subaltern's Log-Book; Including Anecdotes of Well-Known Characters*, 2 vols. (Ridgeway, 1828), vol. 2, p. 163.

35. MSS Brown Correspondence, no. 1,863, J. Dunkan, Quarter-Master of the 74th, to Wilson, October 26, 1845.

36. The tartan's square was to "be only half the size of the square in the men's tartan as I think them rather too large for children." MSS Brown Correspondence, no. 1,863, from J. Dunkan, Quarter-Master of the 74th to Wilson, Portsmouth, July 28, 1846.

37. "There will be an inspection of necessaries, arms and accoutrements, every Monday morning." James, *Regimental Companion*, vol. 3, p. 13.

38. "The corporals are always to have a brush on parade, that the company's clothes may be clean brushed." James, *Regimental Companion*, vol. 1, p. 255.

39. Scottish Record Office GD/174/2,315, *Orders . . . Assisting the Non-Commissioned Officers . . . 79th Regiment*, p. 3.

40. Arthur Wellesley, First Duke of Wellington, *The Prime Minister's Papers: Wellington, Political Correspondence I: 1833—November 1834*, ed. John Brooke and Julia Gandy (London: Her Majesty's Stationery Office, 1975), p. 24.

41. Serg. George Calladine, *The Diary of Colour-Sergeant George Calladine, 19th Foot, 1793–1837*, ed. M. L. Ferrar (London: E. Fisher and Co., 1922), pp. 119–120. Punctuality was also significant for observation and control: "All duties will be regulated by the clock." *General Regulations and Standing Orders for the Garrison of Dublin*, p. 1. Pocket watches were considered essential for sergeant-majors and all superior ranks, and noncommissioned officers carried them in most units. Significantly, soldiers under commissioned rank were exempt from a short-lived tax on watches instituted in 1797. G. O. Rickword, "Clock and Watch Act," *JSAHR* 22 (1944), p. 258. A private with a watch gained a reputation for steadiness and sober conduct, for a drunk would never have saved his money for a watch. John Shipp, *The Path of Glory: Being the Extraordinary Military Career of John Shipp*, ed. C. J. Stranks (London, 1829; reprint ed., London: Chatto and Windus, 1969), p. 42.

42. Pipeclay was often applied twice a day to belts. Lt.-Col. J[onathan] Leach, *Rough Sketches of the Life of an Old Soldier* (London, 1831), p. 111. One officer lauded "the old arrangement" of the army, which "kept a soldier in constant work, when he is not so kept, he is doing mischief." General John Mitchell [Bombardino], "On Military Promotion," *Fraser's Magazine* 8 (1833), p. 312.

43. "Officers and non-commissioned officers must avoid anything to irritate a drunken soldier, who may be a good soldier sober, but get a severe punishment if [he is] provoked and strikes out." Colonel John Rolt, *On Moral Command* (London, 1842), p. 119.

44. "Siege of Badajoz in 1812," *United Services Journal*, pt. 2 (1833), p. 53.

45. "[Drunkenness is] the parent of the majority of military crimes." Sir James E[dward] Alexander, *Passages in the Life of a Soldier: or Military Service in the East and West*, 2 vols. (London, 1857), vol. 2, p. 255.

46. "Gin . . . makes one as tight as if he had a military coat on." John Shipp,

The Military Bijou, or, the Contents of a Soldier's Knapsack: being Gleanings from Thirty-Three Years of Active Service, 2 vols. (London, 1831), vol. 1, p. 166.

47. [Joseph Donaldson], *Recollections of an Eventful Life, Chiefly passed in the Army* (Glasgow, 1824), p. 85.

48. The duke of Kent's *Standing Orders* contained complicated rules that "probed most searchingly into every moment of the soldier's life." This was endured until he closed the dramshops in 1802, and the men mutinied, led by his own corps. The authorities revealed their judgment in this affair by recalling him, which must have been considered necessary to humiliate the king's son. He never again held military command. Roger Fulford, *The Royal Dukes: The Father and Uncles of Queen Victoria*, rev. ed. (London: Fontana Books, 1973), pp. 178–180. This was the second time a mutiny plot was devised in his command as a result of the attempt to abolish grog. A plan to murder the officers and march to the United States was discovered in 1791, when he was commander in chief in Canada. Daniel Green, *Great Cobbett: The Noblest Agitator* (Oxford: Oxford University Press, 1985), p. 69. Cobbett was sergeant-major of the Fifty-fourth Foot in Canada.

49. "An army is a vast body, the soul of which is composed of a world of conflicting passions . . . It is a motley concourse of men . . . perfectly careless of their individual reputations." "Leisure Moments in the Camp, etc.," *Military Panorama* (July 1813), p. 313.

50. Lieutenant-General Sir Thomas Picton, *Memoirs of Lieutenant-General Sir Thomas Picton, G.C.B., etc.*, ed. H[eaton] B[owstead] Robinson, 2nd rev. ed., 2 vols. (London, 1836), vol. 2, p. 140.

51. *Standing Orders . . . 56th Regiment*, p. 189.

52. NLS MSS 9,668 Wilson Papers, 92nd Highlanders, Reg't. Orders, Falmouth, March 11, 1823.

53. *Standing Orders . . . 56th Regiment*, pp. 105–106.

54. "Any man who, for the sake of avoiding water or other bad places, or for any other reason, presumes to step on one side, or quit his proper place in the ranks, must be confined." *Standing Orders as Given Out and Enforced by the Late General Robert Craufurd, for the Use of the Light Division during the Years 1809, 10 and 11* (Corfu, n.d.), p. 13. The same sentence appears in Rolt, *Moral Command*, p. 99.

55. "Artizans," *Military Panorama* (May 1814), p. 142.

56. When Sergeant Taylor of the Fourth Light Dragoons proposed in the late 1820s that a regimental library be established for noncommissioned officers, the colonel exploded with rage. Sergeant-Major William Taylor, *Life in the Ranks* (London, 1843), pp. 285–287. As the times changed and soldiers were better treated, regiments did establish libraries for the Other Ranks.

57. *Hints to Aspirants for the Army, and Young officers on Appointment* (London, 1840), p. 43.

58. Lieutenant John Sinnott, *A Manual of Light Infantry and Other Duties; Originally Compiled for the use of the Non-Commissioned Officers of the Forty-seventh or Lancashire Regiment,* 2nd ed. (London, 1851), p. 111.

59. Rolt, *Moral Command,* p. 113.

60. Sinnott, *Manual of Light Infantry,* p. 107.

61. "Memorandum," *Horse Guards Circular,* April 16, 1832, cited in Ibid., p. 104.

62. NLS MSS 2,873, Regimental Order 2, Cottoura[?], April 7, 1827, pp. 169–170.

63. *Orders for the Assistance . . . of Non-commissioned Officers . . . 79th Regiment* (Colchester, n.d.), p. 20.

64. Ulysses Macnamara, *The British Army: Condition at the Close of the Eighteenth Century, Compared with Its Present State and Prospects* (London, 1839), p. 58.

65. H.O. 50/11, letter to Lord Sidmouth, from [illegible], passed on from the duke of York to Sir John Byng, December 4, 1819.

66. Lord Colonel De Ros, *The Young Officer's Companion; or, Essays on Military Duties and Qualities* (London, 1851), p. 392.

67. Major-General Sir John T[homas] Jones, *A Journal of the Sieges Carried on by the Army under the Duke of Wellington in Spain: 1811–14,* 3rd ed., 3 vols. (London, 1846), vol. 1, p. 205.

68. "It is impossible that a company can advance correctly, while there is in its ranks a single individual whose shoulders and body are not square to the front." Sinnott, *Manual of Light Infantry,* p. 6.

69. *Orders for the Assistance . . . of Non-commissioned Officers . . . 79th Regiment,* p. 17.

70. Lieutenant-Colonel A. Cunningham Robertson, "Military Training," *Journal of the Royal United Service Organization* 5 (1861), p. 94. This refers to the "old (pre-Crimean) British Army." There were factors that mitigated these values in many regiments (see Chapter 6).

71. NLS MSS 2,875, Regimental Orders, 2nd Battalion, Rifle Brigade, February 27, 1840, Order no. 4.

72. Shipp, *Path of Glory,* p. 31. This effect can best be understood by wearing an army coat; the important "proper cut" forces the shoulders back, the head up, and rigidly encases the upper body.

73. Rolt, *Moral Command,* p. 91.

74. For cavalry this included virtually every motion on horseback, from simple mounting and dismounting to "draw swords," "front your horses," "load," "fire," and so on, and included more than a hundred separate motions. These were repeated "until the recruit is perfect in his style." The language implies that the training transcended the need for the proper use of weapons and management of the horse. Pvt. Alexander Somerville, *The Autobiography of a Working Man* (n.p., 1848; reprint ed., London: MacGibbon & Kea, 1967), p. 151.

75. Rolt, *Moral Command*, p. 107.
76. Inspector-General Sir Robert Jackson, *Outline of Hints for the Political Organization and Moral Training of the Human Race* (Edinburgh, 1823), p. 160.
77. Henry Mayhew wrote in the 1850s that the ex-soldier "had all the evidence of drill and barrack life about him." He also noted soldierly dress habits: "Ragged though he may be, there is a certain smartness about [him]." Henry Mayhew, *London Labour and the London Poor*, 4 vols. (New York: Dover Books, 1968), vol. 4, p. 417.
78. John Rees, who led the Newport Rising, was described as such in the *Monmouthshire Merlin*, November 16, 1839; cited in Ivor Hughes Wilkes, "Insurrections in Texas and Wales: The Careers of John Rees," *Welsh History Review: Cychgrawn Hanes Cymru* 11, no. 1 (1982), p. 85.
79. They cost 1s.\1d. each. NLS MSS 2,874, August 30, 1832.
80. Sergeant John Menzies, *Reminiscences of an Old Soldier* (Edinburgh, 1883), p. 7. Calcraft was London's public hangman from 1829 to 1874.
81. Buck Adams, *The Narrative of Private Buck Adams, 7th (Princess Royal's) Dragoon Guards on the Eastern Frontier of the Cape of Good Hope, 1843–48*, ed. A. Gordon Brown (Cape Town: W. J. Van Riebeeck Society Publications, 1941), p. 47.
82. Lieutenant-Colonel George Gawler, *The Essentials of Good Skirmishing*, 2nd ed. (London, 1852), p. 60. Gawler served in the Fifty-second Light Infantry.
83. Mayhew, *London Labour*, vol. 4, p. 417.
84. He agreed when he found out that the new kind cost no more than the old ones. Percival Kirby, *Sir Andrew Smith, M.D., K.C.B.* (Capetown: A. A. Balkema, 1965), p. 296.
85. "The colonel was quite wild at the straggling . . . as if they could help being done up, poor fellows!" Colonel James P. Robertson, *Personal Adventures and Anecdotes of an Old Officer* (London: E. Arnold, 1906), pp. 51–52. The Thirty-first was marching with loaded weapons at the time. In the tropics, concessions were sometimes (but not always) made by using white clothing.
86. Michel Foucault, *Discipline and Punish: The Birth of the Prison* (New York: Vintage Books, 1979). Foucault noted some of the factors in military control as an aspect of his larger discussion but did not delve into the subject.
87. The Adjutant, *Memoranda for the Officers of the Scots Fusilier Guards* (n.p., *c.* 1836), p. 7.
88. Rolt, *Moral Command*, p. 89. For a larger discussion of this curious dance of primate solidarity, see William H. McNeill, *Keeping Together in Time: Dance and Drill in Human History* (Cambridge, Mass.: Harvard University Press, 1995).
89. Calladine, *Diary*, p. 136. Drill was also important on detached duty to give a semblance of routine: "Unvaried routine is the very essence of true discipline." "Discipline in the Army," *United Services Journal* 1 (1833), p. 452.

90. "As regards . . . drill . . . it is not a very pleasant amusement." Sir Phelim O'Doodle [pseud.], *The Subaltern's Check-Book* (London, 1848), p. 38. Many cases exist of privates killing sergeants for over-drilling; two hours was considered the limit that men could endure, but extra drill was a favorite punishment.

91. Somerville noted that "in warm weather this is a terrible punishment." Somerville, *Autobiography*, p. 170.

92. The striking and unmistakable posture and motions might well be the reason New Zealand Maoris in the 1840s thought that soldiers were a race separate from Europeans. Colonel Thomas Bunbury, *Reminiscences of a Veteran*, 3 vols. (London, 1861), vol. 2, p. 54.

93. HEH MS ST 151, John Foster, *The Private Soldier's Monitor or Pocket Companion in Three Parts*, p. 1.

94. Inspector-General Sir Robert Jackson, *A View of the Formation, Discipline and Economy of Armies* (London, 1845), pp. 25 and cxxviii–cxxix.

95. Lieutenant-Colonel Stepney Cowell Stepney, *Leaves from the Diary of an Officer of the Guards* (London, 1854), p. 179.

96. Major-General John Mitchell, *Thoughts on Tactics and Military Organization: Together with an Enquiry into the Power and Position of Russia* (London, 1838), p. 249.

97. Serg. James Bodell, *A Soldier's View of Empire: The Reminiscences of James Bodell*, ed. Keith Sinclair (Toronto: The Bodley Head, 1982), p. 130.

98. Private William Douglas, *Soldiering in Sunshine and Storm* (Edinburgh, 1865), pp. 173–174.

99. Jones, *Journal*, vol. 1, p. 220.

100. *Subaltern's Log-Book*, vol. 2, p. 97.

101. [Tom S.], *A Soldier of the Seventy-First: The Journal of a Soldier of the Highland Light Infantry, 1806–1815*, 2nd ed. (London, 1819; reprint ed., London: Leo Cooper, 1975), p. 29.

102. Combat efficiency "can only be effected by constant and unremitting attention and practice." Leach, *Rough Sketches*, p. 408.

103. Captain Frederick B[rickdale] Doveton, *Reminiscences of the Burmese War in 1824-5-6* (London, 1852), p. 132.

104. Inspector-General Sir Robert Jackson, *A View of the Formation, Discipline and Economy of Armies*, 3rd ed., revised (London, 1845), p. 357.

105. "I am afraid it [flogging] is still too prevalent in our colonies." *Scenes and Sketches of a Soldier's Life in Ireland*, cited in *Naval and Military Magazine* 1 (1827), p. 468.

106. Many examples are mentioned in the narrative (1786–1793) of James Aytoun, *Redcoats in the Caribbean* (Lancashire: Blackburn Recreation Services Department (U.K.), 1984).

107. General Sir Eyre Coote was caught red-handed in a Chelsea boy's school

in 1816, having paid some pupils to beat him and to let him beat them. H.O. 50/11. He escaped court proceedings by being declared insane. Sadism has been perceived as a noteworthy aspect of English culture for centuries. See Ian Gibson, *The English Vice: Beating, Sex and Shame in Victorian England and After* (London: Gerald Duckworth, 1978).

108. A discussion of sadism and two examples of it in the army can be found in Serg. Paul Swanston, *Memoirs of Serjeant Paul Swanston; A Narrative of a Soldier's Life, in Barracks, Ships, Camps, Battles, and Captivity on Sea and Land; with Notices of the Most Adventurous of His Comrades* (London, 1840), pp. 42–50.

109. Macnamara, *British Army*, pp. 27–28.

110. De Ainslie, *Life*, p. 40.

111. O'Doodle, *Subaltern's Check-Book*, p. 49.

112. Major John Patterson, *Camp and Quarters: Scenes and Impressions of Military Life* (London, 1840), p. 312.

113. *Subaltern's Log-Book*, vol. 2, pp. 3–4.

114. He was considered "eccentric." Maj. John Patterson, *The Adventures of Captain John Patterson, with Notices of the Officers, etc., of the 50th Regiment, from 1807 to 1821* (n.p., 1837), pp. 357–378.

115. Private John Harris, *The Recollections of Rifleman Harris, as told to Henry Curling*, ed. Christopher Hibbert (London: Century, 1985), p. 28. To be commanded by a gentleman rather than one of their own also elevated some privates in their own eyes.

116. Major Charles James, *A New and Enlarged Military Dictionary* (London, 1810), p. 154.

117. Many officers disliked light infantry drill, but it was essential for rifle regiments. Lieutenant-Colonel Leach of the Ninety-fifth Rifles wrote: "It is doubtless, vastly pretty to see officers march by and salute gracefully,—to see formations from line into column, and from column into line, executed with accuracy and promptness; but I hold these to be very secondary considerations indeed for a rifle corps." But he added: "Although I am far from thinking that they should be neglected." Leach also wrote that his opinions would be deemed "heresy" by some officers. Leach, *Rough Sketches*, pp. 408 and 410.

118. This consequence was "perhaps an intentional one." George Thomas, the Earl of Albemarle, *Fifty Years of My Life*, 2 vols. (London, 1876), vol. 2, p. 219. Albemarle served in the Sixty-second Foot.

119. Colonel James Campbell, *The British Army as It Was, Is, and Ought to Be* (London, 1840), p. 220.

120. "Our colonel proved to be a thorough coward after landing in China, as all bombastic, bullying martinets are, I [have] never seen such men staunch when danger come[s]." Bodell, *Soldier's View*, p. 49. Many contemporaries

of all ranks made similar assessments. Norman Dixon's *The Psychology of Military Incompetence* (London: Futura, 1976), Chapters 16 and 17, offers the best discussion of this topic.

121. The notion of control through the use of positive means gradually gained ground; one officer declared (somewhat optimistically) that "moral influence has become and must ever be continued to be the ordinary discipline engine for the conduct of common regimental routine." Colonel Arthur W. Torrens, *Six Familiar Lectures for the Use of Young Military Officers* (London, 1851), pp. 1–2.

122. MS 7,311-6-1, Standing Orders of the 15th Regiment, 1813(?)–1845, "Punishments," p. 117. Colonels were more strict about officers' appearing at court-martials and punishments in full-dress. James, *Regimental Companion*, vol. 2, p. 464.

123. The victim had to pay six pence to the executioner for the cats because these were replaced after each flogging. Shipp, *Military Bijou*, p. 193.

124. The Duke of Wellington, *The Despatches, Correspondence, and Memoranda of Field Marshall Arthur, Duke of Wellington K.G.*, edited by his son, 12 vols. (London, 1834–1838), vol. 6, p. 196.

125. Adams, *Narrative*, p. 24. Theft in the army was considered especially odious, and the privates sometimes held informal courts to try offenders, with the two oldest and two youngest soldiers serving as the court. Punishment often consisted of a flogging with a belt. Shipp, *Military Bijou*, p. 187.

126. Private Adams wrote that he assisted in amputations, but that flogging was much worse. Adams, *Narrative*, pp. 15–16. Flogging constituted in a very real sense a form of public torture, and was a subject of controversy throughout the period under discussion. It was gradually reduced after the 1790s, in both the sort of courts that could "award" it and the number of lashes inflicted, until being abolished in 1881. Alan Ramsay Skelley, *The Victorian Army at Home: The Recruitment and Terms and Conditions of the British Regular, 1859–1899* (Montreal: McGill-Queens, 1977), p. 152. The subject is discussed in Harry Hopkins, *Strange Death of Private White: A Victorian Scandal That Made History* (London: Weidenfield and Nicolson, 1977).

127. Shipp, *Path of Glory*, p. 17.

128. Although the colonels often remitted the number of lashes after some had been inflicted, mob interference could create problems, and sometimes resulted in a reduction in the number of strokes inflicted. An example is described in John Green, *The Vicissitudes of a Soldier's Life, or a Series of Occurrences from 1806 to 1815 . . . the Whole Containing a Concise Account of the War in the Peninsula* (Louth, 1827), pp. 15–16.

129. A limit of three hundred lashes was set in 1812; two hundred in 1832. *Report From His Majesty's Commissioners For Inquiring Into The System of Military Punishments In The Army*, March 15, 1836, cited in *United Services Journal* 1 (1836), p. 511.

130. "After a notorious spree of looting [in the Peninsula] in which officers and men both participated, the officers got no punishment . . . [while the Other Ranks were punished]." James, *Military Dictionary*, p. 189. The propensity for drinking among officers was nothing short of legendary, but abated somewhat in the 1820s as growing middle-class values opposed this eighteenth-century fashion: "Hard drinking is everywhere declining in high life, both civil and military." *The Guards: A Novel*, 3 vols. (London, 1827), vol. 1, p. 85.

131. Connolly, *Romance*, vol. 1, p. 139.

132. Rolt, *Moral Command*, p. 46. This was also done to convicts: "The shaving of the head is a . . . punishment directed to the mind." *Parliamentary Papers*, 1810–1811, vol. 3, p. 44, cited in Michael Ignatieff, *A Just Measure of Pain: The Penitentiary in the Industrial Revolution, 1750–1850* (New York: Columbia University Press, 1978), p. 101.

133. *Naval and Military Magazine* 1 (June 1827), p. 620.

134. Edward Costello, *Edward Costello: The Peninsular and Waterloo Campaigns*, ed. Anthony Brett-James (Hamden, Conn.: Connen Books, 1968), p. 7.

135. Royal Fusiliers Archive, file S/13, copied from the *Gibraltar Garrison Orders*. The execution took place on November 7, 1862.

136. Shipp, *Military Bijou*, vol. 2, p. 37.

137. Adjutant-General, *Addendum to the General Regulations and Orders for the Army* (1830), Gen. Order no. 481, August 6, 1829. Before the abolition of the infantry sergeant's halberd in 1830, three halberds were tied together to form a triangle for the punishment, which could occur in the midst of battle. Some regiments used ladders to tie up an offender, or the flogging was administered inside the riding school in some cavalry regiments, with the prisoner manacled to the wall. This latter practice had the advantage of not arousing as much public attention.

138. While in Portugal, the bandmaster Westcott of the Twenty-sixth Foot described flogging: "In the British army [culprits are] tied up naked." BL ADD MSS 32,468, January 1812, p. 135.

139. *Subaltern's Log-Book*, vol. 1, p. 244.

140. As musicians, the drummers were considered more subservient, and their uniforms more closely resembled civilian liveries. Unlike bandsmen, they were "field musicians" transmitting commands by drum. They also had less honor because their job was to play rather than fight. Drummers were technically not combatants but were supposed to fight to the death to preserve their drums (though their short swords made poor weapons). This low status—reinforced by the distasteful duty of inflicting floggings—was probably the reason they tended to be unpopular. "A drummer will be a drummer still, no matter what rank he may attain, and I really think that it is true." Robert Waterfield, *The Memoirs of Private Waterfield, Soldier in Her Majesty's 32nd Regiment of Foot (Duke of Cornwall's Light Infantry) 1842–57*,

ed. Arthur Swinson and Donald Scott (London: Cassell, 1968), p. 125. It would be a rare man who was forced to inflict flogging without also feeling himself degraded. Similarly, farriers had a low status because they did not fight, but instead carried axes and were not supposed to bear swords: "From 1766 it was ruled that 'neither firelock, pistols nor swords to be accounted' for farriers." Michael Barthorp, *British Cavalry Uniforms since 1660* (Poole, Dorset: Blandford Press, 1984), p. 42. Yet some nineteenth-century illustrations show farriers armed with swords. The axes were used to dispatch wounded horses after battle, a menial duty without honor. Their primary job was to shoe horses, with a horseshoe on their caps instead of a plate. The ugliest, shortest men were made farriers.

141. "Neither officers nor men being able to preserve their gravity." Taylor, *Life*, p. 126. Those administering the flogging were alternated every twenty-five strokes to prevent their tiring.

142. Campbell, *British Army*, p. 95.

5. Morale

1. Inspector-General Sir Robert Jackson, *A View of the Formation, Discipline and Economy of Armies*, 3rd ed., revised (London, 1845), pp. 24–25.

2. Off-reckonings refer to the money deducted from a soldier's pay to buy his clothing and necessaries, and for the packing and shipping costs. This is not the place to discuss the reasons for the increased splendor of the military uniform from the late seventeenth century to the first half of the nineteenth century. But this process reveals larger trends in the transition from the Old Regime to the modern world, especially in regard to the relationship between the state and the increasing political power of the public.

3. Charles James, *The Regimental Companion*, 4 vols. (London, 1811–1813), vol. 1, p. 52.

4. This assumption of status by the the elaborateness of dress was a touchy point, however, because incompetent officers could wear a fancy uniform if they could afford the commission and kit; musicians' dress was also an exception, since their clothing was closer to livery and thus conveyed a sense of honor they did not embody.

5. In a proposal for a punishment or *corvée* corps, prisoners would be kept at drudgery, without arms and wearing very plain clothing, the net effect being "an inward consciousness of inferiority." James, *Regimental Companion*, vol. 1, p. lxxviii.

6. M[aurice] Austin, *The Army in Australia: 1840–50* (Canberra: Australian Government Publishing Service, 1979), p. 136.

7. "The dinner was followed by no excess." Letter of March 26, 1827, Prince Pückler-Muskau, *A Regency Visitor: The English Tour of Prince Pückler-Muskau Described in his letters, 1826–8* (New York: E. P. Dutton, 1958),

p. 83. Normally, violations of mess rules resulted in the offender's being fined bottles of wine, which were shared by all.

8. Percy Sumner, "Regimental Orders for Dress, 25th Foot, 1796 and 1828," *JSAHR* 16 (1937), p. 148. It is important to remember that such regulations might be ignored or altered when a new colonel took command.

9. These were the same color as full-dress (although a white version was adopted for the tropics), with bullion lace, although they were not as fancy as full-dress coats. The Sixtieth Rifles claim to have first adopted mess-dress in 1832. "Replies," C. E. A., "Mess Dress—Officers," *JSAHR* 3 (1924), p. 19.

10. This dated from 1746, when part of the unit was massacred while dining on St. John's Island in the West Indies. "Replies," A. C. W., "The Ever-Sworded," *JSAHR* 4 (1925), p. 219.

11. H. F. N. Jourdain, "Replies," "The Toast of 'The King', Captain E. C. B. Merriman," *JSAHR* 3 (1924), p. 13.

12. Major John Patterson, *Camp and Quarters: Scenes and Impressions of Military Life*, 2 vols. (London, 1840), vol. 2, p. 93.

13. "Our streaming white feathers are plain to be seen, and our facings are called the Gosling Green." Sergeant Stephen Morley, *Memoirs of a Serjeant of the 5th Regiment of Foot, Containing an Account of His Services in Hannover, South America, and the Peninsula* (Ashford, Kent, 1842), frontispiece.

14. Philip Henry, Fifth Earl of Stanhope, *Notes of Conversations with the Duke of Wellington, 1831–1851* (London, 1888), p. 252. After the facings reform of 1881, the Thirty-third got white facings like other English regiments, but after lobbying, they regained the red color in 1905. James D. Lunt, *The Duke of Wellington's Regiment (West Riding)* (London: Leo Cooper, 1971), p. 58. Many other units also strived to get the old facings restored. T. H. McGuffie refers to the pride the soldiers attached to their facings as "rather pathetic." T. H. McGuffie, "Recruiting the Ranks of the Regular British Army During the French Wars," *JSAHR* 34 (1956), p. 124. This overlooks or takes for granted the importance of such elements in building morale.

15. Edward Costello, *Edward Costello: The Peninsular and Waterloo Campaigns*, ed. Anthony Brett-James (Hamden, Conn.: Connen Books, 1968), p. 9.

16. Lt.-Col. J[onathan] Leach, *Rough Sketches of the Life of an Old Soldier* (London, 1831), pp. 6–7. The colonel of the Eightieth Foot wrote: "We considered ourselves a crack regiment, and what regiment does not think the same of themselves?" Colonel Thomas Bunbury, *Reminiscences of a Veteran*, 3 vols. (London, 1861), vol. 2, p. 251.

17. He went home and hung it in his hall. *The Subaltern's Log-Book; Including Anecdotes of Well-Known Characters*, 2 vols. (Ridgeway, 1828), vol. 2, p. 207.

18. "The Hermit of London," "The Fellowship and Brotherhood of the Army," *Naval and Military Magazine* 3 (March 1828), p. 77. Even cotton button-laces could be a mark of pride; an officer described an Irish soldier's reaction

to French criticisms of British button-lace: "Faith, then, we have often *worsted* them, and trimmed their jackets into the bargain." *The Guards: A Novel*, 3 vols. (London, 1827), vol. 1, p. 10, footnote.

19. Each battalion had two colours, the king's or queen's colour and the regimental colour. In cavalry units the colours were called a "standard." The first twenty-five or so infantry regiments were more likely to have badges on their appointments; by 1860 all corps had a title. An adjutant-general's memorandum from 1834 indicates that of all infantry units including guards and colonial corps, thirty-two had badges on the officers' forage caps and seventy-six had numbers, with one (the Forty-first Foot) blank. Most (or all) would have had the same ornaments on the Other Ranks' forage caps as well. Lelia A. Ryan, "Forage Cap Badges," *JSAHR* 55 (1972), p. 20.

20. General Sir Garnet Wolseley, *The Story of a Soldier's Life*, 2 vols. (London: A. Constable & Co. Ltd., 1903), vol. 1, p. 19.

21. Captain B. H. Liddell Hart, "Some Extracts from a Military Work of the 18th Century," *JSAHR* 12 (1933), p. 151.

22. Late in the nineteenth century, General Sir Evelyn Wood strongly recommended to the commission examining army headgear that the busby be retained because "everything in the way of a busby makes a man look taller and that adds to his vanity." W.O. 33/68, Minutes of Evidence, question 67, put to General Sir Evelyn Wood, *Report . . . Headdresses*, p. 14. Field Marshal Lord Roberts stated that "the present headdresses ought to be retained for *esprit de corps*, but would not have been chosen otherwise." He added that he had heard everyone say they wished to keep their distinctive headdresses. Question 199, put to Field-Marshall Lord Roberts, p. 19.

23. As a punishment, one colonel took away a cockade from a soldier who "seemed more alive to honor than the rest of his comrades," but instead of feeling remorse, he "was exceedingly grateful; it saved him the trouble of keeping it clean!" Edward Lytton Bulwer, *England and the English* (London, 1833; reprint ed., Chicago: University of Chicago Press, 1970), p. 65. "Cockade" probably meant the cap badge or shako plate.

24. Letter from Colonel E. C. Whinyates, Royal Horse Artillery, November 30, 1842, cited in William Siborne, *Waterloo Letters* (London, 1891), p. 208. The rocket sticks were called "fasces."

25. From the diary of Ensign Edmund Knox, entry of June 16, 1841. One of Them [pseud.], *The Eighty-Fifth King's Light Infantry (now 2d Battn. The King's Shropshire Light Infantry)*, ed. C. R. B. Barrett (London: Spottiswoode and Co., 1913), p. 276.

26. Charles Lethbridge Kingsford, commenting on the Sixth Foot's white stripe, wrote that "the inspecting officer in 1843 did not interfere, noting that it was an old custom." *The Story of the Royal Warwickshire Regiment (formerly the Sixth Foot)* (London: Country Life, Ltd., 1921), p. 88.

27. Each guards company still has its own company color, dating from the seventeenth century.
28. Of the kilt, one remarked, "There is an amaranthine [bright and unfading] charm of moral association interwoven with its warp and with its woof." Speech of Major Burgh, Ninety-third Highlanders, made in Canada on St. Andrew's Day. *Naval and Military Magazine* (January 14, 1843), p. 28.
29. "Editor's Portfolio," *United Services Journal*, pt. 3 (1834), p. 123.
30. Patterson, *Camp and Quarters*, vol. 2, p. 244. Patterson served in an English unit, the Fiftieth, Royal West Kent.
31. Colonel John Rolt, *The Guards and the Bearskin Caps* (London, 1854), p. 4.
32. The kilt was not then as popular as in later years. A commissary named Tidmarsh said in 1816, "Poor highlanders, sir, scarce decent, theirs is the nastiest costume!" and stated that the kilt was worn to save money because they could not afford "small clothes" (underclothing). Benson Hill, *Recollections of an Artillery Officer including Scenes and Adventures in Ireland, America, Flanders and France*, 2 vols. (London, 1836), vol. 2, p. 321.
33. Because of this, their recruits received 1/10s. after being attested fit for service, whereas those of other infantry units got only ten shillings. W.O. 43/741, "War Office Circ.," no. 927 (May 1844), p. 3.
34. Light troops' uniforms also cost more than the heavies'. Col. Armine S. H. Mountain, *Memoirs and Letters of the Late Colonel Armine S. H. Mountain*, ed. Mrs. Armine S. H. Mountain (London, 1858), p. 42. See note 8, Chapter 4, above.
35. Private John Harris, *The Recollections of Rifleman Harris, as told to Henry Curling*, ed. Christopher Hibbert (London: Century, 1985), p. 5.
36. The adjutant-general expected that only the best men would be taken for the rifle regiments. W.O. 3/611, letter from Adjutant-General H. Torrens to Sir Andrew Barnard of the Rifle Brigade, June 11, 1816.
37. Each full-strength line infantry regiment had eight battalion companies and a grenadier and light company.
38. This was done in the Twenty-sixth Foot in 1845. Mountain, *Memoirs*, p. 219.
39. General John Mitchell [Bombardino], "On Military Promotion," *Fraser's Magazine* 8 (1833), p. 323.
40. This was done at a time when many of his men were being punished for crimes. Diary of Captain Robert Dickson, entry of April 21, 1813. Sir Major General Alexander Dickson, *The Dickson Manuscripts: Being Diaries, Letters, Maps, Account Books, with Various other Papers*, 5 vols., ed. Major John H. Leslie (Woolich: The Royal Artillery Institution, 1905–1908; reprint ed., Cambridge: Ken Trotman, 1987–1991), vol. 4, p. 720.
41. "On A Badge of Distinction for General Service," *United Services Journal* 1 (1831), p. 370.

42. *Military Magazine* 2 (December 1811).

43. In the early nineteenth century "forlorn hope" referred only to the initial assault upon a besieged fortress, not the initial attack in battle, as it once had. The Other Ranks got medals after the battle of Seringapatam in 1799 and the Egyptian campaign of 1801, but these had been awarded by the East India Company and the Ottoman Sultan respectively.

44. One writer noted "the degree of interest that his [a soldier's] medal produces, particularly among civilians." *Naval and Military Gazette* 547 (July 1, 1843), p. 407. They served "to increase the distance between soldiers and civilians." Major Charles Dupin, *View of the History and Actual State of the Military Force of Great Britain*, 2 vols. (London, 1822), vol. 2, p. 18.

45. Alfred Brewis, "The Order of Merit—5th Regiment of Foot, 1767–1856," *JSAHR* 2 (1923), p. 118.

46. The best shot in each Rifle Brigade company got a silver medal, and the best regimental marksman received a gilt silver medal. If a man received the award two years in a row it was engraved with his name and became his property. NLS MSS 2,873, Regimental Orders, 2nd Rifle Brigade, Templemore, June 10, 1824, Regimental Order No. 2, pp. 47–48. In 1827, to "still further excite emulation," marksmen were made exempt from fatigue duties. Cottonera, Malta, April 22, 1827.

47. Costello, *Peninsular and Waterloo Campaigns*, p. 7. This was conducted by the colonel of the First Battalion, Ninety-fifth Rifles, after its return from the battle of Corunna. It was the first parade after the men received new uniforms.

48. In 1817, Thomas Peatley and William Morroh of the Fourth Foot received medals inscribed "From his Comrades" rather than from the regiment. B. A. Burke, "A Regimental Medal," *JSAHR* 41 (1963), p. 53. The granting of regimental medals was subject to the adjutant-general's approval. William Grattan, *The Duke of Wellington and the Peninsular Medal* (London, 1845), pp. 38–39. One wonders how often the regiments bothered to seek permission.

49. Colonel Francis Arthur Whinyates, *Corunna to Sebastopol: A History of "C" Battery, "A" Brigade Royal Horse Artillery* (London, 1881), p. 66.

50. All officers who served at Waterloo also received two extra years' seniority, a matter of no small significance to an army soon to be reduced.

51. Grattan, *Peninsular Medal*, p. 22. Many such examples are recorded.

52. A letter-writer demanded to know what right paymasters had to the Waterloo medal, since they were not "fighting characters." Letter to the *Military Register* 5 (August 1816), p. 32.

53. "H," *United Services Journal* 1 (1831), pp. 372–374. His colonel dissuaded him from this. Many Peninsular veterans would have been eager to pay the expense of striking the medal themselves.

54. Grattan, *Peninsular Medal*, p. 40. Two corps at the Cape had a similar affray.

55. General Daniel Lysons, *Early Reminiscences . . . With Illustrations from the Author's Sketches* (London, 1896), pp. 105–106.

56. Grattan, *Peninsular Medal*, p. 22.

57. Serg. T[homas] J. W. Connolly, *The Romance of the Ranks, or Anecdotes, Episodes and Social Incidents of Military Life*, 2 vols. (London, 1859), vol. 2, p. 63. A medal also meant a great difference to a veteran's survival, whether for employment or begging.

58. Two men received fifteen clasps. Major M. L. Ferrar, "War Medals of the British Cavalry," *Cavalry Journal* 75 (1918), pp. 101–102.

59. "General Orders, Circulars, & c[?]: General Order, Horse-Guards, Oct. 16th, 1830," *United Services Journal* 2 (1830), p. 890.

60. "Portfolio of an Officer," *United Services Journal* 1 (1831), p. 447. Another declared: "In all my soldiering (1803–1831) we never had the least notion of getting medals, Victoria Cross, or thanks of Parliament." MS Royal Fusiliers Archive, file H/6, Statement of John Hardy, 2d Batt. Royal Fusiliers, p. 4.

61. "Triumph of Treason! The King against White," *Military Magazine* 2 (December 1811), p. 439.

62. "On a Badge of Distinction for General Service," *United Services Journal* 1 (1831), p. 374.

63. Cited from Ellenborough to Lady Colville, June 8, 1842, I, Ellenborough Papers, Albert H. Imlah, *Lord Ellenborough: A Biography of Edward Law, Earl of Ellenborough, Governor-General of India* (Cambridge, Mass.: Harvard University Press, 1939), pp. 99–100.

64. Letter of September 3, 1813, from 2nd Captain R. M. Cairnes to Major General William Cuppage; from Dickson, *Dickson Manuscripts*, vol. 5, p. 1035.

65. [Captain Joseph Moyle Sherer], *Recollections of the Peninsula*, 4th ed. (London, 1825), p. 297. That he did not link "praise" and "fame" with battle honors shows how rarely they were granted by the sovereign.

66. Britannicus [pseud.], *Military Panorama* (January 1814), p. 467. On badges, a single, especially noteworthy battle-honor was displayed, while the colours bore all the honors.

67. J. H. W. Hall, *Scenes in a Soldier's Life* (Montreal, 1848), p. 357.

68. Pvt. William Wheeler, *The Letters of Private Wheeler*, ed. Capt. B[asil] H. Liddel Hart (Boston: Houghton Mifflin, 1952), p. 21.

69. For example, the Forty-first Foot got the honors of "Detroit," "Queenstown," and "Miami" for the American war. W.O. 3/65, letter from Adjutant-General Cathcart to the Commander-in-Chief, His Highness the Duke of York, April 2, 1816.

70. Lt.-Colonel Joseph [Jocelyn] Anderson, *Recollections of a Peninsular Veteran* (London: Edward Arnold, 1913), pp. 264–265.

71. Buck Adams, *The Narrative of Private Buck Adams, 7th (Princess Royal's)*

Dragoon Guards on the Eastern Frontier of the Cape of Good Hope, 1843–48, ed. A. Gordon Brown (Cape Town: W. J. Van Riebeeck Society Publications, 1941), p. 233.

72. Patterson, *Camp and Quarters*, vol. 2, pp. 93–95.

73. Bunbury, *Reminiscences*, vol. 3, p. 327.

74. John Shipp, *The Path of Glory: Being the Extraordinary Military Career of John Shipp*, ed. C. J. Stranks (London, 1829; reprint ed., London: Chatto and Windus, 1969), p. 117.

75. "The Late Howell Paynter and the Battle of Chillianwallah," *Colburn's United Service Magazine* 362 (January 1859), p. 589.

76. The fakes were discovered, but: "If taken while they are contending with a vastly superior force, as was the case in this instance, it cannot reflect any disgrace." Serg. Thomas Morris, *Recollections of Military Service in 1813, 1814 and 1815, through Germany, Holland, and France; including some details of the Battles of Quatre Bras and Waterloo* (London, 1845), p. 251.

77. Philip J. Haythornthwaite, *British Infantry in the Napoleonic Wars* (New York: Arms and Armour Press, 1987), p. 32. He was also promoted, which was usual in such cases.

78. "The regiment cannot be well said to exist as yet . . . Where are the old non-commissioned officers and the old soldiers on whom the corps is to be formed? It will need much tact and rare skill to restore to the 44th Regiment [its] pride." "Presentation of Colours to the 44th Foot," *Naval and Military Magazine* 534 (1843), p. 200.

79. NAM 7,311–6–1, Standing Orders, 15th Regiment. Presumably, such conduct by an officer was unthinkable.

80. [William Maginn], *The Military Sketch-Book*, 2 vols. (London, 1827), vol. 1, p. 249.

81. *Military Register* 5 (November 1816).

82. Hall, *Scenes*, pp. 80–81.

83. Maj. M. L. Ferrar, "Burial of the Regimental Colours," *JSAHR* 3 (1924), p. 104.

84. Wheeler, *Letters*, pp. 35–36.

85. J. F. R., "Burning Of The Colours Of The Second Battalion King's Regiment, With Prefatory Remarks On The Condition Of The Half-Pay," *United Services Journal* 2 (1830), pp. 537–539.

86. Harris, *Recollections*, p. 35.

87. [Maginn], *Military Sketch-Book*, vol. 1, p. 98.

88. Ibid., pp. 103–104.

89. See Linda Colley, "The Apotheosis of George III: Loyalty, Royalty and the British Nation, 1760–1820," *Past and Present* 102 (1984), pp. 112–113. This has since been expanded upon in her book *Britons: Forging the Nation, 1707–1837* (London: Pimlico, 1992).

90. RSUSM MSS q 355.486 * 213.2, "Scots Greys Regimental Papers . . .

Waterloo and Crimean Campaigns," General Orders, Headquarters, Before Sebastopol, December 24, 1854; War Department, Duke of Newcastle's Dispatch, 27th December, November, 1854.

91. Letter of June 20, 1820, Lady Palmerston (Emily Cowper Temple), *The Letters of Lady Palmerston*, ed. Tresham Lever (London: John Murray, 1957), p. 37.

92. John Mollo, *Military Fashion* (New York: G. P. Putnam's Sons, 1972), p. 30.

93. After the accession of King William IV, the Fiftieth Foot's title was changed from "The Duke of Clarence's" regiment to "The Queen's Own," and its black facings were changed to royal blue. "Promotions," *United Services Journal* 5 (1831), p. 421.

94. Wheeler, *Letters*, p. 237.

95. "An example to royalty in future to enter the battle-field, and share the dangers of war." [Major-General George Bell], *Rough Notes by an Old Soldier, during Fifty Years of Service*, 2 vols. (London, 1867), vol. 2, p. 214.

96. Mourning dress for King George III in 1820 was as follows: the hat lace and sword knot were to be covered with black, the gorget ribbon was to be black, with a black arm band on the left arm, a black crepe scarf was to be draped over the right shoulder, and the colors were to be hung with black crepe. "Mourning the King," *Military Register* 4 (1820), pp. 143–144.

97. Colonel C. P. [Charles Phillip] De Ainslie, *Life As I have Found It* (Edinburgh, 1883), p. 116.

98. Serg. George Calladine, *The Diary of Colour-Sergeant George Calladine, 19th Foot, 1793–1837*, ed. M. L. Ferrar (London: E. Fisher and Co., 1922), pp. 100–102.

99. Queen Victoria to Sir George Grey, July 14, 1848, *Queen Victoria's Early Letters*, ed. John Raymond, rev. ed. (New York: Macmillan, 1963), p. 146.

100. "The Hermit of London," "The Fellowship and Brotherhood of the Army," *Naval and Military Magazine* 3 (1828), p. 77.

101. Lady Canning (Charlotte Stuart) from Florence Nightingale, September 9, 1855. Florence Nightingale, *"I Have Done My Duty": Florence Nightingale in the Crimean War, 1854–56*, ed. Sue M. Goldie (Iowa City, Iowa: University of Iowa Press, 1987), p. 151. No source has been found in this research that contains any expression of disloyalty toward the monarch by soldiers of any rank.

102. Such privileges have done much to shape the army's rich regimental traditions, and today every unit many customs that are unique to it.

103. Royal Fusiliers Archive, file P/Powley, David Powley, "The Royal Regiment of Fusiliers: 1827–1965," (M.A. thesis, Centre of Education, 1976), p. 149.

104. Lieutenant-Colonel Balcarres D. Wardlaw Ramsay, *Rough Recollections of Military Service and Society*, 2 vols. (Edinburgh, 1882), vol. 1, p. 36. When the Eleventh met Prince Albert at Dover in 1840 and escorted him to

Windsor, they gained the title "Prince Albert's Own, Hussars." But three months later the colonel, Lord Cardigan, began a series of notorious episodes that started with the "Black Bottle" affair, "a nine days wonder," which was followed by a string of ugly scandals. There were vehement denunciations in the press, he was hooted at on the streets of Brighton, and a riot ensued when he attended a London theater. See Cecil Woodham-Smith, *The Reason Why* (New York: E. P. Dutton & Co., 1960), pp. 57–83. This might be an example of Wellington's taking advantage of an opportunity to alter a tradition and thus avoid embarrassment—or worse—for both the crown and the army.

105. Such isolated worlds have been called "total institutions." See Erving Goffman, *Asylums: Essays on the Social Situation of Mental Patients and Other Inmates* (New York: Anchor Books, 1961).

106. Sergeant [David] Robertson, *The Journal of Sergeant D. Robertson, late 92nd Foot: comprising the different campaigns, between the Years 1797 and 1818, in Egypt, Walcheren, Denmark, Sweden, Portugal, Spain, France and Belgium* (Perth, 1842), p. 106. A recruiting sergeant of the Twenty-ninth Foot mistakenly took two counterfeit pound notes, and then, having no money to feed his recruits, deserted and tried to starve himself to death while hiding in a ditch: "It hurt his feelings so much that he could not bear it, having been in the regiment ten years, without the least stain on his character." Royal United Service Institution, "Military Extracts," cited in H. Everhard, *History of Thos. Farrington's Regiment, subsequently designated the 29th Regiment (Worcestershire) Foot, 1694 to 1891* (Worcester: Littlebury and Co., 1891), p. 355.

107. RSUSM MSS q 355.486 * 213.2, "Scots Greys Regimental Papers, Relating to the Waterloo and Crimean Campaigns," "Interesting anecdote—Sergeant Wier."

108. Colonel James Campbell, *The British Army as It Was, Is, and Ought to Be* (London, 1840), p. 221.

6. Campaign and Combat

1. Sergeant-Major Timothy Gowing, *A Voice from the Ranks; A Personal Narrative of the Crimean Campaign by a Sergeant of the Royal Fusiliers*, ed. Kenneth Fenwick (London: Folio Society, 1954), p. 3. This reaction was especially noteworthy; Gowing's editor notes: "The 'Manchester School' of political thought, addicted to free trade and laissez-faire, was also noted for its pacifist principles."

2. "The Brothers," *Naval and Military Magazine* 4 (December 1828), p. 497.

3. Gowing, *Voice*, pp. 2–3.

4. The Twenty-third Fusiliers received orders one evening to march the next morning from Colchester to Portsmouth for embarkation abroad. "The

whole night of course was spent in bustle of every description." Capt. Thomas Henry Browne, *The Napoleonic Journal of Captain Thomas Henry Browne, 1807–1816*, ed. Roger Norman Buckley (London: The Bodley Head, 1987), p. 68. Browne's company embarked the next day, and the regiment sailed for Canada three weeks after receiving the orders.

5. W.O. 7/56, Report of July 13, 1811. The last practice gives a strong indication that for cavalry, bayonets were almost exclusively useful for show—or riot duty.

6. Percy Sumner, "Uniforms and Equipment of the 15th Light Dragoons (Hussars) 1808 to 1813; Extracts From the Adjutant's Journals," *JSAHR* 16 (1937), p. 168. After many years of war, the Horse Guards in 1811 finally prohibited the practice of allotting horses to cavalry companies on the basis of color. Instead, they were to be placed immediately in troops "as the circumstances of the service may render most expedient." MS C40, *Addendum . . . Regulations . . . 12 August, 1811*, Circular Letter of October 12, 1811, copied in the *Scots Guards Regimental Orderly Book*, p. 328.

7. The Eleventh Hussars' officers did this in 1854. Cecil Woodham-Smith, *The Reason Why* (New York: E. P. Dutton, 1960), p. 133.

8. When the Fortieth Foot arrived at Montevideo in 1807, long hair and powder were done away with. Sergeant William Lawrence, *The Autobiography of Sergeant William Lawrence, A Hero of the Peninsular and Waterloo Campaigns* (London, 1886; reprint ed., Cambridge, England: Ken Trotman, 1987), p. 23. Queues were also cut off for active service in the eighteenth century.

9. Colonel John Rolt, *The Guards and the Bearskin Caps* (London, 1854), p. 2.

10. W.O. 7/56, Report of February 3, 1812, p. 171; Preben Kannik, *Military Uniforms in Color*, trans. John Hewish, English edition ed. W. Y. Carman (New York: McMillan, 1968), p. 206.

11. This is shown in a print entitled "Second Battalion Grenadier Guards, Fall, 1838" that was made on the spot. Captain Russell Steele, "British Army Uniforms in Canada in 1838," *JSAHR* 23 (1944), p. 123. This seems to have been the practice after 1815.

12. For example, three infantry colonels agreed to experiment by clothing their regiments in different kinds of trousers for the Walcheren expedition of 1809. Lieutenant-Colonel Charles Cadell, *Narrative of the Campaigns of the 28th Regiment since their return from Egypt in 1802* (London, 1835), pp. 83–84.

13. Major-General John Mitchell, *Thoughts on Tactics and Military Organization: Together with an Enquiry into the Power and Position of Russia* (London, 1838), p. 226. Jack boots provided cavalrymen with some leg protection in a skirmish, but they were heavy and awkward, requiring a second pair of shoes for walking.

14. Capt. [Rees Howell] Gronow, *The Reminiscences and Recollections of Captain*

Gronow: Being Anecdotes of the Camp, Court, Clubs and Society, 1810–1860, 2 vols. (London: John C. Nimmo, 1900), vol. 1, p. 80.

15. Tartan trews were worn by mounted field grade officers. Both kilts and trews were sometimes worn on campaign, even in the harshest conditions. Rifleman Harris refers to the Ninety-second and Seventy-ninth Highland regiments during the retreat to Corunna in 1808–1809 as "the kilts." Private John Harris, *The Recollections of Rifleman Harris, as told to Henry Curling*, ed. Christopher Hibbert (London: Century, 1985), p. 66.

16. W.O. 7/56, February 3, 1812, p. 172. The Forty-second wore kilts through-out the Peninsular war; after 1814, kilts, trousers, and trews were all worn by highland regiments on overseas campaigns, with kilts being supplied when units were sent out in some cases, although this depended upon circumstances. The Ninety-third Highlanders wore trews when sent to the West Indies in 1834, and were not required by army regulations to wear kilts. W.O. 7/58, letter of December 1, 1834.

17. John Shipp, *The Path of Glory: Being the Extraordinary Military Career of John Shipp*, ed. C. J. Stranks (London, 1829; reprint ed., London: Chatto and Windus, 1969), p. 106.

18. James recommends these, while stating regulations where they applied. Maj. Charles James, *The Regimental Companion*, 4 vols. (London, 1813), vol. 2, p. 376. Slops were one of the forerunners of mass-produced, ready-made clothing.

19. *Addendum . . . Regulations . . . January 1830–31 March, 1835*, Horse Guards Circular Memorandum, March 12, 1834, copied in the *Scots Guards Orderly Book*, pp. 817–819. A list of "Sea Necessaries" states that canvas frocks were not included when Gibraltar was the destination. *Scots Guards Orderly Book*, pp. 818–819. Marines also wore slops at sea, saving the red coats for shore duty. N. A. M. Rodger, *The Wooden World: An Anatomy of the Georgian Navy* (Annapolis: Naval Institute Press, 1986), p. 215.

20. Nine balls of pipeclay were part of the list of "Sea Necessaries" for voyages to the East Indies. *Scots Guards Orderly Book*, pp. 818–819. When the Thirty-third Foot went to India, Wellington ordered that when on ship-board they were to wear full-dress with accoutrements to divine service. Elizabeth Longford, *Wellington: The Years of the Sword* (New York: Harper and Row, 1969), p. 51. At sea, regiments continued to drill on deck to the extent that space made it possible; this helped to maintain discipline, in addition to keeping the men in practice and maintaining the correct posture.

21. Percy Sumner, "Dress Worn in Hot Climates, Seventeenth and Eighteenth Centuries," *JSAHR* 13 (1934), p. 173.

22. For the late eighteenth century, see Philip J. Haythornthwaite, *Uniforms of the French Revolutionary Wars: 1789–1802* (Poole, Dorset: Blandford Press, 1981), pp. 92 and 102. For the Crimea, see Sir James [Edward] Alexander, *Passages in the Life of a Soldier*, 2 vols. (London, 1857), vol. 1, p. 298. These

summer uniforms were made in Italy and seem to have been an *ad hoc* arrangement.

23. Richard L. Blanco, *Wellington's Surgeon General: Sir James McGrigor* (Durham, N.C.: Duke University Press, 1974), p. 54.

24. "An Account of the Recruiting Depot to be Raised at Sierra Leone or Gorée, for the Enlistment of Men of Colour, for . . . West India Regiments," *Military Panorama* (October 1812), p. 61. Round coats were made without tails. W.O. 7/56, "Clothing and Equipment of Infantry," Report of February 3, 1812. Haythornthwaite, *Uniforms*, p. 92.

25. Guy C. Dempsey, "Mutiny at Malta: The Revolt of Froberg's Regiment, April, 1807," *JSAHR* 67 (1989), p. 20. The Other Ranks were Greeks and Albanians.

26. Certificates of delivery were required by the adjutant-general. W.O. 7/56, Report of February 3, 1812, sec. X, p. 174.

27. *The Subaltern's Log-Book; Including Anecdotes of Well-Known Characters*, 2 vols. (Ridgeway, 1828), vol. 2, p. 240. It is difficult to pinpoint when this was first practiced. John Gilinsky, "Officer's Dress of the 24th Regiment of Foot, India 1820," *JSAHR* 60 (1981), p. 250. Sergeant Pearman recorded in his memoirs that in 1851 treatment at the army hospitals in India was very good, another indication of the company's concern for the soldiers' health. Sgt. John Pearman, *The Radical Soldier's Tale: John Pearman, 1819–1908*, intro. Carolyn Steedman (New York: Routledge, 1988), p. 184.

28. "Costume in India," *Naval and Military Miscellany* 4 (December 1827), p. 612; Gilinsky, "Officer's Dress," p. 250. White clothing was made out of "cotton jean." There were exceptions to the custom of wearing scarlet in the cool season, but some officers took pride in wearing it despite the heat, and everyone had to have a full-dress uniform: "A mans kit in India [in the 1840s] in quarters is . . . 4 white jackets [and] 1 dress coat." Pearman, *Radical Soldier's Tale*, p. 143.

29. John Clark Marshman, *Memoirs of Major-General Sir Henry Havelock, K.C.B.*, new ed. (London, 1885), pp. 281–282. He writes that "every effort" was made to procure slops for the Seventy-eighth; the coats might have been modified to make them more bearable.

30. Capt. Russell Steele, "The Last India Mutiny Survivors at the Royal Hospital, Chelsea," *JSAHR* 35 (1957), p. 138.

31. W.O. 3/27.

32. W.O. 7/56, Report of July 13, 1811, p. 121.

33. Philip J. Haythornthwaite, *British Infantry in the Napoleonic Wars* (New York: Arms and Armour Press, 1987), p. 94. This refers to the York Light Infantry Volunteers, a foreign corps composed of captured Dutch prisoners.

34. This was recommended in Col. Lord W. De Ros, *The Young Officer's Companion: or, Essays on Military Duties and Qualities* (London, 1851), p. 37. Air vents were not added to shakos until the mid-1830s.

35. This is covered for the period of the French wars in David Gates, *The British Light Infantry Arm: c. 1790–1815* (London: B. T. Batsford, 1987).
36. They also had browned muskets, "to prevent them being seen in the woods." Shipp, *Path of Glory*, p. 29.
37. Haythornthwaite, *Uniforms*, p. 110 and plate no. 35.
38. "Round hats" (forerunners of the top hat) were best known as symbols of patriotism, but trousers and gaiters also had this connotation. Henry Cockburn, *Memorials of His Time*, ed. Karl F. C. Miller (London: University of Chicago Press, 1974), p. 62.
39. "He went on to say, that there was nothing we ought to watch more jealously than any infringement on the national uniform, nor anything more important to maintain, than the solidarity and steadiness of our infantry." Chaplain-General G[eorge] Gleig, *The Life of Wellington* (London, n.d.), p. 340. Although it is claimed that he was "utterly heedless of forms and regulations regarding dress" (Longford, *Wellington*, p. 205), this apparently refers to officers' dress on campaign. When a new gentleman volunteer in the Peninsula asked Wellington if he could be assigned to the Ninety-fifth Rifles, the duke replied: "The uniform isn't very smart." On the volunteer's stating that they saw a good deal of the enemy, the duke—who may have been testing him—said that he would be assigned to that regiment. Gerald Fitzmaurice, *Biographical Sketch of Major General John Fitzmaurice K.H., written for Private Circulation* (Anghiari, Italy: Tiber Printing Press, 1908), p. 19. I am indebted to Sheperd Paine and the Military Miniature Society of Illinois for knowledge of this work.
40. Major John Patterson, *Camp and Quarters: Scenes and Impressions of Military Life* (London, 1840), p. 240. Light infantry wore scarlet with a green shako plume in parade dress, indicating that they were light—rather than heavy—infantry.
41. W.O. 7/56, Report of 1810/11, p. 103.
42. Sir Patrick Cadell, "The Beginnings of Khaki," *JSAHR* 31 (1953), pp. 132–133.
43. BL ADD MSS 27,597, 1810/11, "Sir David Dundas's Report on Army Clothing, Etc."
44. Many men were without their helmets, or the crests had been broken or removed, and many lacked belts, canteens, and haversacks; Mercer did not believe combat was the sole cause. General Cavalié [Alexander] Mercer, *Journal of the Waterloo Campaign, kept throughout the Campaign of 1815* (New York: Praeger, 1970), p. 199.
45. Ibid., p. 119.
46. Gronow, *Reminiscences*, vol. 1, pp. 97–98.
47. General Sir John Burgoyne, *Life and Correspondence of Field Marshal Sir John Fox Burgoyne, Bart.*, 2 vols. (London, 1873), vol. 1, p. 223.
48. "We had an arms parade in the evening to keep the men sober!" Robert

Waterfield, *The Memoirs of Private Waterfield, Soldier in Her Majesty's 32nd Regiment of Foot (Duke of Cornwall's Light Infantry) 1842–57*, ed. Arthur Swinson and Donald Scott (London: Cassell, 1968), p. 92.

49. *Hints to Aspirants for the Army, and Young officers on Appointment* (London, 1840), pp. 44–45.

50. In India they were occupied by in 1818 "washing, shaving, and dressing themselves; everlastingly counting over their stock of clothes and folding them carefully." *Subaltern's Log-Book*, vol. 2, p. 34.

51. Crimean officers also wore "fantastic dress" for hunting. Captain Richard Temple Godman, *The Fields of War: A Young Cavalryman's Crimea Campaign*, ed. Philip Warner (London: John Murray, 1977), p. 26.

52. Wearing "jackets of blue, black, green or crimson velvet, with round silver filigree buttons *á la espagnol* as large as plums dangling from small chains, and with breeches of a green, azure, or brown colour, the officers considered themselves perfectly attired for mess." August Ludolf Friedrich Schaumann, *On the Road With Wellington: The Diary of a War Commissary in the Peninsular Campaigns*, ed. and trans. Anthony Ludovici (New York: Alfred A. Knopf, 1924), p. 229.

53. "A friend of mine shaved all the hair off the crown of his head, and *he* was decidedly the most *outre*-looking man amongst us, and consequently the happiest." "Reminiscences of a Subaltern," *United Services Journal* 2 (1830), pp. 826–827.

54. The lieutenant's fellow officers were "completely puzzled by the magic of his toilet." Patterson, *Adventures*, pp. 95–96 and 316–317.

55. This was one cause of Lord Cardigan's numerous scrapes. See Woodham-Smith, *The Reason Why*.

56. Buck Adams, *The Narrative of Private Buck Adams, 7th (Princess Royal's) Dragoon Guards on the Eastern Frontier of the Cape of Good Hope, 1843–48*, ed. A. Gordon Brown (Cape Town: W. J. Van Riebeeck Society Publications, 1941), pp. 224–225.

57. "Worn-out gold and silver lace" was among the booty the British captured from General Soult in 1811. Schaumann, *On the Road*, pp. 294–295.

58. Officers complained of the shoulder-knot partly because "the knot when worn out will hardly burn for a breakfast, whereas the old epaulet will cover the expense of a day's regale." Anti-Shoulder Knot [pseud.], *Military Magazine* 2 (July 1811), p. 26.

59. Sergeant Julius Jefferies, *The British Army in India: Its Preservation* (London, 1858), p. 5.

60. "Costume in India," *Naval and Military Magazine* 4 (1827), p. 612. At social functions it was customary to arrive in uniform and then change into white dress, which a servant brought along.

61. Lt.-Colonel Joseph Anderson, *Recollections of a Peninsular Veteran* (London: Edward Arnold, 1913), p. 198.

62. Colonel Harry Smith in Cape Colony wanted the Seventy-second Foot to wear red for the Sixth "Kaffir" War of 1835—despite the fact that it made an excellent target—because the color would remind Africans of the "great Power beyond the seas." Joseph H. Lehmann, *Remember You Are an Englishman: A Biography of Sir Harry Smith, 1787–1860* (London: Jonathan Cape, 1977), p. 159.

63. "The camp presented a scene of unparalleled confusion, in which it was difficult to say whether the ludicrous or distressing predominated." Sergeant-Major William Taylor, *Life in the Ranks* (London, 1843), p. 171.

64. "Nothing is more harassing [nor] so likely to produce sickness." William Napier, *The Life and Opinions of General Sir Charles Napier*, 4 vols. (London, 1857), vol. 2, p. 235.

65. Serg. T[homas] J. W. Connolly, *The Romance of the Ranks, or Anecdotes, Episodes and Social Incidents of Military Life*, 2 vols. (London, 1859), vol. 1, p. 35.

66. Hall, *Scenes*, p. 252. He does not mention who was responsible for this order to the doomed British force, but the commander General Elphinstone was noted for incompetence.

67. Pearman, *Radical Soldier's Tale*, p. 158; [Tom S.], *A Soldier of the Seventy-First: The Journal of a Soldier of the Highland Light Infantry, 1806–1815*, 2nd ed. (London, 1819; reprint ed., London: Leo Cooper, 1975), p. 74.

68. By contrast, General Wolseley observed that "officers of the East India Company were sensibly dressed." *Story of a Soldier's Life*, 2 vols. (London: A. Constable & Co., Ltd., 1903), vol. 2, pp. 51–52.

69. Col. C[harles] P[hillip] De Ainslie, *The Cavalry Manual*, 3rd ed. (London, 1858), p. 100.

70. Colonel Thomas Bunbury, *Reminiscences of a Veteran*, 3 vols. (London, 1861), vol. 3, pp. 271–272.

71. P. H. Kealey, *General Sir Charles William Pasley, 1780 to 1861* (London, 1930), p. 19; Patterson, *Camp and Quarters*, p. 237.

72. Karl Liebknecht, *Militarism and Anti-Militarism* (New York: Dover, 1972), p. 32. This early-twentieth-century analysis is even more applicable to the early-nineteenth-century British army.

73. Waterfield, *Memoirs*, pp. 44, 42.

74. Captain W. R. King, *Campaigning in Kaffirland, or Scenes and Adventures In The Kaffir War of 1851–2* (London, 1853), p. 110.

75. A corps returning from India in 1820 still wore the pre-1811 shako, and had no new clothing for two years. Serg. George Calladine, *The Diary of Colour-Sergeant George Calladine, 19th Foot, 1793–1837*, ed. M. L. Ferrar (London: E. Fisher and Co., 1922), p. 89. A cap was supposed to last two or three years, but the rate of wear depended on many factors.

76. The loss of the *Prince* on November 14, 1854, off Balaclava Harbor was "incalculable," as it held clothing, including fifty-three thousand "coats or

frocks." In the field "a flannel shirt and drawers were worth their weight in gold." Gowing, *Voice*, pp. 63–64.

77. It is clear that a major change had occurred when one compares the management of the Crimean War and the Persian expedition of 1856 with the Abyssinian campaign of 1867–1868.

78. Leaky boots were sent to the Crimea with soles that lasted only a few days. George Lawson, *Surgeon in the Crimea: The Experiences of George Lawson Recorded in His Letters to his Family, 1854–1855*, ed. Victor Bonham-Carter (London: Military Book Society, 1968), p. 129.

79. Adams, *Narrative*, p. 88. This was a major problem on the eastern frontier of Cape Colony in the wars of the 1840s.

80. Shipp, *Path of Glory*, p. 31.

81. "The novelty of the Peninsular system consisted . . . in the extent to which . . . supply fell upon [the] government." S. G. P. Ward, *Wellington's Headquarters: A Study of Administrative Problems in the Peninsula, 1809–1814* (Oxford: Oxford University Press, 1957), pp. 78, 90.

82. BL ADD MSS 27,597, Dundas Clothing Report, p. 20.

83. W.O. 7/56, Report of May 30, 1815, p. 510.

84. A Private Soldier, "Two Months Recollections of the Late War in Spain and Portugal," *United Services Journal* 1 (1830), p. 288; Cadell, *Narrative*, p. 141. In the former account, the author wrote that these shoes were very clumsy, and that many men were without stockings and had sore feet.

85. Alexander, *Passages*, vol. 1, p. 298.

86. Burgoyne, *Life and Correspondence*, vol. 2, p. 196.

87. Colonel James P. Robertson, *Personal Adventures and Anecdotes of an Old Officer* (London: E. Arnold, 1906), p. 260.

88. G. C. Stent, *Scraps from My Sabretache*, cited in A. C. W., "Dress, 14th Light Dragoons in the Mutiny," *JSAHR* 18 (1939), p. 52.

89. In 1813, a cap worn by Pyrenees mountaineers became "quite the fashion with our officers." [Capt. Joseph Moyle Sherer], *Recollections of the Peninsula*, 4th ed. (London, 1828), p. 346.

90. Calladine, *Diary*, p. 38.

91. Captain Frederick B[rickdale] Doveton, *Reminiscences of the Burmese War in 1824-5-6* (London, 1852), p. 308.

92. Lieutenant-Colonel Geoffrey White, "Lt.-Colonel W. Munro and the Officers of the 39th regiment in the Crimea," *JSAHR* 40 (1961), p. 147. Unless he was poor, an officer might have four to six full-dress coats, or even more; Captain Elers of the Twelfth Foot bought six when commissioned in 1796. Capt. George Elers, *Memoirs of George Elers, Captain of the 12th Regiment of Foot* (New York: D. Appleton and Co., 1903), p. 37.

93. *Subaltern's Log-Book*, vol. 1, p. 263.

94. John Shipp's self-portrait shows him wearing the frock with a shako while in India in 1817. *Path of Glory*, frontispiece. During the mutiny, Colonel

Robertson always fought in an old blue quilted jacket worn over his uniform. Robertson, *Personal Adventures*, p. 243.

95. Patterson, *Adventures*, p. 116.

96. Donaldson, *Recollections*, p. 149.

97. Quoted from Harrowby MSS, vol. 14, Aberdeen to Harrowby, September 30, 1813. Murial E. Chamberlain, *Lord Aberdeen: A Political Biography* (London: Longman, 1983), p. 126.

98. Doveton, *Reminiscences*, p. 49.

99. When Sir Robert Wilson was with a cossack corps in Poland in 1807, his servant took away his light dragoon helmet before combat because, being different from the cossacks' fur hats, it would have made him a target. Michael Glover, *A Very Slippery Fellow: The Life of Sir Robert Wilson, 1777–1849* (Oxford: Oxford University Press, 1977), p. 39.

100. Sir Richard Henegan, *Seven Years Campaigning in the Peninsula and the Netherlands, from 1808 to 1815*, 2 vols. (London, 1846), vol. 2, pp. 8–10.

101. W.O. 5/56, Clothing Board Report (1811), p. 103.

102. "Reminiscences," *United Services Journal* 1 (1832), p. 199. Cavalry trumpeters and buglers were killed off in the Peninsula because they wore colors reversed from the rest of their unit. In a "submission" of September 1811, the prince regent suggested changing the practice and dressing them the same as their units, and this became regulation in October 1814. R. Jones, "Drummer's Coats," *JSAHR* 22 (1944), p. 306. This reverted to the old style after 1815, but in 1836 the recommendation of 1811 again became regulation, for the same reason as before.

103. Schaumann, *On the Road*, p. 229.

104. "Yet this army has met no disaster." Circular from the Duke of Wellington, Frenada, November 29, 1812. BL ADD MSS 35,060, f. 210, Rowland Hill Papers. Private Pearman liked combat because death put the rich and the poor on the same level. Pearman, *Radical Soldier's Tale*, p. 208.

105. "When off duty we had plenty of sports . . . the officers and the men mixing together, the officer[s] do not have so much pride on service." Ibid., p. 162.

106. Adams, *Narrative*, p. 169. Privates were also called "animated food for powder."

107. Edmund Wheatley, *The Wheatley Diary*, ed. Christopher Hibbert (London: Longmans, Green and Co., 1964), p. 85.

108. Patterson, *Adventures*, pp. 57–58.

109. After the fall of San Sebastián in 1813, for days they were "strutting about the roads outside the town in masquerade—some in silks and satins—others as pedlars selling their plunder to the people." *Military Sketch Book*, vol. 2, p. 170.

110. "Reminiscences," *United Services Journal* 2 (1832), p. 338.

111. A sapper private looted the coat of a sergeant from the Twenty-third Foot after the fall of Badajoz in 1812. Connolly, *Romance*, vol. 1, p. 112.

112. "Plunder or booty is absolutely needful . . . to urge the soldiers to enter-prize, because [self-]interest is the greatest stimulant in human nature." Napier, *Life and Opinions*, vol. 1, p. 247.

113. Alexis de Tocqueville, *Democracy in America*, vol. 1 (New York: Vintage Books, 1954), p. 296.

114. Chelsea Pensioner [sergeant, Fifteenth Hussars], *Jottings from My Sabretache* (London, 1847), p. 133.

115. [William Maginn], *The Military Sketch-Book*, 2 vols. (London, 1827), vol. 2, p. 117.

116. After being shot in the face in 1810, Charles Napier wrote: "The scars on my face will be as good as medals, better!" *Life and Opinions*, vol. 1, p. 144.

117. Gronow, *Reminiscences*, vol. 2, p. 218.

118. Col. S. H. Mountain, *Memoirs and Letters of the Late Colonel Armine S. H. Mountain*, ed. Mrs. S. H. Mountain (London, 1858), p. 218. Mountain had a long career as colonel of the Twenty-sixth Foot, and became adjutant-general of the Indian army.

119. Schaumann, *On the Road*, p. xv. This Hanoverian intended his diary not for publication, but only for his family; the editor cross-checked the facts, and believes it has "the stamp of genuineness and accuracy," p. vii.

120. One colonel kept all the clothes and equipment he used while in the same regiment for forty-five years. *Subaltern's Log-Book*, p. 202.

121. *Times*, June 22, 1861. Cited in Alan Ramsay Skelley, *The Victorian Army at Home: The Recruitment and Terms and Conditions of the British Regular, 1859–1899* (Montreal: McGill-Queens, 1977), p. 252. This minority is the equivalent of what those who study political phenomena call "critical mass."

122. Mitchell, *Thoughts*, p. 235.

123. [Major-General George Bell], *Rough Notes by an Old Soldier, during Fifty Years of Service*, 2 vols. (London, 1867), vol. 2, p. 157.

124. Wolseley, *Soldier's Life*, vol. 1, p. 52.

125. W[illiam] H. Russel, *The War: from the Landing at Gallipoli to the Death of Lord Raglan* (London, 1855), p. 118.

126. Gowing, *Voice*, p. 65.

127. W.O. 33/15, *Report into the Effect On Health . . . of Carrying the Accoutrements, Ammunition, and Kit*, Appendix, p. 17.

128. Patterson, *Camp and Quarters*, vol. 2, p. 95.

129. G. M. Trevelyan, *British History in the Nineteenth Century and After: 1782–1919* (London: Penguin Books, 1965), p. 299.

130. Patterson, *Camp and Quarters*, vol. 2, p. 279.

7. CIVIL DISORDER

1. Kenneth O. Fox, *Making Life Possible: A Study of Military Aid to the Civil Power in Regency England* (Kineton, Warwick, 1982), focuses on the army's

police duties in this era. F. C. Mather, *Public Order in the Age of the Chartists* (Manchester: Manchester University Press, 1959), and Stanley H. Palmer, *Police and Protest in England and Ireland, 1780–1850* (Cambridge, England: Cambridge University Press, 1988), treat this topic to a lesser extent. Sometimes historians who study civil disorders tend to give superficial treatment to the army's role, except in using military sources to learn more about rioters, so accounts of events can be somewhat one-sided.

2. Chelsea Pensioner [sergeant, Fifteenth Hussars], *Jottings from My Sabretache* (London, 1847), pp. 122–123.

3. Galen Broeker, *Rural Disorder and Police Reform in Ireland, 1812–36* (Toronto: University of Toronto Press, 1970), p. 31.

4. Frank Ongley Darvell, *Disturbances and Public Order in Regency England* (Oxford: Oxford University Press, 1969), p. 268.

5. "Personal Narrative . . . by Major Mackworth," *United Services Journal* 3 (1831), p. 446.

6. General Sir John Fox Burgoyne, *Aide-Mémoire to the Military Sciences* (London, 1853), p. 584.

7. The officers were concerned enough to obtain "chain reins" covered with leather. Lord William Pitt Lennox, *My Recollections from 1806 to 1873*, 2 vols. (London, 1874), vol. 1, pp. 72–73.

8. A raid on Irish rebels in Kildare in 1814 failed because the soldiers were drunk. Broeker, *Rural Disorder*, p. 64.

9. Malcolm I. Thomis, *The Luddites: Machine Breaking in Regency England* (New York: Schocken Books, 1970), pp. 148, 150.

10. Edward M. Spiers, *The Army and Society, 1815–1914* (London: Longman, 1980), p. 74.

11. George Calladine, *The Diary of Colour-Sergeant George Calladine, 19th Foot, 1793–1837*, ed. M. L. Ferrar (London: E. Fisher and Co., 1922), p. 134.

12. Spiers, *Army and Society*, p. 82.

13. Correlli Barnett, *Britain and Her Army, 1509–1970: A Military, Political and Social Survey* (Middlesex, England: Penguin Books, 1974), p. 279.

14. An example is mentioned in William Napier, *The Life and Opinions of General Sir Charles Napier*, 4 vols. (London, 1857), vol. 2, pp. 71–72.

15. Coroners' inquests after the death of two rioters at Queen Caroline's funeral in September 1820 returned verdicts of manslaughter and willful murder upon unknown privates of the Life Guards. The inquests were said to be "irregular and partisan." *Annual Register*, 1821, p. 128.

16. Opinion of Lord Chief Justice Tindal, H.O. 41/14, letter of August 14, 1839, cited in Mather, *Public Order*, p. 157.

17. HEH MS, "2nd Regt. Buckinghamshire Hussars Regimental Order Book: 1815–1832," "Reply of the Duke of Chandos, Buckingham & Chandos [?] to various congratulations from members of the regiment on his gaining the title of Duke," February 2, 1822.

18. Thomis, *Luddites*, p. 150. In Ireland the problem was sometimes evaded in a fashion that would not have been tolerated elsewhere; officers above the rank of lieutenant were appointed as temporary magistrates in 1819, and ordinary constables were so authorized in 1820–1821. Palmer, *Police and Protest*, p. 221.

19. Broeker, *Rural Disorder*, p. 212.

20. Asa Briggs, *Victorian Cities* (New York: Harper Colophon Books, 1970), pp. 149–150.

21. Mather, *Public Order*, p. 177.

22. An officer estimated that nine-tenths of the recruits regretted their enlistment. Henry Marshall, *Hints to Medical Officers of the Army on the Examination of Recruits* (1828), pp. 89–90, cited in Hew Strachan, *Wellington's Legacy: The Reform of the British Army, 1830–54* (Manchester: Manchester University Press, 1984), p. 57.

23. Elizabeth Longford, *Wellington: Pillar of State* (St. Albans, Herffordshire: Granada Publishing Ltd., 1975), p. 97. In 1803, three hundred men of the Third battalion and thirty or forty from the First battalion of the First Foot Guards were accused of involvement in half-pay officer Colonel Despard's *coup d'état* plot. The accuracy of the charges has been questioned, but the six men tried and executed with Despard were guardsmen. These incidents raise the question of how reliable the Other Ranks of the guards were in the early nineteenth century; one guardsman named his son "Bonaparte." E. P. Thompson, *Making of the English Working Class* (New York: Vintage Books, 1966), p. 483.

24. *Military Register*, October 1, 1820, pp. 428–429. It is significant that the sergeants who led the guards' mutiny were not punished, but merely cashiered by the order of the commander in chief, the duke of York. W.O. 3/20, letter from the Duke of York to the Colonel of the Scots Fusilier Guards, June 21, 1820. A public punishment might have caused a major riot, or a more serious reaction.

25. *Military Register*, October 15, 1820. Neither regimental nor most British army historians have examined these events in the era after Waterloo. An important exception for the late eighteenth century is John Prebble, *Mutiny: Highland Regiments in Revolt, 1743–1804* (Harmondsworth, Middlesex: Penguin Books, 1977).

26. *Military Register* (October 15, 1820). This issue also contains notices of mutinies by the Twentieth and the Eighty-first Foot regiments.

27. He wrote that the Grays would stop illegal acts but not legal ones; his colonel accused him of treason. Alexander Somerville, *The Autobiography of a Working Man* (n.p., 1948; reprint ed., London: MacGibbon & Kee, 1967), p. 159.

28. Broeker, *Rural Disorder*, p. 208.

29. Ivor Wilkes, *South Wales and the Rising of 1839: Class Struggle as Armed*

Struggle (Urbana: University of Illinois Press, 1984), pp. 150–152. The Welshmen underestimated the constraints of army discipline, believing that the soldiers would not fire on them.

30. Two of these regiments were the Eighty-first and the Twentieth Foot (an interesting coincidence, see note no. 25 above) and one of the Rifle corps (Sixtieth or Ninety-fifth).

31. Mick Jenkins, *The General Strike of 1842* (London: Lawrence and Wishart, 1980), p. 171. Mather states that "there is no evidence that the troops ever faltered in their duty when called upon to put down Chartist and other disturbances." *Public Order*, pp. 180 and 178. This might refer to a more narrow context of the actual moment of confrontation in which the mechanisms of discipline were powerful, but the statement is incorrect.

32. H.O. 50/11, letter of March 10, 1817, the Duke of York to Lord Sidmouth concerning William Wright, of the Scots Fusilier Guards, and letter of November 1833 from the Lieutenant-Colonel of the Grenadier Guards. Duke of Wellington, *The Prime Minister's Papers: Wellington, Political Correspondence I: 1833–November 1834*, ed. John Brooke and Julia Gandy (London: Her Majesty's Stationery Office, 1975), pp. 20–24. Neither were officers completely exempt from disaffection; during the Bristol riots of 1831, two were disgraced for not doing their duty out of sympathy for the rioters. Colonel Brereton, commanding the Fourteenth Light Dragoons, was charged with mutiny after he withdrew his troops from the city contrary to orders. Spiers, *Army and Society*, p. 82. After being disgraced, he committed suicide. Higher-ranking officials might also sympathize with rioters; in the contentious year 1798, the duke of Norfolk was removed from the lord lieutenancy of the West Riding of Yorkshire and the colonelcy of the West Yorkshire Militia for openly declaring his opposition to government policy by drinking a toast to "the Sovereinty of the people." J. Ann Hone, *For the Cause of Truth: Radicalism in London, 1796–1821* (Oxford: Oxford University Press, 1982), pp. 39 and 43.

33. W. Y. Baldry, "Regimental Nicknames," *JSAHR* 1 (1921), p. 75.

34. H.O. 41/5/274, unsigned letter to Thomas Horton of November 20, 1819.

35. "His [the soldier's] pride must restrain him from admitting anyone to improper familiarity." Col. C[harles] P[hilip] De Ainslie, *The Cavalry Manual*, 3rd ed. (London, 1858), p. 14. This statement is interesting considering that it was futile to attempt to apply the rule to women attracted by the red coats.

36. Captain May, Order of June 5, 1809, from Dickson, Sir Maj. Gen. Alexander Dickson, *The Dickson Manuscripts: Being Diaries, Letters, Maps, Account Books, with Various other Papers*, 5 vols., ed. Major John H. Leslie (Woolich: The Royal Artillery Institution, 1905–1908; reprint ed., Cambridge: Ken Trotman, 1987–1991), vol. 1, p. 35.

37. *Proceedings of the General Court Martial on the Trial of Captain Wathen,*

Fifteenth Hussars (London, 1834; reprint ed., London: Frederick Muller Ltd., 1970), pp. 3–4.

38. Calladine mentions more than once this exchange of quarters between two regiments. *Diary*, pp. 6–7, 158, and 190.

39. Richard Carlile, "A New Years Address to the Reformers of Great Britain," *Address to the Reformers of Great Britain* (London, 1821), p. 3. It is likely that the attempted insurrection at Spa Fields in 1816 was in part motivated by the belief that the soldiers would sympathize. The activist Samuel Bamford wrote of visiting Knightsbridge barracks in 1817 and distributing radical literature to "delighted" soldiers. He noted that "very soon after this a law was passed, making it death to attempt to seduce a soldier from his duty." Samuel Bamford, *Passages in the Life of a Radical* (Oxford: Oxford University Press, 1984), p. 24. Apparently, he was not alone in his endeavor.

40. See Chapter 3, note 8. The image of the Other Ranks' being predominantly Irish was strong in the first half of the nineteenth century, and the *Times* noted that "the Irish soldier . . . is the chief representative of the valour . . . of the three kingdoms." October 24, 1843, cited in A. H. Saxon, *Enter Foot and Horse: A History of Hippodrama in England and France* (New Haven: Yale University Press, 1968), p. 144.

41. This was noted by Richard Carlile in his *Address*, p. 4.

42. Mather, *Public Order*, p. 179.

43. John Prebble, *The Highland Clearances* (New York: Penguin Books, 1978), p. 251. In 1816 soldiers of the Ninety-third Highlanders showed solidarity with their kin when they refused to reenlist because their families in Strathnaver had been evicted. Ibid., p. 167.

44. An inspecting general noted in his report on the Eighty-seventh Foot that it would be "hazardous to disperse this mainly Irish regiment in Ireland," implying that there was a likelihood of its being sent there. W.O. 27/193, Inspection Report of Major-General Sir. H. Bouverie, November 4, 1829.

45. Copied in the Scots Guards Orderly Book. Horse Guards, *Additional Regulations . . . Jan. 1820 to 1830*, "Circular Letter to Com. Officers of Reg'ts," February 5, 1825, p. 470. The returns were monthly statements of the condition of a corps.

46. Drunken soldiers of the Seventh Dragoon Guards attended an Orange celebration in 1826 and made enough of a scene to attract the notice of the press for singing "obnoxious songs." A year later soldiers were seen in Tipperary with Orange decorations on their uniforms. Broeker, *Rural Disorder*, p. 177.

47. Edward Law, Lord Ellenborough, *A Political Diary, 1828–1830*, ed. Lord Colchester, 2 vols. (London, 1881), vol. 1, p. 184.

48. Calladine, *Diary*, p. 134.

49. An officer in the Eighty-sixth Foot, an Irish corps with not more than "150 Protestants in the whole regiment," noted that an Orange lodge had been

"properly suppressed" in the army in the early 1830s. Colonel W. K. Stuart, *Reminiscences of a Soldier*, 2 vols. (London, 1847), vol. 2, pp. 185–186.

50. Cited from *Report on Orange Lodges IV Report from select Committee . . . in Great Britain*, House of Commons, 1835 [605], xvii, p. xii. Hereward Senior, *Orangeism in Ireland and Britain, 1795–1836* (London: Routledge and Kegan Paul, 1966), pp. 302–303 and 178.

51. This practice was criticized in the House of Commons. *Times*, June 20, 1820, p. 2.

52. Charles Steevens, *Reminiscences of My Military Life from 1795 to 1818*, ed. Nathaniel Steevens (Winchester, 1878), p. 122.

53. Sergeant Calladine mentions that while on antismuggling duty as a militiaman in Essex, he formed an attachment to a smuggler's daughter. *Diary*, pp. 6, 8.

54. This happened during a riot at Cork in 1839. *Naval & Military Gazette*, October 5, 1839, cited in Hew Strachan, *Waterloo to Balaclava: Tactics, Technology, and the British Army, 1815–1854* (Cambridge, England: Cambridge University Press, 1985), p. 29.

55. "Improved Musket and Bayonet," *United Services Magazine* 3 (1834), pp. 546–548.

56. Other long-arms had problems too, and are discussed in Strachan, *Waterloo to Balaclava*, pp. 31–43 and 84–87.

57. Quoted from Lt-Colonel Griffiths, [Scots Grays], 1854, P.R.O. (W.O. 44/701). Col. Edward Cooper Hodge, *'Little Hodge,' Being Extracts from the diaries and letters of Edward Cooper Hodge, written during the Crimean War, 1854–1856*, George C. H. V. Paget, marquess of Anglesey, ed. (London: Leo Cooper, 1971), p. 49.

58. T. J. W. Connolly, *The Romance of the Ranks, or Anecdotes, Episodes and Social Incidents of Military Life*, 2 vols. (London, 1859), vol. 1, pp. 107–108.

59. Fox, *Making Life Possible*, p. 38. I have no evidence indicating that rockets were ever used against rioters. It is significant that these often inaccurate weapons were last used in a European theater—contrary to Wellington's orders—at Waterloo, but were used into the twentieth century in Third World countries because of their intimidating effect upon foes who were unaccustomed to their frightening, noisy display.

60. J. T. Ward, *Chartism* (New York: Barnes and Noble, 1973), p. 121.

61. This could be a dangerous game, and it appears that blanks would not avail in serious, ongoing confrontations after the novelty had worn off. They seem to have been useful against rioters unaccustomed to confronting soldiers; after the Bristol riots, blanks were no longer used. Connolly, *Romance*, vol. 1, p. 103.

62. Spiers, *Army and Society*, p. 84.

63. H.O. 41/7/416, letter of September 24, 1827, to A. Jobson of Wisbeck.

64. Capt. [Rees Howell] Gronow, *The Reminiscences and Recollections of Captain*

Gronow: 1810–1860, Being Anecdotes of the Camp, Court, Clubs and Society, 2 vols. (London: John C. Nimmo, 1900), vol. 2, p. 87.

65. In 1810, an Irish coach was held up by a lone robber who set a row of tall hats on a wall next to the road to give his victims the impression of greater numbers and then fired shots from behind the hats. The coachman later multiplied the number of robbers to four hundred and magnified the hats' proportions, saying they were "towering like a church steeple," thus linking the exaggerated size with his own fright. William Graham, *Travels Through Portugal and Spain, During the Peninsular War* (London, 1820), p. 2.

66. Thomas Richards, *The Commodity Culture of Victorian England: Advertising and Spectacle, 1851–1914* (Stanford: Stanford University Press, 1990), pp. 48–49. Richards belittles the effects of these giant advertisements, claiming that they "usually inspired laughter and derision," yet advertising has always been ridiculed. He notes that "by the 1840s the streets of London were clogged with the effigies of things." Thus it would appear that they were deemed effective by those who paid for them.

67. Anon., *Letter to Lord Castlereagh, Found Near His Lordship's House, in St. Jame's Square* (London, 1820), p. 2. Considering the youth of most soldiers, this assertion is close to being the literal truth and perhaps was intended as irony.

68. He proposed that the infantry wear crested heavy cavalry helmets. Major-General John Mitchell, *Thoughts on Tactics and Military Organization: Together with an Enquiry into the Power and Position of Russia* (London, 1838), pp. 213–237. It is significant that "all troops employed during the railway and coal strikes of 1911" wore the full-dress headdress with their khaki uniform. "Clericus," "Uniform for the Future Army," *Journal for the Royal United Service Institute* 63 (1918), p. 53.

69. "Cavalry," *Military Register* 1 (January 5, 1820), p. 16.

70. "Cavalry Officer," *The Whole Art of Dress, or, The Road to Elegance and Fashion at the Enormous Savings of 30%!!! Being a Treatise Upon that Essential and Much Cultivated Requisite of the Present Day, Gentleman's Costume* (London, 1830), pp. 42–43.

71. Lt.-Col. Basil Jackson, *Notes and Reminiscences of a Staff Officer, chiefly relating to the Waterloo Campaign and to St. Helena matters during the captivity of Napoleon* (London: J. Murray, 1903), p. 15.

72. P.R.O., H.O. 100/236, cited in Broeker, *Rural Disorder*, p. 207.

73. Kenneth Bourne, *Palmerston: The Early Years, 1784–1841* (London: Allen Lane, 1982), p. 41.

74. Maj. John Patterson, *The Adventures of Captain John Patterson, with notices of the officers, etc., of the 50th . . . Regiment, from 1807 to 1821* (n.p., 1837), pp. 6–7.

75. A soldier was severely wounded and a woman and man received sword cuts. "Two officers arriving interfered . . . and ordered full amends to be made

to the wounded parties; and the soldiers soon after left the town for Guildford." *Gentleman's Magazine* 73 (1803), p. 971.

76. Trevor Royle, comp., *A Dictionary of Military Quotations* (New York: Simon & Shuster, 1989), p. 147.

77. Lewis Mumford, *The City in History: Its Origins, Its Transformations, and Its Prospects* (New York: Harcourt, Brace & World, 1961), p. 369.

78. [William Maginn], *The Military Sketch-Book*, 2 vols. (London, 1827), vol. 1, p. 30. Even civilian authorities at a higher level sometimes reacted negatively to uniforms. A London magistrate censured a Royal Navy midshipman early in the Peninsular war merely for wearing a uniform in the city. The officer was told that he could wear his uniform only when conducting business at the Admiralty. Ibid., vol. 2, p. 33.

79. C. T. Atkinson, "A Swiss Officer in Wellington's Army," *JSAHR* 35 (1956), pp. 73, 75.

80. Cited in Asa Briggs, *The Making of Modern England; 1783–1867, The Age of Improvement* (New York: Harper Torchbooks, 1965), p. 161.

81. *Military Sketch-Book*, vol. 1, p. 310.

82. Ibid.

83. "House of Commons Reports on Public Petitions," Petition to Parliament, 1850, no. 512, p. 281, app. 617, April 15, 1850, signed by John Sawyers, Provost of Stirling, with other community leaders. The mention of moral indecency might indicate that the kilt symbolized soldiers' objectionable behavior, as well as a garment that exposed male limbs.

84. H. J. Hanham, "Religion and Nationality in the Mid-Victorian Army," in M. R. D. Foot, ed., *War and Society: Historical Essays in Honour and Memory of J. R. Western* (London: Paul Elek, 1973), pp. 163–164. A gradual transformation took place in public perceptions from the 1850s to the end of the century, in which soldiers were sometimes idealized as "Christian heroes."

85. Robert Huish, *An Authentic History of the Coronation of His Majesty, King George the Fourth: with a full and Authentic Detail of the August Solemnity: An Account of all the Interesting Proceedings; the Adjudication of the Court of Claims, and an Historical Account of the Origin of the Court; A Full and Original Detail of the Regalia, and Other Important Particulars connected with that Magnificent Ceremony* (London, 1821), p. 276.

86. "Bronterre O'Brien's Account of the Radical Meeting at the Crown and Anchor, 28 February 1837," cited in Dorothy Thompson, ed., *The Early Chartists* (Columbia, S.C.: University of South Carolina Press, 1971), p. 58.

87. Lovett Papers, vol. 1, pp. 26–27, cited in Joel Wiener, *The War of the Unstamped: The Movement to Repeal the British Newspaper Tax, 1830–1836* (New York: Cornell University Press, 1969), p. 135.

88. Clowns are an entertainment genre that share this ambiguity; they possess an attraction yet also menace. See William Willeford, *The Fool and His*

Scepter, A Study of Clowns and Jesters and Their Audience (Evanston, Ill.: Northwestern University Press, 1969).

89. In pre–World War I Germany, the radical Karl Liebknecht maintained that the glitter of the military spectacle was essential for internal policing: "War against the external enemy requires men; war against the enemy at home requires slaves, machines. As regards equipment and armament they cannot dispense with the bright uniforms, glittering buttons and helmets, the flags, parade drills, cavalry attacks, and all the rubbish needed to create the necessary spirit in the struggle against the enemy at home." Karl Liebknecht, *Militarism and Anti-Militarism* (New York: Dover Books, 1972), p. 32.

90. "The Finery of War," *Douglas Jerrold's Shilling Magazine* 1 (1845), p. 41.

91. "The headquarters of the Scotch greys: the head of a man full of large lice." [Capt. Francis Grose], *Dictionary of the Vulgar Tongue: A Dictionary of Buckish Slang, University Wit, and Pickpocket Eloquence* (London, 1811; fac. ed., London: Bibliophile Books, 1984).

92. R. R. Madden, *The Life and Times of the United Irishmen*, 2 vols. (n.p.), vol. 2, p. 83. Quoted in Roger Wells, *Insurrection: The British Experience, 1795–1803* (Gloucester: Alan Sutton, 1983), p. 132.

93. Clive Emsley, *British Society and the French Wars: 1793–1815* (Totowa, N.J.: Rowman and Littlefield, 1979), p. 169.

94. Bamford, *Passages*, p. 133.

95. One report mentions a march by ten thousand men at Cappaghwhite. Broeker, *Rural Disorder*, p. 183.

96. *Times*, December 24, 1816, cited in Clifford Morsley, ed., *News from the English Countryside, 1750–1850* (London: Harrap, 1979), p. 204.

97. Thompson, *Working Class*, p. 680.

98. H.O. 41/5/298–9, letter to the Mayor of Leeds acknowledging the receipt of the letter that contained this information.

99. They "organized themselves into sixteen battalions . . . Many [were] old soldiers I knew," with "perfect organization." Lieutenant-General Sir Harry Smith, *The Autobiography of Lieutenant-General Sir Harry Smith, Baronet of Aliwal on the Sutlej, G.C.B.*, 2 vols. (New York: E. P. Dutton & Co., 1902), vol. 1, p. 325.

100. Despard's paramilitary group in 1803 also had regimental organization. Thompson, *Working Class*, pp. 681, 480.

101. *Naval and Military Gazette*, July 8, 1843.

102. *Poor Man's Guardian*, June 2, 1832, p. 413.

103. The *Ashton Reporter*, January 30, 1869. Quoted in James Epstein, "Radical Dining, Toasting, and Symbolic Expression in Early Nineteenth-Century Lancashire: Rituals of Solidarity," *Albion* 20 (Summer 1988), p. 289.

104. Thompson, *Working Class*, p. 680; Bamford, *Passages*, p. 147.

105. Thompson, *Working Class*, p. 680.

106. Sergeant John Menzies, *Reminiscences of an Old Soldier* (Edinburgh, 1883), p. 16. The mob's composition, number, and armaments are stated differently by this eyewitness participant than in P. G. Rogers, *Battle in Bossenden Wood* (London: Oxford University Press, 1962), pp. 132–137, or in a much more comprehensive study, Barry Reay, *The Last Rising of the Agricultural Labourers: Rural Life and Protest in Nineteenth-Century England* (Oxford: Oxford University Press, 1990), "The Rising," pp. 83–109. Both these works cite smaller numbers for the rioters, their composition, weapons, and tactics. Courtenay appealed to rural grievances, promising land and bread; the riot occurred only a few years after the Swing riots, and the authorities had many reasons to downplay it and ascribe the cause to a charismatic lunatic, lest others feel encouraged to revolt.

107. Courtenay, handsome and greatly admired by his female followers, falsely claimed to be a knight of Malta. Rogers, *Battle in Bossenden Wood*, pp. 136–137, 97, and 117.

108. See Emmanuel Le Roy Ladurie, *Carnival in Romans: A People's Uprising, 1579–1580*, trans. Mary Feeney (New York, 1979). The protests of English laborers frequently had an "atmosphere of festiveness, ritual and formality about them, such as the wearing of best clothes [and] ribands." George Rude and Eric Hobsbawm, *Captain Swing: A Social History of the Great English Agricultural Uprisings of 1830* (New York: W. W. Norton, 1978), p. 67.

109. "Though England lacked the festival of carnival proper, it had other festivals which shared its characteristics . . . Hence, the *motifs* of licentiousness, of abandonment of restraint, of liberation . . . singing and dancing in the streets . . . the acting out of aggressiveness, the acceptance of folly and carnival 'madness.' " Douglas A. Reid, "Interpreting the Festival Calendar: Wakes and Fairs as Carnival," in Robert D. Storch, ed., *Popular Culture and Custom in Nineteenth-Century England* (New York: Croom Helm Ltd., 1982), pp. 125, 126. Such activities are mentioned in Dorothy Thompson, *The Chartists: Popular Politics in the Industrial Revolution* (New York: Pantheon Books, 1984), p. 118.

110. John B. Gough, *Autobiography and Personal Recollections of John B. Gough* (Springfield, Mass., 1870), p. 44. Another Guy wore an army corporal's jacket and cap, and they had bands of music. Robert D. Storch, "Please to Remember the Second of November," in Storch, *Popular Culture*, p. 89. Rioters in the 1760s also wore military dress, and there is a strong possibility that some were militiamen, who by wearing uniform actually increased the risk of prosecution. Walter James Shelton, *English Hunger and Industrial Disorders: A Study of Social Conditions During the First Decade of George III's Reign* (Toronto: University of Toronto Press, 1973), pp. 125–126.

111. Bamford, *Passages*, p. 145.

112. Robert Elliot, *The Power of Satire: Magic, Ritual, and Art* (Princeton, N.J.: Princeton University Press, 1960), p. 65. Bamford, *Passages*, p. 155.

113. This might explain why a rioter in the 1760s stole militia clothing. If motivated by greed alone, such a theft would have been a very bad idea, because the wearing of a red coat would help to identify the rioter. Shelton, *English Hunger*, pp. 125–126. That the use of elements of identification was interpreted as a successful assertion of power by rioters is shown by a "Plan of Action of Householders" from the Gordon riots of 1780, where mention is made "to suffer no signs of countenancing the rioters to prevail [such as] wearing badges and huzzing and illuminating." W.O. 34/103 (Amherst Papers), no. 234, letter of June 9, 1780, from B. Kennet, Mayor. This usage would dovetail with the theme of "the world turned upside down" and possibly with the use of army uniforms as a form of parody.

114. Michel Foucault, *Discipline and Punish: The Birth of the Prison*, trans. Alan Sheridan (New York: Vintage Books, 1979), pp. 261–262, mentions a similar practice by early-nineteenth-century French chain-gang convicts. When passing through a town, they decorated their chains with ribbons, braided straw, flowers, and precious cloth, and some made helmets like those of the heavy cavalry. They marched, singing "let the trumpets blow for us" and "the star of liberty will shine for us." The spectacle celebrated an inversion of the social and legal order; Foucault calls this "theater" and the participants "the army of disorder."

115. *Poor Man's Guardian*, December 29, 1832. Another example of the use of marching band music as ridicule comes from London in 1830, cited in *The Place Newspaper Collection*, 31, p. 209, "The State of the Metropolis Last Night," *Chronicle*, November 10, 1830.

116. E. P. Thompson, "Rough Music: Le Charivari Anglais," *Annales* 27 (1972), p. 285ff.

117. Storch, "Please to Remember," p. 79. During the Vietnam war, observers commented on the frequent use of military dress by antiwar demonstrators. This was labeled as inconsistency and hypocrisy, but it can be interpreted in part as a desire to achieve a sense of the personal and corporate power and solidarity that was essential for these groups. This is implicit in uniforms, even if worn only as fragments mixed with other, quite different elements. The protestors' imagery was very different from that of the army, but their display created a distinctive, readily identifiable image. It formed a kind of uniform representing common values, in much the same way a three-piece suit, pressed shirt, and tie are the "uniform" of business.

118. Hugh Cunningham, "The Language of Patriotism, 1750–1914," *History Workshop* 12 (1981), pp. 8–31.

119. Ward, *Chartism*, p. 113.

120. *Nottingham Journal*, May 8, 1846. Cited in George Fellows and Benson

Freeman, *Historical Records of the South Nottinghamshire Hussars Yeomanry, 1794–1924* (Aldershot, 1928), p. 73.

121. The corps had also been very active in quelling the disturbances of 1831. Some of the yeomanry were themselves "reformers," but they did not allow this to interfere with their duty. Oskar Teichman, "The Yeomanry as an Aid to Civil Power: 1795–1867," pt. 2, *JSAHR* 14 (1935), p. 73, emphasizes the significance of the yeomanry in the three especially volatile East Midland shires during the Chartist conflicts. The scale of the disturbances forced the government to employ yeomanry cavalry corps despite a preference for regulars.

122. "The very presence of the yeomanry at the scene of disorder tended to add to the intensity of the conflict." Mather, *Public Order*, p. 148. Napier disliked them for being "overzealous for cutting and slashing." *Life*, vol. 2, p. 73. This phenomenon appears similar to the American public's attitude toward carnivals, where the entertainment is deemed attractive, yet the employees are viewed with mistrust.

123. G. N. Wright, *The Life and Reign of William The Fourth*, 2 vols. (London, 1837), vol. 2, p. 619. Sometimes the soldiers would turn the tables on the spectators, and the spectacle's latent violence would be transformed into threat. At an inspection of the Second Life Guards in 1843, Lieutenant Knox of the Eighty-fifth Foot witnessed a squadron "charging at full speed up to the very carriage [of a spectator?] to the horror of the ladies." Alice Elizabeth Blake, *Memoirs of a Vanished Generation: 1813–1855* (London: John Lane, the Bodley Head, 1909), p. 197.

124. Thomas Carlyle, *Sartor Resartus* (London, 1831; reprint ed., New York: Chelsea House, 1983), p. 32.

8. Entertainment, Power, and Paradigm

1. In 1841 at Dorchester, a cavalry corps' march to church resulted in a fire; when a man frying bacon heard a shout that soldiers were going by he upset the pan and started a grease fire that destroyed a dozen houses. Colonel John Anstruther-Thomson, *Eighty Years' Reminiscences*, 2 vols. (London: Longmans, Green & Co., 1904), vol. 1, p. 77. The impact of British martial spectacle on civilian life during the French wars has received more attention in recent years. Linda Colley's *Britons: Forging the Nation, 1707–1837* (London: Pimlico, 1992), discusses its role in the development of nationalism (see pp. 183–187, 224–226); and Gillian Russell, *The Theaters of War: Performance, Politics and Society, 1793–1815* (Oxford: Oxford University Press, 1995), gives a theater historian's perspective on the prominence of theatricality in the era's warfare, and the influence of the martial spectacle upon the stage.

2. A review held at Hounslow Heath in the summer of 1817 lasted three and

one-half hours. *Times*, July 26, 1817. War had long been a European spectator sport; during the floating battery attack at the siege of Gibraltar in 1782, eighty thousand spectators gathered on the mainland to watch the show. T. H. McGuffie, *The Siege of Gibraltar: 1779–1783* (London: B. T. Batsford, 1965), p. 158.

3. Francis Grose, *The Mirror's Image: Advice to the Officers of the British Army*, 6th ed. (London, 1867), p. 38.

4. [Major-General George Bell], *Rough Notes by an Old Soldier, during Fifty Years of Service*, 2 vols. (London, 1867), vol. 1, pp. 230–231.

5. In 1854, a fashionable young lady stayed at a hotel longer than she had intended because a captain with smallpox was there and she hoped he would die so she could see the funeral. She was "much disappointed" when he recovered. James Howard Harris, Earl of Malmsbury, *Memoirs of an Ex-Minister: an Autobiography*, 2 vols. (London, 1884), vol. 1, pp. 444–445.

6. Thomas W. Laqueur, "The Ideology and Symbolism of Legitimation in England, 1792–1799," in *The Consortium on Revolutionary Europe, Proceedings*, ed. Owen Connelly (Athens, Ga., 1979), p. 276. Often the only infantry units (except the guards) involved in London's wartime reviews were nonprofessional corps. At the grand review of June 10, 1811, volunteer infantry, the Royal Horse Artillery, and regular cavalry participated, but no regular infantry performed. *Times*, June 11, 1811.

7. Henry Cockburn, *Memorials of His Time*, ed. Karl F. C. Miller (London: University of Chicago Press, 1974), pp. 180–181.

8. Phillip Ziegler, *Addington: A Life of Henry, First Viscount Sidmouth* (London: John Day Co., 1965), pp. 200–211. The displays of the nonprofessionals were modeled on the army.

9. Louis Simond, *An American in Regency England: The Journal of a Tour in 1810–1811*, ed. Christopher Hibbert (London: The History Book Club, 1968), p. 146.

10. *Times*, June 11, 1811.

11. General orders were published for the 1811 review. Simond, *An American*, p. 146. The "Official Programme for the Triumphal Entry of the Guards into London, Wednesday, July 9th, 1856," is preserved at the Scottish United Services Museum at Edinburgh Castle, file F.G. 856.1.

12. *Times*, July 26, 1817.

13. David Cannadine's essay "The Context, Performance and Meaning of Ritual: The British Monarchy and the 'Invention of Tradition' *c.* 1820–1977," in *The Invention of Tradition*, ed. Eric Hobsbawm and Terence Ranger (Cambridge, England: Cambridge University Press, 1984), pp. 101–164, has overlooked the role of the grand military review as a part of the public ceremonial of the crown. Cannadine's description of the reign of William IV leaves the impression that he avoided all such public events (p. 118)—though he did avoid army uniform, preferring naval dress. The

king attended a series of grand reviews after his accession in the summer of 1830 and was the centerpiece of the show, displaying great interest in the proceedings: "His Majesty walked up and down the ranks, paying the most minute attention to the military and clean appearance of the men." *Times,* July 23, 1830. A Royal Horse Guards (Blue) private wrote: "Our late lamented sovereign . . . during the latter years of his life was particularly partial to military shows." Col. Charles Cozens, *Adventures of a Guardsman* (London, 1848), p. 32. This disputes Cannadine's statement that William "loathed ceremonial and ostentation" (p. 118). Rather, the king did not want an elaborate coronation because of the "useless . . . expense" that would be "ill-timed": "excitement and agitation . . . must attend and arise from that ceremony, at a period [the Reform Bill debate] when it is so desirable to avoid all that can promote popular effervescence." Sir H. Taylor to Earl Grey, St. James, July 2, 1831. Henry Earl Grey, ed., *The Reform Act, 1832: The Correspondence of the late Earl Grey with His Majesty King William IV and with Sir Herbert Taylor,* 2 vols. (London, 1867), vol. 1, p. 301.

14. *Times,* July 23, 1830.
15. *Times,* July 27, 1830. If the entire regiment was at hand, this made a total of nearly one thousand men on crowd control.
16. *John Bull* (August 1, 1830).
17. "The Editor's Portfolio," *United Services Journal* 2 (1830), p. 239.
18. "Boat Lancers," *Naval and Military Magazine* 4 (September 1828), p. li.
19. Item, *United Services Journal* 2 (1831), p. 266.
20. Robert Blake, *Disraeli* (New York: St. Martin's Press, 1967), p. 151.
21. A dinner and ball were held by the officers. Robert Waterfield, *The Memoirs of Private Waterfield, Soldier in Her Majesty's 32nd Regiment of Foot (Duke of Cornwall's Light Infantry) 1842–1857,* ed. Arthur Swinson and Donald Scott (London: Cassell, 1968), pp. 18–19.
22. Charles Dickens, *The Posthumous Papers of the Pickwick Club* (London, 1849; reprint ed., New York: A. I. Burt and Co., n.d.), p. 48.
23. Major John Patterson, *Camp and Quarters: Scenes and Impressions of Military Life* (London, 1840), vol. 1, pp. 101–102.
24. James Walvin, *Leisure and Society, 1830–1950* (London: Longman, 1978), p. 103. See also Colley, *Britons,* pp. 307–308.
25. Many elements of nineteenth-century European military imagery (and heraldry), including hussar and lancer dress, the grenadier cap, the shako, and the mameluk sword and trousers, and so on, originated in—or were transmitted through—the Islamic states and the borderlands between Christian Europe and the Middle East. Military bands constitute a significant cultural manifestation of "orientalism."
26. For example, see George Calladine, *The Diary of Colour-Sergeant George Calladine, 19th Foot, 1793–1837,* ed. M. L. Ferrar (London: E. Fisher and Co., 1922), p. 186.

27. Donald Thomas, *Cardigan: A Life of Lord Cardigan of Balaclava* (New York: Viking Press, 1974), p. 95.

28. He wrote: "A 'civilian' has no more 'right' to their music than the Coldstream have to insist on *his* playing the fiddle to *them*." "Regimental Music at the Tower," *United Services Journal* 2 (1829), p. 240.

29. This incident is enshrined in a contemporary caricature: "The Wimbledon Hoax! or Waterloo Review!!! !!!, June 18th, 1816," published by J. Johnston, George Cruikshank, artist. Huntington Library print, Pr. Box 216/60.

30. "The Troops and the Weather," *Punch* 9 (1845), p. 84.

31. Excerpt from the *York Herald*, April 1846, quoted in Colonel John Vandeleur, *Letters of Colonel John Vandeleur, 1810–1846* (London, 1846), p. 185.

32. Henry Ross Lewin, *Life of a Soldier. A Narrative of Twenty-Seven Years' Service . . . By a Field Officer*, 3 vols. (London, 1834; new ed., Dublin: Hodges, Figgis, 1904), vol. 1, p. 2.

33. The soldier had died after a flogging. Harry Hopkins, *Strange Death of Private White: A Victorian Scandal That Made History* (London: Weidenfield and Nicolson, 1977), p. 100.

34. J. H. Plumb, "The Commercialization of Leisure," "The New World of Children," in Neil McKendrick, John Brewer, and J. H. Plumb, *The Birth of a Consumer Society: The Commercialization of Eighteenth-Century England* (Bloomington: University of Indiana Press, 1982), p. 310. A child who had heard that the Crimean army needed reinforcements sent a wooden soldier to Florence Nightingale. Florence Nightingale, *"I Have Done My Duty": Florence Nightingale in the Crimean War, 1854–56*, ed. Sue M. Goldie (Iowa City, Iowa: University of Iowa Press, 1987), p. 144.

35. The expensive dolls were elaborate wax or earthenware models, some with jointed bodies and wardrobes. "Dolly Dearest," exhibition of Victorian dolls, City of London Museum, 1986; Plumb, "The New World of Children," p. 310.

36. *Army and Navy ABC*, Dean's Movable Books (n.p., n.d.).

37. These were made of wood, costing from a few shillings to a pound. Pamphlets of dialogue together with punch-out paper "actors" were sold separately for a few pennies. Texts were always "strictly subservient to the spectacle," with instructions on making fires, explosions, and other special effects. See *Pollock's Characters & Scenes in the Battle of Waterloo*, with an introduction by Eric Underwood (London, 1842; reprint ed., London: B. Pollock, 1970), p. iv. Henry Mayhew interviewed the inventor, Henry Mayhew, "The Toy-Makers," Eileen Yeo and E. P. Thompson, *The Unknown Mayhew* (New York: Schocken Books, 1972), pp. 286–287. See also George Speaight, *The History of the English Toy Theater*, rev. ed. (Boston: Plays Inc., 1969).

38. The famous actor David Garrick played Othello wearing English regimen-

tals. George Rowell, *The Victorian Theater, 1792–1914: A Survey*, 2nd ed. (Cambridge, England: Cambridge University Press, 1978), p. 15.

39. Soldiers performed on stage in Dublin. *Roscius*, February 1, 1825, cited in A. H. Saxon, *The Life and Art of Andrew Ducrow & the Romantic Age of the English Circus* (Hamden, Conn.: Archon Books, 1978), p. 127. "No soldier is to appear on the stage of the theater in any part of his regimentals except when on duty." "Memorandum of Instructions to the Officers of the Scots Fusilier Guards" (1830), p. 52.

40. *Punch* 29 (1855), p. 76.

41. The composer Georg Frederick Handel wrote a march in 1745 for a London volunteer regiment. Henry George Farmer, "The Martial Music of the Georges," *JSAHR* 42 (1964), pp. 203, 204.

42. For an example, see Nicol Smith, "The British Grenadiers," *JSAHR* 6 (1927), pp. 23–30.

43. Harry Austin, *Guards Hussars and Infantry: Adventures of Harry Austin*, 3 vols. (London, 1838), vol. 3, p. 290.

44. The queen noted: "Never did I see such enormous crowds at night." Letter of April 19, 1855; Queen Victoria, *Letters from a Journal* (New York: Farrar Straus & Co., 1961), pp. 53–54.

45. One veteran considered this influence important enough to complain that exhibitions of Waterloo shown in Edinburgh a few months after the battle distorted the facts. Only Scotsmen were portrayed as having been significant in the victory. The Scots Grays and the highlanders were depicted as giants in the foreground, and "John Bull and Pat [the Irish] were little better than idle spectators on the left," and depicted as "pigmies" in the background. Lt.-Col. J[onathan] Leach, *Rough Sketches of the Life of an Old Soldier* (London, 1831), p. 399.

46. Anthony D. Hippisley Coxe, "Equestrian Drama and the Circus," in David Bradby, Louis James, and Bernard Sharratt, eds., *Performance and Politics in Popular Drama* (Cambridge, England: Cambridge University Press, 1980), p. 109.

47. Rowell, *Victorian Theater*, p. 9.

48. Benson Earle Hill, *Playing About; or, Theatrical Anecdotes and Adventures, with Scenes of a General Nature from the Life*, 2 vols. (London, 1840), vol. 1, p. 234.

49. Saxon, *Foot and Horse*, pp. 141, 144.

50. Austin, *Guards Hussars*, vol. 3, p. 311.

51. *Drama or Theatrical Pocket Magazine* (June 1824), cited in Saxon, *Enter*, pp. 137 and 140; Thomas Moore, *Memoirs, Journals and Correspondence of Thomas Moore*, ed. Lord John Russell, 8 vols. (London, 1853–1856), vol. 6, p. 61.

52. Erroll Sherson, *London's Lost Theaters of the Nineteenth Century* (London: John Lane, 1925), p. 61.

53. Cremorne Gardens in Chelsea put on *The Storming of Mooltan*, the Surrey

Zoological Gardens did *The Siege of Badajos*, and Astley's staged a "New Grand Equestrian Military Spectacle" entitled *Mooltan and Goojerat, or the Conquest of the Sikhs*, "The Fortunes of War," *Punch* 17 (1850), p. 11.

54. Coxe, "Equestrian Drama," p. 112.

55. John Malcolm Bullock, "Soldiering and Circuses," *JSAHR* 8 (1929), pp. 183–189.

56. Saxon, *Ducrow*, pp. 131–132.

57. Plumb, "The New World of Children," p. 308.

58. It was shown at Edinburgh, Glasgow, Dublin, Belfast, Bury St. Edmunds, Liverpool, Chester, Sheffield, Tavistock, and Plymouth, but was probably displayed in other places too. Ralph Hyde, *Panoramania!: The Art and Entertainment of the 'All Embracing' View* (London: Trefoil, 1988), p. 65.

59. The panorama "The Siege of Brussels" was reviewed in the "Fine Arts" section of *Athenaeum* (March 16, 1833), p. 171.

60. After 1815, patrons considered martial themes in painting to be militaristic, but the topic gradually became more popular. As a less exalted medium, the print was more acceptable for martial themes. J. W. M. Hishberger, *Images of the Army: The Military in British Art, 1815–1914* (Manchester: Manchester University Press, 1988), pp. 12–13 and 52–53.

61. This was seen by General Thomas Picton, who could not bear to watch: "A battle is nothing to that." H[eaton] [Bowstead] Robinson, *Memoirs of Lieutenant-General Sir Thomas Picton, G.C.B.&c. including His Correspondence*, 2nd rev. ed., 2 vols. (London, 1836), vol. 1, p. 406.

62. The "captain" of the "Society of Goffers" at Blackheath became a "captain-general" in 1808, wearing epaulets and a medal as badges of office. Paul Goldman, *Sporting Life: An Anthology of British Sporting Prints* (London: British Museum, 1983), prints 9, 116, and 117.

63. Army Museum's Ogilby Trust, *Index to British Military Costume Prints, 1500–1914* (London: Robert Ogilby Trust, 1972), pp. 200–219; the Anne S. K. Brown Collection also houses an important collection of music covers with martial themes that include many British items from this era. See Peter Harrington, *Catalogue to the Anne S. K. Brown Military Collection, Vol. 1: The British Prints, Drawings and Watercolors* (New York: Garland Publishing, 1987).

64. George Cruikshank, *A Pop-gun Fired off by George Cruickshank in Defence of the British Volunteers of 1803* (London, 1866), p. 11.

65. Gavin Gleig, *Folk Songs of the North-East*, 3 vols. (Peterhead, 1907), vol. 1, pt. 25, p. 2.

66. Quoted by Charles Hindley, *The History of the Catnach Press* (1887), p. xxviii, cited in E. D. Mackerness, *A Social History of English Music* (London: Routledge and Kegan Paul, 1964), p. 135.

67. George Hogarth, *The Songs of Charles Dibdin*, 2 vols. (London, 1848), vol. 2, p. 383.

68. Sergeant Paul Swanston, *Memoirs of Serjeant Paul Swanston; being A Narrative of a Soldier's Life in Barracks, Ships, Camps, Battles, Captivity on Sea and Land; with Notices of the Most Adventurous of his Comrades* (London, 1840), p. 240.

69. James White, *Adventures of Sir Pumpkin Frizzle; Nights in the Mess and Other Tales* (Edinburgh, 1836), p. 1.

70. S. G. P. Ward, "Major Monsoon," *JSAHR* 59 (1981), p. 65.

71. Hishberger, *Images of the Army*, p. 6.

72. George III was colonel of this unit. John Aston, *Old Times: A Picture of Social Life at the End of the Eighteenth Century* (London: J. C. Nimmo, 1885; reprint ed., Detroit: Singing Tree Press, 1969), pp. 63–64. By the late 1790s, wealthy men wore this court livery in society, a development that appears in part to have been a way for them to avoid unfavorable comparisons with the brilliant appearance of soldiers, but it also served as a mark of loyalty to the Crown during the conflict with France. Charles Mansel, "Monarchy, Uniform and the Rise of the *Frac*, 1760–1830," *Past and Present* 96 (August 1982), pp. 115–116.

73. The sumptuary laws forbade too close an imitation of either the Windsor uniform or army dress. Such restrictions were not limited to Britain; while at Ravenna in 1820, Lord Byron's liverymen looked so much like the Papal Guard Carabiniers that they petitioned the local cardinal against the liveries. Lord Byron, *Byron's Letters and Journals*, ed. Leslie A. Marchand, 8 vols. (Cambridge, Mass.: Harvard University Press, 1977), vol. 7, p. 118.

74. He quit after being posted to one of those unbearably desolate places so typical of the remote stations of the army—Manchester. Willard Connely, *The Reign of Beau Brummell* (New York: Greystone Press, 1940), p. 45.

75. Ellen Moers, *The Dandy: Brummell to Beerbohm* (London: Secker and Warburg, 1960), pp. 33–34. Brummell was influenced by military dress in some details, adopting tasseled "Hessian" (hussar) boots and the *chapeau bras*.

76. A fashion historian described it as "a certain swaggering flashiness and exaggeration of effect . . . reflected from the theatricality of uniforms on to the latest clothing for civilian men." Geoffrey Squire, *Dress and Society: 1560–1970* (New York: Viking Press, 1974), p. 138.

77. Thomas Moore, *Journal of Sir Valentine Sleek* (n.p., 1818), cited in ibid., p. 142.

78. "Military Uniforms," *Blackwood's Magazine* 23 (January 1818), pp. 92–93.

79. An Officer, *Observations on the Army* (London, 1825), p. 24. The ringmaster Widdecombe also wore a moustache and was often called a dandy: "the very Brummell and D'Orsay of the ring." *Ear*, July 12, 1840, as cited in Saxon, *Ducrow*, p. 132.

80. Letter from "An Half-Pay Officer," *New Military Register* (London), April 14, 1819. Some soldiers were horrified and complained to the press. C. H., "Medal or Other Distinction for Service," *United Services Journal* 2 (1830),

p. 881. Many second-hand uniforms were available after the postwar reductions, and penniless, half-pay officers often supplemented their incomes by selling them to old-clothes dealers.

81. Eric J. Hobsbawm, *The Age of Capital, 1848–1875* (New York: Mentor Books, 1979), p. 238.

82. Anne Hollander, *Seeing Through Clothes* (New York: Avon Books, 1978), p. 474.

83. Quentin Bell, *Of Human Finery*, 2nd rev. ed. (New York: Schocken Books, 1976), p. 43. The creation of uniforms—along with sports clothes and the sewing machine—is considered the most significant factor in the development of male dress in the past 300 years. See Penelope Byrde, *The Male Image: Men's Fashion in Britain, 1300–1970* (London: B. T. Batsford, 1979), p. 73.

84. Philip Haythornthwaite, *Uniforms of the French Revolutionary Wars: 1793–1802* (Poole, Dorset: Blandford Press), p. 110.

85. Letter of September 3, 1805. Lady Maria Nugent, *Lady Nugent's Journal of Her Residence in Jamaica from 1801 to 1805*, new, rev. ed., Philip Wright, ed. (Kingston: Institute of Jamaica, 1966), p. 253.

86. In Bath in 1812 a Canadian saw "crowds of ladies" wearing "pelisses laced with gold cords and hussar's hats." Thomas Ridout, *Ten Years of Upper Canada in Peace and War, 1805–1815, Being the Ridout Letters*, ed. Matilda Edgar (Toronto, 1890; reprint ed., Toronto: Coles Publishing Co., 1970), pp. 90–91.

87. William Donaldson, *The Jacobite Song: Political Myth and National Identity* (Aberdeen: Aberdeen University Press, 1988), p. 92.

88. Orlo Williams, *Life and Letters of John Rickman* (Boston: Houghton Mifflin Co., 1912), p. 126.

89. C. Willett Cunningham, *English Women's Clothing in the Nineteenth Century* (London: Saber and Saber, 1937), p. 439.

90. Elizabeth Ewing, *Women in Uniform* (Totowa, N.J.: Rowman and Littlefield, 1975), p. 64.

91. Elizabeth Ewing, *History of Children's Costume* (New York: Scribner, 1977), p. 82.

92. Plumb, "The New World of Children," p. 311.

93. Ewing, *Children's Costume*, p. 82.

94. Mary Russell Mitford, *Our Village* (London, 1824; reprint ed., Philadelphia), p. 58.

95. *York Herald*, April 1846, quoted in Vandeleur, *Letters*, p. 186.

96. Seaton Papers, General Sir Henry Hardinge to Lord Seaton, June 16, 1853, cited in Hew Strachan, *Wellington's Legacy: The Reform of the British Army, 1830–54* (Manchester: Manchester University Press, 1984), p. 167.

97. *Punch* 24 (1853), p. 3.

98. *Punch* 25 (1853), p. 92.

99. *Douglas Jerrold's Shilling Magazine* I (1845), p. 40.

100. J. M., "Fragments from the Portfolio of a Field Officer," *United Services Journal* I (1831), p. 304.

101. G. Kitson Clark, *The Making of Victorian England* (New York: Athenaeum, 1974), p.88.

102. Both quoted in W. L. Burn, *The Age of Equipoise: A Study of the Mid-Victorian Generation* (New York: W. W. Norton Co., 1965), p. 65.

103. Walter E. Houghton, *The Victorian Frame of Mind, 1830–1870* (New Haven: Yale University Press, 1985), p. 198.

104. Because the image was a matter of regulation, the soldiers' own feelings were irrelevant to the message, much as an advertising model's opinion about a product being promoted has no bearing upon the image created, although the model's appearance and speech are designed to convey the illusion of an objective message.

105. Thomas Carlyle, *Past and Present*, ed. Richard D. Altick (New York: New York University Press, 1977), p. 267.

106. "Society: The Roots of Honour," John Ruskin, *Selections and Essays*, ed. Frederick William Roe (New York: Charles Scribner's Sons, 1946), pp. 316–317.

107. James Montgomery, *The Carding and Spinning Master's Assistant: Or the Theory and Practice of Cotton Spinning* (Glasgow, 1832), reprinted in Alfred D. Chandler, ed., *Precursors of Modern Management* (New York: Arno Press, 1979), p. 221.

108. G. M. Young, *Victorian England: Portrait of an Age* (Oxford: Oxford University Press, 1964), p. 27.

109. Ruskin, *Selections and Essays*, p. 316.

110. Quoted in N. McKendrick, "Josiah Wedgwood and Factory Discipline," *Historical Journal* I (1960), p. 35.

111. *New Moral World* XI (March 4, 1843), cited in J. F. C. Harrison, *Quest for the New Moral World: Robert Owen and the Owenites in Britain and America* (New York: Charles Scribner's Sons, 1969), p. 187.

112. Margaret Cole, *Robert Owen* (New York: Oxford University Press, 1953), pp. 84–85.

113. Robert Owen, *A New View of Society* (New York: J. M. Dent and Sons, 1927), p. 291.

114. Frank Podmore, *Robert Owen: A Biography* (New York: Appleton and Co., 1924), p. 144.

115. Carlyle, *Past and Present*, pp. 208, 268–269, and 271.

116. Hobsbawm, *Age of Capital*, p. 238.

117. Karl Marx and Friedrich Engels, *The Communist Manifesto* (Baltimore: Penguin Books, 1969), pp. 87–88.

118. Stanley H. Palmer, *Police and Protest in England and Ireland: 1780–1850* (Cambridge, England: Cambridge University Press, 1988), points out that

the Irish police (essentially martial in character) were the primary prototype for the English police.

119. Michael Ignatieff, *A Just Measure of Pain: The Penitentiary in the Industrial Revolution, 1750–1850* (New York: Columbia University Press, 1978), pp. 191–192.

120. Thomas Bakewell, *A Letter addressed to the Chairman of the Select Committee of the House of Commons, appointed to enquire into the State of Madhouses: to which is subjoined Remarks on the Nature, Causes and Cure of Mental Derangement* (Stafford, 1815), p. 53, cited in William Parry-Jones, *The Trade in Lunacy: A Study of Private Madhouses in England in the Eighteenth and Nineteenth Centuries* (London: Routledge and Kegan Paul, 1972), p. 175.

121. Asa Briggs, *Victorian People: A Reassessment of Persons and Themes, 1851–1867*, rev. ed. (Chicago: University of Chicago Press, 1972), p. 116.

122. *Duty, With Illustrations of Courage, Patience, and Endurance* (New York, 1881), *Character* (New York, n.d.), and *Self-Help* (New York, n.d.). He even found one for *Thrift* (New York, 1876), p. 152, although soldiers were scarcely famous for frugality.

123. Briggs, *Victorian People*, pp. 127–128.

124. Samuel Smiles, *Duty, with illustrations of Courage, Patience, and Endurance* (New York, 1881), pp. 12, 19. Did the idea for the United States' World War II slogan "Work To Keep Free," which the Nazis adopted ("Arbeid Makt Frei") and painted on the entrance signs of the death camps, originate from Smiles?

125. Thomas Walter Laqueur, *Religion and Respectability: Sunday Schools and Working Class Culture, 1780–1850* (New Haven, Conn.: Yale University Press, 1976), p. 219.

126. The conductor, Sir George Smart, adopted similar traits, being known for "extreme punctuality"; "a more rigid man and methodical man of business I never met." Henry Phillips, *Musical Recollections during Half a Century*, 2 vols. (London, 1865), vol. 1, pp. 213–214.

127. [Isabella] Beeton, *The Book of Household Management* (London, 1861; facs. ed., London: Jonathan Cape Ltd., 1968), p. 1; [Isabella] Beeton, *Beeton's Every-Day Cookery and Housekeeping Book* (London, 1865; facs. ed., London: Gallery Books, 1984), pp. i–vii.

128. Geoffrey Best, *War and Society in Revolutionary Europe, 1770–1870* (Harmondsworth, Middlesex: Fontana, 1982), p. 235.

129. Ian F. W. Beckett, *Riflemen Form: A Study of the Rifle Volunteer Movement, 1859–1908* (Aldershot: Ogilby Trust, 1982), p. 198.

130. Hugh Cunningham, *The Volunteer Force: A Social and Political History, 1859–1908* (Hamden, Conn.: Archon, 1975), p. 64. The author assumes that the factory was the model for the volunteers—rather than both the factory and the regulars having influenced the volunteers—whereas the factory itself imitated the army.

131. Beckett, *Riflemen Form*, pp. 108–109, and *Volunteer Service Gazette* (1859), p. 351, cited on p. 109.

132. Cited in Cunningham, *Volunteer Force*, p. 82.

133. Peter Bailey, *Leisure and Class in Victorian England: Rational Recreation and the Contest for Control, 1830–1885* (New York: Methuen Books, 1978), p. 139.

134. Bruce Haley, *The Healthy Body and Victorian Culture* (Cambridge, Mass.: Harvard University Press, 1978), p. 170. The Oundle school chapel, for example, is dedicated to officers who fell in the Second World War.

135. H. J. Hanham, "Religion and Nationality in the Mid-Victorian Army," in M. R. D. Foot, *War and Society: Historical Essays in Honour and Memory of J. R. Western, 1928–1971* (London: Paul Elek, 1973), p. 172.

136. Cited from the *Post, Punch* 44 (1863), p. 61.

137. The Archbishop of Canterbury observed that Booth's "peculiar mode of proceeding was such as might have considerable influence over uncultivated minds." But the parades created much resentment when residents were awakened on Sunday mornings by the army's "unbearable" din. An opposition group calling itself the "Skeleton Army" armed themselves with a black skull and crossbones, flag, mud, stones, dead cats, paint, and live coals and fought the paraders. *Hansard's Parliamentary Debates* 269 (1882), col. 822, cited in Donald C. Richter, *Riotous Victorians* (Athens, Ohio: Ohio University Press, 1981), pp. 74–75. Salvation army bandsmen wore second-hand army uniforms before getting their own. Ewing, *Women in Uniform*, p. 59.

138. Carlyle, *Past and Present*, p. 260.

139. Dickens, *Pickwick Papers*, pp. 48, 50.

140. Kipling shared Smiles's sharp ambivalence toward the martial model; he "would have abhorred the form right-wing corporativism took under Hitler in Germany," and the story includes Jewish schoolboys' winning a military exercise contest. But the vision's allure affected Kipling's judgment. It marked a "significant decline in artistic balance," being "absurd and remote from the facts of English life." Angus Wilson, *The Strange Ride of Rudyard Kipling* (New York: Penguin Books, 1979), pp. 241–243.

141. There were of course mistakes made at reviews, and some were deliberate— such as officers' appearing in mufti instead of uniform. But the spectacle was based on an idealized image, and, like any other show, it rarely reached the perfection it was supposed to embody. Jeffery L. Lant has discussed the problems at royal spectacles in *Insubstantial Pageant: Ceremony & Confusion at Queen Victoria's Court* (New York: Taplinger Publishing Co., 1980).

142. Carlyle, *Past and Present*, pp. 255, and 258.

143. Serg. Robert Blatchford, *My Life in the Army* (London: The Clarion Press, 1910), p. 139.

144. The scene was rendered comicical when the spectators were saluted with a volley of blank cartridges, and at the discharge "something" whistled past Mr. Winkle's ear. The troops then charged with fixed bayonets directly at the spot where the Pickwickians were standing, and they fled for their lives. Dickens, *Pickwick Papers*, pp. 48–51.

145. Quoted in Briggs, *Victorian People*, p. 127. Henry Havelock's history of the First Burmese War prompted anger; his brother was bluntly asked at the Horse Guards, "Is he tired of his commission? . . . The book brought him neither profit nor promotion." John Clark Marshman, *Memoirs of Major-General Sir Henry Havelock, K.C.B.* (London, 1885), p. 31. British officers were among the most poorly educated in Europe, preferring to play field sports rather than learn their duty. Only the absolute necessity of changing techniques in war eventually forced the army to demand a modest degree of education from its officers.

146. Blatchford, *Life*, p. 139.

147. See William McNeill, *Keeping Together in Time: Dance and Drill in Human History* (Cambridge, Mass.: Harvard University Press, 1995), especially pp. 131–132.

148. Walter Bagehot, *The English Constitution* (London, 1867; reprint ed., Ithaca, N.Y.: Cornell University Press, 1976), pp. 63–64.

149. Colley, *Britons*, p. 187.

150. Carlyle, *Past and Present*, p. 249.

151. Although these groups claimed that they met to enjoy African dances, the links with the tradition of Latin carnival and the "world turned upside down" are strong. Lord Mordaunt Fraser, *History of Trinidad*, vol. 1 (1781–1813) (1891; reprint ed., London: Cass, 1971), pp. 268–269.

152. Terence Ranger, "The Invention of Tradition in Colonial Africa," in Hobsbawm and Ranger, *Invention of Tradition*, pp. 245–246. The impact of military rule on seventeenth-century colonies is treated in Stephen Saunders Webb, *The Governors-General: The English Army and the Definition of Empire, 1569–1681* (Chapel Hill: Institute of Early American History and Culture, 1979), but the significant effects of martial culture and institutions on indigenous cultures and peoples around the world, as well as its role in the development of colonial societies, have not been much studied. A noteworthy exception for Canada is Elinor Kyte Senior, *British Regulars in Montreal: An Imperial Garrison, 1832–1854* (Montreal: McGill-Queens, 1981).

153. Klaus Theweleit in *Male Fantasies I: Women, Floods, Bodies, History*, vol. 1, trans. Stephen Conway (Cambridge, England: Polity Press, 1987), writes that for the German working class, "anyone wearing a uniform must be an oppressor. That was all there was to it" (p. 147), and "that stereotype of the imperial age, the young lieutenant who is the heartthrob of all the girls, may have had some basis in reality in smaller garrison towns." though this

did not apply in "urbanized working-class settlements" (p. 151). No evidence is cited to substantiate these claims. Robert Eben Sacket, in *Popular Entertainment and Politics in Munich, 1990–1923* (Cambridge, Mass.: Harvard University Press, 1982), writes "'Old Bavaria' liked to think of sexuality in terms of a few basic, unquestioned natural principles. That women found men in uniform irresistible was one of these principles" (p. 58). This statement seems absolute and simplistic, but the appeal of uniforms cannot be dismissed as simply a matter of class. Theweleit also overlooks the fact that the appeal—or threat—of the uniform depends upon the context in which it appears, as well as who is wearing it, for those who oppose the state and its army sometimes don this guise of solidarity and strength, symbolically absorbing the army's power, an almost universal practice in the history of conflict. This has also been a recurrent theme among women cross-dressers and lesbians for centuries.

154. [William Maginn], *Tales of Military Life*, 3 vols. (London, 1829), vol. 1, p. 82.

155. *Narrative of a Private Soldier in His Majesty's 92nd Regiment of Foot, Written by Himself*, 2nd ed. (Glasgow, 1820), p. 23. British army service was still relatively new for Catholics, having only been legalized in the 1780s. The fear of being drilled provides an interesting insight into the Irish revolutionary tradition, and adds an intriguing dimension to the traditional stereotype of the "wild Irish." This example highlights the organizational dilemma of a people who fear the tyranny of regimentation when confronted with a professional line army.

156. See John M. MacKenzie, ed., *Popular Imperialism and the Military: 1850–1950* (Manchester: Manchester University Press, 1992); for boys' books, see Guy Arnold, *Held Fast for England: G. A. Henty, Boys' Writer* (London: Hamish Hamilton, 1980).

157. Ewing, *Women in Uniform*, p. 58. "There was a passion for uniforms in the second half of the nineteenth century. 'Everybody' they say, 'who did anything special in those days wore clothing that indicated his occupation . . . From lift boys to funeral undertakers, from policemen, postmen, seamen, and dustmen, to the Speaker of the House of Commons . . . men proclaimed their calling in the way they dressed." Quoted from Catherine Booth, from Reginald Woods, ed., *Harvest of the Years* (London: Salvationist Pub. and Supplies, 1960).

158. A basic feature was the notion of civilizing soldier-Christians' bringing the True Faith to the non-European world, while sacrificing their own comfort and safety to fight against the evil-doers who were presumed to dominate the "uncivilized regions." One example of the many books then published along these lines is Marshman, *Henry Havelock*.

159. Houghton, *Victorian Frame of Mind*, p. 203.

160. Michael Rosenthal, *The Character Factory: Baden-Powell and the Origins of the Boy Scout Movement* (New York: Pantheon Books, 1984), pp. 164–165.

161. Carlyle, *Past and Present*, pp. 249, 261, and 259.

162. Albert J. LaValley, *Carlyle and the Idea of the Modern: Studies in Carlyle's Prophetic Literature and Its Relations to Blake, Nietzsche, Marx, and Others* (New Haven: Yale University Press, 1968), p. 10.

163. The advent of World War I saw a decline in some of the elements of the show, and except for the highly visible guards units, the old scarlet and blue uniforms went into store and were abolished after the war ended. Brightly colored martial display still exists, but compared with the nineteenth century it is much reduced, less imposing, and more subtle in its impact. In modern war, machines have increasingly displaced dress as the show's focal point, and soldiers have become attendants for the terrible machines of death. But despite the growing importance of camouflage in twentieth-century warfare, reflecting and symbolizing the weapons' enormous power, British army spectacle retains more of its nineteenth-century character than most other contemporary armies, and much less emphasis is placed upon the display of high-tech weapons. Unlike the American army, each regiment still maintains a band that wears traditional uniforms and appears in a variety of public contexts. When regular units appear in public they usually wear the their best dress, consisting of blue patrol jackets—the successor of the frock coat. The show of the last century thus continues to be popular, and not primarily as a draw for tourists, either, although the obligatory photos of guardsman in tourist pamphlets might give the opposite impression. At the "Trooping to the Colours" ceremony only ticket-holders are admitted (tickets are distributed free of charge to Britons and are unavailable to tourists). I am indebted to Sheperd Paine for this information.

Conclusion: The Martial Vision

1. Perhaps it is the impressive power of the machine paradigm, with its idealized notions that glorify and legitimize dehumanization, that has induced many to believe that martial management is a "science." The logic of this view is that continued refinements in technique will allow it finally to take its place with the other sciences in the measurement and manipulation of the physical world.

2. Walter Bagehot, *The English Constitution* (Ithaca, N.Y.: Cornell University Press, 1976), pp. 63–64.

3. Raymond Frith, *Symbols: Public and Private* (Ithaca, N.Y.: Cornell University Press, 1973), p. 88, citing C. Wright Mills, *The Sociological Imagination* (New York, 1961, n.p.).

4. Frith, *Symbols*, p. 88, citing Kingsley Martin, *The Crown and the Establishment* (Harmondsworth, 1963, n.p.).

5. It is both curious and remarkable that this martial show was displayed before a civilian audience that so often viewed soldiers with revulsion, yet was also a source of delight, and had a greater influence on their culture and mentality, even though no other aim was sought than to manage the army and advertise its image to the public. Some soldiers believed that the army and its ways were superior to the civilian world, but beyond such officially sanctioned chauvinism, no evidence has surfaced indicating that commanders utilized these advertisements for any reason other than that of military management and public relations.

6. Eric Hobsbawm, *The Age of Capital: 1848–1875* (Mentor Books, 1979), pp. 235–236.

7. This illustrates a fundamental problem in the attempt to create a truly classless society in an era of increasingly centralized economic and political power. The organizational dictates of centralization will assure for any group attempting to "build a new world" the formation of institutional hierarchies, which have a strong tendency to serve their own interests first—regardless of the consequences. Thus the best of intentions will necessarily tend to result in the replication of a fundamental—yet destructive—feature of the old system it was meant to replace and improve.

8. See Introduction, note 57.

9. Robert W. Malcomson, *Popular Recreations in English Society, 1700–1850* (Cambridge, England: Cambridge University Press, 1973), pp. 89–90.

10. Karl Marx and Friedrich Engels, *The Communist Manifesto* (Baltimore: Penguin Books, 1969), p. 99.

11. Lewis Mumford, *The Myth of the Machine: The Pentagon of Power* (New York: Harcourt, Brace, Jovanovich, 1970), p. 150.

12. For example, see L. Carl Brown, *The Tunisia of Ahmad Bey, 1837–1855* (Princeton, N.J.: Princeton University Press, 1974), pp. 265–266 and 355. This process has sometimes been accompanied by attempts to impose Western dress on civilian populations, often with tragi-comic results.

13. David I. Kertzer, *Ritual, Politics and Power* (New Haven: Yale University Press, 1988), p. 8. "And what political environment could be more dependent on symbolism than one in which our decision whether to pat a person on the back or to shoot him in the back depends on the color of the uniform he wears? With the increase in the size of the state and the growth of bureaucracy, Michael Walzer observes, politics is transformed 'from a concrete activity into what Marx once called the fantasy of everyday life." Ibid, cited from Michael Walzer, "Politics in the Welfare State," *Dissent* no. 15, p. 36.

14. Charles Tilly, *Popular Contention in Great Britain, 1758–1834* (Cambridge,

Mass.: Harvard University Press, 1995), p. 388. Quoted from Linda Colley, *Britons: Forging the Nation, 1707–1837* (London: Pimlico, 1994), p. 312.

15. *Oxford English Dictionary*, 2nd ed. (Oxford: Oxford University Press, 1989), vol. 9, p. 185.

16. Two of the Oxford dictionary's examples also make reference to the state: "Oh Royall Peece: There's Magick in thy Maiestie" (1611), and: "Civility is a strong Political Magick" (1702), Ibid.

ACKNOWLEDGMENTS

I am indebted to many people for the assistance and encouragement that culminated in this study. I wish first to thank David Shibley of Santa Monica College, whose inspiration was a major factor in my decision to pursue historical work, and Geoffrey Symcox of U.C.L.A., who gave me the encouragement to continue when I needed it. Hew Strachan was most helpful in making suggestions on research strategy, and his own works on the British army were of incalculable value.

A number of institutions aided in my research; the staff of the Public Record Office at Kew was always helpful and efficient, as was that of the British Museum Library. I am indebted to the National Army Museum in Chelsea, to J. F. Russell and the staff of the National Library of Scotland, to Mrs. Philip and Allan Carswell of the Royal Scottish United Services Museum at Edinburgh Castle, and to the Scottish Record Office. I also wish to thank J. C. Andrews, the director of the Ministry of Defence Library at Whitehall, who assisted me with some very useful documents. Carl Benn, T. MacDonnell, and the staff of Historic Fort York, Toronto, Canada, were also most helpful, as were Peter Harrington, the curator of the Brown Collection, Cathy Cherbosque, the curator of prints and drawings at the Huntington Library, and Pamela Clark of the Royal Archive at Windsor.

I received a very courteous reception at the headquarters of the Royal Fusiliers Regiment, at the Tower of London, and wish to thank Col. Pettifar and the regimental clerk, Mr. Gibson. I also appreciate the help of Maj. J. T. Morton of the Royal Scots Dragoon Guards. The Scots Guards headquarters provided me with access to nineteenth-century *General Regulations*, which were not available elsewhere in London.

While in London, I benefited from membership at the University of London's Institute for Historical Research, and from the advice of some of the Institute's members, including Rohan McWilliams, Kelly Boyd, and Arnold Harvey. The University of London Library was also very useful, and I especially wish to thank Steve Clews.

John Reed read an earlier draft of this book, as did Sheperd Paine, who photographed the plates for the illustrations, and whose knowledge of the history of the military uniform is most impressive; he made sensible suggestions and intelligent observations that helped me avoid some pitfalls.

I would like to thank Geoffrey Parker, Roger Norman Buckley, and Mark Blum for their useful suggestions, and Philip J. Haythornthwaite, Susan Ranson of Claydon House, Buckinghamshire, and M. A. Loveday for sending me useful information from Britain.

The staffs of the libraries and inter-library loan offices of the Universities of Illinois and Louisville were very helpful, as were the librarian Jim Millhorn, and Sachi Yagyu of the Von der Ahe Library at Loyola-Marymount University in Los Angeles. I also wish to thank Peter Stearns of the *Journal of Social History* for allowing me to use material from my article "'The Eye Must Entrap the Mind': Army Spectacle and Paradigm in Nineteenth-Century Britain," vol. 26, no. 1 (Fall 1992), in Chapter 8.

Kimberley Hunt provided invaluable editorial help on earlier drafts, together with her assistant, Trevor Hunt. I would also like to thank my parents, Jim Irving and Marilyn Hughes Myerly, and my brothers, Kevin Frederick and Jim Irving Myerly, as well as Robert and Betty Hunt, of Lena, Illinois, for their support. Jonathan and Eleana Howarth of Chiswick, Mr. and Mrs. John Bojanic of Acton, Lucian and Barbara Mudza, and Timothy and Anna Fernyhough were all courteous hosts during my visits to Britain. Thanks are due Alexis Dolan for proofreading the final manuscript, and to my editor, Christine Thorsteinsson.

Finally, I owe a great debt to Walter L. Arnstein, and especially to Tamara L. Hunt, without whom this work would not have been written, and who has done so much to help see me through a long journey.

INDEX

287